5th Workshop on Natural Language Processing Techniques for Educational Applications (NLPTEA 2018)

Held at ACL 2018

Melbourne, Australia
19 July 2018

ISBN: 978-1-5108-6724-6

ACL 2018

Natural Language Processing Techniques for Educational Applications

Proceedings of the Fifth Workshop

July 19, 2018
Melbourne, Australia

Preface

Welcome to the 5th Workshop on Natural Language Processing Techniques for Educational Applications (NLPTEA 2018), with a Shared Task on Chinese Grammatical Error Diagnosis.

The development of Natural Language Processing (NLP) has advanced to a level that affects the research landscape of many academic domains and has practical applications in many industrial sectors. On the other hand, educational environment has also been improved to impact the world society, such as the emergence of MOOCs (Massive Open Online Courses). With these trends, this workshop focuses on the NLP techniques applied to the educational environment. Research issues in this direction have gained more and more attention, examples including the activities like the workshops on Innovative Use of NLP for Building Educational Applications since 2005 and educational data mining conferences since 2008.

This is the fifth workshop held in the Asian area, with the first one NLPTEA 2014 workshop being held in conjunction with the 22nd International Conference on Computer in Education (ICCE 2014) from Nov. 30 to Dec. 4, 2014 in Japan. The second edition NLPTEA 2015 workshop was held in conjunction with the 53rd Annual Meeting of the Association for Computational Linguistics and the 7th International Joint Conference on Natural Language Processing (ACL-IJCNLP 2015) from July 26- 31 in Beijing, China. The third version NLPTEA 2016 workshop was held in conjunction with the 26th International Conference on Computational Linguistics (COLING 2016) from December 11- 16 in Osaka, Japan. The fourth edition NLPTEA 2017 workshop was held in conjunction with the 8th International Joint Conference on Natural Language Processing (IJCNLP 2017) from November 27- December 1 in Taipei, Taiwan. This year, we continue to promote this research line by holding the workshop in conjunction with the ACL 2018 conference and also holding the fourth shared task on Chinese Grammatical Error Diagnosis. We receive 33 valid submissions for research issues, each of which was reviewed by at least two experts, and have 12 teams participating in the shared task and submitting their task reports. In total, there are 10 oral papers and 20 posters accepted. We also organize a keynote speech in this workshop. The invited speaker Professor Yuji Matsumoto is expected to deliver a great talk entitled as "Multi-word Expressions in Second Language Learning".

We would like to thank the program committee members for their hard work in completing the review tasks. Their collective efforts achieved quality reviews of the submissions within a few weeks. Great thanks should also go to the speaker, authors, and participants for the tremendous supports in making the workshop a success.

Welcome you to the Melbourne city, and wish you enjoy the city as well as the workshop.

NLPTEA 2018 Workshop Chairs
Yuen-Hsien Tseng, National Taiwan Normal University
Hsin-Hsi Chen, National Taiwan University
Vincent Ng, The University of Texas at Dallas
Mamoru Komachi, Tokyo Metropolitan University

Organization

Workshop Organizers:

Yuen-Hsien Tseng, National Taiwan Normal University
Hsin-Hsi Chen, National Taiwan University
Vincent Ng, The University of Texas at Dallas
Mamoru Komachi, Tokyo Metropolitan University

Shared Task Organizers:

Gaoqi Rao, Beijing Language and Culture University
Qi Gong, Beijing Language and Culture University
Baolin Zhang, Beijing Language and Culture University
Endong Xun, Beijing Language and Culture University

Program Committee:

David Alfter, University of Gothenburg
Chris Brockett, Microsoft Research
Christopher Bryant, Cambridge University
Tao Chen, John Hokins University
Vidas Daudaravicius, VTeX Solutions for Science Publishing
Mariano Felice, Cambridge University
Cyril Goutte, National Research Council Canada
Homa B. Hashemi, University of Pittsburgh
Trude Heift, Simon Fraser University
Tomoyuki Kajiwara, Tokyo Metropolitan University
Herbert Lange, University of Gothenburg
John Lee, The City University of Hong Kong
Lung-Hao Lee, National Taiwan University
Chen Li, Microsoft, USA
Chuan-Jie Lin, National Taiwan Ocean University
Shervin Malmasi, Harvard University
Tomoya Mizumoto, Tohoku University
Courtney Napoles, John Hopkins University
Gustavo Paetzold, University of Sheffield
Livy Real, IBM Research, Brazil
Elizabeth Salesky, Massachusetts Institute of Technology
Yukio Tono, Tokyo University of Foreign Studies
Elena Volodina, University of Gothenburg
Thuy Vu, University of California, Los Angles
Mats Wiren, Stockholm University
Shih-Hung Wu, Chaoyang University of Technology
Huichao Xue, Google, USA
Jui-Feng Yeh, National Chiayi University
Dong Yu, Beijing Language and Culture University
Liang-Chih Yu, Yuan Ze University
Zheng Yuan, Cambridge University
Marcos Zampieri, University of Wolverhampton

Invited Speaker

Yuji Matsumoto, Professor of Information Science, Nara Institute of Science and Technology

Title:

Multi-word Expressions in Second Language Learning

Abstract:

Multi-word Expressions (MWEs) pose difficult problems to the learners of a second language. Effective learning of MWEs is important for them to become fluent speakers or writers. In this talk, I will discuss what kinds of resource and functionality are useful in computational assistance to language learners, and present our experiences on construction of MWE resources, MWE usage classification, MWE-aware error correction and proper usage suggestion.

Biography:

Yuji Matsumoto is currently a Professor of Information Science, Nara Institute of Science and Technology, and a Team Leader of the Knowledge Acquisition Team at Riken AIP. He received his M.S. and Ph.D. degrees in information science from Kyoto University in 1979 and in 1989. He joined Machine Inference Section of Electrotechnical Laboratory in 1979. He has then experienced an academic visitor at Imperial College of Science and Technology, a deputy chief of First Laboratory at ICOT, and an associate professor at Kyoto University. His main research interests are natural language understanding and machine learning. He is an ACL fellow and a fellow of Information Processing Society of Japan.

Table of Contents

Workshop Program

Thursday, July 19, 2018

09:20–09:30 Opening Remarks

09:30–10:30 Invited Talk

09:30–10:30 *Multi-word Expressions in Second Language Learning*
Yuji Matsumoto

10:30–11:00 Coffee Break

11:00–12:40 Regular Paper Session

11:00–11:20 *Generating Questions for Reading Comprehension using Coherence Relations*
Takshak Desai, Parag Dakle and Dan Moldovan

11:20–11:40 *Syntactic and Lexical Approaches to Reading Comprehension*
Henry Lin

11:40–12:00 *Feature Optimization for Predicting Readability of Arabic L1 and L2*
Hind Saddiki, Nizar Habash, Violetta Cavalli-Sforza and Muhamed Al Khalil

12:00–12:20 *A Tutorial Markov Analysis of Effective Human Tutorial Sessions*
Nabin Maharjan and Vasile Rus

12:20–12:40 *Thank "Goodness"! A Way to Measure Style in Student Essays*
Sandeep Mathias and Pushpak Bhattacharyya

Thursday, July 19, 2018 (continued)

12:40–14:10   **Lunch**

14:10–15:30   **Shared Task Session**

14:10–14:30   *Overview of NLPTEA-2018 Share Task Chinese Grammatical Error Diagnosis*
Gaoqi RAO, Qi Gong, Baolin Zhang and Endong Xun

14:30–14:45   *Chinese Grammatical Error Diagnosis using Statistical and Prior Knowledge driven Features with Probabilistic Ensemble Enhancement*
Ruiji Fu, Zhengqi Pei, Jiefu Gong, Wei Song, Dechuan Teng, Wanxiang Che, Shijin Wang, Guoping Hu and Ting Liu

14:45–15:00   *A Hybrid System for Chinese Grammatical Error Diagnosis and Correction*
Chen Li, Junpei Zhou, Zuyi Bao, Hengyou Liu, Guangwei Xu and Linlin Li

15:00–15:15   *Ling@CASS Solution to the NLP-TEA CGED Shared Task 2018*
Qinan Hu, Yongwei Zhang, Fang Liu and Yueguo Gu

15:15–15:30   *Chinese Grammatical Error Diagnosis Based on Policy Gradient LSTM Model*
Changliang Li and Ji Qi

15:30–16:00   **Coffee Break**

16:00–17:00   **Poster Session**

The Importance of Recommender and Feedback Features in a Pronunciation Learning Aid
Dzikri Fudholi and Hanna Suominen

Selecting NLP Techniques to Evaluate Learning Design Objectives in Collaborative Multi-perspective Elaboration Activities
Aneesha Bakharia

Augmenting Textual Qualitative Features in Deep Convolution Recurrent Neural Network for Automatic Essay Scoring
Tirthankar Dasgupta, Abir Naskar, Lipika Dey and Rupsa Saha

Thursday, July 19, 2018 (continued)

17:00–17:10   Closing Remarks

Generating Questions for Reading Comprehension using Coherence Relations

Takshak Desai   **Parag Dakle**   **Dan I. Moldovan**
Department of Computer Science
The University of Texas at Dallas
Richardson TX
{takshak.desai, paragpravin.dakle, moldovan} @ utdallas.edu

Abstract

We propose a technique for generating complex reading comprehension questions from a discourse that are more useful than factual ones derived from assertions. Our system produces a set of general-level questions using coherence relations. These evaluate comprehension abilities like comprehensive analysis of the text and its structure, correct identification of the author's intent, thorough evaluation of stated arguments; and deduction of the high-level semantic relations that hold between text spans. Experiments performed on the RST-DT corpus allow us to conclude that our system possesses a strong aptitude for generating intricate questions. These questions are capable of effectively assessing student interpretation of text.

1 Introduction

The argument for a strong correlation between question difficulty and student perception comes from Bloom's taxonomy (Bloom et al. (1964)). It is a framework that attempts to categorize question difficulty in accordance with educational goals. The framework has undergone several revisions over time and currently has six levels of perception in the cognitive domain: Remembering, Understanding, Applying, Analyzing, Evaluating and Creating (Anderson et al. (2001)). The goal of a Question Generation (QG) system should be to generate meaningful questions that cater to the higher levels of this hierarchy and are therefore adept at gauging comprehension skills.

The scope of several QG tasks has been severely restricted to restructuring declarative sentences into specific level questions. For example, consider the given text and the questions that follow.

Input: The project under construction will raise Las Vegas' supply of rooms by 20%. Clark county will have 18000 new jobs.

Question 1: What will raise Las Vegas' supply of rooms by 20%?

Question 2: Why will Clark County have 18000 new jobs?

From the perspective of Bloom's Taxonomy, questions like Question 1 cater to the 'Remembering' level of the hierarchy and are not apt for evaluation purposes. Alternatively, questions like Question 2 would be associated with the 'Analyzing' level as these would require the student to draw a connection between the events, 'increase in room supply in Las Vegas' and 'creation of 18000 new jobs in Clark County'. Further, such questions would be more relevant in the context of an entire document or paragraph; and serve as better reading comprehension questions.

This paper describes a generic framework for generating comprehension questions from short edited texts using coherence relations. It is organized as follows: Section 2 elaborates on previously designed QG systems and outlines their limitations. We also discuss Rhetorical Structure Theory (RST), which lays the linguistic foundations for discourse parsing. In Section 3, we explain our model and describe the syntactic transformations and templates applied to text spans for performing QG. In Section 4, we discuss experiments performed on the annotated RST-DT corpus and measure the quality of questions generated by the system. Proposed evaluation criteria address both the grammaticality and complexity of generated questions. We have also compared our system with a baseline to show that our system is able to generate complex questions. Finally, in Section 5, we provide our conclusions and suggest potential avenues for future research.

1

Proceedings of the 5th Workshop on Natural Language Processing Techniques for Educational Applications, pages 1–10
Melbourne, Australia, July 19, 2018. ©2018 Association for Computational Linguistics

2 Related Work

2.1 Previous QG systems

Previous research work done in QG has primarily focused on transforming declarations into interrogative sentences, or on using shallow semantic parsers to create factoid questions.

Mitkov and Ha (2003) made use of term extraction and shallow parsing to create questions from simple sentences. Heilman and Smith (2010) suggested a system that over-generates questions from a sentence. Firstly, the sentence is simplified by discarding leading conjunctions, sentence-level modifying phrases, and appositives. It is then transformed into a set of candidate questions by carrying out a sequence of well-defined syntactic and lexical transformations. Then, these questions are evaluated and ranked using a classifier to identify the most suitable one.

Similar approaches have been suggested over time to generate questions, like using a recursive algorithm to explore parse trees of sentences in a top-down fashion (Curto et al. (2012)), creating fill-in-the-blank type questions by analyzing parse trees of sentences and thereby identifying answer phrases (Becker et al. (2012)); or using semantics-based templates (Lindberg et al. (2013); Mazidi and Nielsen (2014)). A common drawback associated with these systems is that they create factoid questions from single sentences and focus on grammatical and/or semantic correctness, not question difficulty.

The generation of complex questions from multiple sentences or paragraphs was explored by Mannem et al. (2010). Discourse connectives such as 'because', 'since' and 'as a result' signal explicit coherence and can be used to generate Why-type questions. Araki et al. (2016) created an event-centric information network where each node represents an event and each edge represents an event-event relation. Using this network, multiple choice questions and a corresponding set of distractor choices are generated. Olney et al. (2012) suggested the use of concept maps to create inter-sentential questions where knowledge in a book chapter is represented as a concept map to generate relevant exam questions. Likewise, Papasalouros et al. (2008) and Stasaski and Hearst (2017) created questions utilizing information-rich ontologies.

Of late, several encoder-decoder models have been used in Machine Translation (Cho et al. (2014)) to automatically learn the transformation rules that enable translation from one language to another. Yin et al. (2015) and Du et al. (2017) argue that similar models can be used to automatically translate narrative sentences into interrogative ones.

2.2 Rhetorical Structure Theory

In an attempt to study the functional organization of information in a discourse, a framework called Rhetorical Structure Theory (RST) was proposed by Thompson and Mann (1987). The framework describes how short texts written in English are structured by defining a set of coherence relations that can exist between text spans. Typically, relations in RST are characterized by three parameters: the nucleus, the satellite and the rhetorical interaction between the nucleus and the satellite. The nucleus is an action; the satellite either describes this action, provides the circumstance in which this action takes place or is a result of the performed action. Notable exceptions are relations such as Contrast, List, etc. which are multinuclear and do not involve satellites.

In order to describe the complete document, these relations are expressed in the form of a discourse graph, an example of which is shown in Figure 1 (O'Donnell, 2000).

We simplify the task of QG by focusing only on the relations given in Table 1. We have condensed some of the relations defined in the RST manual (Thompson and Mann, 1987) and grouped them into new relation types as shown. A complete definition of these relation types can be found in Carlson et al. (2003).

Relation (N,S)	Obtained from
Explanation (N,S)	Evidence, Reason, Explanation
Background (N,S)	Background, Circumstance
Cause (N,S)	Cause, Purpose
Result (N,S)	Result, Consequence
Solutionhood (N,S)	Problem-Solution
Condition (N,S)	Condition, Hypothetical
Evaluation (N,S)	Evaluation, Conclusion

Table 1: Set of relations used by our system. Here, N represents the Nucleus and S represents the Satellite

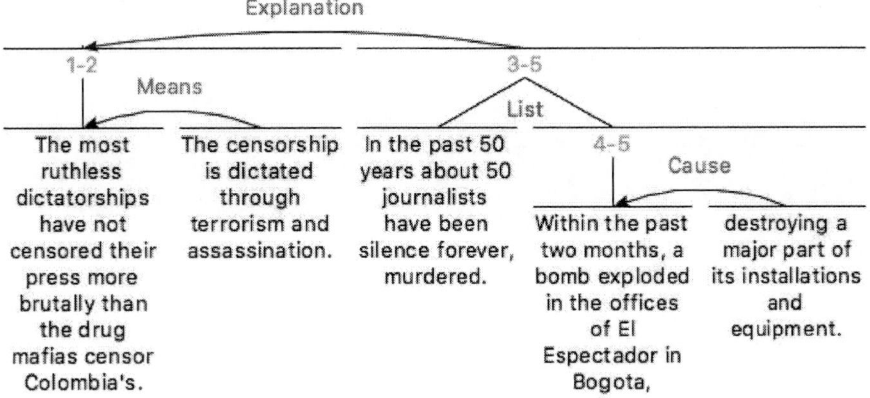

Figure 1: An example of discourse graph for a text sample from the RST-DT corpus

3 Approach

3.1 System Description

The text from which questions are to be generated goes through the pipeline shown in Figure 2. A detailed description of each module/step in the pipeline is described in the subsequent subsections.

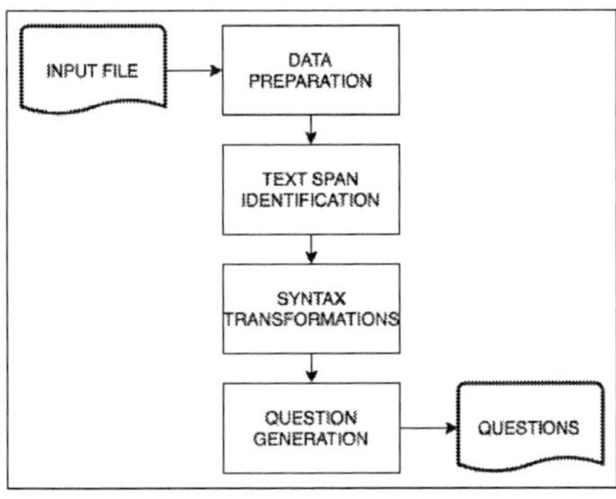

Figure 2: System pipeline

3.1.1 Data Preparation

Here the discourse graph associated with the document is input to the system, which in turn extracts all relevant nucleus-satellite pairs. Each pair is represented as the tuple: Relation (Nucleus, Satellite).

Prior to applying any syntactic transformations on the text spans, we remove all leading and/or trailing conjunctions, adverbs and infinitive phrases from the text span. Further, if the span begins or ends with transition words or phrases like 'As a result' or 'In addition to', we remove them as well.

The inherent nature of discourse makes it difficult to interpret text spans as coherent pockets of information. To facilitate the task of QG, we have ignored text spans containing one word. Further, in several cases, we observe that the questions make more sense if coreference resolution is performed: this task was performed manually by a pair of human annotators who resolved all coreferents by replacing them with the concepts they were referencing. Two types of coreference resolution are considered: event coreference resolution (where coreferents referring to an event are replaced by the corresponding events) and entity coreference resolution (where coreferents referring to entities are replaced by the corresponding entities). Also, to improve the quality of generated questions, annotators replaced some words by their synonyms (Glover et al. (1981); Desai et al. (2016)).

3.1.2 Text-span Identification

We associate each text span with a *Type* depending on its syntactic composition. The assignment of Types to the text spans is independent of the coherence relations that hold between them. Table 2 describes these Types with relevant examples.

3.1.3 Syntax transformations

If the text span is of Type 1 or Type 2, we analyze its parse tree and perform a set of simple surface syntax transformations to convert it into a form suitable for QG. We first use a dependency parser to find the principal verb associated with the span,

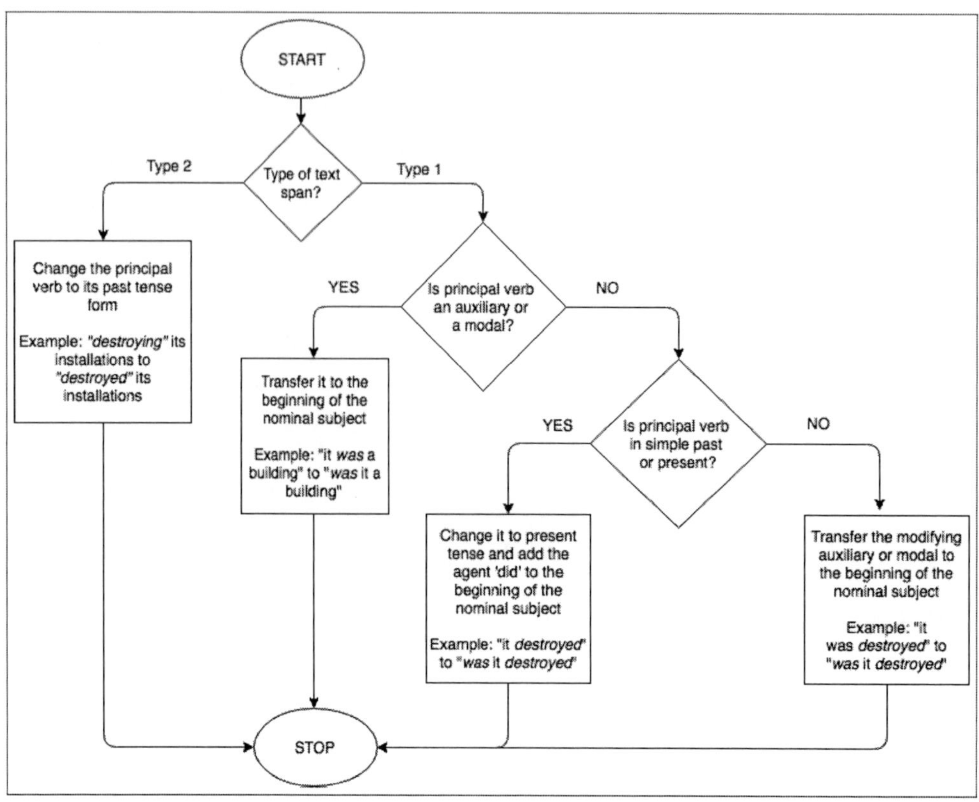

Figure 3: Syntactic transformations applied on text spans. These transformations convert the spans to a form suitable for QG.

Span type	Characteristic of span	Example
Type 0	A group of many sentences	A bomb exploded in the building. It destroyed its installations.
Type 1	One sentence, or a phrase or clause not beginning with a verb, but containing one	The bomb destroyed the building.
Type 2	Phrase or clause beginning with a verb	destroyed the buildings
Type 3	Phrase or clause that does not contain a verb	destruction of the building

Table 2: Text span Types with relevant examples

its part-of-speech tag and the noun or noun phrase it is modifying. Then, according to the obtained information, we apply a set of syntactic transformations to alter the text. Figure 3 describes these transformations as a flowchart.

No syntactic transformations are applied on text spans of Type 0 or Type 3. We directly craft questions from text spans that belong to these Types.

3.1.4 Question Generation

Upon applying the transformations described in Figure 3, we obtain a text form suitable for QG. A template is applied to this text to formulate the final question. Table 3 defines these templates. The design of the chosen templates depends on the relation holding between the spans, without considering the semantics or the meaning of the spans. This makes our system generic and thereby scalable to any domain.

3.2 Example

As an example, consider the same discourse graph from Figure 1. We show how our system will gen-

Relation	Template for type 0	Template for type 1	Template for type 2	Template for type 3
Explanation	[Nucleus]. What evidence can be provided to support this claim?	Why [Nucleus]?	What [Nucleus]?	What caused [Nucleus]?
Background	[Nucleus]. Under what circumstances does this happen?	Under what circumstances [Nucleus]?	What circumstances [Nucleus]?	What circumstances led to [Nucleus]?
Solutionhood	[Nucleus]. What is the solution to this problem?	What is the solution to [Nucleus]?	What solution [Nucleus]?	What is the solution to the problem of [Nucleus]?
Cause	[Satellite]. Explain the reason for this statement.	Why [Satellite]?	What [Satellite] ?	Explain the reason for [Satellite]?
Result	[Nucleus]. Explain the reason for this statement.	Why [Nucleus]?	What [Nucleus] ?	Explain the reason for [Nucleus]?
Condition	[Nucleus]. Under what conditions did this happen ?	Under what conditions [Nucleus]?	What conditions [Nucleus] ?	What conditions led to [Nucleus]?
Evaluation	[Nucleus]. What lets you assess this fact?	What lets you assess [Nucleus]?	What assessment [Nucleus]?	What assessment can be given for [Nucleus]?

Table 3: Templates for Question Generation.

erate questions for a causal relation that has been isolated in Figure 4.

For the given relation, we begin by associating the satellite: "destroying a major part of its installations and equipment" with Type 2. The principal verb 'destroying' is changed to past tense form 'destroyed' and the pronoun 'it' is replaced by the entity it is referencing i.e. 'the offices of El Especatador', to obtain the question stem: 'destroyed a major part of the installations and equipment of the offices of El Especatador'.

We use the template for the cause relation for Type 2 to obtain the question: "What destroyed the installations and equipment of the offices of El Especatador?". Similar examples have also been provided in Table 4.

4 Experimental Results

4.1 Data

For the purpose of experimentation, we used the RST-DT corpus (Carlson et al. (2003)) that contains annotated Wall Street Journal articles. Each article is associated with a discourse graph that describes all the coherence relations that hold between its components. We used these discourse graphs for generating questions. As described in a previous section, we filtered certain relations, and did not consider those relations in which the template is to be applied to text spans containing only one word.

4.2 Implementation

Part-of-Speech tagging and Dependency parsing were performed using Stanford's Part-of-Speech tagger (Toutanova et al. (2003)) and Dependency Parser (Nivre et al. (2016); Bird (2006)) respectively. We used the powerful linguistics library provided by NodeBox (Bleser et al. (2002)) to convert between verb forms. We have used a heavily annotated corpus and made several amendments ourselves, by performing coreference resolution and paraphrasing. This is due to the inability of modern discourse parsers to perform these tasks with high accuracy. While advances have been made in discourse parsing (Rutherford and

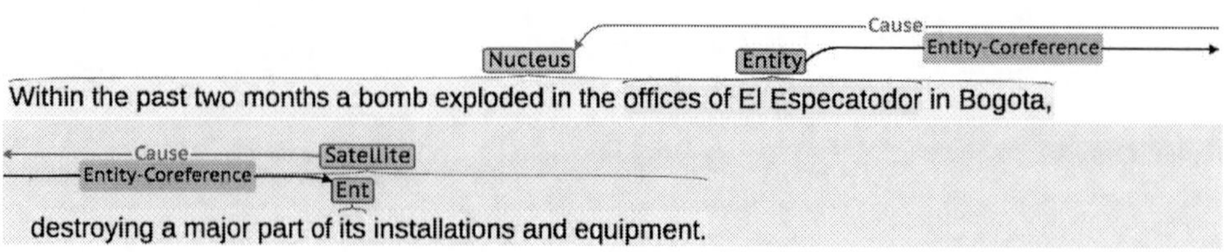

Figure 4: Example of a cause relation from the document

Metric type	Relation	Generated Question	Evaluation
Nature of coherence relation	Nucleus: they are going to be in big trouble with unionists over any Jaguar deal. Satellite: If they try to build it somewhere else in Europe besides the U.K., Relation: Condition	Under what conditions are **General Motors and Ford Motor Co.** going to be in big trouble with unionists over any Jaguar deal?	This is an example of an explicit relation, made apparent through the use of discourse connective 'If' in the satellite
Nature of question	Nucleus: **As a result,** Colombia will earn $500 million less from its coffee this year than last. Satellite: The 27-year old coffee cartel had to be formally dissolved this summer. Relation: Result	Why will Colombia earn $500 million less from its coffee this year than last?	Here, both the question and answer are derived from text spans belonging to different sentences. Thus the score assigned will be 1.
Number of inference steps	Nucleus: **Then,** when it would have been easier to resist them, nothing was done Satellite: and **my** brother was **murdered** by the mafia three years ago Relation: Explanation	Why was **the author's** brother **killed** by the mafia three years ago?	The student should be able to correctly resolve the pronoun 'my' to 'the author' and know that 'killed' is a synonym of 'murdered'. Thus two semantic concepts, paraphrase detection and entity co-reference resolution, are tested here.

Table 4: Examples for metric evaluation

Xue (2014); Li et al. (2014)), such models make several simplifying assumptions about the input. Likewise, coreference resolution (Bengtson and Roth (2008); Wiseman et al. (2016)) is also an uphill task in discourse parsing.

4.3 Evaluation Criteria

To evaluate the quality of generated questions, we used a set of criteria that are defined below. We considered and designed metrics that measure both the correctness and difficulty of the question.

All the metrics use a two-point scale: a score of 1 indicates the question successfully passed the metric, a score of 0 indicates otherwise.

- Grammatic correctness of questions: This metric checks whether the question generated is only syntactically correct. We do not take into account the semantics of the question.

- Semantic correctness of questions: We account for the meaning of the generated question and whether it makes sense to the reader.

It is assumed if a question is grammatically incorrect, it is also semantically incorrect.

- Superfluous use of language: Since we are not focusing on shortening sentences or removing redundant data from the text, generated questions may contain information not required by the student to arrive at the answer. Such questions should be refined to make them shorter and sound more fluent or natural.

- Question appropriateness: This metric judges whether the question is posed correctly i.e. we check if the question is not ambivalent and makes complete sense to the reader.

- Nature of coherence relation: Coherence relations are classified into two categories: explicit (the relations that are made apparent through using discourse connectives) and implicit (the relations that require a deep understanding of the text). Questions generated through explicit coherence relations are easier to attempt as compared to the ones generated via implicit coherence relations. We assign a score of 1 to a question generated from an implicit coherence relation and 0 to that generated from an explicit relation.

- Nature of question: We check for the nature of generated question: If both the answer and question are derived from the same sentence, we assign a score of 0, otherwise the score will be 1.

- Number of inference steps (Araki et al. (2016)): To evaluate this metric, we consider three semantic concepts: paraphrase detection, entity co-reference resolution and event co-reference resolution. We consider a score for each concept: 1 if the concept is required and 0 if not. We take the arithmetic mean of these scores to get the average number of inference steps for a question.

4.4 Example

As an example, consider some of the tuples obtained from the RST-DT corpus. Table 4 explains how the generated questions evaluate against some of our criteria.

4.5 Results and Analysis

We generated questions for the entire corpus using our system. For the 385 documents it contains, a total of 3472 questions were generated. Table 5 describes the statistics for the questions generated for each relation type.

Relation type	Fraction of generated questions
Explanation	0.282
Background	0.263
Solutionhood	0.014
Cause	0.164
Result	0.156
Condition	0.067
Evaluation	0.054

Table 5: Statistics for Generated Questions

For evaluating our system (represented as QG), we considered the system developed by Heilman and Smith (2010) as a baseline (represented as MH). We sampled 20 questions for each relation type. Note that we did not consider the last four metrics for comparison purposes as these metrics were designed keeping question complexity in mind: MH never addressed this issue and hence such a comparison would be unfair. Table 6 summarizes the results obtained for our system against each relation type. The process was done by two evaluators who are familiar with the evaluation criteria, and are well versed with the corpus and nature of generated questions. The table reports the average scores, considering the evaluation done by each evaluator.

An analysis of the results reveals that many questions are syntactically and semantically well-formed and our results are comparable to that of MH. QG does outperform MH in several cases: however these performance gains are incremental. Issues commonly arose due to errors made by the parser; and the inability of NodeBox to convert between verb forms. Additionally, in some cases, the templates designed were unable to handle all text span Types either due to poor design or because the text span did not follow either definition of the defined Types. For example, some text spans were phrased as questions and some had typographical errors (originally in the text): this led to the generation of unnatural questions. Further, some text spans were arranged in a way such that the main clause appeared after the subordinate clause (For example, the sentence 'If I am hungry, I will eat a cake'): handling such text spans would require us to modify the text such that the subordinate clause

Evaluation criteria	System	R1	R2	R3	R4	R5	R6	R7	Average
Grammatical Correctness	MH	**0.95**	**0.94**	**0.91**	**0.98**	**0.98**	**0.9**	**0.84**	**0.95**
	QG	**0.95**	0.92	**0.91**	**0.98**	0.97	0.87	0.8	0.94
Semantic Correctness	MH	**0.95**	**0.91**	0.97	0.88	**0.94**	**0.88**	**0.8**	**0.93**
	QG	0.93	**0.91**	**0.98**	**0.92**	**0.94**	0.87	**0.8**	0.91
Superfluity of language	MH	**0.84**	**0.81**	0.77	**0.82**	**0.71**	0.9	**0.83**	0.66
	QG	0.81	0.69	**0.78**	**0.82**	0.68	**0.96**	0.8	**0.7**
Question Appropriateness	QG	**0.93**	0.83	**0.95**	0.75	0.78	0.87	0.6	**0.85**
Nature of coherence relation	QG	**0.79**	0.38	**1.0**	0.33	0.27	0.22	**0.94**	0.52
Nature of Question	QG	**0.71**	0.37	**1.0**	0.24	0.24	0.4	**0.88**	0.45
Average no. of inference steps	QG	**0.43**	**0.46**	**0.42**	**0.56**	**0.39**	**0.33**	**0.27**	**0.42**

Table 6: Average score for the evaluation criteria. Here R1: Explanation, R2: Background, R3: Solutionhood, R4: Cause, R5: Result, R6: Condition, R7: Evaluation. The average scores for each criterion are indicated in the last column.

follows the main clause (In this example's case, 'I will eat a cake if I am hungry'). However, to the best of our knowledge, there are no known transformations that allow us to achieve this rearrangement.

Table 7 provides some statistics on common error sources that contributed to semantic (and/or grammatical) errors in generated questions.

Source of Error	Percentage of incorrect questions
NodeBox errors	6.7%
Parsing errors	8.3%
Poor template design	13.3%
Incorrect Type Identification	13.3%
Clause rearrangement	57.3%
Other minor errors	1.0%

Table 7: Common error sources: The percentage of incorrect questions is the ratio of incorrect to total questions with semantic/grammatic errors.

Superfluity of language is of concern, as generated questions often contained redundant information. However, identifying redundant information in a question would require a deep understanding of the semantics of the text spans and of the relation that holds between them. Currently, modern discourse parsers are inept at handling this aspect.

The latter four metrics depend heavily on the corpus, and not the designed system. QG, because of its ability to create inter-sentential questions and handle complex coherence relations, was given a moderate to good score by both evaluators. Depending on the text and its relations, these scores may vary. We expect these scores to increase considerably for a corpus containing many implicit relations between text spans that are displaced far apart in the text.

5 Conclusions and future work

We used multiple sources of information, namely a cognitive taxonomy and discourse theory to generate meaningful questions. Our contribution to the task of QG can be thus summarized as:

- As opposed to generating questions from sentences, our system generates questions from entire paragraphs and/or documents.

- Generated questions require the student to write detailed responses that may be as long as a paragraph.

- Designed templates are robust. Unlike previous systems which work on structured inputs such as sentences or events, our system can work around mostly any type of input.

- We have considered both explicit coherence relations that are made apparent through discourse connectives (Taboada (2009)), and implicit relations that are difficult to realize.

- Our system generates inter-sentential questions. To the best of our knowledge, this is the first work to be proposed that performs this task for a generic document.

There are several avenues for potential research. We have focused only a subset of relations making up the RST-DT corpus. Templates can also be defined for other relations to generate more questions. Further, Reed and Daskalopulu (1998) argue RST can be complemented by defining more relations or relations specific to a particular domain. We also wish to investigate the effectiveness of encoder-decoder models in obtaining questions from Nucleus-Satellite relation pairs. This might eliminate the need for manually performing coreference resolution and/or paraphrasing.

We also wish to investigate other performance metrics that could allow us to measure question complexity and extensibility. Further, we have not addressed the task of ranking questions according to their difficulty or complexity. We wish to come up with a statistical model that analyzes questions and ranks them according to their complexity or classifies them in accordance with the levels making up the hierarchy of Bloom's taxonomy (Thompson et al. (2008)).

References

Lorin W Anderson, David R Krathwohl, P Airasian, K Cruikshank, R Mayer, P Pintrich, James Raths, and M Wittrock. 2001. A taxonomy for learning, teaching and assessing: A revision of blooms taxonomy. *New York. Longman Publishing. Artz, AF, & Armour-Thomas, E.(1992). Development of a cognitive-metacognitive framework for protocol analysis of mathematical problem solving in small groups. Cognition and Instruction* 9(2):137–175.

Jun Araki, Dheeraj Rajagopal, Sreecharan Sankaranarayanan, Susan Holm, Yukari Yamakawa, and Teruko Mitamura. 2016. Generating questions and multiple-choice answers using semantic analysis of texts. In *COLING.* pages 1125–1136.

Lee Becker, Sumit Basu, and Lucy Vanderwende. 2012. Mind the gap: learning to choose gaps for question generation. In *Proceedings of the 2012 Conference of the North American Chapter of the Association for Computational Linguistics: Human Language Technologies.* Association for Computational Linguistics, pages 742–751.

E. Bengtson and D. Roth. 2008. Understanding the value of features for coreference resolution. In *EMNLP*.

Steven Bird. 2006. Nltk: the natural language toolkit. In *Proceedings of the COLING/ACL on Interactive presentation sessions.* Association for Computational Linguistics, pages 69–72.

Frederik De Bleser, Tom De Smedt, and Lucas Nijs. 2002. Nodebox version 1.9.5 for mac os x. http://nodebox.net.

Benjamin Samuel Bloom, Committee of College, and University Examiners. 1964. *Taxonomy of educational objectives*, volume 2. Longmans, Green New York.

Lynn Carlson, Daniel Marcu, and Mary Ellen Okurowski. 2003. Building a discourse-tagged corpus in the framework of rhetorical structure theory. In *Current and new directions in discourse and dialogue*, Springer, pages 85–112.

Kyunghyun Cho, Bart Van Merriënboer, Caglar Gulcehre, Dzmitry Bahdanau, Fethi Bougares, Holger Schwenk, and Yoshua Bengio. 2014. Learning phrase representations using rnn encoder-decoder for statistical machine translation. *arXiv preprint arXiv:1406.1078* .

Sérgio Curto, Ana Cristina Mendes, and Luisa Coheur. 2012. Question generation based on lexico-syntactic patterns learned from the web. *Dialogue & Discourse* 3(2):147–175.

Takshak Desai, Udit Deshmukh, Mihir Gandhi, and Lakshmi Kurup. 2016. A hybrid approach for detection of plagiarism using natural language processing. In *Proceedings of the Second International Conference on Information and Communication Technology for Competitive Strategies.* ACM, New York, NY, USA, ICTCS '16, pages 6:1–6:6.

Xinya Du, Junru Shao, and Claire Cardie. 2017. Learning to ask: Neural question generation for reading comprehension. *arXiv preprint arXiv:1705.00106* .

John A Glover, Barbara S Plake, Barry Roberts, John W Zimmer, and Mark Palmere. 1981. Distinctiveness of encoding: The effects of paraphrasing and drawing inferences on memory from prose. *Journal of Educational Psychology* 73(5):736.

Michael Heilman and Noah A Smith. 2010. Good question! statistical ranking for question generation. In *Human Language Technologies: The 2010 Annual Conference of the North American Chapter of the Association for Computational Linguistics.* Association for Computational Linguistics, pages 609–617.

Jiwei Li, Rumeng Li, and Eduard H Hovy. 2014. Recursive deep models for discourse parsing. In *EMNLP.* pages 2061–2069.

David Lindberg, Fred Popowich, John Nesbit, and Phil Winne. 2013. Generating natural language questions to support learning on-line .

Prashanth Mannem, Rashmi Prasad, and Aravind Joshi. 2010. Question generation from paragraphs at upenn: Qgstec system description. In *Proceedings of QG2010: The Third Workshop on Question Generation*. pages 84–91.

Karen Mazidi and Rodney D Nielsen. 2014. Linguistic considerations in automatic question generation. In *ACL (2)*. pages 321–326.

Ruslan Mitkov and Le An Ha. 2003. Computer-aided generation of multiple-choice tests. In *Proceedings of the HLT-NAACL 03 workshop on Building educational applications using natural language processing-Volume 2*. Association for Computational Linguistics, pages 17–22.

Joakim Nivre, Marie-Catherine de Marneffe, Filip Ginter, Yoav Goldberg, Jan Hajic, Christopher D Manning, Ryan T McDonald, Slav Petrov, Sampo Pyysalo, Natalia Silveira, et al. 2016. Universal dependencies v1: A multilingual treebank collection. In *LREC*.

Michael O'Donnell. 2000. Rsttool 2.4: a markup tool for rhetorical structure theory. In *Proceedings of the first international conference on Natural language generation-Volume 14*. Association for Computational Linguistics, pages 253–256.

Andrew M Olney, Arthur C Graesser, and Natalie K Person. 2012. Question generation from concept maps. *Dialogue & Discourse* 3(2):75–99.

Andreas Papasalouros, Konstantinos Kanaris, and Konstantinos Kotis. 2008. Automatic generation of multiple choice questions from domain ontologies. In *e-Learning*. Citeseer, pages 427–434.

Chris Reed and Aspassia Daskalopulu. 1998. Modelling contractual arguments. In *PROCEEDINGS OF THE 4TH INTERNATIONAL CONFERENCE ON ARGUMENTATION (ISSA-98). SICSAT*. Citeseer.

Attapol Rutherford and Nianwen Xue. 2014. Discovering implicit discourse relations through brown cluster pair representation and coreference patterns. In *EACL*. volume 645, page 2014.

Katherine Stasaski and Marti A Hearst. 2017. Multiple choice question generation utilizing an ontology. In *Proceedings of the 12th Workshop on Innovative Use of NLP for Building Educational Applications*. pages 303–312.

Maite Taboada. 2009. Implicit and explicit coherence relations. *Discourse, of course. Amsterdam: John Benjamins* pages 127–140.

Errol Thompson, Andrew Luxton-Reilly, Jacqueline L Whalley, Minjie Hu, and Phil Robbins. 2008. Bloom's taxonomy for cs assessment. In *Proceedings of the tenth conference on Australasian computing education-Volume 78*. Australian Computer Society, Inc., pages 155–161.

Sandra A Thompson and William C Mann. 1987. Rhetorical structure theory. *IPRA Papers in Pragmatics* 1(1):79–105.

Kristina Toutanova, Dan Klein, Christopher D Manning, and Yoram Singer. 2003. Feature-rich part-of-speech tagging with a cyclic dependency network. In *Proceedings of the 2003 Conference of the North American Chapter of the Association for Computational Linguistics on Human Language Technology-Volume 1*. Association for Computational Linguistics, pages 173–180.

Sam Wiseman, Alexander M Rush, and Stuart M Shieber. 2016. Learning global features for coreference resolution. *arXiv preprint arXiv:1604.03035* .

Jun Yin, Xin Jiang, Zhengdong Lu, Lifeng Shang, Hang Li, and Xiaoming Li. 2015. Neural generative question answering. *arXiv preprint arXiv:1512.01337* .

Syntactic and Lexical Approaches to Reading Comprehension

Henry Lin

esotericbubba@hotmail.com

Hackley School, Tarrytown, New York

Abstract

Teaching reading comprehension in K – 12 faces a number of challenges. Among them are identifying the portions of a text that are difficult for a student, comprehending major critical ideas, and understanding context-dependent polysemous words. We present a simple, unsupervised but robust and accurate syntactic method for achieving the first objective and a modified hierarchical lexical method for the second objective. Focusing on pinpointing troublesome sentences instead of the overall readability and on concepts central to a reading, we believe these methods will greatly facilitate efforts to help students improve reading skills.

1 Introduction

Teaching reading comprehension and readability research are related but also different. Readability research generally focuses on ranking the difficult level of a passage while reading comprehension education more directly aims at helping students read better.

Although readability metrics offer a good indication of a passage's difficulty level, a more useful approach for teaching comprehension is to pick out those difficult sentences for specific, targeted learning. Although vocabulary is an important factor in making a sentence difficult, it also often happens that a sentence, either with no unknown words or after all the words have been looked up, is still difficult to understand. The following is an example from a 6th grade history reading:

"Nor have legitimate grounds ever failed a prince who wished to show colorable excuse for the non-fulfillment of his promise."[1]

-----

[1] Niccolo Machiavelli, *The Prince*, Chapter XVII.

Even though the main idea was more or less clear, sentences like this were, in general, difficult for 6th graders.

Sufficient background and vocabulary are two prerequisites of reading success, but beyond these two, what textual features are there that make a sentence hard? This is one question this paper addresses. The second question is how to help students understand all major critical ideas in a reading because in a passage, in addition to the main idea, there are major supporting details that are crucial to comprehension. For example, in Martin Luther King Jr.'s *Beyond Vietnam* speech, the main idea is to oppose the war in Vietnam and there are four major reasons given. Understanding these four reasons is as integral to the passage's comprehension as the main idea. The third question we address is how to help students understand in-context polysemous words. Together, this paper makes the following contributions:

- A set of simple and accurate statistics that identifies, within a passage, the sentences that are challenging.
- A set of interesting findings about the standardized reading tests.
- A modified hierarchical lexical clustering method to find critical concepts in a reading.
- A word2vec application for selecting in-context meaning of a word.

2 Previous Work

One focus of the previous NLP work on accessing text difficulties is readability ranking. For example, Lexile (Lennon, 2004), Flesch-Kincaid (Kincaid, 1975), Dale-Chall (Dale, 1948), Coleman-Liau (Coleman, 1975), and SMOG (McLaughlin, 1969) largely rely on words and sentence length. Since one or two long sentences or difficult words do not necessarily make a passage difficult, those systems give rankings for an entire passage or a

Proceedings of the 5th Workshop on Natural Language Processing Techniques for Educational Applications, pages 11–19

Melbourne, Australia, July 19, 2018. ©2018 Association for Computational Linguistics

book and are not aimed at pinpointing difficult sentences.

Recently, Pitler et. al. (2008), Peterson et. al. (2009), Kate et. al. (2010), Feng (2010), and Dascalu et. al. (2013) addressed the readability problem using supervised data and a richer set of linguistic features. However, their systems still focus on giving a readability score of the overall article, not individual sentences from which students can improve their reading comprehension. Pitler et. al. (2008) and Tanaka-Ishii et. al. (2010) also built comparators to decide relative difficulty between two sentences. Both and Tanaka-Ishii et. al. (2010) especially make heavy use of lexical features. All these models also require supervised data and vocabulary acquisition.

Works by François et. al. (2014), Siddharthan et. al. (2014), and Vajjala et. al. (2014) have focused on sentence simplification instead of sentence selection for the purpose of teaching reading comprehension. This paper provides a simple and robust method for identifying difficult sentences in a reading passage. We incorporate some of the standard features seen in previous work such as tree depth, but we also devise new features such as abstract appositives. While much of the previous research has made use of both lexical and syntactic features, our focus is on an in-depth study on syntax phenomena that contribute to sentence complexity.

In addition to individual sentences that are hard to read, scattered concepts are also challenging to a reader. An author often develops a critical idea in several paragraphs using paraphrases, synonyms, and related ideas. When a reader cannot see the relation among these words and phrases, he will have difficulty grasping that concept. For this problem, we propose a word2vec-based (Mikolov, 2013) modified hierarchical clustering model to find clusters of concepts in a reading passage.

3 The Syntactic Features

We present a set of simple and robust features able to identify the difficult sentences in a reading. We show the efficacy of these features in a series of tests on grade-level readings.

3.1 The Features

Figures 1a – 1f depict each feature in action. In the figure, each rectangular box describes what the feature is and how the feature is determined.

3.2 Feature Performance

Our goal is to find candidate sentences that are challenging for a young reader. This task is difficult to evaluate for two reasons: the lack of labeled data at sentence level and probably more importantly, the lack of a methodology for creating such a dataset. The creation of supervised data involves judgment from a young reader (under 16 years of age). First, young children often cannot articulate what they find difficult. Second, they sometimes think they understand a sentence while they don't. An attempt was made at a local tutoring center for children 11-16. Fifty-two children were given a grade-level passage and an above-grade passage (e.g. a hard SAT passage). They were asked to pick out the sentences they didn't understand. For both passages, more than 80% of the children either said they understood everything or they found the passage hard but couldn't tell where the difficulties were. They were then given multiple-choice questions. Fewer than 5% of the children who claimed they understood everything scored perfectly on the test. For more than 50% of the mistakes made, more than half the children claimed that it was not because they didn't understand the passage but because they were careless. This attempt showed that human judgment from a young reader is hard to obtain. Secondly, an approximation of difficulty via test performance is problematic. Perhaps, a possible approach is to convene expert reading teachers and ask them to, based on their field experiences, rank each sentence's difficulty level for each grade. This would require these teachers to have intimate knowledge of how children process sentences. For these reasons, we first evaluate the features by measuring how well they correspond to the changes in reading levels. We then use the features to rank the difficulty of each sentence and perform a qualitative assessment.

For the first part of the evaluation, we look for data that correlate well with grade levels. Representative grade-level readings are not easy to collect because readers in each grade vary greatly in their reading abilities[2]. We thus use passages in standardized tests. In this section, we present data from passages on the New York State ELA tests, which are annual tests given to students from grades 3 to 8. For high school reading data, we

---

[2] For example, according to Lexile, the range for 7th grade reading is 300L to 1330L, a difference between *Three Billy-Goats Gruff* (340L) and *Understanding Hume* (1290L).

use the SAT test, a national test for high school students. Thus, the data represent standard reading levels of grades 3 to high school. We first run the Stanford parser (Manning et. al.,2014). We then collect statistics of the nine features on each sentence. The data statistics and feature performance are

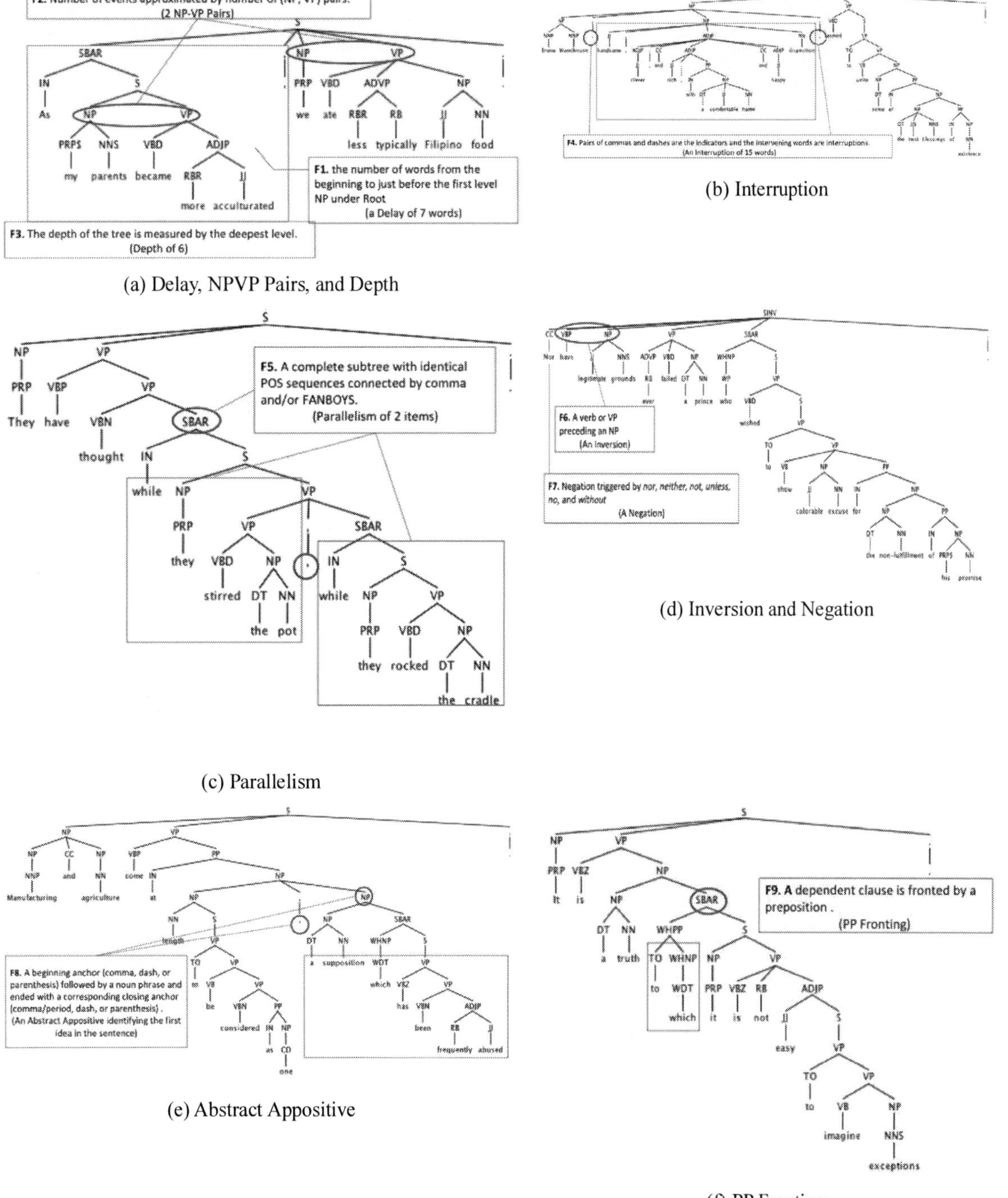

(a) Delay, NPVP Pairs, and Depth

(b) Interruption

(c) Parallelism

(d) Inversion and Negation

(e) Abstract Appositive

(f) PP Fronting

Figure 1. Syntactic Features

presented in Table 1 and Figures 2a-2c. *p*-values of *t*-test at α=0.05 are shown in Tables 2a − 2c. For example, the increase in Delay from Grade 5 to Grade 6 is 95% statistically significant (p-value 0.003 < 0.05 in Table 2a). All significant changes are in bold. While the general trend is increasing through grades, sometimes decreases are observed in two adjacent grades. Many of the decreases are statistically insignificant such as the decrease in Delay from G3 to G4 with *p*-value of 0.13.

It is noticeable that in grades 3 – 12, standard readings contain virtually none of the more specialized features of 1c-1f. These features are more prominent in older and more mature readings such as those in 19th-century literature. In section 5, we use only features in 1a and 1b.

Grade	Test Year	#Sentences	#Tokens
3	2006 – 10	975	9,967
4	2006 – 10	1,729	20,533
5	2006 – 10	1,131	14,972
6	2006 – 10	1,145	17,306
7	2006 – 10	1.296	20,256
8	2006 – 10	1,636	26,812
9+	2009,12, 16	1,397	35,415

Table 1. Data Statistics

Grade	Delay	Pair NP-VP	Depth
3→4	0.13	**1.76e-11**	**3.47e-11**
4→5	0.48	**0.035**	**1.48e-7**
5→6	**0.003**	**0.002**	**0.002**
6→7	0.38	**0.011**	**0.011**
7→8	0.59	0.68	0.68
8→9+	**2.64e-9**	**1.09e-38**	**2.26e-55**

Table 2a. *p*-values

Grade	Inversion	Parallel	Interruption
3→4	0.10	0.61	0.20
4→5	0.25	**0.015**	**0.008**
5→6	0.31	0.31	0.04
6→7	0.08	0.08	0.58
7→8	0.83	0.83	0.05
8→9+	**1.80e-14**	**1.80e-14**	**3.10e-6**

Table 2b. *p-values*

Grade	Negation	Abstract Appositive	PP Fronting
3→4	0.07	**0.008**	0.10
4→5	0.45	0.08	0.83
5→6	0.28	0.33	0.75
6→7	0.06	0.76	0.14
7→8	0.30	0.35	0.24
8→9+	**9.52e-12**	0.87	**7.68e-9**

Table 2c. *p-values*

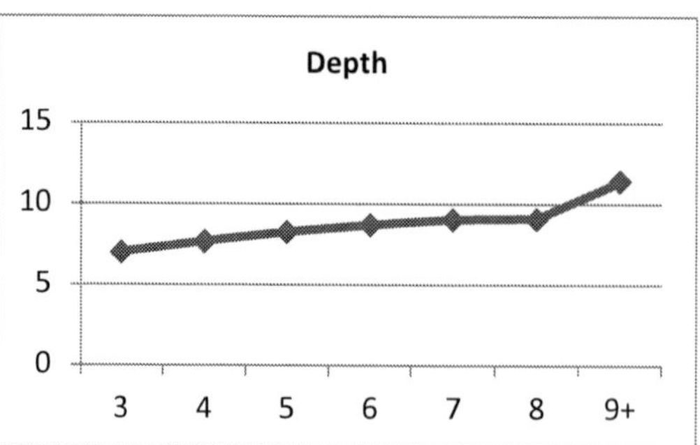

Figure 2a. Depth

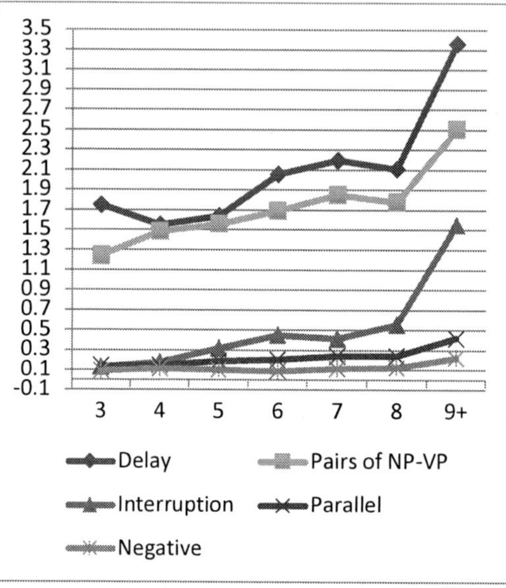

Figure 2b. Delay, NPVP, Interruption, Parallel, and Negation

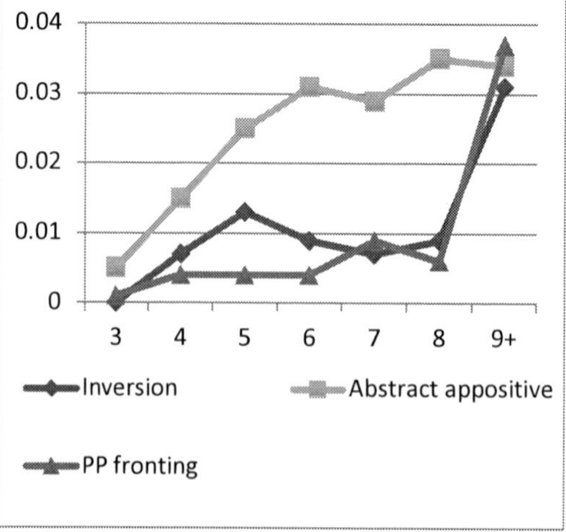

Figure 2c. Inversion, Abstract Appositive, and PP Fronting

Next we rank the sentences. Each sentence has a vector of nine feature scores. Although many different weighing schemes are possibilities, we take the simple approach of uniform weights. We compare the top-3 most difficult sentences ranked by the nine features to those ranked by sentence length and tree depth. For lower-grade texts, there is almost no difference in the order. But for more complex passages, more significant differences start to show. Through this exercise, we also find a qualitative value of the nine features. Even when the rankings by our nine features agree with the length-based rankings, we can point out more specifically what makes these sentences difficult. These specifics are shown as Notes in Table 3. We believe the ability to locate these syntax phenomena for students should be helpful in improving their reading skills.

Rank	Sentence
Top 1 by both	<u>Deeming that a serene and unconscious contemplation of him would best beseem me, and would be most likely to quell his evil mind,</u> I advanced with that expression countenance, and was rather congratulating myself on my success, <u>when suddenly the knees of Trabb's boy smote together,</u> <u>his hair uprose, his cap fell off,</u> he trembled violently in every limb, staggered out into the road, and crying to the populace, "Hold me!"
Notes:	Specifically, in addition to a depth of 17 levels, two long delay (underlined), and a parallel phrase (double underlined).
Top 2 by length and depth	Words cannot state the amount of aggravation and injury wreaked upon me by Trabb's boy, when, passing abreast of me, he pulled up his shirt collar, twined his side-hair, stuck an arm akimbo, and smirked extravagantly by, wriggling his elbows and body, and drawling to his attendants, "Don't know yah, don't know yah, 'pon my soul don't know yah!"
Top 2 by nine features	The disgrace <u>attendant on his immediately afterwards taking so <u>crowing and pursuing me across the bridge with crows,</u> as from an exceedingly dejected fowl who had known me when I was a blacksmith,</u> culminated the disgrace *with which* I left the town, and was, so to speak, ejected by it into the open country.
Notes:	a long interruption of 18 words (underlined), one parallel phrase ("crowing and pursuing", double underline), and one PP fronting ("with which", italicized).
Top 3 by both	One or two of the tradespeople even darted out of their shops, and went a little way down the street before me, that they might turn, as if they had forgotten something, and pass me face to face – *on which* occasions I don't know whether they or I made the worse pretence; <u>they of doing it, or I of not seeing it.</u>
Notes:	Specific features are PP fronting (italicized) and one parallel phrase (underlined).

Table 3. Sentence Ranking Example

4 The Lexical Approach

We now turn to finding critical ideas in a reading. Our concern is to find related and paraphrased words that contribute to the same idea.

4.1 An Example

We distinguish critical ideas from the main idea of a reading. Critical ideas are any ideas that the author develops to some extent. A crude definition is that a critical idea is an idea that the author mentions more than once. They may or may not be the main idea, but they should all contribute to the main idea. In the following short passage, there is one main idea and several critical ideas.

"Black holes are the most efficient engines of destruction known to humanity. Their intense gravity is a one-way ticket to oblivion, and material spiraling into them can heat up to millions of degrees and glow brightly. Yet, they are not all-powerful. Even supermassive black holes are minuscule by cosmic standards. They typically account for less than one percent of their galaxy's mass. Accordingly, astronomers long assumed that supermassive holes, let alone their smaller cousins, would have little effect beyond their immediate neighborhoods. So it has come as a surprise over the past decade that black hole activity is closely intertwined with star formation occurring farther out in the galaxy." (SAT 2009 Practice Test)

The main idea is the last sentence of the passage, but the many critical ideas that the author develops are: "black holes", "destruction", and "intertwined with star formation".

4.2 Finding Critical Ideas

The word2vec model (Mikolov, 2013) has been a widely used statistical model for encoding word meanings. We use a modified hierarchical clustering algorithm using word2vec[3] as a representation of each word. First, cosine distances are computed on every word pair in the passage (after removing stopwords), resulting in an $n \times n$ matrix where n is the number of words. Unlike the traditional hierarchical clustering where the end result is a tree structure, our clustering is more flat and does not build a hierarchy. The linking criteria are two: (1) the distance between two words must exceed a minimum and (2) the distance between a word and an existing cluster must exceed a minimum percentage of the best pair in the cluster. The algorithm is in Figure 3.

```
Make an empty Critical Cluster list
While (1) {
    (w_i, w_j) = next best word pair in the matrix
    score_ij = score of (w_i, w_j)
    if (score_ij < minimum_score_threshold) {
            break;
    }
    if (neither wi nor wj is in any cluster) {
        make a new cluster (w_i, w_j);
                add to Critical Cluster list;
    }
    else if (w_i or w_j is in a cluster) {
        cluster_k = the cluster w_i or w_j is in
                if (score_ij >= cluster_k's score) {
                    add w_i or w_j to cluster_k
    }
    else {
        cluster_i = the cluster wi is in;
                cluster_j = the cluster wj is in;
        if (score_ij >= cluster_i's score or
            score_ij >= cluster_j's score) {
                merge clusteri and clusterj
        }
    }
}
```

Figure 3. Word2Vec Modified Clustering

5 Applications, Experiments and Results

In addition to identifying troublesome sentences, there are many other useful things possible with these features. Interesting experiments include comparing tests across many dimensions such as across geography and across standards.

5.1 State Difference?

The National Assessment of Educational Progress, or NEAP offers reading assessments to 4th and 8th graders nationwide. In 2015, all 52 states participated. A state may score higher than another state for a variety of reasons, economic, political, etc. In this experiment, we're interested in seeing if there might be any meaningful correlation at all between a state's NAEP score and the difficulty level of its state ELA[4] tests. To this end, we select Massachusetts, the top-ranking state whose NAEP score of 235 is considerably higher than the national average of 221, and compare its state ELA passages to those of New York whose score is 223. The data comparison is shown in Table 4a. The metrics are shown in Tables 4b and 4c where p-values are at 95% and the bold values indicate statistical significance. Again, the more specialized feature 'Inversion' is not a significant factor in 4th and 8th grade readings[5].

Grade	Sentences	Words
NY 4th	1,729	20,533
MA 4th	1,093	16,593
NY 8th	1,636	26,812
MA 8th	908	17,594

Table 4a. NY and MA ELA Passages

Metric	NY 4th	MA 4th	*p-value*
Delay	1.551	2.083	**9.26e-5**
Interruption	0.180	0.527	**3.54e-7**
Pairs NP VP	1.484	1.765	**7.68e-11**
Depth	7.723	8.662	**1.85e-15**
Inversion	0.002	0.002	0.80

Table 4b. NY and MA 4th grade comparison

Metric	NY 8th	MA 8th	*p-value*
Delay	2.110	2.613	**0.016**
Interruption	0.557	1.116	**1.71e-6**
Pairs NP VP	1.778	2.074	**5.46e-7**
Depth	9.114	9.809	**1.26e-5**
Inversion	0.004	0.007	0.46

Table 4c. NY and MA 8th grade comparison

It's interesting to see that for both 4th and 8th grades, there is a progression of text difficulty from NY's ELA tests to MA's ELA tests. There are many reasons, both educational and non-educational, that come into play to influence one

---

[3] This is the Google News word2vec at https://github.com/mmihaltz/word2vec-GoogleNews-vectors

[4] English Language Arts
[5] At the time of the paper, only the 4th and 8th grade ELA from Massachusetts tests are publically available online.

state's performance. Perhaps this could be a first step in better understanding the impact of increased level of difficulty on student reading performance.

5.2   SAT or ACT?

The SAT and the ACT are standardized tests college-bound juniors and seniors take. One common section in both tests is the Reading section where students are given passages to read and multiple-choice questions to answer. Students and parents have long wondered which test is easier. A simple online search of "SAT reading vs. ACT reading" yields many comparisons. The question of which test is easier depends on many factors such as timing, question types, and so on. What this paper is concerned with is not necessarily the simple yes/no answer to the question of which test is easier, but rather with comparing the passages on each reading test. From a simple survey at a local test preparation center, students who choose ACT all report that the ACT passages are more straightforward than those on the SAT, and those who take the SAT report that some SAT passages are harder to read, specifically in genres such as pre-1900 fictions and history. This fact does not directly lead to a judgment of which test is easier, simply that the ACT passages are easier to read[6]. To test this hypothesis and to quantify how much easier or harder the reading passages differ on each test, we collect passages from both tests and run the feature analysis on them. The data information is presented in Table 5a.

Test	Year of Test	Number of passages	Number of words
SAT	2015 – 16 Official Practice	40	26,862
ACT	2015 – 17 Official Released Tests	40	28,752

Table 5a. SAT and ACT Passage Data

Feature	SAT	ACT	*p-value*
Delay	3.364	2.570	**0.0006**
Interruption	1.552	1.214	**0.014**
Pairs NP-VP	2.502	2.068	**2.92e-12**
Depth	11.403	10.264	**1.92e-12**
Inversion	0.009	0.008	0.728

Table 5b. SAT and ACT

Feature	SAT	ACT
Delay	2.397	1.248
Interruption	1.349	0.841
Pairs NP VP	0.893	0.425
Depth	2.179	1.490
Inversion	0.031	0.021

Table 5c. SAT and ACT Standard Deviation

The results of the analysis are shown in Table 5b. ACT passages score uniformly lower than those on the SAT with majority of the difference being statistically significant. Table 5c shows that the standard deviations of the SAT are higher, indicating that the SAT passages have more variations. The two excerpts from each test in Table 6 give a qualitative view of the phenomenon where * indicates an example of increased complexity.

ACT Humanities	In 2008, the prodigiously gifted bassist, singer, and composer Esperanza Spalding released her major-label debut. Esperanza, which she recorded as a twenty-three-year-old instructor at the Berklee College of Music.
ACT Science	Pikas, a diminutive alpine-dwelling rabbit relative. are unique among alpine mammals in that they gather up vegetation throughout summer—including flowers, grasses, leaves, evergreen needles, and even pine cones – and live off the hay pile throughout winter, rather than hibernating or moving downslope.
* SAT Humanities:	But of all relations, that between men and women, being the nearest and most intimate, and connected with the greatest number of strong emotions, was sure to be the last to throw off the old rule, and receive the new; for, in proportion to the strength of a feeling is the tenacity with which it clings to the forms and circumstances with which it has even accidentally become associated …
SAT Science	Nearly a half-century ago, Peter Higgs and a handful of other physicists were

---

[6] Independent of the level of the passages, the questions can still be hard. Therefore, the level of passages is but one factor among many that a student takes into account in deciding which test to take.

trying to understand the origin of a basic physical feature: mass. You can think of mass as an object's heft or, a little more precisely, as the resistance if offers to having its motion changed.

Table 6. SAT and ACT Passage Difference Examples

5.3 Automatic Vocabulary Response

It is labor intensive to manually evaluate the efficacy of the word2vec-based lexical approach. While we annotate data for further research, we meanwhile evaluate the idea on vocabulary questions on the 8 released SAT official tests (CollegeBoard, 2009). These vocabulary questions ask the meaning of a word in the context of a given passage. The majority of the choices consist of one word each. Our baseline approach is to measure the vector cosine score between the word in question and the words in each choice. The choice with the greatest similarity score is chosen as the answer. When a choice has more than one word, we first remove the function words and then take the average of the vector scores.

We then apply a contextual word2vec model to the questions. For each word in a vocabulary question, we locate the sentence that the word occurs in and add up the vectors of all the content words in that sentence. The resultant vector is then compared to each choice in the vocabulary question. Table 7 shows that the context model outperforms baseline significantly. This experiment shows the power of combining context and a computable meaning representation such as the word2vec.

28 Vocabulary Questions from 8 official SAT tests		
Method	Num. Correct	Accuracy
Baseline	5	17.86%
Context	20	71.43%

Table 7. Word2Vec-based Vocabulary Performance

One reason the baseline performs poorly is that almost all words tested in the SAT vocabulary questions are polysemous. The word2vec is trained on mostly news data which biases the meaning of a word toward a typical news-oriented meaning. For example, the word 'consumption', without context, is most intuitively associated with consumer and commerce. In this question, of the five choices, "destruction", "viewing", "erosion", "purchasing", and "obsession", the most

likely context-independent choice is "purchasing" and that is what the baseline model chooses. In the given passage, however, the enclosing sentence is "According to [this thesis], television consumption leads above all to moral dangers." After adding up all the vectors of the contextual words, the correct answer "viewing" surfaces and the context-model is able to answer that question correctly. This model makes concrete what the English teachers have meant when they instruct the students to look at the context. It also represents nicely the idea that the meaning of a word is *selected* by its surrounding words (the context).

6 Conclusion and Future Work

We present a set of straightforward and novel features to identify difficult sentences in a reading passage. In our experiments, the features correlate well with the actual grade of each text. We are also able to quantify and make more concrete of the differences between Common Core and pre-Common Core standards, and between different states. In the future, we hope to not only put all in an application for real use but also to incorporate general-purpose lexical features to further enhance reading comprehension education. Secondly, we intend to continue to investigate using word2vec as a stepping stone to distributed meaning representation. For example, extend critical ideas to multi-word phrases and tackle reading comprehension questions such as those on the SAT.

Acknowledgments

This work would not have been possible without the patient and generous help from my mentor Dr. Scott McCarley from IBM Research.

References

Coleman, Meri; and Liau, T. L. 1975. *A computer readability formula designed for machine scoring*, Journal of Applied Psychology, Vol. 60, pp. 283–284.

CollegeBoard, 2009. *The Official SAT Study Guide*. 2nd edition, Macmillan Publishing

Common Core. *Common Core State Standards* 2010 National Governors Association Center for Best Practices, Council of Chief State School Officers, Washington D.C.

Dale E, Chall J. 1948. *A Formula for Predicting Readability*. Educational Research Bulletin. 27. pp. 11–20.

Dascalu, M., P. Dessus, S. Trausan-Matu, M. Bianco, and A. Nardy. 2013. *Readerbench, an environment for analyzing text complexity and reading strategies*. In Artificial Intelligence in Education, pages 379–388. Springer

Feng, Lijun. 2010. *Automatic Readability Assessment*. Dissertation Thesis, City University of New York, NY.

François, T. et Bernhard, D. (eds.), 2014. *Recent Advances in Automatic Readability Assessment and Text Simplification*. In International Journal of Applied Linguistics (Special issue), 165:2

Kate, Rohit. J., Luo, X., Patwardhan, S., Franz, M., Florian, R., Mooney, R. J., Welty, C. 2010. *Learning to predict readability using diverse linguistic features*. In the 23rd International Conference on Computational Linguistics, p. 546–554

Kincaid, J.P., Fishburne, R.P., Rogers, R.L., and Chissom, B.S. 1975. *Derivation of new readability formulas (automated readability index, fog count, and flesch reading ease formula) for Navy enlisted personnel*. Research Branch Report 8–75. Chief of Naval Technical Training: Naval Air Station Memphis.

Lennon, Colleen and Hal Burdick. 2004. *The Lexile Framework as an Approach to Reading Measurement and Success*. https://cdn.lexile.com/cms_page_media/135/The%20Lexile%20Framework%20for%20Reading.pdf

Manning, Christopher D., Mihai S., John Bauer, Jenny Finkel, Steven J. Bethard, and David McClosky. 2014. *The Stanford CoreNLP Natural Language Processing Toolkit*. In Proceedings of the 52nd Annual Meeting of the Association for Computational Linguistics: System Demonstrations, pp. 55-60.

McLaughlin, G. Harry. 1969. *SMOG Grading — a New Readability Formula*. Journal of Reading. 12 (8): 639–646.

Mikolov T., Ilya Sutskever, Kai Chen, Greg Corrado, and Jeffrey Dean. 2013 *Distributed Representations of Words and Phrases and their Compositionality*. In NIPS, pages 3111–3119

Petersen, S.E., Ostendorf, M. 2009. *A machine learning approach to reading level assessment*. Computer Speech and Language, 23: 89-106.

Pitler, Emily and Ani Nenkova. 2008. *Revising Readability: A Unified Framework for Predicting Text Quality*. Conference on Empirical Methods in Natural Language Processing, Honolulu, Hawaii.

Siddharthan A., Angrosh Mandya. 2014. *Hybrid text simplification using synchronous dependency grammars with hand-written and automatically harvested rules*. In Proceedings of the 14th Conference of the European Chapter of the ACL, Gothenburg, Sweden.

Tanaka-Ishii, K., Tezuka, S., and Terada, H. 2010. *Sorting texts by readability*. Computational Linguistics, 36(2), pp. 203-227

Vajjala Sowmya, Detmar Meurers 2014. *Assessing the relative reading level of sentence pairs for text simplification*. In Proceedings of the 14th Conference of the European Chapter of the ACL, Gothenburg, Swede.

Feature Optimization for Predicting Readability of Arabic L1 and L2

Hind Saddiki,[†‡] **Nizar Habash,**[†] **Violetta Cavalli-Sforza,**[⋆] **and Muhamed Al Khalil**[†]
[†]New York University Abu Dhabi
[‡]Mohammed V University in Rabat   [⋆]Al Akhawayn University in Ifrane
{hind.saddiki,nizar.habash,muhamed.alkhalil}@nyu.edu, v.cavallisforza@aui.ma

Abstract

Advances in automatic readability assessment can impact the way people consume information in a number of domains. Arabic, being a low-resource and morphologically complex language, presents numerous challenges to the task of automatic readability assessment. In this paper, we present the largest and most in-depth computational readability study for Arabic to date. We study a large set of features with varying depths, from shallow words to syntactic trees, for both L1 and L2 readability tasks. Our best L1 readability accuracy result is 94.8% (75% error reduction from a commonly used baseline). The comparable results for L2 are 72.4% (45% error reduction). We also demonstrate the added value of leveraging L1 features for L2 readability prediction.

1 Introduction

The purpose of studies in readability is to develop and evaluate measures of how well a reader can understand a given text. Computational readability measures, historically shallow and formulaic, are now leveraging machine learning (ML) models and natural language processing (NLP) features for automated, in-depth readability assessment systems. Advances in readability assessment can impact the way people consume information in a number of domains. Prime among them is education, where matching reading material to a learner's level can serve instructors, book publishers, and learners themselves looking for suitable reading material. Content for the general public, such as media and news articles, administrative, legal or healthcare documents, governmental websites and so on, needs to be written at a level accessible to different educational backgrounds. Efforts in building computational readability models and integrating them in various applications continue to grow, especially for more resource-rich languages (Dell'Orletta et al., 2014a; Collins-Thompson, 2014).

In this paper, we present a large-scale and in-depth computational readability study for Arabic. Arabic, being a relatively low-resource and morphologically complex language, presents numerous challenges to the task of automatic readability assessment. Compared to work done for English and other European languages, efforts for Arabic have only picked up in recent years, as better NLP tools and resources became available (Habash, 2010). We evaluate data from both Arabic as a First Language (L1) and Arabic as a Second or Foreign Language (L2) within the same experimental setting, to classify text documents into one of four levels of readability in increasing order of difficulty (level 1: easiest; level 4: most difficult). This is a departure from all previously published results on Arabic readability, which have only focused on either L1 or L2. We examine a larger array of predictive features combining language modeling (LM) and shallow extraction techniques for lexical, morphological and syntactic features. Our best L1 Readability accuracy result is 94.8%, a 75% error reduction from a baseline feature set of raw and shallow text attributes commonly used in traditional readability formulas and simpler computational models (Collins-Thompson, 2014). The comparable results for L2 are 72.4%, a 45% error reduction from the corresponding baseline performance in L2. We leverage our rich Arabic L1 resources to support Arabic L2 readability. We increase the L2 accuracy to 74.1%, an additional 6% error reduction, by augmenting the L2 feature set with features based on L1-generated language models (LM).

Proceedings of the 5th Workshop on Natural Language Processing Techniques for Educational Applications, pages 20–29
Melbourne, Australia, July 19, 2018. ©2018 Association for Computational Linguistics

	Corpus			Depth of Features			LM	Results
	Size (tokens)	L1	L2	*Raw*	*Morph*	*Syn*	Features	Reported
Al-Khalifa and Al-Ajlan (2010)	150 docs (57,089)	✓		✓			✓	Accuracy: 77.8%
Al Tamimi et al. (2014)	1,196 docs (432,250)	✓		✓				Accuracy: 83.2%
Cavalli-Sforza et al. (2014)	114 docs (49,666)		✓	✓	✓			Accuracy: 91.3%
Forsyth (2014)	179 docs (74,776)		✓	✓	✓			F-Score: 71.9%
Saddiki et al. (2015)	251 docs (88,023)		✓	✓	✓			F-Score: 73.4%
El-Haj and Rayson (2016)	73,000 lines (1,8M)	✓		✓	✓			Spearman R: .329
Nassiri et al. (2017)	230 docs (60,000)		✓	✓	✓			F-Score: 90.5%
Our Work	**L1: 27,688 docs (6.9M)** **L2: 576 docs (186,125)**	✓	✓	✓	✓	✓	✓	**L1 Accuracy: 94.8%** **L2 Accuracy: 72.4%**

Table 1: Comparative summary of recent work and our current study on computational readability for Arabic in terms of corpus size, focus on L1 or L2, use of shallow vs. deep features requiring heavier processing for extraction from the text, use of language models in generating features. Results reported are presented for reference rather than direct comparison.

2 Background and Related Work

Computational readability assessment presents a growing body of work leveraging NLP to extract complex textual features, and ML to build readability models from corpora, rather than relying on human expertise or intuition (Collins-Thompson, 2014). Approaches vary depending on the purpose of the readability prediction model, e.g., measuring readability for text simplification (Aluisio et al., 2010; Dell'Orletta et al., 2014a; Al Khalil et al., 2017), selecting more cognitively-predictive features for readers with disabilities (Feng et al., 2009) or for self-directed language learning (Beinborn et al., 2012). Features used in predicting readability range from surface features extracted from raw text (e.g. average word count per line), to more complex ones requiring heavier text processing such as syntactic parsing features (Heilman et al., 2007, 2008; Beinborn et al., 2012; Hancke et al., 2012). The use of language models is increasingly favored in the literature over simple frequency counts, ratios and averages commonly used to quantify features in traditional readability formulas (Collins-Thompson and Callan, 2005; Beinborn et al., 2012; François and Miltsakaki, 2012). We evaluate features extracted using both methods in this study.

There is a modest body of work on readability prediction for Arabic with marked differences in modeling approaches pursued, feature complexity, dataset size and type (L1 vs. L2), and choice of evaluation metrics. We build our feature set with predictors frequently used for Arabic readability studies in the literature, and augment it with features from work carried out on other languages.

We do organize our feature set on two dimensions: *(a)* the way features are quantified: basic statistics for frequencies and averages, or **language modeling** perplexity scores; *(b)* the **depth of processing** required to obtain said features: directly from raw text, morphological analysis, or syntactic parsing. In Table 1, using these two dimensions, we situate ours and previous work and establish a common baseline of raw base features (i.e. traditional measures (DuBay, 2004)) to compare to.

Use of Language Modeling Features such as frequency counts, averages and other ratios seem to dominate the literature for *Arabic readability*. These are usually referred to as traditional, shallow, basic or base features in the literature for their simplicity. In contrast, Al-Khalifa and Al-Ajlan (2010) add word bi-gram perplexity scores to their feature set, a popular readability predictor in English and other languages.

Depth of Features The set of features used in previous readability studies exhibit a range of complexity in terms of depth of processing needed to obtain them. While some studies have relied on raw text features requiring shallow computations (Al-Khalifa and Al-Ajlan, 2010; Al Tamimi et al., 2014; El-Haj and Rayson, 2016), most augment their feature set with lexical and morphological information by processing the text further and extracting features such as lemmas, morphemes, and part-of-speech tags (Cavalli-Sforza et al., 2014; Forsyth, 2014; Saddiki et al., 2015; Nassiri et al., 2017). We add another level of feature complexity by extracting features from syntactic parsing, used in readability assessment for other languages but so far untried for Arabic (Table 1).

3 Features for Readability Prediction

Textual features associated with degree of readability range from surface attributes such as text length or average word length, to more complex ones quantifying cohesion or higher-level text pragmatics. Naturally, the shallower attributes are also the easiest and least costly to extract from a text, as opposed to the deeper and more computationally challenging features.

Notation We define the notation used in the remainder of this paper to describe features, ranges of features and classification feature sets:

- An individual feature is expressed as F[i], $i \in [1, 146]$ is a number assigned to the feature as defined in Table 2; e.g., **F[1]** for number of characters per document

- A feature range is expressed as F[i-j], $1 \leq i \leq j \leq 146$ and indicates a group of features similar in nature with numbers assigned to them as defined in Table 2

- A classification feature set or subset is expressed as FEAT $_{Subscript}^{Superscript}$. The superscript indicates whether the set contains features that are {Raw, Morph, Syn or all three Raw.Morph.Syn}. The subscript indicates whether the features are computed as {Base, LM, or both Base.LM} quantities.

The feature list we have compiled (Table 2) is inspired by previous work for Arabic and other languages, and is organized by category as discussed in the previous section.

Base features FEAT $_{Base}$ range from shallow estimates, like word count or average sentence length, to others requiring more advanced processing, e.g. average parse tree depth for sentences in a document. LM-based features FEAT $_{LM}$ are a range of 12 perplexity scores obtained on n-gram models (uni-, bi- and tri-grams) built per level of readability. For instance, the first 3 features in the range F[51-62] are the following: F[51] Level 1 character unigrams, F[52] Level 1 character bigrams, F[53] Level 1 character trigrams.

We also distinguish three category labels for the depth of NLP-based processing required to extract the different features:

- FEAT ^{Raw} : raw text extraction with minimal processing: Several formulas making use of raw text features have been successfully

8 FEAT $_{Base}^{Raw}$ *	
F[1] Characters	F[5] $\frac{Tokens}{Sentences}$
F[2] Tokens	F[6] Al-Heeti Formula
F[3] Characters/Tokens	F[7] ARI Formula
F[4] Sentences	F[8] AARI Formula
20 FEAT $_{Base}^{Morph}$ *	
F[9] Morphemes	F[19] $\frac{Verbs}{Tokens}$
F[10] Lemma Types	F[20] $\frac{Pronouns}{Tokens}$
F[11] $\frac{LemmaTypes}{Tokens}$	F[21] Psv. Verbs
F[12] $\frac{Morphemes}{Sentences}$	F[22] $\frac{PsvVerbs}{Tokens}$
F[13] Open-class Tokens	F[23] Perf. Verbs
F[14] Closed-class Tokens	F[24] $\frac{PerfVerbs}{Tokens}$
F[15] Nouns	F[25] Imperf. Verbs
F[16] Verbs	F[26] $\frac{ImperfVerbs}{Tokens}$
F[17] Pronouns	F[27] Cmd Verbs
F[18] $\frac{Nouns}{Tokens}$	F[28] $\frac{CmdVerbs}{Tokens}$
10 FEAT $_{Base}^{Syn}$	
F[29-36] CATiB dependency	
F[37] Average parse tree breadth	
F[38] Average parse tree depth	
24 FEAT $_{LM}^{Raw}$	
F[39-50] LM perplexity of Characters	
F[51-62] LM perplexity of Words *	
48 FEAT $_{LM}^{Morph}$	
F[63-74] LM perplexity of morphemes	
F[75-86] LM perplexity of lemmas	
F[87-98] LM perplexity of POS	
F[99-110] LM perplexity of lemma-POS mix	
36 FEAT $_{LM}^{Syn}$	
F[111-122] LM perplexity of CATiB POS	
F[123-134] LM perplexity of CATiBx POS	
F[135-146] LM perplexity of CATiB dependency	

Table 2: Our feature set organized by category. All features are calculated per document, and sentence level features are averaged per document. Feature sets or features marked by an * are inspired by previous work on Arabic readability.

adopted and adapted in English and other languages, their appeal largely due to them being easy to understand and compute.

- FEAT ^{Morph} : morphological analysis providing lexical and morpho-syntactic information: Readability is heavily influenced by vocabulary and word-level information (DuBay, 2007). Having word-level lexical and morpho-syntactic information can better inform the predictions.

- FEAT ^{Syn} : syntactic parsing providing parse tree information and dependencies: Syntactic features have shown promise in improving readability prediction, especially for L2 reading. (Hancke et al., 2012) (Heilman et al.,

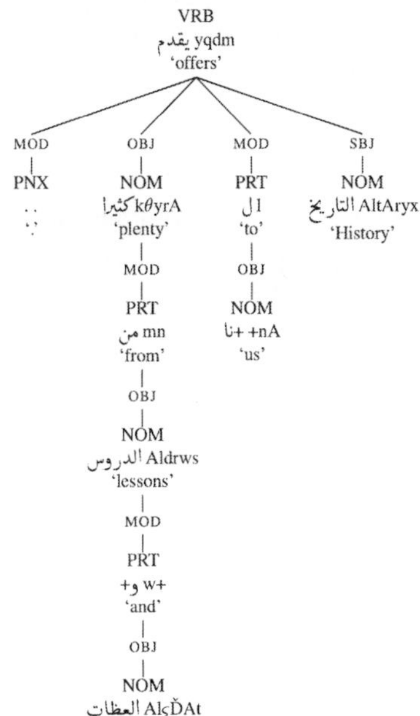

| | Word | Morph | POS$_6$ | English |
	Lemma	Morph POS	POS$_{34}$	
1	AltAryx	Al+tAriyx+u	NOM	history
	tAriyx	DET+NOUN	noun	
		+CASE$_{DEF.NOM}$		
2	yqdm	yu+qad$\sim$im+u	VRB	offers
	qad$\sim$am	IV3MS+IV	verb	
		+IVSUFF$_{MOOD:I}$		
3	lnA	la+nA	PRT	to, for
	li	PREP	prep	us
		+PRON$_{1P}$		
4	kθyrA	kaθiyr+Aã	NOM	plenty,
	kaθiyr	ADJ	adj	many
		+CASE$_{INDEF.ACC}$		
5	mn	min	PRT	from, of
	min	PREP	prep	
6	Aldrws	Al+duruws+i	NOM	lessons
	dars	DET+ NOUN	noun	
		+CASE$_{DEF.GEN}$		
7	wAlςǓAt	wa+Al+çiǓ+At+i	NOM	sermons
	çiǓaħ	CONJ+DET+NOUN	noun	
		+NSUFF$_{FEM.PL}$		
		+CASE$_{DEF.GEN}$		
8	.	.	PNX	.
	.	PUNC	punc	

FEAT $_{Base}^{Raw}$ **Features computed for the example sentence**

F[1] Characters	35	F[5] $\frac{Tokens}{Sentences}$		8.0
F[2] Tokens	8	F[6] Al-Heeti Formula $F[3] \times 4.414 - 13.468$		5.8
F[3] $\frac{Characters}{Tokens}$	4.4	F[7] ARI Formula $F[3] \times 4.71 + F[5] \times 0.5 - 21.43$		3.2
F[4] Sentences	1	F[8] AARI Formula $\frac{F[1] \times 3.28 + F[3] \times 1.43 + F[5] \times 1.24 + 472.42}{1046.3}$		0.6

Figure 1: TOP: Example of linguistic annotations for the sentence التاريخ يقدم لنا كثيرا من الدروس والعظات. 'History offers us plenty of lessons and sermons.'; BOTTOM: Table of FEAT $_{Base}^{Raw}$ feature values computed for the example sentence given.

2007)

In Table 2, most base features are computed simply by counting occurrences within the document. Ratios are expressed as mathematical fractions, such as F[3], F[5], F[11] and so on. LM perplexity is computed per readability level(1, 2, 3, and 4) on (uni-, bi- and tri-)grams language models, generating 4 level scores per n-gram and a total of 12 perplexity scores per feature. Figure 1 gives an idea of the linguistic annotation extracted for an example sentence and illustrates how feature values are computed for the FEAT $_{Base}^{Raw}$ subset. The annotation was generated using the CamelParser. POS tagsets used are POS$_6$ (Habash and Roth, 2009) and a higher granularity POS$_{34}$ (Habash et al., 2012). We refer the user to Shahrour et al. (2016) for further details.

We elaborate next on the feature names in Table 2:

- F[6] Al-Heeti readability formula for Arabic as presented by Al-Khalifa and Al-Ajlan

(2010) and other subsequent work.

- F[7], F[8] represent the Automated Readability Index (ARI) readability formula for English, and the Arabic ARI (AARI) readability formula for Arabic, both discussed at length by Al Tamimi et al. (2014).

- F[9] Morphemes - approximated by counting $proclitics + enclitics + stem$ for any given token, first explored by Cavalli-Sforza et al. (2014) and Forsyth (2014), further tested by Saddiki et al. (2015) and Nassiri et al. (2017).

- All features in FEAT $_{Base.LM}^{Morph}$ follow the MADAMIRA POS$_{34}$ tag set (Pasha et al., 2014).

- F[13], F[14] Open and closed class tokens are determined by POS$_{34}$ tag

- F[21], F[22] Marking passive voice as one of the few cases where diacritic marks are typically provided for disambiguation in otherwise undiacritized text intended for adult readers of Arabic. It is also a frequently used indicator of difficult or poor readability in other languages (DuBay, 2007; Aluisio et al., 2010).

- F[23-28] Marking verb aspect (perfective, imperfective, imperative) as an indicator used with some success in other languages (Dell'Orletta et al., 2014a).
- F[29-36] Columbia Arabic Treebank (CATiB) tagset (Habash and Roth, 2009).
- F[63-74] A morpheme language model is generated with the higher granularity Morph-POS tagset (illustrated in Figure 1) based on (Buckwalter, 2002).
- F[99-110] A lemma-POS mixed language model is generated with the lemma of open-class tokens and the POS_{34} (Habash et al., 2012) for closed-class tokens.
- F[111-122] A POS-based language model is generated with the CATiB POS tagset (Habash and Roth, 2009).
- F[123-134] A POS-based language model is generated with the extended CATiB POS tagset presented in (Marton et al., 2013).
- F[135-146] A dependency language model is generated on the CATiB dependency tags in F[29-36] to get different levels of dependency context information, the most salient one being dependency information for parent-child nodes in the parse tree.

4 Modeling Readability

We evaluate readability prediction as a classification problem on a large feature set for documents in two text corpora designed for L1 and L2 reading, and labelled with readability levels 1, 2, 3 and 4 in increasing difficulty.

4.1 L1 and L2 Data

We leverage the L1 leveled reading corpus built by Khalil et al. (2018) based on grades 1 through 12 of an Arabic school curriculum and a collection of adult-level fiction. The corpus was split across 4 levels of readability in increasing order of difficulty: level 1 (905 documents), level 2 (1,192 documents), level 3 (2,054 documents) and level 4 (18,089 documents). The first three levels are sourced from curricular texts, grades 1-4, 5-8 and

9-12. The fourth considerably larger level contains novels suitable for post-secondary readers.

For L2, we work with an augmented version of the corpus used by Forsyth (2014), Saddiki et al. (2015) and Nassiri et al. (2017). It is comprised of 576 documents, leveled according to the Interagency Language Roundtable (ILR) scale for foreign language proficiency.[1] With documents in the L2 corpus averaging 250 words, the L1 corpus was split accordingly for better comparability in our experiments.

Both the L1 and L2 datasets underwent an 80-10-10 random stratified split over the four levels for training (80%), development (10%) and testing (10%). The L1 corpus, partially sourced from textbook material from three different subjects, was also split across the three subjects to ensure a balanced sample of all three: *Arabic, Social Studies, Islamic Studies*.

4.2 Feature Extraction

The datasets are first enriched with several layers of linguistic annotation (e.g. Fig. 1) in preparation for feature extraction. Then, both raw text and annotations from the training set are used to build LMs for each of the 4 levels of readability (Table 3) with the SRILM toolkit (Stolcke et al., 2002). At this point, we begin extracting features from the various configurations of annotation and language models we generated:

- $\text{FEAT}_{Base.LM}^{Raw}$ features are extracted directly from the raw text, e.g. total number of characters in a document.
- $\text{FEAT}_{Base.LM}^{Morph}$ text is annotated with morphological, lexical and morpho-syntactic information using the MADAMIRA tool (Pasha et al., 2014) for morphological disambiguation.
- $\text{FEAT}_{Base.LM}^{Syn}$ text is annotated with syntactic parsing information using the Camel-Parser tool (Shahrour et al., 2016).

All $\text{FEAT}_{Base}^{Raw.Morph.Syn}$ features are obtained from computing occurrences, averages and other ratios over: raw text (FEAT_{Base}^{Raw}); lemmatization, tokenization and morpho-syntactic annotation ($\text{FEAT}_{Base}^{Morph}$); syntactic parsing annotation (FEAT_{Base}^{Syn}). All $\text{FEAT}_{LM}^{Raw.Morph.Syn}$ features

---

[1] The scale goes from 0 (no proficiency) to 5 (native or bilingual proficiency) with + designation for intermediate levels, for further details http://www.govtilr.org/skills/ILRscale1.htm

L1 Corpus					L2 Corpus			
Level	Source	Docs	Tokens		Level	Source	Docs	Tokens
1	K12 grades 1-4 (textbooks)	1,230	297,772		1	0 or 0+ (No proficiency)	31	2,462
2	K12 grades 5-8 (textbooks)	1,683	412,942		2	1 or 1+ (Elementary proficiency)	177	40,816
3	K12 grades 9-12 (textbooks)	2,553	628,978		3	2 or 2+ (Limited working proficiency)	290	105,277
4	Original literary texts (novels)	22,222	5,594,310		4	3 or 3+ (Professional working proficiency)	78	37,570
		27,688	**6,934,002**				**576**	**186,125**

Table 3: Descriptive corpus statistics for our L1 and L2 data.

are obtained from computing perplexity scores per document over the LMs generated using either raw text or text annotation (lemmas, POS, etc).

In total, there were 146 features extracted for each document. We perform three main experiments, described next, to determine their efficacy in the classification task for L1 and L2.

4.3 Experiment Setup

First, we build classifiers on the full feature set $\text{FEAT}\,_{Base.LM}^{Raw.Morph.Syn}$ to determine best performance for L1 and L2. All classification experiments are carried out within the WEKA environment (Hall et al., 2009). We test classification algorithms used with some success in previous work (*D.Tree* decision tree, *Rnd.F* random forest, *kNN* k-nearest-neighbour, *SVM* support vector machine). We include two baseline classifiers for reference: *zeroR* (a simple classifier predicting the majority class for all instances) and *oneR* (a 1-rule classifier using the feature with least error to predict the correct class).

Then, we test the performance of the feature subsets to assess the predictive power of different feature configurations for L1 and L2. We perform feature selection in two ways:

- Manually, following the categorization we defined in Table 2 and resulting in 12 combinations of feature sets to be tested: feature subsets (i, j) with i in {Raw, Morph, Syn} and j in {Base, LM} with $\text{FEAT}\,_{Base}^{Raw}$ as the performance baseline for evaluating all feature subsets; composite subsets (i) with i in {Raw, Morph, Syn} or (j) in {Base, LM}; and finally the full feature set $\text{FEAT}\,_{Base.LM}^{Raw.Morph.Syn}$.

- Automatic feature selection using correlation-based feature selection (CFS) $\text{FEAT}\,_{Base.LM}^{Correl}$ implemented as CfsSubsetEval in WEKA with a BestFirst backward search through the feature space (Hall, 1999).

Finally, we experiment with the potential of using L1 $\text{FEAT}\,_{LM}^{Raw.Morph.Syn}$ to improve L2 readability predictions. First, we calculate perplexity scores for L2 documents using L1 LMs. We add these perplexity scores as features to the original L2 feature set, bringing the total set size to 254 features. Then, using this $\text{FEAT}\,_{Base.LM.LM_{L1}}^{Raw.Morph.Syn}$ feature set, we: (1) rerun the classifier performance experiment to see if any overall performance improvement is achieved; (2) run CFS feature selection on the L1-based LM subset to examine which features correlate the most with L2 readability classes. All experiments are reported in terms of F-score in addition to % Accuracy and F-score to give a better sense of prediction performance while accounting for class imbalance in the corpus.

5 Results and Discussion

In this section we present and discuss the results of experiments previously described in Section 5.3, which we organize as follows: results to optimize for classifier choice, results to optimize for features choice, and finally results on leveraging L1-based features for L2 readability prediction.

5.1 Classifier Choice Optimization

The classification results in Table 4 show that SVM performs best on overall accuracy for both L1 and L2 predictions. For L1, SVM achieves error reduction of 76% to the zeroR baseline, 64 % to the oneR baseline, while outperforming other classifiers from the literature by varying degrees. Performance over the 4 levels of readability, measured in precision, recall and F-score, is as follows:

- Precision: Level 1 (78.3%), Level 2 (81.8%), Level 3 (89.4%) and Level 4 (97.5%)

- Recall: Level 1 (78.8%), Level 2 (68.9%), Level 3 (81.7%) and Level 4 (100%)

- F-score: Level 1 (78.5%), Level 2 (74.8%), Level 3 (85.4%) and Level 4 (98.7%)

Taking a closer look at misclassified documents, mostly from Levels 1, 2 and 3, we find the ma-

L1 FEAT $_{Base.LM}^{Raw.Morph.Syn}$	Accuracy	Average F1
ZeroR	77.9	21.9
OneR	85.4	52.1
D.Tree (C=0.25, M=12)	72.2	50.4
Rndm Frst (I=500)	94.6	83.6
kNN (k=9)	93.8	80.4
SVM (C=5.0, rbfKernel)	**94.8**	**84.4**

L2 FEAT $_{Base.LM}^{Raw.Morph.Syn}$	Accuracy	Average F1
ZeroR	50.0	16.7
OneR	34.5	24.4
D.Tree (C=0.25, M=2)	31.0	21.7
Rndm Frst (I=100)	50.0	55.0
kNN (k=2)	67.2	61.1
SVM (C=1.0, rbfKernel)	**72.4**	**60.5**

Table 4: Comparison of different classifiers using the full feature set FEAT $_{Base.LM}^{Raw.Morph.Syn}$ for L1 (left) and L2 (right). Baseline performance is that of classifiers ZeroR and OneR. Performance is reported in terms of Accuracy (%) and F1-score (%) averaged over the 4 classification levels.

L1 SVM Classifier		
Feature Subset	Accuracy	Average F1
FEAT $_{Base.LM}^{Raw.Morph.Syn}$	**94.8**	**84.4**
FEAT $_{LM}^{Raw.Morph.Syn}$	94.3	83.3
FEAT $_{Base.LM}^{Morph}$	94.3	83.1
FEAT $_{LM}^{Morph}$	93.8	81.6
FEAT $_{Base.LM}^{Raw}$	88.6	61.4
FEAT $_{LM}^{Raw}$	87.2	50.5
FEAT $_{Base.LM}^{Correl}$	85.3	42.6
FEAT $_{Base}^{Raw.Morph.Syn}$	83.4	40.7
FEAT $_{Base.LM}^{Syn}$	82.7	39.7
FEAT $_{LM}^{Syn}$	82.0	37.3
FEAT $_{Base}^{Morph}$	81.8	33.7
FEAT $_{Base}^{Raw}$	**79.3**	**28.1**
FEAT $_{Base}^{Syn}$	78.0	22.5

Table 5: Comparison of different feature subsets using SVM Classifier for L1 (based on best performance results from Table 4). Baseline performance is that of subset FEAT $_{Base}^{Raw}$. Performance is reported in terms of Accuracy (%) and F1-score (%) averaged over the 4 classification levels.

L2 SVM Classifier		
Feature Subset	Accuracy	Average F1
FEAT $_{Base.LM}^{Raw.Morph.Syn}$	**72.4**	**60.5**
FEAT $_{Base}^{Raw.Morph.Syn}$	70.7	38.6
FEAT $_{LM}^{Raw.Morph.Syn}$	67.2	53.7
FEAT $_{Base.LM}^{Correl}$	67.2	37.3
FEAT $_{Base.LM}^{Morph}$	67.2	36.4
FEAT $_{Base.LM}^{Syn}$	67.2	35.7
FEAT $_{Base.LM}^{Raw}$	63.8	35.1
FEAT $_{LM}^{Morph}$	63.8	34.6
FEAT $_{LM}^{Raw}$	60.3	33.2
FEAT $_{Base}^{Morph}$	51.7	19.6
FEAT $_{LM}^{Syn}$	50.0	16.9
FEAT $_{Base}^{Raw}$	**50.0**	**16.7**
FEAT $_{Base}^{Syn}$	50.0	16.7

Table 6: Comparison of different feature subsets using SVM Classifier for L2 (based on best performance results from Table 4). Baseline performance is that of subset FEAT $_{Base}^{Raw}$. Performance is reported in terms of Accuracy (%) and F1-score (%) averaged over the 4 classification levels.

jority mostly off by no more than 1 level. For intance, the bulk of misclassified documents for Level 1 are labeled as Level 2. This can be in part due to the high similarity between the highest grade in Level 1 (Grade 4) and the lowest grade in Level 2 (Grade 5), considering that Level 2 contains both Primary and Preparatory grades. Another typically misclassified document type is one containing mainly instructional text and intended learning outcomes for the lessons. This is a language and style of writing that is particular to textbooks and repeated throughout the curriculum. Level 2 shows more dispersion in the misclassifications across other levels. Considering that Level 2 combines a portion of upper Primary and lower Preparatory grades, we expect some interference from the proximity in style and content in Grade4-Grade5 and Grade8-Grade9. The inclu-

sion of more excerpts of original literary texts, especially in the Preparatory grades, could help explain why Level 4 predictions were obtained for some documents. Level 3 classification errs predominantly towards Level 4, this is also a plausible outcome considering that Arabic textbooks delve further into literature and include much longer excerpts of original fiction, and keeping in mind that some works of fiction are plausibly accessible to readers nearing the end of their K12 education.

Results for L2 remain consistent with 45% and 58% error reduction to the zeroR and oneR baselines, respectively.

We find that all misclassified documents are only off by 1 level and often due to the intermediate proficiency levels marked by a '+' being too close in difficulty to the next level up (e.g. a '1+' proficiency document misclassified as '2' accord-

	L2 Feat $_{Base.LM}^{Raw.Morph.Syn}$		L2 Feat $_{Base.LM.LM_{L1}}^{Raw.Morph.Syn}$	
	Accuracy	**Average F1**	**Accuracy**	**Average F1**
ZeroR	50.0	16.7	50.0	16.7
OneR	34.5	24.4	34.5	24.4
D.Tree	31.0	21.7	31.0	21.7
R.Forest	50.0	55.0	72.4	**67.9**
kNN	67.2	**61.1**	**74.1**	66.2
SVM	**72.4**	60.5	72.4	60.5

Table 7: L2 results with different classifiers on Feat $_{Base.LM.LM_{L1}}^{Raw.Morph.Syn}$. Comparison of different classifiers using the augmented feature set Feat $_{Base.LM.LM_{L1}}^{Raw.Morph.Syn}$ for L2 (L2 features + L1 LM features). Baseline performance is that of classifiers ZeroR and OneR. Performance is reported in terms of Accuracy (%) and F1-score averaged over the 4 classification levels.

ing to the scale in 3). Evaluating L2 readability is a worthwile experiment which is hindered mostly by data sparsness.

5.2 Feature Optimization

Feature optimization experiments are carried out with SVM classification using the best performing parameter configurations for L1 and L2. Tables 5 and 6 show performance results of various feature subsets in comparison with the baseline Feat $_{Base}^{Raw}$. We make the following noteworthy observations:

- A combination of LM-based, NLP-based and traditional features Feat $_{Base.LM}^{Raw.Morph.Syn}$ performs best in readability prediction: 75% and 45% error reduction on Feat $_{Base}^{Raw}$ for L1 and L2 respectively

- LM Features Feat $_{LM}^{Raw.Morph.Syn}$ are better predictors than base features: performance is second-best for L1 and third-best for L2

- NLP-based features (Feat $_{LM}^{Raw.Morph.Syn}$, Feat $_{Base.LM}^{Morph}$, Feat $_{Base.LM}^{Syn}$) are better predictors than raw shallow features Feat $_{Base}^{Raw}$: this is true overall, with heavier influence in L2 prediction

- Features based on syntactic parsing Feat $_{Base.LM}^{Syn}$ inform readability predictions, more so for L2 than for L1: 16% and 34% error reduction on Feat $_{Base}^{Raw}$ for L1 and L2 respectively

Feat $_{Base.LM}^{Correl}$ for L1 is a subset of 10 features[2] achieving 29% error reduction on the Feat $_{Base}^{Raw}$

baseline. All features are LM-based, with 50% of them extracted from raw text, ideal for low-cost performance with minimal NLP effort. This can be useful in lightweight web-based readability tools. We also noted with interest an 80%-20% split into vocabulary-based and syntax-based features, suggesting that vocabulary plays a more dominant role in readability than grammar.

Feat $_{Base.LM}^{Correl}$ for L2 achieves 34% error reduction on the Feat $_{Base}^{Raw}$ baseline with 29 features,[3] dominated largely by LM-based attributes. Some interesting predictive features from Feat $_{Base}^{Morph}$ are lemma type count per document indicating lexical richness, Verb-to-Token ratio and Pronoun-to-Token ratio. Mixed LMs built with lemmas of open-class tokens and the POS of closed-class tokens for readability levels 2, 3 and 4 correlate highly with L2 predictions but did not figure in L1 Feat $_{Base.LM}^{Correl}$ which relied more on raw word LMs.

5.3 L1-based Features for L2 Readability

Table 7 presents the results of augmenting L2 with L1 LM-based features. Adding L1 features to the L2 feature set did not degrade performance for any of the classifiers. While D.Tree and SVM classification did not show any significant improvement, the L1 features drastically improved prediction accuracy and F-score for Random Forest (Accuracy: 45% error reduction, F-score: 28.6% error reduction) and kNN (Accuracy: 21% error reduction, F-score: 13% error reduction) classification.

Looking into LM-based L1 features[4] that correlate the most with L2 readability levels, we find that the most predictive of these features are mostly based on L1 readability levels 1 and 4, and distributed among raw character features, word features (raw and lemma), POS features, and parsing dependency features. Results from L2 using L1 encourage further exploration of L1 feature use in L2 readability prediction. It is worthwhile to explore the performance of classifying L1 documents on an L2 scale validated by expert judgment. Given the considerably smaller size of L2 resources in comparison with L1 texts, we can potentially mine L1 for L2-suitable material, thereby increasing the pool of texts available to L2 readers.

---

[2]L1 CFS-based subset of 10 features: F[41, 56, 58, 61, 62, 68, 71, 86, 123, 141], numbered according to Table 2

[3]L2 CFS-based subset of 29 features: F[10, 19, 20, 26, 37, 41, 47, 50, 55, 56, 58, 59, 62, 65, 67, 68, 73, 74, 82, 83, 86, 97, 103, 107, 109, 113, 124, 134, 137].

[4]L2 subset of L1-based features: F[46-50, 53, 55, 76, 85, 87, 92, 112, 120, 122-124, 126, 132, 141, 144-146].

6 Conclusion and Future Work

We have presented the largest and most in-depth computational readability study for Arabic to date. We studied a wide set of features with varying depths from shallow words to syntactic trees for both L1 and L2 readability tasks. Our best L1 Readability accuracy result is 94.8% (75% error reduction from a commonly used baseline). The comparable results for L2 are 72.4% (45% error reduction). We demonstrated the added value of using L1 features for L2 readability prediction by increasing the L2 accuracy to 74.1% (an additional 6% error reduction).

The next step in improving model robustness and performance would be to address the dataset imbalance among the four levels for both L1 and L2 by adjusting sampling (He and Garcia, 2009). We are also considering a cost-sensitive prediction model: for instance, by assigning different costs to misclassification scenarios, we can penalize the model more heavily for errors in sparser levels.

In the future, we plan to employ our best results in the development of online tools to support an effort for text simplification for pedagogical purposes. Going forward in this direction, we expect to widen our range to include different levels of document granularity: 500-word to 1K-word size documents, as well as sentence-level readability (Dell'Orletta et al., 2014b).

References

Hend S Al-Khalifa and Amani A Al-Ajlan. 2010. Automatic readability measurements of the Arabic text: An exploratory study. *Arabian Journal for Science and Engineering*, 35(2 C):103–124.

Muhamed Al Khalil, Nizar Habash, and Hind Saddiki. 2017. Simplification of Arabic masterpieces for extensive reading: A project overview. *Procedia Computer Science*, 117:192–198.

Abdel Karim Al Tamimi, Manar Jaradat, Nuha Al-Jarrah, and Sahar Ghanem. 2014. AARI: automatic Arabic readability index. *Int. Arab J. Inf. Technol.*, 11(4):370–378.

Sandra Aluisio, Lucia Specia, Caroline Gasperin, and Carolina Scarton. 2010. Readability assessment for text simplification. In *Proceedings of the NAACL HLT 2010 Fifth Workshop on Innovative Use of NLP for Building Educational Applications*, pages 1–9. Association for Computational Linguistics.

Lisa Beinborn, Torsten Zesch, and Iryna Gurevych. 2012. Towards fine-grained readability measures for self-directed language learning. In *Proceedings of the SLTC 2012 workshop on NLP for CALL; Lund; 25th October; 2012*, 080, pages 11–19. Linköping University Electronic Press.

Tim Buckwalter. 2002. Buckwalter Arabic Morphological Analyzer Version 1.0. Linguistic Data Consortium, University of Pennsylvania, 2002. LDC Catalog No.: LDC2002L49.

Violetta Cavalli-Sforza, Mariam El Mezouar, and Hind Saddiki. 2014. Matching an Arabic text to a learners' curriculum. In *Proc. 5th Int. Conf. on Arabic Language Processing (CITALA), Oujda, Morocco*, pages 79–88.

Kevyn Collins-Thompson. 2014. Computational assessment of text readability: A survey of current and future research. *ITL-International Journal of Applied Linguistics*, 165(2):97–135.

Kevyn Collins-Thompson and Jamie Callan. 2005. Predicting reading difficulty with statistical language models. *Journal of the Association for Information Science and Technology*, 56(13):1448–1462.

Felice Dell'Orletta, Simonetta Montemagni, and Giulia Venturi. 2014a. Assessing document and sentence readability in less resourced languages and across textual genres. *ITL-International Journal of Applied Linguistics*, 165(2):163–193.

Felice Dell'Orletta, Martijn Wieling, Giulia Venturi, Andrea Cimino, and Simonetta Montemagni. 2014b. Assessing the readability of sentences: Which corpora and features? In *BEA@ ACL*, pages 163–173.

William H DuBay. 2004. *The Principles of Readability*. Impact Information.

William H DuBay. 2007. *Unlocking Language*. Impact Information.

Mahmoud El-Haj and Paul Rayson. 2016. Osman: A novel Arabic readability metric. In *Proceedings of the Tenth International Conference on Language Resources and Evaluation (LREC 2016)*, Paris, France. European Language Resources Association (ELRA).

Lijun Feng, Noémie Elhadad, and Matt Huenerfauth. 2009. Cognitively motivated features for readability assessment. In *Proceedings of the 12th Conference of the European Chapter of the Association for Computational Linguistics*, pages 229–237. Association for Computational Linguistics.

Jonathan Forsyth. 2014. Automatic readability prediction for modern standard Arabic. In *Proceedings of the First Workshop on Free/Open-Source Arabic Corpora and Corpora Processing Tools (LREC 2014), Reykjavik, Iceland*.

Thomas François and Eleni Miltsakaki. 2012. Do nlp and machine learning improve traditional readability formulas? In *Proceedings of the First Workshop on Predicting and Improving Text Readability for target reader populations*, pages 49–57. Association for Computational Linguistics.

N. Habash, O. Rambow, and R. Roth. 2012. MADA+ TOKAN Manual. Technical report, Technical Report CCLS-12-01, Columbia University.

Nizar Habash and Ryan M Roth. 2009. CATiB: The Columbia Arabic Treebank. In *Proceedings of the ACL-IJCNLP 2009 Conference Short Papers*, pages 221–224. Association for Computational Linguistics.

Nizar Y Habash. 2010. *Introduction to Arabic natural language processing*, volume 3. Morgan & Claypool Publishers.

Mark Hall, Eibe Frank, Geoffrey Holmes, Bernhard Pfahringer, Peter Reutemann, and Ian H Witten. 2009. The weka data mining software: an update. *ACM SIGKDD explorations newsletter*, 11(1):10–18.

Mark Andrew Hall. 1999. *Correlation-based feature selection for machine learning*. Ph.D. thesis, University of Waikato Hamilton.

Julia Hancke, Sowmya Vajjala, and Detmar Meurers. 2012. Readability classification for german using lexical, syntactic, and morphological features. In *COLING*, pages 1063–1080.

Haibo He and Edwardo A Garcia. 2009. Learning from imbalanced data. *IEEE Transactions on knowledge and data engineering*, 21(9):1263–1284.

Michael Heilman, Kevyn Collins-Thompson, Jamie Callan, and Maxine Eskenazi. 2007. Combining lexical and grammatical features to improve readability measures for first and second language texts. In *Human Language Technologies 2007: The Conference of the North American Chapter of the Association for Computational Linguistics; Proceedings of the Main Conference*, pages 460–467.

Michael Heilman, Kevyn Collins-Thompson, and Maxine Eskenazi. 2008. An analysis of statistical models and features for reading difficulty prediction. In *Proceedings of the Third Workshop on Innovative Use of NLP for Building Educational Applications*, pages 71–79. Association for Computational Linguistics.

Muhamed Al Khalil, Hind Saddiki, Nizar Habash, and Latifa Alfalasi. 2018. A Leveled Reading Corpus of Modern Standard Arabic. In *Proceedings of the International Conference on Language Resources and Evaluation (LREC 2018)*.

Yuval Marton, Nizar Habash, and Owen Rambow. 2013. Dependency parsing of modern standard Arabic with lexical and inflectional features. *Computational Linguistics*, 39(1):161–194.

Naoual Nassiri, Abdelhak Lakhouaja, and Violetta Cavalli-Sforza. 2017. Modern standard Arabic readability prediction. In *International Conference on Arabic Language Processing*, pages 120–133. Springer.

Arfath Pasha, Mohamed Al-Badrashiny, Mona Diab, Ahmed El Kholy, Ramy Eskander, Nizar Habash, Manoj Pooleery, Owen Rambow, and Ryan M Roth. 2014. MADAMIRA: A Fast, Comprehensive Tool for Morphological Analysis and Disambiguation of Arabic. In *Proceedings of the Language Resources and Evaluation Conference (LREC), Reykjavik, Iceland*.

Hind Saddiki, Karim Bouzoubaa, and Violetta Cavalli-Sforza. 2015. Text readability for Arabic as a foreign language. In *Proceedings of the IEEE/ACS 12th International Conference of Computer Systems and Applications (AICCSA), Marrakech, Morocco*, pages 1–8. IEEE.

Anas Shahrour, Salam Khalifa, Dima Taji, and Nizar Habash. 2016. Camelparser: A system for arabic syntactic analysis and morphological disambiguation. In *Proceedings of COLING 2016, the 26th International Conference on Computational Linguistics: System Demonstrations*, pages 228–232.

Andreas Stolcke et al. 2002. Srilm-an extensible language modeling toolkit. In *Interspeech*, volume 2002, page 2002.

A Tutorial Markov Analysis of Effective Human Tutorial Sessions

Nabin Maharjan and Vasile Rus
Department of Computer Science / Institute for Intelligent Systems
The University of Memphis
Memphis, TN, USA
{nmharjan,vrus}@memphis.edu

Abstract

This paper investigates what differentiates effective tutorial sessions from less effective sessions. Towards this end, we characterize and explore human tutors' actions in tutorial dialogue sessions by mapping the tutor-tutee interactions, which are streams of dialogue utterances, into streams of actions, based on the language-as-action theory. Next, we use human expert judgment measures, *evidence of learning* (EL) and *evidence of soundness* (ES), to identify effective and ineffective sessions. We perform sub-sequence pattern mining to identify sub-sequences of dialogue modes that discriminate good sessions from bad sessions. We finally use the results of sub-sequence analysis method to generate a tutorial Markov process for effective tutorial sessions.

1 Introduction

Identifying effective instructional strategies, i.e., strategies that induce learning gains, has been a key research question in the Intelligent Tutoring Systems (ITSs) community. There are two common approaches used to address this research question: (1) hypothesize and validate through experimentation strategies guided by sound pedagogical theory (Aleven et al., 2001; Rus et al., 2017a) and (2) discover strategies employed by expert tutors (Boyer et al., 2011; Rus et al., 2015; Ohlsson et al., 2007). In our work, we adopt the latter approach which typically consists of mining patterns associated with successful tutorial sessions in large collections of recorded human tutoring sessions. (Boyer et al., 2011; Cade et al., 2008; Rus et al., 2015; Ohlsson et al., 2007).

It is important to note that discovering effective tutoring strategies by studying the strategies used by expert tutors is challenging because what characterizes tutoring expertise is still an open question to some degree (Rus et al., 2015). A tutor who employs sound strategies may appear less expert when working with students having low abilities or lacking in motivation. On the other hand, an average tutor may seem expert if s/he only works with high ability and highly motivated students. We lack student ability and prior knowledge information in our data and therefore focus on *effective tutoring* rather than *expert tutoring*. *Effective tutoring* refers to tutoring that yields learning gains. In sum, we study in this paper strategies of effective tutors as reflected in effective tutorial sessions.

In this paper, we worked with an annotated corpus of human tutoring sessions from which we identified effective sessions based on human expert judgments (see Section 5). We mapped tutorial sessions onto sequences of dialogue acts and dialogue modes (Cade et al., 2008), explained later, using a predefined coding taxonomy (see Section 3). We then conducted sub-sequence pattern mining to identify sub-sequences of dialogue modes that occur in effective tutoring sessions but not in ineffective tutoring sessions. We used these distinctive sub-sequences of modes to build a Markov process for effective tutorial sessions. Finally, using the tutorial Markov process, we analyzed and searched for dialogue mode patterns associated with effective tutoring sessions.

2 Related Work

Discovering the structure of tutorial dialogues and tutors' strategies has been a main goal of the intelligent tutoring research community from the very beginning because such tutorial session structures and strategies must be understood in order to be replicated in the development of effective

Proceedings of the 5th Workshop on Natural Language Processing Techniques for Educational Applications, pages 30–34
Melbourne, Australia, July 19, 2018. ©2018 Association for Computational Linguistics

ITSs. Graesser et al. (1995) proposed a five-step general structure of collaborative problem solving during tutoring. Cade et al. (2008) examined likely sequences of dialogue modes in expert tutoring. Boyer and colleagues (2009; 2010) applied hidden Markov models to discover effective dialogue modes inherent in the tutoring sessions. Rus et al. (2017b) used a supervised machine learning method to automatically map tutorial sessions into dialogue acts, sub-acts and modes and then analyzed human tutoring sessions using profile comparison and sequence logos to discover effective tutorial strategies in terms of dialogue acts and modes. Our work further contributes to this area of research by characterizing effective tutorial sessions in terms of dialogue mode sequential patterns and tutorial Markov processes.

3 Coding Taxonomy

The role of the coding taxonomy is to help us map tutors and tutees' utterances in tutorial dialogues onto actions, i.e., dialogue acts, based on the language-as-action theory (Austin, 1975; Searle, 1969) according to which *when we say something we do something*. For example, the utterance: *"There is an useful idea called 'conservation of energy'"* is categorized as an *Assertion* dialogue act, i.e., the utterance is making an assertion. Because the assertion is about *"conservation of energy"*, a *Concept*, we consider this as a specialized assertion about a concept, i.e., an Assertion-Concept dialogue act-subact combination.

We group sequences of dialogue acts and sub acts into higher level constructs, i.e., dialogue modes. Dialogue modes represent contiguous sequences of dialogue acts-subacts that together serve particular pedagogical purposes, e.g., a sequence of hints in the form of questions may reflect a scaffolding instructional strategy in which the tutee works mostly by herself on the current instructional task while the tutor offers help, when needed, through such hints.

The dialogue act and mode taxonomies are adapted to our context from a set of earlier taxonomies which were created to analyze a large corpus of online tutoring sessions conducted by human tutors in the domains of Algebra and Physics (Morrison et al., 2014). There are 17 top level expert-defined dialogue act categories. Each dialogue act category may have 4 to 22 subcategories or sub-acts. For example, we dis-

Annotation	Agreement (%)	Kappa
Act	77	0.72
Act-subact	62	0.60
Mode	44	0.37
Mode*	53.8	0.48
Mode**	64.3	0.60

Table 1: Average Inter Annotator Agreement Between Two Independent Annotators. Mode* and Mode** represent dialogue mode agreement between verifier and first annotator and, verifier and second annotator respectively.

tinguish *Assertions* that reference aspects of the tutorial process itself *(Assertion:Process)*; domain concepts *(Assertion:Concept)*, or the the use of lower-level mathematical calculations *(Assertion:Calculation)*. Further, we have a set of 17 dialogue modes: *Assessment, Closing, Fading, ITSupport, Metacognition, MethodID, Modeling, OffTopic, Opening, ProblemID, ProcessNegotiation,RapportBuilding, RoadMap, SenseMaking, Scaffolding, SessionSummary* and *Telling*. A detailed description of the dialogue modes is described by Morrison and colleagues (Morrison et al., 2014).

4 Data

A large corpus of about 19K tutorial sessions between professional human tutors and actual college-level, adult students on Algebra domain was collected via an online human tutoring service. 500 tutorial sessions containing 31,299 utterances were randomly selected for annotation. The sessions were manually labeled by a team of 6 subject matter experts (SMEs). They were trained on the taxonomy of dialogue acts, sub-acts, and modes. Each session was manually tagged by two independent annotators without looking at each other's tags to eliminate any labeling bias problems. The tags of the two independent annotators were double-checked by a verifier who resolved discrepancies in tags, if any. It should be noted that though the average inter-annotator agreement is apparently low, the final agreement of annotators with the verifier is higher (see Table 1). The verifier also happened to be the designer of our dialogue taxonomy. In this paper, dialogue mode should be interpreted as dialogue mode-switch.

Mode sub-sequences (p-value in bracket)
Fading-Closing (0.0002)
Scaffolding-Scaffolding (0.0008)
Fading (0.0009)
Scaffolding-Fading (0.0055)
Fading-Fading (0.01)
ProblemID-Fading (0.02)
ProblemID-Scaffolding-Scaffolding(0.0362)
Closing (0.05)
Fading-RapportBuilding (0.05)
Fading-ProcessNegotiation (0.06)
Fading-Scaffolding (0.07)
Fading-ProcessNegotiation-Closing (0.07)
Fading-Fading-Scaffolding (0.08)
ProblemID-Fading-Scaffolding (0.10)
Fading-Scaffolding-Fading (0.14)
Scaffolding-Closing (0.15)
Opening-ProblemID-Fading (0.18)
RapportBuilding (0.18)
Fading-Scaffolding-Closing (0.18)
Scaffolding-Fading-Scaffolding (0.20)
Scaffolding-RapportBuilding (0.23)
Fading-Scaffolding-ProcessNegotiation (0.26)
RapportBuilding-Closing(0.37)

Table 2: Discriminant mode sub-sequences.

5 Markov Analysis of Tutorial Sessions

In order to identify effective sessions, the SMEs also rated each tutorial session using a 1-5 scale (5 being best score) along two dimensions: evidence of learning (EL) and evidence of soundness (ES). The ES score is supposed to measure the degree to which the tutor applied pedagogically sound tactics. On the other hand, the EL score indicates whether there is strong evidence that the student learned from the tutoring session. The ES and EL distinction was designed in order to separate confounding factors such as learners' engagement in the session. For instance, a tutor may apply sound pedagogy but the student may not learn as all they might be interested is to find a quick answer to their (homework) problem. It should be noted that most of the sessions we had access to were in the context of homework help. That is, students start a session by asking for help with a particular problem. While EL and ES were supposed to capture different things, the EL and ES scores were found to be highly correlated (Pearson co-efficient of 0.7).

We used both EL and ES to capture overall qual-ity of tutoring sessions. We categorized all sessions having ES and EL scores ≤ 2 as ineffective, and all sessions rated with ES = 5 and EL ≥ 4 as effective.

We conducted discriminant mode sub-sequence analysis using *Traminer* package in R. It should be noted that a sub-sequence is not necessarily a contiguous sequence of observations, however, the order of the observations is preserved. For example, (*Fading*)-(*Closing*) is a valid sub-sequence of dialogue modes formed from the (*Fading*)-(*ProcessNegotiation*)-(*Closing*) contiguous session fragment. We generated sub-sequences up to length 7 from all annotated tutorial sessions.

The *Traminer* algorithm first finds the most frequent sub-sequences by counting their distinct occurrences and then applies a Chi-squared test (Bonferroni-adjusted) to identify sub-sequences that are statistically more (or less) frequent in each group. We used a p-value < 0.4 to generate a sufficient number of likely distinctive sub-sequences of modes (Table 2). Once the significant sub-sequences were identified, we generated a state transition matrix, explained next.

5.1 State Transition Matrix

We created a state transition matrix with modes as the states. We ignored sub-sequences of unit length as they don't indicate an observed transition. For sub-sequences spanning more than two states, we split them into multiple bi-gram sub-sequences. For example, we obtained bigram sub-sequences *Opening-ProblemID* and *ProblemID-Fading* from the *Opening-ProblemID-Fading* sub-sequence. We discarded self-transition paths since modes are actually mode switches in our case. Therefore, we discarded transition path *Scaffolding-Scaffolding* from the *ProblemID-Scaffolding-Scaffolding* sub-sequence.

We used confident scores of discriminant sub-sequences to compute transition probabilities. The confidence score of a discriminant sub-sequence is the probability that the sub-sequence is coming from an effective session, i.e., 1 - p-value. We computed a confidence score of a path as the confidence score of the discriminant sub-sequence the path belongs to. For example, for *Opening-ProblemID-Fading* (0.18), the confidence score of paths *Opening-ProblemID* and *ProblemID-Fading* is 1-0.18 = 0.82. We weighted an edge as the cumulative sum of its confi-

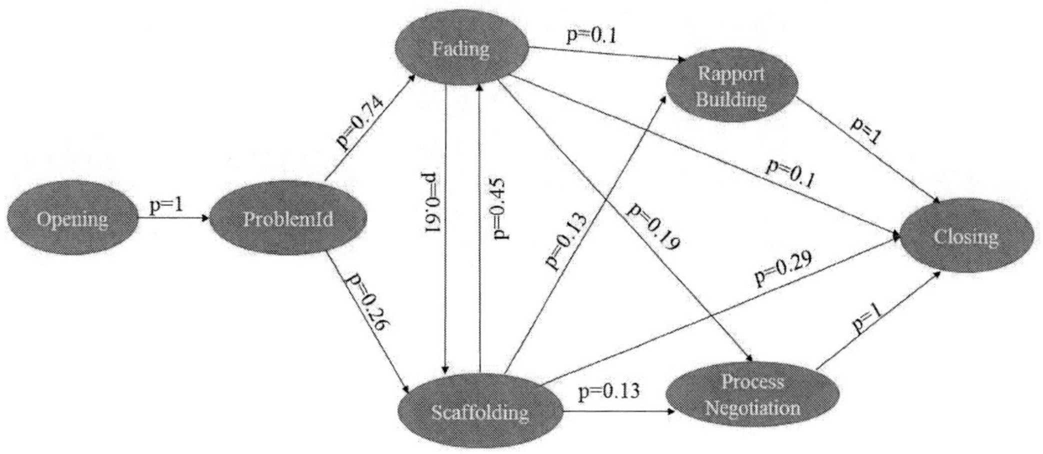

Figure 1: Tutorial Markov Process for effective tutorial sessions.

dence scores from all the sub-sequences where the path is present. For example, path *ProblemID-Fading* is present in sub-sequences *ProblemID-Fading* (0.02) and *Opening-ProblemID-Fading* (0.18). So, the weight of the path *ProblemID-Fading* is: 0.98 + 0.82 = 1.8. Finally, we normalized the weight of each path A-B to represent transition probability by dividing it by the sum of the weights of all possible transitions from A. For example, the weight of the path *ProblemID-Fading* is normalized by dividing it by the sum total of weights of all the transitions from *ProblemID* state.

5.2 Tutorial Markov Interpretation

Figure 1 shows the state transition graph of the underlying Markov process corresponding to the above state transition matrix. In the figure, the states are dialogue modes whereas transitions are generated using only the discriminant sub-sequences of modes. Each path has been labeled with the corresponding transition probabilities.

The Markov process reveals that any sequence of modes it can generate starts with an *Opening* and ends with a *Closing* state and is likely to have a large number of *Scaffolding - Fading* switches/transitions. This result partly supports theoretical expert tutoring models based on the *modeling-scaffolding-fading* paradigm (Rogoff and Lave, 1984). The high occurrences of these modes provide evidence that effective tutors monitor and engage students more and provide help only when needed. Cade et al. (2008) also found that *Scaffolding* was a highly occur-

ring mode in expert tutoring. They found a relatively low occurrence of the *Fading* mode, which they suggested might be explained by time constraints, i.e. the tutoring session prevented tutors from spending too much time in the *Fading* mode.

The Markov process also resembles to some degree Graesser's (Graesser et al., 1995) 5-step dialogue framework, which captures the tutorial phases prevalent in collaborative problem-solving tutoring: *i) Tutor asks question, ii) Student answers question, iii) Tutor gives short feedback, iv)Tutor and student collaboratively improve the quality of the answer, v) Tutor assesses student's understanding.* One probable effective tutorial path from the Markov process, which might be comparable to Graesser's framework, is *Opening - ProblemId - Fading - Scaffolding - Fading - ProcessNegotiation - Closing.* Indeed, the subpath *ProblemId - Fading - Scaffolding - Fading - ProcessNegotiation* resembles Graesser's 5-step framework.

The first 3 phases in Graesser's framework don't align with the initial modes of the suggested learning path. This might be because of the difference in the tutoring environment. Graesser assumed tutor-driven sessions, which with a tutor first asking a question or presenting a problem for the learner to solve, followed by a student answer, etc. In our case, it is the students who are seeking help from tutors on specific problems. Initially, in our case, the tutor works together with the student to understand the problem (*ProblemId*). Then, the tutor fades, allowing the student to work on the problem by herself (*Fading*). The tutor may switch between *Scaffolding* and *Fading* to provide help (*Scaffolding*), only when needed. In this sense, the last two elements in Graesser's framework can be considered to be aligned with the *Scaffolding - Fading* pattern.

The additional benefit of this Markov process representation is that it suggests multiple possible paths or meta-strategies that can lead to learning gains.

6 Conclusion

We used human expert judgment scores to identify effective and ineffective tutoring sessions. We conducted discriminant mode sub-sequence analysis based on which we generated a Markov process for effective tutorial sessions. We found that sequences of dialogue modes derived from the Markov process are most likely to have many *Scaffolding* and *Fading* modes. Furthermore, the inferred Markov process suggests a new model for tutoring when students ask for help as opposed to tutor-driven sessions, which was modeled in the past. Our future work is to expand our understanding of the effective strategies in effective tutorial sessions while accounting for other factors such as students' prior knowledge.

Acknowledgments

This work was partially supported by The University of Memphis and a contract from the Advanced Distributed Learning Initiative of the United States Department of Defense.

References

Vincent Aleven, Octav Popescu, and Kenneth R Koedinger. 2001. Towards tutorial dialog to support self-explanation: Adding natural language understanding to a cognitive tutor. In *Proceedings of Artificial Intelligence in Education*, pages 246–255.

John Langshaw Austin. 1975. *How to do things with words*. Oxford university press.

Kristy Elizabeth Boyer, Eunyoung Ha, Michael D Wallis, Robert Phillips, Mladen A Vouk, and James C Lester. 2009. Discovering tutorial dialogue strategies with hidden markov models. In *AIED*, pages 141–148.

Kristy Elizabeth Boyer, Robert Phillips, Amy Ingram, Eun Young Ha, Michael Wallis, Mladen Vouk, and James Lester. 2010. Characterizing the effectiveness of tutorial dialogue with hidden markov models. In *International Conference on Intelligent Tutoring Systems*, pages 55–64. Springer.

Kristy Elizabeth Boyer, Robert Phillips, Amy Ingram, Eun Young Ha, Michael Wallis, Mladen Vouk, and James Lester. 2011. Investigating the relationship between dialogue structure and tutoring effectiveness: a hidden markov modeling approach. *International Journal of Artificial Intelligence in Education*, 21(1-2):65–81.

Whitney Cade, Jessica Copeland, Natalie Person, and Sidney DMello. 2008. Dialogue modes in expert tutoring. In *Intelligent tutoring systems*, pages 470–479. Springer.

Arthur C Graesser, Natalie K Person, and Joseph P Magliano. 1995. Collaborative dialogue patterns in naturalistic one-to-one tutoring. *Applied cognitive psychology*, 9(6):495–522.

Donald Morrison, Benjamin Nye, Borhan Samei, Vivek Varma Datla, Craig Kelly, and Vasile Rus. 2014. Building an intelligent pal from the tutor. com session database phase 1: Data mining. In *Educational Data Mining 2014*.

Stellan Ohlsson, Barbara Di Eugenio, Bettina Chow, Davide Fossati, Xin Lu, and Trina C Kershaw. 2007. Beyond the code-and-count analysis of tutoring dialogues. *Artificial intelligence in education: Building technology rich learning contexts that work*, 158:349.

Barbara Ed Rogoff and Jean Ed Lave. 1984. *Everyday cognition: Its development in social context*. Harvard University Press.

Vasile Rus, Rajendra Banjade, Nobal Niraula, Elizabeth Gire, and Donald Franceschetti. 2017a. A study on two hint-level policies in conversational intelligent tutoring systems. In *Innovations in Smart Learning*, pages 171–181. Springer.

Vasile Rus, Nabin Maharjan, and Rajendra Banjade. 2015. Unsupervised discovery of tutorial dialogue modes in human-to-human tutorial data. In *Proceedings of the Third Annual GIFT Users Symposium*, pages 63–80.

Vasile Rus, Nabin Maharjan, Tamang Lasang, Michael Yudelson, Susan Berman, Fancsali Stephen, and Steve Ritter. 2017b. An analysis of human tutors actions in tutorial dialogues. In *Proceedings of the Thirtieth International Florida Artificial Intelligence Research Society Conference*.

John R Searle. 1969. *Speech acts: An essay in the philosophy of language*, volume 626. Cambridge university press.

Thank "Goodness"! A Way to Measure Style in Student Essays

Sandeep Mathias, Pushpak Bhattacharyya
Centre for Indian Language Technology
Department of Computer Science and Engineering
Indian Institute of Technology, Bombay
{sam,pb}@cse.iitb.ac.in

Abstract

Essays have two major components for scoring - content and style. In this paper, we describe a property of the essay, called **goodness**, and use it to predict the score given for the style of student essays. We compare our approach to solve this problem with baseline approaches, such as language modeling and also a state-of-the-art deep learning system, proposed by Taghipour and Ng (2016). We show that, despite being quite intuitive, our approach is very powerful in predicting the style of the essays.

1 Introduction

The first Automatic Essay Grading (AEG) system was Project Essay Grade developed by Ellis Page in 1966 (Page, 1966). Page (1966) believed that there are two major components to an essay, namely content (what the essay is about) and style (how well the essay is written). Style consists of two major parts, namely sentence fluency and word choice.

In 2012, a competition was organized by Kaggle. This competition, called the Automated Student Assessment Prize (ASAP), had multiple essays written by high school students of classes 7 to 10. The dateset for this competition has led to a large amount of research in AEG and automatic short-answer scoring in the last few years.

In this paper, we discuss one of the aspects of essay-writing, namely style, and how we can predict it automatically. In addition, we also look at two of the major components of style, namely word choice and sentence fluency. Style is necessary for providing a rich and diverse structure to the writing of the essay. Proficient and crisp vocabulary, as well as good sentence fluency is a

mark of a writer being able to express his / her thoughts in the language of their writing.

Style is necessary for providing a rich and diverse structure to the writing of the essay. Proficient and crisp vocabulary, as well as good sentence fluency is a mark of a writer being able to articulate his / her thoughts well in the language of their writing.

There has been a fair bit of recent work in predicting other aspects of the essay, such as coherence (Somasundaran et al., 2014), organization (Persing et al., 2010), etc. However, not much work has been done for grading either style, sentence fluency, or word choice in student essays.

The central contribution of our paper is the definition of **goodness** and its use in predicting the style, word choice and sentence fluency scores of student essays. We define the **goodness** of a word (or phrase) as the weighted average of the count of the word (or phrase), weighted by score of the essay (either style, or word choice, or sentence fluency). In this way, words or phrases that occur more often in essays with a better score, get scored higher. Using this property, we show a significant improvement over our baseline measures, as well as a state-of-the-art deep learning system, developed by Taghipour and Ng (2016).

The rest of the paper is organized as follows. Section 2 defines the problem statement of our paper - in particular the terms style, word choice and sentence fluency. Section 3 describes our approach to predict the **goodness** scores of essays. Section 4 describes other features that we use, as well as a state-of-the-art system. Section 5 describes the dataset used. Section 6 describes the experiments that we performed. Section 7 gives our results and provides an analysis on the goodness of words and other features, and how they impact the sentence fluency score of essays. We also use ablation tests to find out which is the most

35

Proceedings of the 5th Workshop on Natural Language Processing Techniques for Educational Applications, pages 35–41
Melbourne, Australia, July 19, 2018. ©2018 Association for Computational Linguistics

important feature set. Section 8 describes related work in solving this problem. We conclude the paper in Section 9.

2 Problem Definition

We define style as the quality that measures how well the essay is written with respect to its language, vocabulary, sentences, etc. Hence, we say that style consists of 2 parts, namely word choice and sentence fluency.

Word choice is a quality in the essay where precise vocabulary is used. For example an essay using the word "express" ("Sally Yates expressed her concern about Michael Flynn's ties with Russia.") has a better word choice than if it were to use the word "say" ("Sally Yates said that she was concerned about Michael Flynn's ties with Russia.").

Sentence fluency is the quality of an essay that measures the writer's command of the language that they are writing in. A writer who is proficient in writing, will be able to form good quality phrases, construct sentences quite easily, and show a flow between the sentences that they write.

We model each of these as an ordinal classification problem, where each score point corresponds to a class.

3 Goodness

We hypothesize that essays with a better score in style, word choice or sentence fluency make use of words and phrases that have a higher goodness score. Goodness of a word (or phrase) W, is defined as the weighted average of W, weighted by the score of the essay. Hence, goodness is calculated using the formula:

$$Goodness(W) = \frac{\sum\limits_{i} i * C_i(W)}{\sum\limits_{i} C_i(W)},$$

where $Goodness(W)$ is the goodness of the word (or phrase) W, $C_i(W)$ is the count of word (or phrase), in essays scored with a score of i with respect to the relevant task (either style, word choice or sentence fluency).

For training, we run two passes over our dataset. In the first pass, we assign each word the same score of the essay (i.e. all words are assigned a score of i in essays with a score of i). Once this is done, we then construct the vocabulary in the second pass. In the second pass, we assign a score for each word in the vocabulary as the mean of the scores of the word throughout its occurrence in the

training data. In this way, we learn the **goodness** scores of words and phrases.

For an unknown essay, we first score each word with the same score it has in the training data, it occurs in the training data set. Unknown words (or phrase) are scored as follows:

1. In case it is an **unknown word**, we find the most similar word to the unknown word using GloVe word vectors (Pennington et al., 2014) that is also present in the training data.

2. In case it is a **spelling mistake**. In case an unknown word does not exist in our set of word embeddings, we tag such a word as a spelling mistake, and assign a goodness score of 0.

3. In case it is an **unknown phrase**. In case there is a phrase that is not present in the training data, then it is marked as an unknown phrase. The score given to it is the mean score of its corresponding words.

We calculate the overall goodness score of the essay as the mean of the goodness scores of all the relevant words and phrases in the essay.

4 Additional Features

In addition to calculating the goodness, we also include the following add-on features to help improve our predictions of style, word choice and sentence fluency:

4.1 Essay statistics

These are length-based statistics about the essays, namely the number of words and sentences. We use these statistics because we observed that essays which were scored low (i.e. getting a 1) have a very low length, as compared to the average length of the essay. Similarly, essays that are scored high have a large number of words and sentences as well.

4.2 Punctuation features

In addition to the length-based features, we also count the number of commas, explanation points, question marks, and quotations. We believe that usage of these punctuation marks will help in detecting different kinds of sentences, like questions, exclamations, etc.

Prompt ID	Score Range	Essays	Average Length	Quantities Predicted
7	1-4	1569	250	Style
8	1-6	723	600	Word Choice & Sentence Fluency

Table 1: Properties of the data that we used.

4.3 Complexity features

Complexity measures, like the Flesch Reading Ease Score (FRES) are also used as features in our system. In addition to those, we also looked at parse tree features, like the average parse tree depth and the number of subordinate clauses (SBAR) in the text.

4.4 Language modeling features

These are language modeling features of the essay using the English Wikipedia from the Leipzig corpus (Goldhahn et al., 2012). These features are the output from the SRILM toolkit (Stolcke et al., 2002). We use the following features:

1. Number of sentences per essay.

2. Number of words per sentence.

3. Number of OOVs in the sentence.

4. Language model score.

5. Perplexity of the text.

6. Average perplexity per words of the text.

4.5 Coherence-based Features

We define sentence flow as the content word similarity between two adjacent sentences. For every pair of adjacent sentences, we find out $MaxSim$ and $MeanSim$, which are the maximum and mean similarity values between the content words of the 2 sentences (Pitler et al., 2010). We use the GloVe pre-trained word embeddings (Pennington et al., 2014) for the vectors of the content words.

In addition to the above, we also construct PoS-tag and lemma vectors of each of the sentences, and calculate the average similarity between adjacent sentences (Pitler et al., 2010).

We also look at entity grid features (Barzilay and Lapata, 2005). An entity grid is a 1-0 grid of sentences × entities. A cell ($E[i][j]$) in the grid is a 1 if the entity i is present in the sentence j, and 0 otherwise. We count the number of sequences of length between 2 to 4, that have at least one 1 and use them as features. A sequence of multiple 1s denote that an entity is referred to in a lot of consecutive sentences. On the other hand, sequences with a solitary 1 mean that the entity is mentioned just once, and never again in the adjacent sentences. The length of the sequence determines how many adjacent sentences we are considering at a time.

4.6 LSTMs - The State-of-the-Art

Deep learning networks, like LSTMs are quite good in predicting the score of the essays. We perform the experiments done by Taghipour and Ng (2016)[1]. We ran multiple configurations of their system. We used the default hyperparameters as described in Section 5.1 of Taghipour and Ng (2016). For pre-trained word embeddings, we ran experiments using

1. No pre-trained word embeddings

2. The same word embeddings that Taghipour and Ng (2016) used; and

3. GloVe word embeddings (Pennington et al., 2014)

The word-embeddings dimension for the lookup table layer was 50 for the first 2 experiments, and 300 for the experiment using GloVe.

5 Dataset

The complete ASAP training data set consists of nearly 13,000 essays, across 8 different essay prompts. The essays were written by students from classes 7 to 10. Things like dates, times, percentages, numbers, etc. were also anonymized.

Despite the fact that there are nearly 13,000 essays that have been graded in the data set, there are only two prompts (prompts #7 and #8) of 1569 and 723 essays, in which individual scores are given for each attribute or the essay. Since the scoring range is between 0 - 3 for prompt #7, we transform it to a range of 1 - 4, so that we can assign a **goodness** score of 0 to spelling errors, rather than to words belonging to the lowest-scoring essays.

---

[1] The system can be downloaded from https://github.com/nusnlp/nea

Experiment	Style	Word Choice	Sentence Fluency
Baseline Experiments			
Taghipour and Ng (2016)	0.4902	0.2511	0.3463
All features other than Goodness	0.5485	0.3433	0.3886
Goodness			
Goodness using only content words	0.2259	0.3323	0.3586
Goodness using all words	0.2821	0.3557	0.3984
Goodness using all words and content phrases	0.0792	0.1785	0.2241
ALL features	**0.5617**	**0.4233**	**0.4443**
Other human rater	0.5444	0.4816	0.5091

Table 2: Results of our experiments. These are the mean QWK scores. Numbers in **bold** denote the best system (excluding the human inter-rater agreement).

Table 1 describes the properties of the different different from which we score style, word choice and sentence fluency. Each of these scores were assigned by 2 annotators. For our experiments, we make use of Cohen's Kappa with Quadratic Weights - the Quadratic Weighted Kappa (QWK) (Cohen, 1968). The human inter-annotator agreement for style was 0.5444, word choice was 0.4816, and sentence fluency was 0.5091 between the human raters.

6 Experiment Setup

We model this problem as an ordinal classification problem where we consider each score to correspond to a class. We then classify the essay into the appropriate class that corresponds to its score.

This is not a run-of-the-mill classification problem as the values of the scores are ordered ($1 < 2 < 3 < ...$), and not independent. This is also not a regression problem, because the scores are discrete variables, and not continuous values. In regression, for instance, we could end up with scores higher than the maximum score possible. For instance, if the highest score was 4, if we are to use regression, we could end up scoring that essay 4.5!

We make use of the Ordinal Class Classifier (Frank and Hall, 2001) on Weka (Frank et al., 2016). The Ordinal Class Classifier is a meta-classifier that pre-processes the input data and transforms the input classes from ordinal to categorical classes before running the classification on an internal classifier. We ran our experiments using three classifiers, namely a Naïve Bayes Classifier (John and Langley, 1995), a Random Forest Classifier (Breiman, 2001), and a Multinomial Logistic Regression Classifier (le Cessie and van Houwelingen, 1992) as the internal classifier. The best classifiers were the Naïve Bayes Classifier for measuring style, and the Random Forest Classifier for measuring word choice and sentence fluency. We use *stratified* five-fold cross-validation. The results of our classification are given in Table 2.

7 Results and Analysis

The results of the 5-fold cross-validation of the training set are as shown in Table 2. The first block is the baseline experiments. The reported result for the neural network corresponds to the **best** neural network architecture - namely an LSTM with a CNN layer using GloVe pre-trained word embeddings due to space constraints. Block 2 features only goodness, and block 3 shows the results with all the features and compares it to the agreement with the other human rater.

In 2 out of the 3 tasks, using **goodness** without any additional features, we are able to outperform the baseline and Taghipour and Ng (2016)'s system. In the third task, while goodness is not able to outperform the baseline as well as the deep learning system, with the aid of language modeling, we are able to outperform the baseline when predicting style. This is because language modeling is able to reward / penalize style by itself.

7.1 Analysis of Goodness Scores

Table 3 gives examples of different words and their corresponding goodness scores for a single training fold for sentence fluency. Words with the lowest goodness scores tend to be spelling mistakes or out-of-context words. For instance, the word *computers* has the lowest goodness score of 1. This is because, in that fold it only occurs in a single training essay with word choice and sentence fluency scores of 1.

Range	Example Words	Example Phrases
1 - 2	ower, rumers, computers	sameting funing, adefokil stoeshi, feel happy we
2 - 3	tho, trash, reward	love laughter, a good thing, laugh that much
3 - 4	ok, fair, forever	make me happy, a joke, love to laugh
4 - 5	cherish, role, obvious	cherish forever, the center of attention
5 - 6	dire, aggressively, anguish	one of utter sarcasm, went on similarly, something ridiculous

Table 3: Example words with goodness scores for a single training fold in sentence fluency.

An interesting feature with respect to phrases is that the constituents of a phrase may have a lower score as compared to the overall goodness score of the phrase. For example, the words *cherish* and *forever* have mean goodness scores of 4.4 and 3.9 respectively, while the phrase *cherish forever* has a mean goodness score of 4.5.

7.2 Predictions Using Goodness Scores

If an essay contains a significant number of spelling errors (like *rumers*), or out-of-context words (like *computers*), the goodness score of the essay will be lowered and it will be predicted to have a lower style, word choice and sentence fluency score.

Unknown word handling allows us to handle spelling errors, as well as score words that are not present in the training data. For example *aggressively* has a mean goodness score of 5.5 across all training folds for both reviewers in the task of sentence fluency (out of 6). However, there may be a training fold in which it is not present. In one such fold, the synonym was *vigorously*, which also had a very high score of 4.5. In the absence of unknown word handling, we would skip it entirely.

When it came to using phrases, one of the challenges that we faced was data sparsity. For example, a phrase with a goodness score of 4.5, like *cherish forever* was ignored because the only essays that it occurred in were in the same fold. Hence, when any of those essays were encountered in testing, the phrases were tagged as an unknown phrase and skipped. Because of this, the results degraded when we used phrases.

To find out which of the feature sets worked best, we also ran ablation tests. We found out, that for style and word choice, goodness was the most important feature, and was the second-most important feature after the entity grid feature set, for sentence fluency.

Overall, we were able to consistently outperform the State-of-the-Art system, by using all our features in all three tasks.

7.3 Adversarial Essays

An adversarial essay is one where a human rater would rate it low but our system would be fooled into rating it high. A key question to ask here is: *Can a cunning student easily con the entire system into giving a good grade by submitting rubbish?* The answer is probably no. At least not easily. While it is possible for the writer to write an essay using *only* good words, this may not necessarily translate to a higher score than what he would have scored had he written the essay sincerely.

There are many ways to generate adversarial essays. Taghipour (2017) suggests using context-free grammars, and language modeling to create spurious essays, before trying to detect whether an input essay is spurious or not. Farag et al. (2018) construct adversarial essays by permuting the sentences of good scoring essays.

We created our own version of adversarial essays, by constructing essays that were long, but contained only "good" words (i.e. words with a high goodness score).

In order to see if such a thing would be possible we generated a set of 100 essays (50 from each prompt). These essays were generated from a vocabulary of *good* words, having above average length sentences and a reasonably large word count. We then graded these essays, using the original ASAP data for training. Table 4 shows **how much** is the average score, over the median score of the original essays.

Output	Goodness	Goodness++
Style	1.20	0.42
Sentence Fluency	1.96	1.22
Word Choice	2.05	1.36

Table 4: Adversarial Essays Average score increase using ONLY goodness scores (Goodness) and ALL features (Goodness++).

From this table we see that using all our features tends to make an average gain in score of about 1 point (out of 6 in sentence fluency and word choice) and 0.42 points (out of 4 in style) when we make use of all our features. In short, the easiest way for a cunning student to *beat* our system is for him / her to **write well**.

8 Related Work

As mentioned in Section 1, one of the major components of an essay is its style. While there has been work done in evaluating different sub-problems with respect to style, there hasn't been too much work done with respect to evaluating style.

With respect to sentence fluency, Chae and Nenkova (2009) came up with a set of syntactic features to predict sentence fluency. They focused mainly on machine translation and articles written by people. However, the source of their articles was *published* articles from the Wall Street Journal (WSJ). WSJ articles are written by adults, proof-read, and edited before publication. We focus on essays written by children studying in class 10 *as is* without any proof-reading or editing. Hence, they are expected to have a large number of errors, as compared to WSJ articles, which can serve as a discriminating factor between well and badly written essays.

In sentiment analysis, properties of adjectives have been used to predict the intensity of sentiment of a review as well (i.e. does the review *just* like the item or does he *really* like the item). Sharma et al. (2015) showed how intensity of adjectives could be a good predictor of deciding how positive or negative something is. Our approach - measuring the **goodness** of words / phrases to predict the style score of essays - is analogous to the Weighted Normal Polarized Intensity (WNPI) that they used.

In recent years, there has been a reasonable amount of research work done using deep learning to solve the problem of overall essay grading. However, not much has been done in the area of style, word choice or sentence fluency. Dong and Zhang (2016) describe a system for calculating the overall essay score using CNNs while Taghipour and Ng (2016) use LSTMs for predicting the overall score of essays.

9 Conclusions

We have defined a property of the essay called the **goodness** score, and use it as a way to score the style, word choice and sentence fluency of essays. We show that, by using goodness, we are able to predict the scores of the essays significantly better than the state-of-the-art system in essay grading, namely Taghipour and Ng (2016)'s essay grading system. Our system was able to achieve results that were close to human inter-rater agreement with respect to sentence fluency and word choice, and outperformed the human raters with respect to style.

References

Regina Barzilay and Mirella Lapata. 2005. Modeling local coherence: An entity-based approach. In *Proceedings of the 43rd Annual Meeting of the Association for Computational Linguistics (ACL'05)*, pages 141–148, Ann Arbor, Michigan. Association for Computational Linguistics.

Leo Breiman. 2001. Random forests. *Machine Learning*, 45(1):5–32.

S. le Cessie and J.C. van Houwelingen. 1992. Ridge estimators in logistic regression. *Applied Statistics*, 41(1):191–201.

Jieun Chae and Ani Nenkova. 2009. Predicting the fluency of text with shallow structural features: Case studies of machine translation and human-written text. In *Proceedings of the 12th Conference of the European Chapter of the ACL (EACL 2009)*, pages 139–147, Athens, Greece. Association for Computational Linguistics.

Jacob Cohen. 1968. Weighted kappa: Nominal scale agreement provision for scaled disagreement or partial credit. *Psychological bulletin*, 70(4):213.

Fei Dong and Yue Zhang. 2016. Automatic features for essay scoring – an empirical study. In *Proceedings of the 2016 Conference on Empirical Methods in Natural Language Processing*, pages 1072–1077, Austin, Texas. Association for Computational Linguistics.

Youmna Farag, Helen Yannakoudakis, and Ted Briscoe. 2018. Neural automated essay scoring and coherence modeling for adversarially crafted input. In *Proceedings of the 2018 Conference of the North American Chapter of the Association for Computational Linguistics: Human Language Technologies*, New Orleans, Louisiana, USA. Association for Computational Linguistics.

Eibe Frank and Mark Hall. 2001. A simple approach to ordinal classification. In *12th European Conference on Machine Learning*, pages 145–156. Springer.

Eibe Frank, Mark A. Hall, and Ian H. Witten. 2016. The weka workbench. online appendix for "data mining: Practical machine learning tools and techniques " morgan kaufmann, fourth edition, 2016.

Dirk Goldhahn, Thomas Eckart, and Uwe Quasthoff. 2012. Building large monolingual dictionaries at the leipzig corpora collection: From 100 to 200 languages. In *LREC*, pages 759–765.

George H. John and Pat Langley. 1995. Estimating continuous distributions in bayesian classifiers. In *Eleventh Conference on Uncertainty in Artificial Intelligence*, pages 338–345, San Mateo. Morgan Kaufmann.

Ellis B Page. 1966. The imminence of... grading essays by computer. *The Phi Delta Kappan*, 47(5):238–243.

Jeffrey Pennington, Richard Socher, and Christopher Manning. 2014. Glove: Global vectors for word representation. In *Proceedings of the 2014 Conference on Empirical Methods in Natural Language Processing (EMNLP)*, pages 1532–1543, Doha, Qatar. Association for Computational Linguistics.

Isaac Persing, Alan Davis, and Vincent Ng. 2010. Modeling organization in student essays. In *Proceedings of the 2010 Conference on Empirical Methods in Natural Language Processing*, pages 229–239, Cambridge, MA. Association for Computational Linguistics.

Emily Pitler, Annie Louis, and Ani Nenkova. 2010. Automatic evaluation of linguistic quality in multi-document summarization. In *Proceedings of the 48th Annual Meeting of the Association for Computational Linguistics*, pages 544–554, Uppsala, Sweden. Association for Computational Linguistics.

Raksha Sharma, Mohit Gupta, Astha Agarwal, and Pushpak Bhattacharyya. 2015. Adjective intensity and sentiment analysis. In *Proceedings of the 2015 Conference on Empirical Methods in Natural Language Processing*, pages 2520–2526, Lisbon, Portugal. Association for Computational Linguistics.

Swapna Somasundaran, Jill Burstein, and Martin Chodorow. 2014. Lexical chaining for measuring discourse coherence quality in test-taker essays. In *Proceedings of COLING 2014, the 25th International Conference on Computational Linguistics: Technical Papers*, pages 950–961, Dublin, Ireland. Dublin City University and Association for Computational Linguistics.

Andreas Stolcke et al. 2002. Srilm-an extensible language modeling toolkit. In *Interspeech*, volume 2002, page 2002.

Kaveh Taghipour. 2017. *Robust Trait-Specific Essay Scoring Using Neural Networks and Density Estimators*. Ph.D. thesis.

Kaveh Taghipour and Hwee Tou Ng. 2016. A neural approach to automated essay scoring. In *Proceedings of the 2016 Conference on Empirical Methods in Natural Language Processing*, pages 1882–1891, Austin, Texas. Association for Computational Linguistics.

Overview of NLPTEA-2018 Share Task Chinese Grammatical Error Diagnosis

Gaoqi Rao   Qi Gong   Baolin Zhang   Endong Xun
Beijing Language and Culture University
{raogaoqi , gongqi , zhangbaolin , xunendong}@blcu.edu.cn

Abstract

This paper presents the NLPTEA 2018 shared task for Chinese Grammatical Error Diagnosis (CGED) which seeks to identify grammatical error types, their range of occurrence and recommended corrections within sentences written by learners of Chinese as foreign language. We describe the task definition, data preparation, performance metrics, and evaluation results. Of the 20 teams registered for this shared task, 13 teams developed the system and submitted a total of 32 runs. Progress in system performances was obviously, reaching F1 of 36.12% in position level and 25.27% in correction level. All data sets with gold standards and scoring scripts are made publicly available to researchers.

1   Introduction

Automated grammar checking for learners of English as a foreign language has achieved obvious progress. Helping Our Own (HOO) is a series of shared tasks in correcting textual errors (Dale and Kilgarriff, 2011; Dale et al., 2012). The shared tasks at CoNLL 2013 and 2014 focused on grammatical error correction, increasing the visibility of educational application research in the NLP community (Ng et al., 2013; 2014).

Many of these learning technologies focus on learners of English as a Foreign Language (EFL), while relatively few grammar checking applications have been developed to support Chinese as a Foreign Language(CFL) learners. Those applications which do exist rely on a range of techniques, such as statistical learning (Chang et al, 2012; Wu et al, 2010; Yu and Chen, 2012),

rule-based analysis (Lee et al., 2013), neuro network modelling (Zheng et al., 2016; Zhou et al., 2017) and hybrid methods (Lee et al., 2014).

In response to the limited availability of CFL learner data for machine learning and linguistic analysis, the ICCE-2014 workshop on Natural Language Processing Techniques for Educational Applications (NLP-TEA) organized a shared task on diagnosing grammatical errors for CFL (Yu et al., 2014). A second version of this shared task in NLP-TEA was collocated with the ACL-IJCNLP-2015 (Lee et al., 2015), COLING-2016 (Lee et al., 2016). Its name was fixed from then on: Chinese Grammatical Error Diagnosis (CGED). As a part of IJCNLP 2017, the shared task was organized (Rao et al., 2017). In conjunction with NLP-TEA workshop in ACL 2018, CGED is organized again. The main purpose of these shared tasks is to provide a common setting so that researchers who approach the tasks using different linguistic factors and computational techniques can compare their results. Such technical evaluations allow researchers to exchange their experiences to advance the field and eventually develop optimal solutions to this shared task.

The rest of this paper is organized as follows. Section 2 describes the task in detail. Section 3 introduces the constructed datasets. Section 4 proposes evaluation metrics. Section 5 reports the results of the participants' approaches. Conclusions are finally drawn in Section 6.

2   Task Description

The goal of this shared task is to develop NLP techniques to automatically diagnose (and furtherly correct) grammatical errors in Chinese sentences written by CFL learners. Such errors are defined as

Proceedings of the 5th Workshop on Natural Language Processing Techniques for Educational Applications, pages 42–51
Melbourne, Australia, July 19, 2018. ©2018 Association for Computational Linguistics

PADS: redundant words (denoted as a capital "R"), missing words ("M"), word selection errors ("S"), and word ordering errors ("W"). The input sentence may contain one or more such errors. The developed system should indicate which error types are embedded in the given unit (containing 1 to 5 sentences) and the position at which they occur. Each input unit is given a unique number "sid". If the inputs contain no grammatical errors, the system should return: "sid, correct". If an input unit contains the grammatical errors, the output format should include four items "sid, start_off, end_off, error_type", where start_off and end_off respectively denote the positions of starting and ending character at which the grammatical error occurs, and error_type should be one of the defined errors: "R", "M", "S", and "W". Each character or punctuation mark occupies 1 space for counting positions. Example sentences and corresponding notes are shown as Table 1 shows. This year, we only have one track of HSK.

<table>
<tr><td colspan="1" align="center">HSK (Simplified Chinese)</td></tr>
<tr><td>

Example 1
Input: (sid=00038800481)　我根本不能了解这妇女辞职回家的现象。在这个时代，为什么放弃自己的工作，就回家当家庭主妇？
Output: 00038800481, 6, 7, S
　　　　00038800481, 8, 8, R
(Notes: "了解"should be "理解". In addition, "这" is a redundant word.)

Example 2
Input: (sid=00038800464)我真不明白。她们可能是追求一些前代的浪漫。
Output: 00038800464, correct

Example 3
Input: (sid=00038801261)人战胜了饥饿，才努力为了下一代作更好的、更健康的东西。
Output: 00038801261, 9, 9, M
　　　　00038801261, 16, 16, S
(Notes: "能" is missing. The word "作"should be "做". The correct sentence is "才能努力为了下一代做更好的")

Example 4
Input: (sid=00038801320)饥饿的问题也是应该解决的。世界上每天由于饥饿很多人死亡。
Output: 00038801320, 19, 25, W
(Notes: "由于饥饿很多人" should be "很多人由于饥饿")

</td></tr>
</table>

Table 1: Example sentences and corresponding notes

3　Datasets

The learner corpora used in our shared task were taken from the writing section of the HSK (Pinyin of *Hanyu Shuiping Kaoshi*, Test of Chinese Level) (Cui et al, 2011; Zhang et al, 2013).

Native Chinese speakers were trained to manually annotate grammatical errors and provide corrections corresponding to each error. The data were then split into two mutually exclusive sets as follows.

(1) Training Set: All units in this set were used to train the grammatical error diagnostic systems.

Each unit contains 1 to 5 sentences with annotated grammatical errors and their corresponding corrections. All units are represented in SGML format, as shown in Table 2. We provide 402 training units with a total of 1,067 grammatical errors, categorized as redundant (208 instances), missing (298), word selection (474) and word ordering (87).

In addition to the data sets provided, participating research teams were allowed to use other public data for system development and implementation. Use of other data should be specified in the final system report.

#Units	#Correct	#Erroneous

| 3,549 (100%) | 1,562 (44.01%) | 1,987 (55.99%) |

Table 3: The statistics of correct sentences in testing set.

Test Set: This set consists of testing units used for evaluating system performance. Table 3 shows statistics for the testing set for this year. According to the sampling in the writing sessions in HSK, over 40% of the sentences contain no error. This was simulated in the test set, in order to test the performance of the systems in false positive identification. The distributions of error types (shown in Table 4) are similar with that of the training set. The proportion of the correct sentences is sampled from data of the online Dynamic Corpus of HSK[1].

Error Type	
#R	1,119 (22.20%)
#M	1,381 (27.40%)
#S	2,167 (43.00%)
#W	373 (7.40%)
#Error	5,040 (100%)

Table 4: The distributions of error types in testing set.

4 Performance Metrics

Table 5 shows the confusion matrix used for evaluating system performance. In this matrix, TP (True Positive) is the number of sentences with grammatical errors are correctly identified by the developed system; FP (False Positive) is the number of sentences in which non-existent grammatical errors are identified as errors; TN (True Negative) is the number of sentences without grammatical errors that are correctly identified as such; FN (False Negative) is the number of sentences with grammatical errors which the system incorrectly identifies as being correct.

The criteria for judging correctness are determined at three levels as follows.

(1) Detection-level: Binary classification of a given sentence, that is, correct or incorrect, should be completely identical with the gold standard. All error types will be regarded as incorrect.

(2) Identification-level: This level could be considered as a multi-class categorization problem. All error types should be clearly identified. A correct case should be completely identical with the gold standard of the given error type.

(3) Position-level: In addition to identifying the error types, this level also judges the occurrence range of the grammatical error. That is to say, the system results should be perfectly identical with the quadruples of the gold standard.

Besides the traditional criteria in the past share tasks, Correction-level was introduced to CGED 2018.

(4) Correction-level: For the error types of Selection and Missing, recommended corrections are required. At most 3 recommended corrections are allowed for each S and M type error. In this level the amount of the corrections recommended would influent the precision and F1 in this level. The trust of the recommendation would be test.

The following metrics are measured at all levels with the help of the confusion matrix.

- False Positive Rate = FP / (FP+TN)
- Accuracy = (TP+TN) / (TP+FP+TN+FN)
- Precision = TP / (TP+FP)
- Recall = TP / (TP+FN)

F1 = 2*Precision*Recall / (Precision + Recall)

- False Positive Rate (FPR) = 0 (=0/1)
- Detection-level
  - Accuracy = 1 (=4/4)
  - Precision = 1 (=3/3)
  - Recall = 1 (=3/3)
  - F1 = 1 (= (2*1*1)/(1+1))
- Identification-level
  - Precision = 0.8 (=4/5)
  - Recall = 0.8 (=4/5)
  - F1 = 0.8 (= (2*0.8*0.8)/(0.8+08))
- Position-level
  - Precision = 0.3333 (=2/6)
  - Recall = 0.4 (=2/5)
  - F1=0.3636 (=(2*0.3333*0.4)/(0.3333+0.4))
- Correction-level
  - Precision = 0.125 (=1/8)
  - Recall = 0.3333 (=1/3)
  - F1=0.1818 (=(2*0.3333*0.125)/(0.3333+0.125))

---

[1] http://bcc.blcu.edu.cn/hsk

- Correction-level (Top3)
  - Precision = 0.3333 (=1/3)
  - Recall = 0.3333 (=1/3)
- F1=0.3333
  (=(2*0.3333*0.3333)/(0.3333+0.3333))

```
<DOC>
<TEXT id="2003071095232000140_2_2x3">
因为养农作物时不用农药的话，生产率较低。那肯定价格要上升，那有钱的人想吃多少，就
吃多少。左边的文中已提出了世界上的有几亿人因缺少粮食而挨饿。
</TEXT>
<CORRECTION>
因为种植农作物时不用农药的话，生产率较低。那价格肯定要上升，那有钱的人想吃多少，
就吃多少。左边的文中已提出了世界上有几亿人因缺少粮食而挨饿。
</CORRECTION>
<ERROR start_off="3" end_off="3" type="S"></ERROR>
<ERROR start_off="22" end_off="25" type="W"></ERROR>
<ERROR start_off="57" end_off="57" type="R"></ERROR>
</DOC>

<DOC>
<TEXT id="200210543634250003_2_1x3">
对于"安乐死"的看法，向来都是一个极具争议性的题目，因为毕竟每个人对于死亡的观念都
不一样，怎样的情况下去判断，也自然产生出很多主观和客观的理论。每个人都有着生存的
权利，也代表着每个人都能去决定如何结束自己的生命的权利。在我的个人观点中，如果一
个长期受着病魔折磨的人，会是十分痛苦的事，不仅是病人本身，以致病者的家人和朋友，
都是一件难受的事。
</TEXT>
<CORRECTION>
对于"安乐死"的看法，向来都是一个极具争议性的题目，因为毕竟每个人对于死亡的观念都
不一样，无论在怎样的情况下去判断，都自然产生出很多主观和客观的理论。每个人都有着
生存的权利，也代表着每个人都能去决定如何结束自己的生命。在我的个人观点中，如果一
个长期受着病魔折磨的人活着，会是十分痛苦的事，不仅是病人本身，对于病者的家人和朋
友，都是一件难受的事。
</CORRECTION>
<ERROR start_off="46" end_off="46" type="M"></ERROR>
<ERROR start_off="56" end_off="56" type="S"></ERROR>
<ERROR start_off="106" end_off="108" type="R"></ERROR>
<ERROR start_off="133" end_off="133" type="M"></ERROR>
<ERROR start_off="151" end_off="152" type="S"></ERROR>
</DOC>
```

Table 2: A training sentence denoted in SGML format.

Confusion Matrix		System Results	
		Positive (Erroneous)	Negative(Correct)
Gold Standard	Positive	TP (True Positive)	FN (False Negative)
	Negative	FP (False Positive)	TN (True Negative)

Table 5: Confusion matrix for evaluation.

5 Evaluation Results

Table 6 summarizes the submission statistics for the 12 participating teams including 10 from universities and research institutes in China (AutoNLP, BUPT, CYUT-III, ECNU, HFL, CMMC, NCYU, NTOU, PkU_ICL), 1 from the U.S. (UIUC) and 1 from India (IIT). Two teams (HFL and DM_NLP) of enterprises are all from China. In the official testing phase, each participating team was allowed to submit at most three runs. Of the 12 registered teams, 8 teams submitted their testing results in Correction-level, for a total of 32 runs.

Participant (Ordered by names)	#Runs	Correction-level
AutoNLP	3	√
BUPT	3	√
CYUT-III	3	√
DM_NLP	3	√
ECNU	3	-
HFL	3	√
IIT (BHU)	1	√
CMMC-BDRC	3	√
NCYU	3	√
NTOU	1	-
PkU_ICL	3	√
UIUC	2	-
Walker	1	-

Table 6: Submission statistics for all participants.

Table 7 shows the testing results of the CGED2018. The CYUT-III achieved the lowest false positive rate (denoted as "FPR") of 0.0499, about half of the lowest FPR in the CGED 2017. Detection-level evaluations are designed to detect whether a sentence contains grammatical errors or not. A neutral baseline can be easily achieved by reporting all testing sentences containing errors. According to the test data distribution, the baseline system can achieve an accuracy of 0.5599. However, not all systems performed above the baseline. The system result submitted by HFL achieved the best detection accuracy of 0.7578 and CMMC-BDRC in F1 of 0.7563. For identification-level evaluations, the systems need to identify the error types in a given unit. The system developed by HFL provided the highest F1 score of 0.5503 for grammatical error identification. For position-level evaluations, HFL achieved the best F1 score of 0.3612. Perfectly identifying the error types and their corresponding positions is difficult in part because no word delimiters exist among Chinese words in the given sentences.

In correction-level, DM_NLP achieved best precision (0.2932 and 0.3077) in correction and top3 correction track. HFL's runs reached best F1 of 0.1723 and 0.2527.

10 participants submitted 11 reports on their systems. Though neural networks achieved good performances in various NLP tasks, traditional statistic models and pipe-lines were still widely implemented in the CGED task. LSTM+CRF has been a standard implementation. Unlike CGED 2017, participants began to rethink the importance of the feature selection and statistics.

In summary, none of the submitted systems provided superior performance using different metrics, indicating the difficulty of developing systems for effective grammatical error diagnosis, especially in CFL contexts. From organizers' perspectives, a good system should have a high F1 score and a low false positive rate. Overall, HFL, DM_NLP, and CMMC-BDRC achieved relatively better performances.

TEAM	Runs	FPR	Detection				Identification			Position		
			Acc.	pre	rec	F1	pre	re	F1	pre	rec	F1
AutoNLP	run1	0.3301	0.5131	0.6349	0.4232	0.5079	0.4792	0.1995	0.2817	0.1185	0.0442	0.0644
	run2	0.1642	0.4897	0.6698	0.2494	0.3634	0.5139	0.1323	0.2105	0.1585	0.0331	0.0547
	run3	0.4715	0.4996	0.6346	0.5426	0.5850	0.4735	0.2646	0.3395	0.1129	0.0609	0.0792
BUPT	run1	0.8412	0.5711	0.5752	0.8953	0.7004	0.3506	0.5663	0.4331	0.0482	0.0882	0.0623
	run2	0.5019	0.6005	0.6331	0.6809	0.6562	0.4134	0.3519	0.3802	0.0608	0.0504	0.0551
	run3	0.5480	0.6236	0.6377	0.7584	0.6929	0.4084	0.4161	0.4122	0.0630	0.0609	0.0620
CYUT-III	run1	0.0499	0.4683	0.6953	0.0896	0.1587	0.5426	0.0418	0.0776	0.0586	0.0032	0.0060
	run2	0.1780	0.6016	0.7535	0.4282	0.5461	0.5433	0.2790	0.3687	0.1470	0.0711	0.0959

TEAM	Runs											
	run3	1.0000	0.4728	0.5805	0.8448	0.6881	0.2589	0.2640	0.2614	0.0070	0.0173	0.0100
DM_NLP	run1	0.3214	0.6131	0.6897	0.5617	0.6191	0.4038	0.3657	0.3838	0.2924	0.1842	0.2260
	run2	0.2183	0.6174	0.7399	0.4882	0.5882	0.5943	0.3113	0.4086	0.3900	0.1777	0.2441
	run3	0.2279	0.6238	0.7390	0.5073	0.6016	0.5877	0.3242	0.4179	0.3855	0.1850	0.2500
ECNU	run1	0.3470	0.5923	0.6663	0.5445	0.5993	0.4767	0.2836	0.3556	0.1238	0.0667	0.0867
	run2	0.3873	0.5796	0.6452	0.5536	0.5959	0.4452	0.2740	0.3392	0.0901	0.0506	0.0648
	run3	0.1255	0.5762	0.7760	0.3417	0.4745	0.6139	0.1818	0.2805	0.3745	0.0858	0.1397
HFL	run1	0.1613	0.7101	0.8276	0.6090	0.7017	0.7107	0.4173	0.5259	0.5341	0.2729	0.3612
	run2	0.7554	0.6436	0.6171	0.9572	0.7504	0.3931	0.7331	0.5118	0.1441	0.3886	0.2102
	run3	0.1754	0.7278	0.8254	0.6517	0.7283	0.6874	0.4588	0.5503	0.4752	0.2906	0.3606
IIT (BHU)	run1	0.4190	0.4483	0.5668	0.3889	0.4613	0.2737	0.1705	0.2102	0.0071	0.0030	0.0042
CMMC-BDRC	run1	0.5314	0.6889	0.6736	0.8621	0.7563	0.4834	0.5952	0.5335	0.2741	0.3177	0.2943
	run2	0.3547	0.6988	0.7266	0.7408	0.7336	0.5831	0.4955	0.5357	0.3839	0.2966	0.3346
	run3	0.3470	0.6630	0.7109	0.6709	0.6903	0.4853	0.4096	0.4442	0.2482	0.1814	0.2096
NCYU	run1	0.9987	0.5596	0.5598	0.9985	0.7174	0.2381	0.9749	0.3828	0.0030	0.0390	0.0056
	run2	0.9994	0.5599	0.5599	0.9995	0.7177	0.2382	0.9752	0.3828	0.0030	0.0384	0.0056
	run3	0.9994	0.5599	0.5599	0.9995	0.7177	0.2382	0.9752	0.3828	0.0030	0.0380	0.0055
NTOUA	run1	0.9481	0.5323	0.5497	0.9099	0.6854	0.3297	0.5812	0.4207	0.0065	0.0191	0.0096
PkU_ICL	run1	0.5538	0.6388	0.6448	0.7901	0.7101	0.4483	0.4737	0.4607	0.1642	0.1605	0.1624
	run2	0.2298	0.6317	0.7432	0.5229	0.6139	0.5567	0.3018	0.3914	0.2868	0.1309	0.1797
	run3	0.5679	0.6267	0.6359	0.7796	0.7004	0.4433	0.4710	0.4567	0.1615	0.1615	0.1615
UIUC	run1	0.1274	0.5540	0.7519	0.3035	0.4324	0.6311	0.1696	0.2673	0.2385	0.0536	0.0875
	run2	0.1274	0.5540	0.7519	0.3035	0.4324	0.6311	0.1696	0.2673	0.2385	0.0536	0.0875
walker	run1	0.9309	0.5441	0.5562	0.9179	0.6926	0.3144	0.6266	0.4187	0.0078	0.0189	0.0110

Table7. Results of CGED 2018 in Detection-level, Identification-level and Position-level

TEAM	Runs	Correction			Top3 Correction	
		pre	rec	F1	pre	F1
AutoNLP	run1	0.1667	0.0110	0.0206	0.1667	0.0206
	run2	0.1626	0.0113	0.0211	0.1626	0.0211
	run3	0.1626	0.0113	0.0211	0.1626	0.0211
BUPT	run1	0.0046	0.0093	0.0062	0.0046	0.0062
	run2	0.0033	0.0028	0.0030	0.0033	0.0030
	run3	0.0092	0.0087	0.0090	0.0092	0.0090
CYUT-III	run1	0.0040	0.0008	0.0014	0.0040	0.0014
DM_NLP	run1	0.2603	0.0161	0.0303	0.2701	0.0314
	run2	0.2932	0.0158	0.0299	0.3077	0.0314
	run3	0.2700	0.0180	0.0338	0.2832	0.0355
HFL	run1	0.2087	0.1468	0.1723	0.3059	0.2527
	run2	0.0386	0.1696	0.0629	0.0722	0.1177
	run3	0.1509	0.1400	0.1453	0.2391	0.2301

Team	Run					
IIT (BHU)	run1	0.0000	0.0000	0.0000	0.0000	0.0000
CMMC-BDRC	run1	0.1364	0.1651	0.1494	0.1432	0.1569
	run2	0.1852	0.1609	0.1722	0.1934	0.1798
	run3	0.2126	0.1395	0.1685	0.2190	0.1735
NCYU	run1	1.2079E-05	0.0003	2.3164E-05	3.6236E-05	6.9493E-05
	run2	3.6235E-05	8.4531E-04	6.9490E-05	1.0870E-04	2.0847E-04
	run3	3.6235E-05	8.4531E-04	6.9490E-05	1.0870E-04	2.0847E-04
PkU_ICL	run1	0.0296	0.0775	0.0429	0.0822	0.1189
	run2	0.0556	0.0662	0.0604	0.1522	0.1655
	run3	0.0316	0.0814	0.0456	0.0881	0.1270

Table 8. Results of CGED 2018 in Correction-level

6 Discussions

Table 9 summarizes the approaches and resources for each of the submitted systems, according to their 1st draft of system reports (some details were not clearly described yet). PkU_ICL, NCYU and IIT(BHU) did not submit reports on their systems. Though neural networks achieved good performances in various NLP tasks, traditional pipe-lines were still widely implemented in the CGED task. CRF, as a sequence labelling model with flexible feature space, was chosen by DM_NLP, CMMC, ECNU, HFL, walker and UIUC in their system pipe-lines. Further, UIUC applied its pipe-line only with CRF and post processing, achieving comparable results. NTOU conducted their runs based on frequent subsentences matching in internet corpus.

For LSTM modelling, feature choice played an important role, influencing the system performance a lot. Besides character and word, part of speech (POS) based on the segmentation, are widely selected. ePMI, cPMI, Adjacent Word Collocation (AWC), Dependent Word Collocation (DWC), Contextualized Char Representation are newly implemented features in this task.

For LSTM itself, AutoNLP applied policy gradient in modelling. Some participant added additional memory gate in the neuro, a quite normal trick in machine translation, helping their system achieve high F1 score over 50% in position-level and over 40% in correction-level. The submissions were withdrawn, due to the suspected overfitting of testing set. Although it cannot reflect the real achievement in this task, the phenome is still meaningful in particular context, like computer assistant essay correction[2].

In correction-level, DM_NLP applied rule-based, NMT and SMT models and merge the generated results in hybrid pipe-line. HFL also followed the strategy of multi-model merging, using PMI scoring and a seq2seq network Their pipelines are shown in Fig.1.

More various additional resources appeared in CGED 2018. Besides Gigawords and Wikipedia Corpus, Google Ngram, People's Daily, Chinese 5gram are newly introduced resources in this task. More impressively, CMMC utilized domain dictionary in L2 teaching to form pseudo writing data for training set enhancement, improving their performances in all aspects.

Team	Approach	Features	Correction Model	Additional Resources
Ali_GM	BiLSTM+CRF	Char, POS, AWC, DWC	Rule-System, NMT, SMT	Gigawords, Lang8
AutoNLP	Policy Gradient LSTM model			

---

[2] In the widely existing scenario of large scale examination correction, users may manually correct some submissions for pre-training, then the model with additional memory mechanism can automatically finish the rest with a high F1 score.

System	Approach	Features	Additional methods	Resources
BUPT	bi-LSTM	Contextualized Char Representation		Wiki Corpus
CMMC	LSTM+CRF (Seq2Seq & Seq Label)	Char, POS		People's Daily, Domain Dictionaries in L2 Teaching, Self-generated corpus
CYUT-III	LSTM	Word		
ECNU	LSTM+CRF	Char, POS, Dependency, BOW5		
HFL	BiLSTM+CRF	Gaussian ePMI, POS, PMI, BOW	PMI Scoring, Seq2Seq Networks	external corpus (unclear), Zuowen & Baike (unpublic)
NTOU	Rule-system	Frequent string matching		Chinese Web 5-grams
UIUC	CRF+Rule-system	Word, Char		Google Chinese N-grams
walker	BiLSTM+CRF			

Table 9: Summary of approaches and additional resources used by the submitted systems.

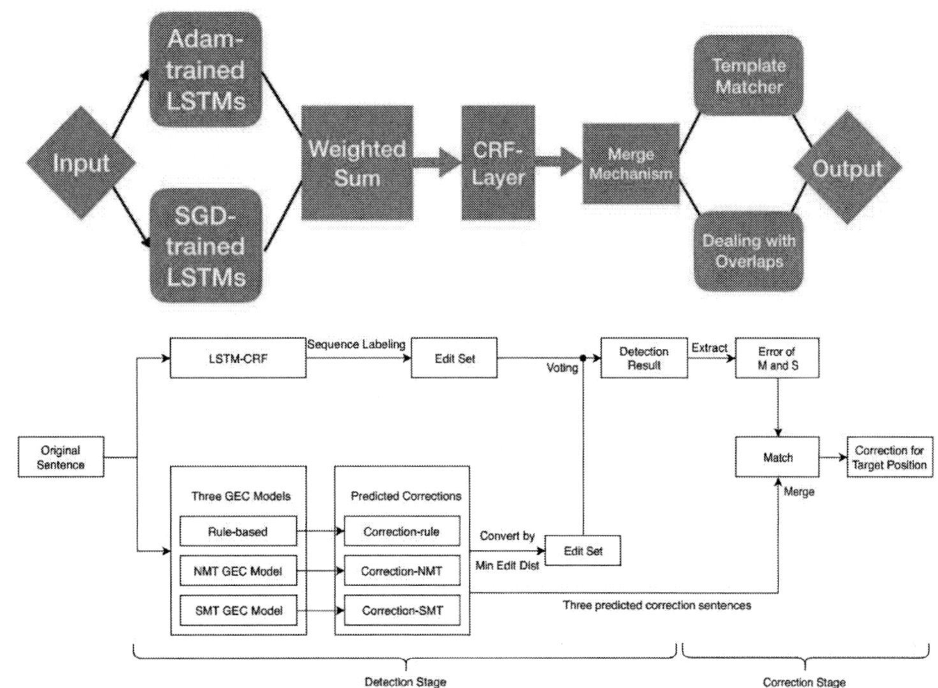

Fig.1 Pipe-lines of the HFL (up) and DM_NLP

7 Conclusion

This study describes the NLP-TEA 2018 shared task for Chinese grammatical error diagnosis, including task design, data preparation, performance metrics, and evaluation results. Regardless of actual performance, all submissions contribute to the common effort to develop Chinese grammatical error diagnosis system, and the individual reports in the proceedings provide useful insights into computer-assisted language learning for CFL learners.

We hope the data sets collected and annotated for this shared task can facilitate and expedite future development in this research area. Therefore, all data sets with gold standards and scoring scripts are publicly available online at http://www.cged.science.

Acknowledgments

We thank all the participants for taking part in our shared task. We would like to thank Kuei-Ching Lee for implementing the evaluation program and the usage feedbacks from Bo Zheng (in the CGED 2016). Lung-Hao Lee contributed a lot in consultation and bidding.

This study was supported by the projects from Beijing Advanced Innovation Center for Language Resources (KYD17004), Institute Project of Beijing Language and Culture University (18YJ060001), Social Science Funding of China (16AYY007), Social Science Funding of Beijing (15WYA017), National Language Committee Project (ZDI135-58, ZDI135-3), MOE Project of Key Research Institutes in Universities (16JJD740004).

References

Ru-Yng Chang, Chung-Hsien Wu, and Philips Kokoh Prasetyo. 2012. Error diagnosis of Chinese sentences usign inductive learning algorithm and decomposition-based testing mechanism. *ACM Transactions on Asian Language Information Processing*, 11(1), article 3.

Xiliang Cui, Bao-lin Zhang. 2011. The Principles for Building the "International Corpus of Learner Chinese". *Applied Linguistics*, 2011(2), pages 100-108.

Robert Dale and Adam Kilgarriff. 2011. Helping our own: The HOO 2011 pilot shared task. *In Proceedings of the 13th European Workshop on Natural Language Generation(ENLG'11)*, pages 1-8, Nancy, France.

Reobert Dale, Ilya Anisimoff, and George Narroway. 2012. HOO 2012: A report on the preposiiton and determiner error correction shared task. *In Proceedings of the 7th Workshop on the Innovative Use of NLP for Building Educational Applications(BEA'12)*, pages 54-62, Montreal, Canada.

Hwee Tou Ng, Siew Mei Wu, Ted Briscoe, Christian Hadiwinoto, Raymond Hendy Susanto, and Christopher Bryant. 2014. The CoNLL-2014 shared task on grammatical error correction. *In Proceedings of the 18th Conference on Computational Natural Language Learning (CoNLL'14)*: Shared Task, pages 1-12, Baltimore, Maryland, USA.

Hwee Tou Ng, Siew Mei Wu, Yuanbin Wu, Christian Hadiwinoto, and Joel Tetreault. 2013. The CoNLL-2013 shared task on grammatical error correction. *In Proceedings of the 17th Conference on Computational Natural Language Learning(CoNLL'13)*: Shared Task, pages 1-14, Sofia, Bulgaria.

Lung-Hao Lee, Li-Ping Chang, and Yuen-Hsien Tseng. 2016. Developing learner corpus annotation for Chinese grammatical errors. *In Proceedings of the 20th International Conference on Asian Language Processing (IALP'16)*, Tainan, Taiwan.

Lung-Hao Lee, Li-Ping Chang, Kuei-Ching Lee, Yuen-Hsien Tseng, and Hsin-Hsi Chen. 2013. Linguistic rules based Chinese error detection for second language learning. *In Proceedings of the 21st International Conference on Computers in Education(ICCE'13)*, pages 27-29, Denpasar Bali, Indonesia.

Lung-Hao Lee, Liang-Chih Yu, and Li-Ping Chang. 2015. Overview of the NLP-TEA 2015 shared task for Chinese grammatical error diagnosis. *In Proceedings of the 2nd Workshop on Natural Language Processing Techniques for Educational Applications (NLP-TEA'15)*, pages 1-6, Beijing, China.

Lung-Hao Lee, Liang-Chih Yu, Kuei-Ching Lee, Yuen-Hsien Tseng, Li-Ping Chang, and Hsin-Hsi Chen. 2014. A sentence judgment system for grammatical error detection. *In Proceedings of the 25th International Conference on Computational Linguistics (COLING'14)*: Demos, pages 67-70, Dublin, Ireland.

Lung-Hao Lee, Rao Gaoqi, Liang-Chih Yu, Xun, Eendong, Zhang Baolin, and Chang Li-Ping. 2016. Overview of the NLP-TEA 2016 Shared Task for Chinese Grammatical Error Diagnosis. *The Workshop on Natural Language Processing Techniques for Educational Applications (NLP-TEA'16)*, pages 1-6, Osaka, Japan.

Gaoqi Rao, Baolin Zhang, Endong Xun, Lung-Hao Lee. IJCNLP-2017 Task 1: Chinese Grammatical Error Diagnosis. *In Proceedings of the IJCNLP 2017*, Shared Tasks, Taipei, Taiwan: 1-8

Chung-Hsien Wu, Chao-Hong Liu, Matthew Harris, and Liang-Chih Yu. 2010. Sentence correction incorporating relative position and parse template language models. *IEEE Transactions on Audio, Speech, and Language Processing*, 18(6), pages 1170-1181.

Chi-Hsin Yu and Hsin-Hsi Chen. 2012. Detecting word ordering errors in Chinese sentences for learning Chinese as a foreign language. *In Proceedings of the 24th International Conference on Computational Linguistics (COLING'12)*, pages 3003-3017, Bombay, India.

Liang-Chih Yu, Lung-Hao Lee, and Li-Ping Chang. 2014. Overview of grammatical error diagnosis for learning Chinese as foreign language. *In Proceedings of the 1stWorkshop on Natural Language Processing Techniques for Educational Applications (NLP-TEA'14)*, pages 42-47, Nara, Japan.

Bao-lin Zhang, Xiliang Cui. 2013. Design Concepts of "the Construction and Research of the Inter-language Corpus of Chinese from Global Learners". *Language Teaching and Linguistic Study*, 2013(5), pages 27-34.

Bo Zheng, Wanxiang Che, Jiang Guo, Ting Liu. 2016. Chinese Grammatical Error Diagnosis with Long Short-Term Memory Networks. *In proceedings of 3rd Workshop on Natural Language Processing Techniques for Educational Applications (NLPTEA2016)*, Osaka, Japan, December 2016, pages 49–56.

Xin Zhou, Jian Wang, Xu Xie, Changlong Sun, Luo Si. Alibaba at IJCNLP-2017 Task 2: A Boosted Deep System for Dimensional Sentiment Analysis of Chinese Phrases. In proceedings of the IJCNLP 2017, Shared Tasks, Taipei, China: 100–10.

Chinese Grammatical Error Diagnosis using Statistical and Prior Knowledge driven Features with Probabilistic Ensemble Enhancement

†Ruiji Fu, ‡Zhengqi Pei, †Jiefu Gong, §Wei Song, ♮Dechuan Teng, ♮Wanxiang Che, †Shijin Wang, †Guoping Hu, ♮Ting Liu

† Joint Laboratory of HIT and iFLYTEK, iFLYTEK Research, Beijing, China
‡ Engineering Science Division, Faculty of Applied Science and Engineering,
University of Toronto, Toronto, Canada
§ Information Engineering, Capital Normal University, Beijing, China
♮ Research Center for Social Computing and Information Retrieval,
Harbin Institute of Technology, Harbin, China

{rjfu, jfgong, sjwang3, gphu}@iflytek.com, zhengqi.pei@mail.utoronto.ca,
wsong@cnu.edu.cn, {dcteng, car, tliu}@ir.hit.edu.cn

Abstract

This paper describes our system at NLPTEA-2018 Task #1: Chinese Grammatical Error Diagnosis. Grammatical Error Diagnosis is one of the most challenging NLP tasks, which is to locate grammar errors and tell error types. Our system is built on the model of bidirectional Long Short-Term Memory with a conditional random field layer (BiLSTM-CRF) but integrates with several new features. First, richer features are considered in the BiLSTM-CRF model; second, a probabilistic ensemble approach is adopted; third, Template Matcher are used during a post-processing to bring in human knowledge. In official evaluation, our system obtains the highest F_1 scores at identifying error types and locating error positions, the second highest F_1 score at sentence level error detection. We also recommend error corrections for specific error types and achieve the best F1 performance among all participants.

1 Introduction

Chinese Language is commonly regarded as one of the most complicated languages. Its sentence structures are not so strict like English. Also, word segmentation usually has to be processed before deeper analysis, since word boundaries are not explicitly given in Chinese which is also different from English. In recent years, more and more people coming from overseas become interested in learning Chinese as a second language. The complicatedness of Chinese language makes it challenging to learn it well for the ones with different language and knowledge background. The learners are unavoidable to make grammatical errors during learning. Therefore, it is necessary to develop automated tools help identifying and correcting grammatical errors. Such tools not only benefit learners also release the burden of teachers.

Deep Learning-based models (Hinton and Salakhutdinov, 2016) has recently become popular due to its powerful capability of capturing features automatically, which demonstrates its excellency in many areas especially in huge-scale data mining. Such models also gain superior performance in previous Grammatical Error Diagnosis system (Zheng et al.,2016). However, prior knowledge is also important, especially when the scale of available data is limited.

This paper introduces our system at NLPTEA-2018 Chinese Grammatical Error Diagnosis task. We will describe how to combine the knowledge that learned from large scale text data and handcraft heuristics with deep learning framework. Different ensemble strategies are also discussed, which have different preferences and achieves variant performances.

2 Chinese Grammatical Error Diagnosis

This shared task aims at developing new NLP techniques to automatically diagnose Chinese grammatical errors in sentences written by Chi-

Proceedings of the 5th Workshop on Natural Language Processing Techniques for Educational Applications, pages 52–59
Melbourne, Australia, July 19, 2018. ©2018 Association for Computational Linguistics

```
<DOC>
<TEXT id="200307109523200140_2_2x3">
因为养农作物时不用农药的话，生产率较低。那肯定价格要上升，那有钱的人想吃
多少，就吃多少。左边的文中已提出了世界上的有几亿人因缺少粮食而挨饿。
</TEXT>
<CORRECTION>
因为种植农作物时不用农药的话，生产率较低。那价格肯定要上升，那有钱的人想
吃多少，就吃多少。左边的文中已提出了世界上有几亿人因缺少粮食而挨饿。
</CORRECTION>
<ERROR start_off="3" end_off="3" type="S"></ERROR>
<ERROR start_off="22" end_off="25" type="W"></ERROR>
<ERROR start_off="57" end_off="57" type="R"></ERROR>
</DOC>
```

Figure 1: Sample training unit.

nese as a Foreign Language(CFL) learners. The error types include R (redundant words), M (missing words), S (word selection), and W (word ordering errors). The target of the task is to detect the error type and its position exactly.

The performances of each team will be evaluated based on the confusion matrix. TP (True Positive) means the number of error-sentences that are correctly identified; FP (False Positive) is the number of error-sentences that are incorrectly identified as correct sentences; TN (True Negative) is the number of correct-sentences that are correctly identified; FN (False Negative) is the number of correct-sentences that are incorrectly identified as containing grammatical errors. The metrics that are used to measure a system's performance has three levels: detection, identification, and position. Each level is evaluated with the help of the confusion matrix based on these metrics (Lee et al.,2016):

- FPR = FP/(FP+TN)
- Accuracy = (TP+TN)/(TP+FP+TN+FN)
- Precision = TP/(TP+FP)
- Recall = TP/(TP+FN)
- F_1 = 2*Precision*Recall/(Precision+Recall)

For instance, the format of the Training Set is shown in Figure 1. Each unit inside was used to train the CGED system.

3 Methodology

3.1 BiLSTM-CRF

The combination of a bidirectional Long Short-Term Memory (Bi-LSTM) network (Hochreiter and Schmidhuber,1997) and a conditional random field (CRF) network (Yu and Chen, 2012) to form a BiLSTM-CRF model can efficiently use past and future information via a Bi-LSTM layer and connecting consecutive output layers from Bi-LSTM via a CRF layer such that the sequence tagging problems can be solved better. Two kinds of potentials are defined in the BiLSTM-CRF model (Huang et al.,2015): emission and transition potentials. The emission potential P is the matrix of scores output by the Bi-LSTM network, of size n × k, where k in the size of distinct tags. Specifically, $P_{i,j}$ represents the emission score of the ith word to the jth tag in an input sequence. The transition potential A is the matrix of transition scores that correspond to the transitions among tags. For instance, $A_{i,j}$ represents the transition score from the ith tag to j^{th} tag. The score of a sequence of predictions is defined as

$$s(X, Y) = \sum_{i=0}^{n} A_{y_i,y_{i+1}} + \sum_{i=1}^{n} P_{i,y_i} \qquad (1)$$

Hence the conditional probability computed by the CRF layer can be defined in favor of the predictive score illustrated above

$$P(Y|X) = \frac{\exp(Score(X,Y))}{\sum_{Y' \in Y_X} \exp(Score(X,Y'))} \qquad (2)$$

where Y_X corresponds to all possible tag sequences for an input sequence X. The training process maximizes the log-probability of the conditional probability computed above upon the correct tag sequence.

$$\log(P(Y|X)) =$$

$$S(X, Y) - \log\left(\sum_{Y' \in Y_X} \exp(Score(X, Y'))\right) \qquad (3)$$

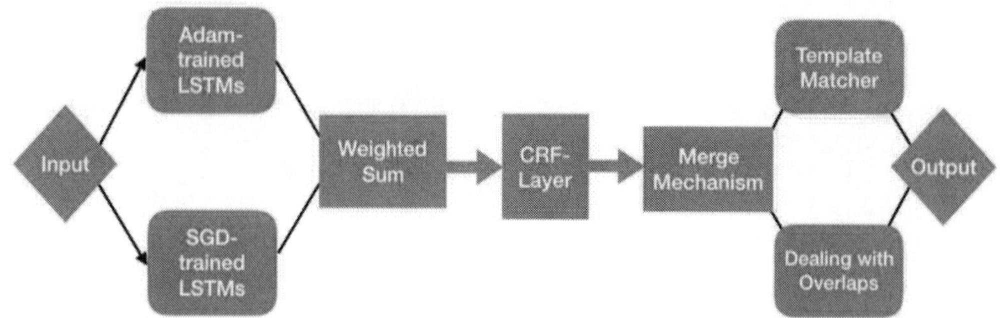

Figure 2: Flowchart of whole forwarding process. Feature-based Inputs are processed firstly via trained single models, whose LSTM-outputs are weighted before producing the tags via CRF-layer. The CRF-outputs are merged and post-processed using our novel methods, generating the desired predictions.

Dynamic programming and Viterbi Decoding (Huang et al., 2015) are used to compute the summation in above equation, and to predict the output tag sequence that obtains the maximum score. The entire training data is divided into batches whose units are processed one by one at each epoch. Each batch contains a list of sentences or sequence-forms. We first run this model forward to obtain the emission matrix P that contains relations between each tag and each position that corresponds to each input word. Then Back-propagation (Hecht-Nielsen, 1992) along with Viterbi Decoding process in the learning phase, updating the network parameters that include the transition matrix A, the weights for Bi-LSTM, and the randomized embedding for input features.

Figure 2 shows the flowchart of our proposed method.

3.2 Novel Features

The task heavily depends on the prior knowledge that can be represented by the selection of features. In practice, feature selection is straightforward phase to affects the model's performance. Better task-specific features simplify the complexity of a model, whereby improve the performance in all levels. Besides the feature engineering introduced by ALI team (Yang et al., 2017), we design several additional features that will be discussed next.

Word Segmentation. we found that sentences in segments are essential to solving the grammatical task due to Chinese's words being combined without segmented spaces that help to indicate the exact meaning of the sentence without ambiguity. We used LTP segmenter[1] to split the input sentences and label each char-gram with the combination of its corresponding segment (word-gram) and its position indicator using BIO-tagging scheme. E.g., a Chinese sequence $A_1A_2B_1B_2B_3C_1D_1$ that can be segmented to $A_1A_2\_B_1B_2B_3\_C_1\_D_1$, then the segmenting feature for char B_2 shall be $I\_word2vec(B_1B_2B_3)$, likewise the segmenting feature for char A_1 shall be $B\_word2vec(A_1A_2)$.

Gaussian ePMI. we use trainable weighted Gaussian distribution to leverage words' distance.

$$GSeP(w_i, w_j) =$$

$$\mu_{ij}\mathcal{N}(j-i) \times ePMI(w_i, w_j; j-i) \qquad (4)$$

The ePMI (exact PMI) measures the co-occurrence of words w_i and w_j when the word interval between them is j - i exactly. We trained six GSeP matrices using an external data consisting of millions of student essays, which store the GSeP scores of each word-pairs varying in distance. Position indicators are also attached to the feature, note that we adjust the scattering rate when mapping the scores into discrete embedding labels based on model's performance. For a target word, we compute ePMI together with neighbor words and map them to discrete value internals as features.

Combination of POS and PMI. our intuition is that the efficiency of PMI-score (Church and Hanks,

---

[1] http://www.ltp-cloud.com/

1990) between words is more relevant to what their POSs (Ferraro et al., 2014) exactly are; PMI-scores for different POS-pairs have different meaning, even though the POS-pairs have identical PMI score. To avoid this ambiguity, we take $POS(w_i)\_POS(w_j)\_PMI(w_i, w_i)$ as a supplementary PMI-feature. E.g., for char B_2 from word B whose POS is n, and its left-adjacent word A whose POS is v, right-adjacent word C whose POS is d, the compound-PMI feature for char B_2 shall be described as

$$cPMI(B_2) = \left\langle \begin{matrix} n\_v\_PMI(B,A) \\ n\_d\_PMI(B,C) \end{matrix} \right\rangle \tag{5}$$

We concatenate the adjacent ePMIs into one single label using the same mapping method as the other feature.

3.3 Ensemble Mechanism

To maximize the performance of single BiLSTM-CRF model, we design two ensemble strategies including the probabilistic-ensemble method and the ranking-based merge method.

Probabilistic-Ensemble. To alleviate the scattering pattern of the LSTM predictive outputs for each tag that will efficiently improve the model's performance on precision-related metrics, we integrate the LSTM-outputs probabilities with weighted sum based on each model's characteristics. Specifically, given n different trained single BiLSTM-CRF models that might have various hyperparameters setting during training phase.

$$M_1, M_2, M_3 \ldots M_n \tag{6}$$

And an input sequence $\mathbb{I}^{k \times l}$ in matrix form, where k is the number of tag the sequence contains, and l is the total size of each tag's dimension. We randomly initialize a grouping vector $\mathcal{G}^{1 \times n}$ uniquely belongs to the n models group and responsible for optimizing their ensemble performance via dot product. For each tag $t^{1 \times l}$ from $\mathbb{I}^{k \times l}$, the corresponding ensemble LSTM output from all single models is defined as

$$\phi_j = \sum_{i=1}^{k} \mathcal{G}_i^{1 \times n} M_i(t_j^{1 \times l}) \tag{7}$$

Then the weighted LSTM outputs are passed onto the fixed CRF-layer, which describes the transition matrix among target tags, as its input features. Given a group of fixed single models, we first train their grouping vector $\mathcal{G}^{1 \times n}$ via strategy above, then we save this $\mathcal{G}^{1 \times n}$ with these single models, and next time when we need the probabilistic-ensemble results of these models we will run this architecture forward to obtain the desired high-precision tagging predictions.

Ranking-based Output Ensemble. This strategy was inspired by ALI team in 2017. We found that the single models trained via Adam optimizer (Kingma and Ba, 2014) perform better on recall-related metrics compared with the ones trained with Stochastic Gradient Descent(SGD). According to experimental results, the Adam-trained models appear to have obvious advantage over the SGD-trained models on both Detection and Identification levels, however, merging-all the results straightforwardly from Adam-trained models lead to drastic decrease on precision-related scores. We tackle this issue with applying ranking method vertically and horizontally on the merge-to-be results upon each input sequence. To be clear, given each prediction with a CRF-score, we keep the top-40% predictions generated by single models and delete the others for each sentence (vertical ranking), and we delete the final-20% predictions for each model such that those low-confidence noisy predictions can be smoothed over (horizontal ranking). Since the SGD-based model is precision-prone due to its stochastic properties capable of capturing detailed task-specific features, we additionally merge the results obtained from selected BiLSTM-CRF models trained with SGD optimizer, improving the ensemble results on precision-related metrics upon all evaluating levels. An input sequence will not be labelled as 'correct' unless all candidate models tag it with a correct label. This correct-tagging scheme successfully balances the evaluating metrics via improving the overall recall-related metrics based on our experimental results.

3.4 Model Selection

Due to random initialization and various manual seeds, as well as different hyperparameters setting, each model has its unique properties toward the task and performs distinctively on each sequential testing unit. More models shall be trained to obtain better ones that capable of achieving higher performance. Generally, we trained 240 SGD-based models and 240 Adam-based models in total using 10 different hyperparameters groups and 24 different manual seed for each optimizer group. Then we selected

40 best models based on customized evaluating criterion on development datasets for each optimizer, calling them 40-SGD group and 40-Adam Group. Next, we applied probabilistic-Ensemble method on each group's models with 4-model, 5-model, and 6-model combinational settings respectively; for each setting, we tried hundreds of combinations and finally we obtained 120 best probabilistic-Ensemble model-groups (pEMGs) each optimizer group. We permutated each pEMG to find out three groups of IEMGs with merging methods, specifically,

- group of 30 best pEMGs being merged-all on P-Level from 120 SGD-IEMGs.

- group of 30 best pEMGs being merged-all on I-Level from 120 Adam-pEMGs.

- group of 30 best pEMGs being rank-merged on P-Level from all 240 pEMGs.

3.5 Post-Processing

When we obtain the results generated by our deep learning models, we will post-process them explicitly using following approaches to tackle with the issues caused by ensemble mechanism.

- **Template Matcher**

We found that many essential grammatical rules cannot be learnt thoroughly from automatic learning process via deep learning models due to the restriction of training data provided. Therefore, we handcrafted several rule-based matchers to add high-precision predictions based on prior knowledge about Chinese grammar, i.e., for a sequence "快乐 的 吃" ("eat happy"), we know that "快乐" is an adjective and "吃" is a verb, and we also definitely know the grammatical rule that an adjective and a verb shall be connected with the word "地" rather than "的" or "得", thereby the word "的" is definitely a Mis-Selection error and shall be replaced by "地". We built hundreds of grammatical matchers based on actual Chinese grammar rules; this approach heavily depends on the excellency of POS-tagging toolkit, the mis-tagging of which would directly interfere with the Template Matcher performance.

- **Dealing with Ensemble Overlaps**

Merging-all the results from different models can cause overlaps. For instance, one model predicts an error with position from 4 to 8, another one predicts it as 6 to 9, however, it is obvious that one of them is incorrect since grammatical errors are considered as independent. Hence, we need strategies to make decision that which predicted error shall be kept.

When overlap happens, we first confirm the overlapping region, then we delete those errors that violate the word segmentations, i.e., we shall delete an error whose positional prediction is 4 to 8 while more than one segmented words exist within this positional range. Subsequently we make decision about the error via voting method; the error that has heaviest vote shall be kept.

3.6 Error Correction

Compared with previous CGED-task, this year the systems are also required to recommend corrections for S-type and M-type errors. We apply two methods to deal with this. The generated results of these two methods are merged and sorted based on their corresponding confidence-value via a voting mechanism.

- **PMI-based Approach**

For each input Chinese sequence, we first locate the error position, then we generate a list of recommended word candidates based on the ePMI values of the neighbor words within a specific window size. We used a student essay dataset (ten million Chinese essay sentences written by Chinese high school students), Baike datasets (two million sentences obtained from Encyclopedia of China), and past CGED training datasets to build the ePMI matrices. Each neighbor word (root-word) recommend a list of collocational supplements (child-word) based on the scores via looking up its corresponding ePMI matrices. Next, we organize all the recommended candidates based on the weights of their root words, generating the final sorted correction list.

- **Seq2Seq with Attention Mechanism**

In order to memorize fixed collocations, we also used Seq2Seq (Sutskever et al., 2014) network, in which two RNNs are combined together to store information from input to output. The encoder RNN reads an input sequence and output its corresponding contextual vector, which is decoded via the decoder RNN to produce an output sequence. We also utilize Attention mechanism to alleviate the burden of the contextual vector by focusing on specific part of the encoder's output for every step of decoding phase. This approach efficiently stores sentences provided in training datasets, helping the system produce exact correction on high precision.

4 Experiment

4.1 Data preparation

We trained our single models using training units that contain both the erroneous and the corrected sentences from 2016, 2017 and 2018 training datasets provided. Furthermore, we collected the sentences from 2016 and 2017 testing datasets, and for each correct-labelled sentence, we randomly handcrafted its erroneous form based on basic Chinese grammatical errors patterns and used it as one of the training units. We pretrained char embedding, word embedding, and bigram embedding via external datasets that include five million sentences from Chinese essays written by Native Chinese high school students in their daily assignment and fine-tuned them during training phase.

	Detection Level			Identification Level			Position Level		
	Precision	Recall	F1	Precision	Recall	F1	Precision	Recall	F1
S	0.8321	0.6070	0.7019	0.6032	0.4547	0.5185	0.4903	0.2967	0.3697
A	0.5271	0.8993	0.6646	0.3957	0.7829	0.5257	0.2016	0.4136	0.2711
S+P	**0.8574**	0.5678	0.6832	**0.6428**	0.3948	0.4892	**0.5703**	0.2832	0.3785
A+P	0.5542	0.8043	0.6562	0.4366	0.7041	0.5390	0.2568	0.3841	0.3078
S+P+M	0.8568	0.6123	0.7142	0.6322	0.4596	0.5323	0.5437	0.3052	**0.3909**
S+A+P+RM	0.6519	**0.9233**	**0.7642**	0.4259	**0.8021**	**0.5564**	0.2074	**0.4908**	0.2916

Table 1: Validation Results using single models and ensemble methods. "S" denotes for SGD-based single model, "A" denotes for Adam-based single model, "P" denotes for probabilistic-ensemble method, "M" denotes for simply merge-all, "RM" denotes for ranking-based output ensemble.

	Detection Level			Identification Level			Position Level		
	Precision	Recall	F1	Precision	Recall	F1	Precision	Recall	F1
baseline	0.8212	0.5673	0.671	0.6086	0.4092	0.4894	0.463	0.2559	0.3296
ePMI	0.821	0.6092	0.6994	**0.6034**	0.4525	0.5172	**0.4815**	0.2693	0.3454
ePMI+Matcher	**0.8322**	**0.6095**	**0.7036**	0.6008	**0.4723**	**0.5289**	0.4712	**0.2962**	**0.3637**

Table 2: Matcher and ePMI Performances of Single model on our Validation dataset. The baseline model is the basic BiLSTM-CRF model described in this article without ePMI feature.

4.2 Validation Results

To demonstrate contributions of our novel features, ensemble mechanism and post-processing approach, we used collections from 2017 Testing datasets, 2016 Testing datasets and other handcrafted datasets based on HSK past topics to customize our validation sets. Table 1 and Table 2 show our results on validation sets. The SGD-based single model performs well on precision-related metrics at all levels and performs much better with probabilistic-Ensemble method. The Adam-based models are superior in recall-related metrics and achieve best D and I scores among all methods. Generally, we found that SGD-based single models being processed with probabilistic-Ensemble method achieve highest precision-related scores at all levels and applying Rank-Merge method on both SGD-based and Adam-based models achieve highest recall-related metrics at all levels. Except for the Adam-based with probabilistic-ensemble, each other ensemble method achieves at least one highest score.

We also evaluated the contributions of the proposed novel features, i.e. the ePMI feature and Template matchers. Table 2 shows the results. We can see that adding ePMI features can improve the performance at all levels. Using template machers at the post processing phase gains further improvements. This confirms the effectiveness of the proposed strategy. It also implies that exploiting external data resource and bringing in humor knowledge are promising for this task.

4.3 Testing Results

As shown in Table 3, our system achieves the best F1 scores at all levels except for the detection level and achieves the best Precision scores at all levels except for the correction level. Instead of Run #3, our Run #1 has best F1 score at P level, and precision scores at all levels, revealing that the testing results can be affected by the components of the provided testing datasets. Although we achieve the highest P-level F1 score at 0.3612 among all teams, there still has wide gap for this task-specific system to overcome in actual NLP application. The reason includes that this task is pretty hard and more than one correction for each sentence shall be considered.

	Detection Level			Identification Level			Position Level		
	Precision	Recall	F1	Precision	Recall	F1	Precision	Recall	F1
Run #1	**0.8276**	0.6090	0.7017	**0.7107**	0.4173	0.5259	**0.5341**	0.2729	**0.3612**
Run #2	0.6171	**0.9572**	**0.7504**	0.3931	**0.7331**	0.5118	0.1441	**0.3886**	0.2102
Run #3	0.8254	0.6517	0.7283	0.6874	0.4588	**0.5503**	0.4752	0.2906	0.3606
Best Team	0.8276	0.9995	0.7563	0.7107	0.9752	0.5503	0.5341	0.3886	0.3612

	Correction			Top-3 Correction		
	Precision	Recall	F1	Precision	Recall	F1
Run #1	**0.2087**	0.1468	**0.1723**	**0.3059**	\	**0.2527**
Run #2	0.0386	**0.1696**	0.0629	0.0722	\	0.1177
Run #3	0.1509	0.1400	0.1453	0.2391	\	0.2301
Best Team	0.2932	0.1696	0.1723	0.3077	\	0.2527

Table 3: Performances of Submitted Runs on Official Evaluation Testing datasets. Yellow-labelled scores represent the best scores we have achieved among all participant teams. "Best Team" row records the best scores among all participant teams at each task-specific evaluating metric.

5 Conclusion and Future Work

This paper describes our system on NLPTEA-2018 CGED task, which combines deep learning mechanism and prior knowledge. We also designed model selection and several ensemble strategies to maximize the model's capability. At all four evaluating levels, we have the best F1 scores in three levels, and the second-highest F1 score in the detection level.

In the future, we are planning to build a more powerful grammatical error diagnosis system with more training data and improve the system's ability with more detailed Template Matchers.

Acknowledgments

Special thanks to the organizers of CGED 2018 for their great job. We also thank the anonymous reviewers for insightful comments and suggestions.

References

Kenneth Ward Church and Patrick Hanks. 1990. Word association norms, mutual information, and lexicog- raphy. Computational linguistics,

16(1):22–29.

Gabriela Ferraro, Rogelio Nazar, Margarita Alonso Ramos, and Leo Wanner. 2014. Towards advanced collocation error correction in spanish learner corpora. Language resources and evaluation, 48(1):45–64.

Robert Hecht-Nielsen. 1992. Neural networks for perception (vol. 2). chapter Theory of the Back- propagation Neural Network, pages 65–93. Harcourt Brace & Co., Orlando, FL, USA.

G. E. Hinton and R. R. Salakhutdinov. 2006. Reducing the Dimensionality of Data with Neural Networks. Science, 313(5786):504–507.

Sepp Hochreiter and Ju͏̈rgen Schmidhuber. 1997. Long short-term memory. Neural computation, 9(8):1735–1780.

Zhiheng Huang, Wei Xu, and Kai Yu. 2015. Bidirectional lstm-crf models for sequence tagging. arXiv preprint arXiv:1508.01991.

Diederik Kingma and Jimmy Ba. 2014. Adam a method for stochastic optimization. arXiv preprint arXiv:1412.6980.

Lung-Hao Lee, RAO Gaoqi, Liang-Chih Yu, XUN Endong, Baolin Zhang, and Li-Ping Chang. 2016. Overview of nlp-tea 2016 shared task for chi- nese grammatical error diagnosis. In Proceed- ings of the 3rd Workshop on Natural Language Processing Techniques for Educational Applications (NLPTEA2016), pages 40–48.

Yi Yang, Pengjun Xie, Jun Tao, Guangwei Xu, Linlin Li, and Si Luo. 2017. Embedding Grammatical Features into LSTMs for Chinese Grammatical Error Diagnosis Task. IJCNLP-2017, page 41.

Chi-Hsin Yu and Hsin-Hsi Chen. 2012. Detecting. word ordering errors in chinese sentences for learning chi- nese as a foreign language. In COLING, pages 3003–3018.

Bo Zheng, Wanxiang Che, Jiang Guo, and Ting Liu. 2016. Chinese grammatical error diagnosis with long short-term memory networks. NLPTEA 2016, page 47.

A Hybrid System for Chinese Grammatical Error
Diagnosis and Correction

Chen Li[*]   **Junpei Zhou**[*†]   **Zuyi Bao**   **Hengyou Liu**   **Guangwei Xu**   **Linlin Li**

Alibaba Group

969 West Wenyi Road, Hangzhou, China

{puji.lc, zuyi.bzy, hengyou.lhy, linyan.lll}@alibaba-inc.com

jpzhou1996@gmail.com   kunka.xgw@taobao.com

Abstract

This paper introduces the DM_NLP team's system for NLPTEA 2018 shared task of Chinese Grammatical Error Diagnosis (CGED), which can be used to detect and correct grammatical errors in texts written by Chinese as a Foreign Language (CFL) learners. This task aims at not only detecting four types of grammatical errors including redundant words (R), missing words (M), bad word selection (S) and disordered words (W), but also recommending corrections for errors of M and S types. We proposed a hybrid system including four models for this task with two stages: the detection stage and the correction stage. In the detection stage, we first used a BiLSTM-CRF model to tag potential errors by sequence labeling, along with some handcraft features. Then we designed three Grammatical Error Correction (GEC) models to generate corrections, which could help to tune the detection result. In the correction stage, candidates were generated by the three GEC models and then merged to output the final corrections for M and S types. Our system reached the highest precision in the correction subtask, which was the most challenging part of this shared task, and got top 3 on F1 scores for position detection of errors.

1 Introduction

More and more people are learning a second or third language as an interest, a career plus, or even a challenge to oneself. Chinese is one of the oldest and most versatile languages in the world. Many people choose to learn Chinese, and the number of CFL leaner grows rapidly.

However, it would be difficult to learn Chinese, because Chinese has a lot of differences from other languages. For example, Chinese has neither the change of singular and plural, nor the tense change of the verb. It has quite flexible expressions and loose structural grammar. These traits bring a lot of trouble to CFL learners, so the demands for Chinese Grammatical Error Diagnosis (CGED) as well as Correction (CGEC) is growing rapidly. GEC for English has been studied for many years, with many shared tasks such as CoNLL-2013 (Ng et al., 2013) and CoNLL-2014 (Ng et al., 2014), while those kinds of studies on Chinese is less yet.

This CGED shared task (Gaoqi et al., 2017; Lee et al., 2016, 2015; Yu et al., 2014) gives researchers an opportunity to build the system and exchange opinions in this field. It could make the community more flourish which benefits all CFL learners. Compared with previous years, this year's NLPTEA CGED shared task requests participants to generate candidate corrections for errors of M and S types. This correction subtask is more challenging and valuable, so we focused on this subtask and got the highest precision in this subtask.

This paper is organized as follows: Section 2 describes some related works in English as well as Chinese. Dataset will be described in Section 3. Section 4 illustrates our hybrid system with two stages, including four models. Section 5 shows the evaluation and discussion of the hybrid model. Section 6 concludes the paper and discusses the future work.

2 Related Work

Earlier attempts to GEC involve rule-based models (Heidorn et al., 1982; Bustamante and León, 1996) and classifier-based approaches (Han et al., 2004; Rozovskaya and Roth, 2011), which can cope with

---

[*]Equal Contribution

[†]This work was done while the author at Alibaba Group

Proceedings of the 5th Workshop on Natural Language Processing Techniques for Educational Applications, pages 60–69

Melbourne, Australia, July 19, 2018. ©2018 Association for Computational Linguistics

Table 1: Typical examples for four types of errors

Error	Original Sentence	Correct Sentence
M	中国已成了世界拥有最多"烟民"的国家。	中国已成了世界上拥有最多"烟民"的国家。
R	孩子的教育不能只靠一个**学校**老师。	孩子的教育不能只靠一个老师。
S	父母对孩子的**爱情**是最重要的。	父母对孩子的**关爱**是最重要的。
W	生产率较低，那肯定**价格**要上升。	生产率较低，那**价格**肯定要上升。

only specific type of errors.

As a sentence may contain multiple errors of different types, a practical GEC system should be able to cope with most of those errors, which is difficult to be achieved by rule-based or classifier models alone. The combination of rule-based and classifier models (Rozovskaya et al., 2013) can correct multiple errors, but it is useful only when the errors are independent of each other, which means that it is unable to solve the problem of dependent errors.

To address more complex errors, MT models are proposed and developed by many researchers. Statistical Machine Translation (SMT) has been dominant for the past two decades. In the work of Brockett et al. (2006), they propose an SMT model used for GEC, and later the round-trip translation is also used in GEC (Madnani et al., 2012). A POS-factored SMT system is proposed (Yuan and Felice, 2013) to correct five types of errors in the text. In the work of Felice et al. (2014), they propose a pipeline of the rule-based system and a phrase-based SMT system augmented by a sizeable web-based language model. The word-level Levenshtein distance between source and target can be used as a translation model feature (Junczys-Dowmunt and Grundkiewicz, 2014) to enhance the model. Rule-based method and n-gram statistical method are combined (Wu et al., 2015) to get a hybrid system for CGED shared task. Recently Napoles and Callison-Bursh (2017) propose a lightweight approach to GEC called Specialized Machine translation for Error Correction.

Nevertheless, Neural Machine Translation (NMT) systems have achieved substantial improvements in this field (Sutskever et al., 2014; Bahdanau et al., 2014). Inspired by this phenomenon, Sun et al. (2015) utilize the Convolutional Neural Network (CNN) for the article error correction. The Recurrent Neural Network (RNN) is also used (Yuan and Briscoe, 2016) to map the sentence from learner space to expert space. Recently Ji et al. (2017) propose a hybrid neural model with nested attention layers for GEC.

3 Dataset Description

The dataset is provided by the 5th Workshop on Natural Language Processing Techniques for Educational Applications (NLPTEA) 2018 with a Shared Task for CGED. The NLPTEA CGED has been held since 2014, and it provides several sets of training data for this field.

Each instance in the CGED training dataset is composed of an original sentence with a unique sentence number 'sid', some 'target edits', and a correction sentence. The original sentence contains grammatical errors in Chinese sentences written by CFL learners. All errors are divided into four types, including redundant words (denoted as R), missing words (M), word selection errors (S), and word ordering errors (W). Some typical examples are shown in Table 1.

Each edit in the 'target edits' indicates the error type and the position at which it occurs in the original sentence. If an input sentence contains one or more grammatical errors, the 'target edits' will include many items, each of which is in the form of [start-off, end-off, error-type], where start-off and end-off respectively denote the starting and ending position of the grammatical error, and the error-type is in the set of R, M, S, and W. For each original sentence given in the test dataset, the developed system should predict the 'target edits' in the format which is same as the training set, and for the error type of S and M, the system should predict the candidate corrections.

We also used an external dataset Lang-8[1] to train our GEC models, which contains more than 700,000 items, and each item consists of an original sentence and corresponding corrected sentences. Each original sentence has k correction

---

[1] provided by NLPCC 2018 GEC shared task

Figure 1: The pipeline of our hybrid system

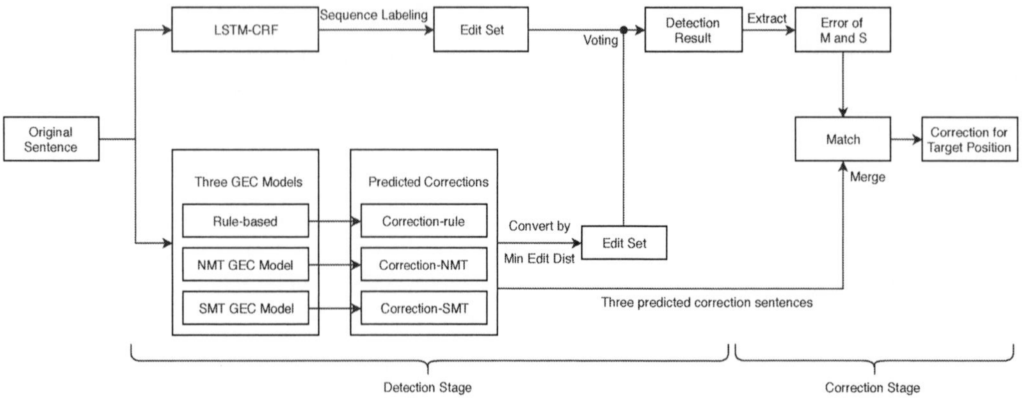

sentences, where $k \geq 0$.

4 System Description

We proposed a hybrid system for the CGED shared task this year, which contained two stages: the detection stage and the correction stage. In the detection stage, given a sentence s_i, which is composed of characters as $[c_1, c_2, ..., c_n]$, our system generates an edit set E_i which contains one or more errors of this sentence in the form of $[sid, start, end, err]$, where $start$ and end denote a specific part of this sentence $[c_{start}, c_{end}]$ has the error of type err. Then, in the correction stage, for the $err \in \{M, S\}$, our system can generate candidate corrections for $[c_{start}, c_{end}]$. If err is M, c_{start} must be equal to c_{end}, and the correction will be inserted at this position. The whole pipeline of our hybrid system is shown in Figure 1.

Our model consists of four models, including the BiLSTM-CRF model for tagging possible errors by sequence labeling at the detection stage, and three GEC models to convert the Chinese sentence from the 'learner space' to the 'expert space'. Those GEC models not only generate candidate corrections for M and S errors at the correction stage, but also help the BiLSTM-CRF model to tag the possible error position at the detection stage. The three GEC models are Rule-based model, NMT model, and SMT model, which are able to cope with different types of grammatical errors.

4.1 BiLSTM-CRF

In the detection stage, we treated the error detection problem as a sequence labeling problem and utilized the BiLSTM-CRF model (Huang et al., 2015) to get the corresponding label sequence in the form of BIO encoding (Kim et al., 2004). More specifically, given an input sentence which is composed of characters as $[c_1, c_2, ..., c_n]$, we utilized this model to predict the label L_i of c_i, for $i \in 1, 2, ..., n$. Since the prior knowledge can be used in this task, we incorporated many additional features for this sequence labeling problem, including Char Bigram, Part-of-speech (POS) tagging, POS score, Adjacent Word Collocation (AWC), Dependent Word Collocation (DWC), as used in (Xie et al., 2017).

4.2 Rule-based Model

The rule-based model starts by segmenting Chinese characters into chunks, which incorporates useful prior grammatical information to identify possible out-of-vocabulary errors. The segments are looked up in the dictionary built by Gigawords (Graff and Chen, 2005), and if a segment is out of vocabulary, it will go through the following steps:

1. If the segment consists of two or more characters, and turn out to be in the dictionary by permuting the characters, it will be added to the candidate list.

2. If the concatenation with a previous or next segment is in the dictionary, it will be added to the candidate list.

3. All possible keys in the dictionary with

the same or similar Pinyin (the Romanization system for Standard Chinese) or similar strokes to the segment are generated. The generated keys for the segment itself, concatenated with those of previous or next segments, will be added to the candidate list of possible corrections.

After the steps, a candidate list of all possible corrections will be processed to identify whether there might be out-of-vocabulary error and it's probability using a language model. The negative log likelihood of a size-5 sliding window suggests whether the top-scored candidate should be a correction of the original segment.

4.3 NMT GEC Model

The NMT model can capture complex relationships between the original sentence and the corrected sentence in GEC. We used the encoder-decoder structure (Bahdanau et al., 2014) with the general attention mechanism (Luong et al., 2015). We used two-layer LSTM model for both encoder and decoder. To enhance the ability of NMT models, we trained four NMT models with different parallel data pairs and configurations as described in Section 5.1. Those four NMT models were denoted as N_j, where $j \in \{1, 2, 3, 4\}$ was the model index. The correction result of sentence s_i generated by N_j was denoted as C_{iN_j}.

We used the character-based NMT because most characters in Chinese has its meaning, which is quite different from English characters, and the Chinese word's meaning often depends on the meaning of its characters. For example, we have two characters 昨天 (yesterday), and we can split it as [yester] + [day]. As in English, the second character 天 means day, and the first one is not a word if taken alone. But it is sufficiently unique to give the whole word its meaning. On the other hand, the errors in original sentences can make the word-based tokenization worse, which will introduce larger and lower quality vocabulary list. So, we chose to use char-based NMT for the CGEC problem.

4.4 SMT GEC Model

The SMT model consists of two components. One is a language model and the other one is a translation model. The language model is learned from a monolingual corpus of the target language, while the parameters of the translation model are calculated from the parallel corpus. We used the noisy channel model (Brown et al., 1993) to combine the language model and the translation model, and incorporated beam search to decode the result.

To explore the ability of SMT models with different configurations, we trained six SMT models with different data granularity and monolingual dataset as described in Section 5.1. Those six SMT models were denoted as S_j, where $j \in \{1, 2, 3, 4, 5, 6\}$ was the model index. The correction result of sentence s_i generated by S_j was denoted as C_{iS_j}.

4.5 Grammatical Error Detection and Correction

For the detection stage, we used the BiLSTM-CRF model as described in Section 4.1 to tag possible errors, by generating labels for each character in sentence s_i. Then each sequence labeling was converted to the editing format $[s_{id}, start, end, err]$. Next, we used the correction results generated by our three different GEC models to help to tune the detection result. For an original sentence s_i, we predicted the corrected sentence C_{iM} with our GEC model M, where M could be NMT N_j or SMT S_j. After getting the predicted correction sentence, we converted it to the editing format $[s_{id}, start, end, err]$, which was consistent with the detection result of the BiLSTM-CRF model.

The conversion from C_{iM} to editing format is based on the minimum editing distance, and we only focused on the error whose type is R, M, or S. On one side, these three types of errors are simple and clear, which can be generated by comparing the s_i and C_{iM} with high confidence. On the other side, the error of type W is more complicated, and the diversity of our GEC model would introduce a great number of noises into the original result on this type of error. Considered that there may exist many kinds of edit trace between a specific pair of s_i and C_{iM}, we kept tracing the edit list which minimized the editing distance between s_i and C_{iM}.

With the edits e_{ij} of sentence s_i, which are generated by BiLSTM-CRF and GEC models, the next step of our system is to ensemble all those edits. When it comes to the ensemble, we tried two methods. One is merging, which combines all detections generated by BiLSTM-CRF model as well as those GEC models, and take the union of their editing sets. The other is voting, in which we

Table 2: Configurations of four NMT models

Model	Network	Embed	Dataset
N_1	LSTM	no	$data_{ed}$
N_2	BiLSTM	enc-dec	$data_{ed}$
N_3	BiLSTM	enc-dec	$data_{all}$
N_4	BiLSTM	dec	$data_{all}$

Table 3: Configurations of six SMT models

Model	Granularity	Corpus	Dataset
S_1	char	Gigawords	$data_{all}$
S_2	char	ChineseWiki	$data_{all}$
S_3	char	CGED+NLPCC	$data_{all}$
S_4	phrase	Gigawords	$data_{all}$
S_5	phrase	ChineseWiki	$data_{all}$
S_6	phrase	CGED+NLPCC	$data_{all}$

set a voting threshold $thre$ and accept the edit with $T_{ij} \geq thre$, where T_{ij} is the times of appearance of edit e_{ij} for sentence s_i.

In the correction stage, we used the editing set E_i generated in the detection subtask. For the edit e_{ij} in E_i whose error type is M or S, we selected the candidate characters in the corresponding correction sentence predicted by our GEC models. Finally, all candidates of corrections generated by different GEC models will be collected and merged to create the submission file with detections as well as corrections.

5 Evaluation and Discussion

5.1 Data Split and Experiment Setting

To train the BiLSTM-CRF model, we collected several datasets of CGED, which are 2015, 2016, 2017, and 2018. We split 20% of the 2017 training data as the validation dataset, which is denoted as '17-dev', and all the rest as training. We used the character embeddings and word embeddings pre-trained on the Gigawords and fixed them. For other parameters, we initialized them randomly.

To train our GEC models, we used the external Lang-8 dataset as explained in Section 3. Because each original sentence could have more than one corrected sentences, we used two approaches to generate parallel data pairs to train our GEC models. The first choice is to use only the correct sentence whose edit distance is smallest from the original sentence. The training data generated by the first choice is denoted as $data_{ed}$. The second choice is to use all the correct sentences of the corresponding original sentence. The training data generated by the first choice is denoted as $data_{all}$.

For the NMT model, we used the pre-trained embedding in different parts of the model. The first choice was to use it for the whole model, which forced the model to learn a proper embedding by itself. Considering the dataset is not large enough for the model to learn the embedding from scratch, we also tested the pre-trained embedding

used for both encoder and decoder parts. But the embedding was trained on the Gigaword (Graff and Chen, 2005), which was quite different from the sentences written by CFL learners, so we also used the pre-trained embedding only in the decoder part. The configurations of our four different NMT GEC models $N_j, j \in \{1, 2, 3, 4\}$ are shown in Table 2. For the 'Network' column, the 'BiL-STM' means bi-directional LSTM (Schuster and Paliwal, 1997), and for the 'Embed' column, the 'enc-dec' means using pre-trained embedding for both encoder and decoder part in our model.

For the SMT model, we trained the language model part on different corpora, including the Gigaword, the Chinese Wikipedia corpus (Denoyer and Gallinari, 2006), and the corpus consists of CGED as well as Lang-8 correct sentences which are constructed by ourselves. Besides, we also tested different granularities of the model, which means, used char-level or phrase-level translation model. It is worth to mention that we found that using $data_{all}$ outperformed $data_{ed}$ significantly, so we only did detailed experiments on $data_{all}$ because of the time limitation of the contest. The configurations of our six different SMT models $S_j, j \in \{1, 2, 3, 4, 5, 6\}$ are shown in Table 3

Many excellent tools can emancipate us from the heavy burden of implementing models from scratch. For those NMT GEC models, we implemented it with the *OpenNMT* (Klein et al., 2017) toolkit, and for those SMT GEC models, we implemented the language model with *KenLM* (Heafield, 2011) toolkit and translation model with *Moses* (Koehn et al., 2007).

For the Lang-8 dataset, we found that in those 717,241 lines data, 474,638 lines contained traditional Chinese. The traditional Chinese cannot convey more information than its corresponding simplified Chinese, but will make the size of vocabulary much larger. So, we used the *opencc*

Table 4: Experiments of Grammatical Error Detection on 17-dev dataset by merging eleven models. The corresponding configuration of the models in 'NMT-type' and 'SMT-type' can be found in Table 2 and Table 3. The values for 'Detection', 'Identification', and 'Position' columns are all F_1 values.

NMT-type	SMT-type	FP-rate	Detection	Identification	Position
N_2	S_2	**0.7868**	0.6721	0.3511	0.1846
N_3	S_3	0.8032	**0.6747**	0.3512	0.1853
N_2	S_6	0.8160	0.6719	**0.3566**	0.1834
N_3	S_2	0.8028	0.6746	0.3513	**0.1856**

Table 5: Experiments of Grammatical Error Detection on 17-dev dataset by voting eleven models. The corresponding configuration of the models in 'NMT-type' and 'SMT-type' can be found in Table 2 and Table 3. The values for 'Detection', 'Identification', and 'Position' columns are all F_1 values.

Threshold	NMT-type	SMT-type	FP-rate	Detection	Identification	Position
2	N_4	S_2	0.3336	0.6414	0.4597	**0.2648**
2	N_1	S_6	0.3452	0.6472	**0.4669**	0.2643
2	N_3	S_6	0.3560	**0.6494**	0.4656	0.2643
4	N_4	S_2	**0.1036**	0.4799	0.3435	0.2297

toolkit to convert all the traditional Chinese to simplified Chinese.

5.2 Experiment Result

The evaluation metrics for NLPTEA CGED shared task consists of four subtasks: 'Detection' (determine if the sentence contains errors), 'Identification' (determine the error types), 'Position' (determine the position of errors), and 'Correction' (determine the candidate corrected words for M and S error types). Those four subtasks are from easy to hard, and the last metric is the most valuable, which will be paid more attention by us. The former three metrics are related to the detection stage, and the last metric is related to the correction stage.

Grammatical Error Detection

We used different parameters and initial states of BiLSTM-CRF model to get eight different results on detection stage. Each of three GEC models can generate the result in the editing format as described in Section 4.5. We utilized different methods to ensemble those eleven models, including merging and voting as explained in Section 4.5. Because both NMT and SMT models have different configurations, we tried all combinations of $N_j, j \in \{1, ..., 4\}$ and $S_j, j \in \{1, ..., 6\}$, with the fixed rule-based model, and part of the experiment result with merging is shown in Table 4, while voting method is shown in Table 5.

It's shown in Table 4 and 5 that voting method is more powerful than the merging method on all metrics except for the 'Detection', which is the easiest subtask. We also found out that different combinations of models can cope with different types of errors, and can generate results good at different subtasks. To better utilize the correction generated by our translation model, we preferred the model which performs best on the 'Position' metric, so we chose to use the voting method with threshold 2 to operate on the test dataset with N_2 and S_4.

Grammatical Error Correction

We found that our GEC models can focus on different type of errors, as shown in the Table 6 on the official testing data of CGED 2018, which is denoted as '18-test'. The Table 7 shows some cases in which our different models generated various types of corrections for the original sentence.

As shown in Table 6, the rule-based model can correct those word selection errors which share similar morphology or pronunciation with the ground truth characters. The rule-based model focuses on the correction of word selection errors, so it is able to yield high precision for the error correction problem. The SMT model can handle some errors whose type is R, even that part seems reasonable in the local context. The NMT model is good at correcting many types of errors, including simple errors of word missing or word redun-

Table 6: The cases which can be corrected by our GEC model

Model	Original Sentence	Translation Sentence
Rule	我就会完全知道他的性格，他的爱好，和不好的**密秘**。	我就会完全知道他的性格，他的爱好，和不好的**秘密**。
Rule	学生早恋这问题是很难**结决**的。	学生早恋这问题是很难**解决**的。
Rule	不过我觉得没有个性的文化**是也**没有意义的。	不过我觉得没有个性的文化**也是**没有意义的。
Rule	没有人可以**帮住我**，我是多么的辛苦，多么的劳累啊！	没有人可以**帮助我**，我是多么的辛苦，多么的劳累啊！
NMT	我们**能会做到得**！	我们**能做到**！
NMT	这种措施对个人健康和公众利益有所**好的影响**。	这种措施对个人健康和公众利益有所**好处**。
NMT	这个问题真是个难以解决的。	这个问题真是个难以解决的**问题**。
NMT	这表示你的肺部不是**正常**。	这表示你的肺部不是**正常的**。
NMT	我们从父母学会很多事情	我们从父母**那里**学会很多事情
NMT	我想**也抽烟**不好，但是不能这样对烟民。	我想**抽烟也**不好，但是不能这样对烟民。
NMT	随着社会的变化两代人之间的差异越来越大了。	随着社会的变化，两代人之间的差异越来越大了。
NMT	我觉得父母给孩子的**最主要东西**应该是极强的思维方式和美好的内心。	我觉得父母给孩子**最主要的东西**应该是极强的思维方式和美好的内心。
SMT	从小我**也**学会有好的爱清洁的习惯。	从小我学会有好的爱清洁的习惯。
SMT	因为化肥和农药，空气污染了很**严重**。	因为化肥和农药，空气污染很**严重**。
SMT	有些流行歌曲，或是些个体，出的歌曲**的中**带有不文明的话与语言。	有些流行歌曲，或是些个体，出的歌曲**中**带有不文明的话与语言。

Table 7: The same original sentence corrected by different GEC models

Model	Original Sentence	Translation Sentence
Rule	青少年看他们抽烟，引起自己的好奇，后来试抽一次，再抽一次，已经**瘾上**了。	青少年看他们抽烟，引起自己的好奇，后来试抽一次，再抽一次，已经**上瘾**了。
SMT	青少年看他们抽烟，引起自己的好奇，后来试抽一次，再抽一次，已经**瘾上**了。	青少年看他们抽烟，引起自己的好奇，后来试抽一次，再抽一次，已经**迷上**了。
NMT	下面我来具体**的**写一下我的理由。	下面我来具体**地**写一下我的理由。
SMT	下面我来具体**的**写一下我的理由。	下面我来具体写一下我的理由。
NMT	我**想**这样的态度是对自己和国家都不好。	我**认为**这样的态度对自己和国家都不好。
SMT	我想这样的态度**是**对自己和国家都不好。	我想这样的态度对自己和国家都不好。

Table 8: Ablation Tests of Correction Subtask

Method	Precision	Recall	F_1
Rule	0.215	0.00395	0.00775
N_4	0.299	0.0124	0.0238
S_2	**0.348**	0.0178	0.0338
$N_4 + S_2$	0.303	0.0248	0.0459
Rule $+ N_4$	0.281	0.0161	0.0304
Rule $+ S_2$	0.313	0.0217	0.0406
Rule $+ N_4 + S_2$	0.292	**0.0285**	**0.0519**

dancy. It is worth mentioning that the NMT model can correct some more complicated problems including phrase editing and word reordering. For example, it can correct 能会做到得 to 能做到, and also can correct 也抽烟不好 to 抽烟也不好. It can also add punctuations in the middle of the original sentence.

In Table 7, it shows that in some cases, given an original sentence, different GEC models can give different corrections. For the first two rows, the rule-based model and the SMT model give different corrections for the same position of the original sentence, and both of those corrections are reasonable. For the last two rows, the NMT model and the SMT model give corrections at different positions of the original sentence. The ensemble of those models could be helpful because they can generate corrections for many parts of the original sentences, and if they produce different candidates for the same position, we use the voting method to determine the final output.

We explored the ablation test after the release of CGED 2018 ground truth labels. Given error detection results generated by BiLSTM-CRF in the detection stage, we used different combination of three GEC models to generate the candidate corrections for errors of S and M. As we mentioned before, we picked the model combination that performed best on the 'Position' metric in Table 5 to better utilize the candidates generated by our GEC models. It's worth to mention that our rule-based GEC model is not customized for this dataset and the errors made by CFL learners are quite different from native speakers, which leads to relatively low precision. The result of the combination of all three models is slightly better than the version we submitted to CGED shared task because we fixed a small bug in the GEC model. From the ablation study, it showed that the combination of three GEC models improved the F_1 score of Correction

Subtask significantly.

6 Conclusion and Future Work

This paper describes our system approach in NLPTEA 2018 shared task of CGED. We proposed a two-stage hybrid system which combined the BiLSTM-CRF model and three GEC models. In the detection stage, we utilized the correction results generated by GEC models to tune the error tags generated by the BiLSTM-CRF model. While in the correction stage, outputs of our GEC models were merged to generate candidate corrections for errors whose type were S or M. Our system achieved the highest precision in the 'Correction' subtask, which is the most challenging part of this shared task and got top 3 on F1 scores for position detection of errors.

In the future, we will further explore the strengths as well as limitations of three GEC models in our system and find a better method to combine them.

References

Dzmitry Bahdanau, Kyunghyun Cho, and Yoshua Bengio. 2014. Neural machine translation by jointly learning to align and translate. *arXiv preprint arXiv:1409.0473*.

Chris Brockett, William B Dolan, and Michael Gamon. 2006. Correcting esl errors using phrasal smt techniques. In *Proceedings of the 21st International Conference on Computational Linguistics and the 44th annual meeting of the Association for Computational Linguistics*, pages 249–256. Association for Computational Linguistics.

Peter F Brown, Vincent J Della Pietra, Stephen A Della Pietra, and Robert L Mercer. 1993. The mathematics of statistical machine translation: Parameter estimation. *Computational linguistics*, 19(2):263–311.

Flora Ramírez Bustamante and Fernando Sánchez León. 1996. Gramcheck: A grammar and style checker. In *Proceedings of the 16th conference on Computational linguistics-Volume 1*, pages 175–181. Association for Computational Linguistics.

Ludovic Denoyer and Patrick Gallinari. 2006. The wikipedia xml corpus. In *International Workshop of the Initiative for the Evaluation of XML Retrieval*, pages 12–19. Springer.

Mariano Felice, Zheng Yuan, Øistein E Andersen, Helen Yannakoudakis, and Ekaterina Kochmar. 2014. Grammatical error correction using hybrid systems and type filtering. In *Proceedings of the Eighteenth Conference on Computational Natural Language Learning: Shared Task*, pages 15–24.

RAO Gaoqi, Baolin Zhang, XUN Endong, and Lung-Hao Lee. 2017. Ijcnlp-2017 task 1: Chinese grammatical error diagnosis. *Proceedings of the IJCNLP 2017, Shared Tasks*, pages 1–8.

David Graff and Ke Chen. 2005. Chinese gigaword. *LDC Catalog No.: LDC2003T09, ISBN*, 1:58563–58230.

Na-Rae Han, Martin Chodorow, and Claudia Leacock. 2004. Detecting errors in english article usage with a maximum entropy classifier trained on a large, diverse corpus. In *LREC*.

Kenneth Heafield. 2011. Kenlm: Faster and smaller language model queries. In *Proceedings of the Sixth Workshop on Statistical Machine Translation*, pages 187–197. Association for Computational Linguistics.

George E. Heidorn, Karen Jensen, Lance A. Miller, Roy J. Byrd, and Martin S Chodorow. 1982. The epistle text-critiquing system. *IBM Systems Journal*, 21(3):305–326.

Zhiheng Huang, Wei Xu, and Kai Yu. 2015. Bidirectional lstm-crf models for sequence tagging. *arXiv preprint arXiv:1508.01991*.

Jianshu Ji, Qinlong Wang, Kristina Toutanova, Yongen Gong, Steven Truong, and Jianfeng Gao. 2017. A nested attention neural hybrid model for grammatical error correction. *arXiv preprint arXiv:1707.02026*.

Marcin Junczys-Dowmunt and Roman Grundkiewicz. 2014. The amu system in the conll-2014 shared task: Grammatical error correction by data-intensive and feature-rich statistical machine translation. In *Proceedings of the Eighteenth Conference on Computational Natural Language Learning: Shared Task*, pages 25–33.

Jin-Dong Kim, Tomoko Ohta, Yoshimasa Tsuruoka, Yuka Tateisi, and Nigel Collier. 2004. Introduction to the bio-entity recognition task at jnlpba. In *Proceedings of the international joint workshop on natural language processing in biomedicine and its applications*, pages 70–75. Association for Computational Linguistics.

Guillaume Klein, Yoon Kim, Yuntian Deng, Jean Senellart, and Alexander M Rush. 2017. Opennmt: Open-source toolkit for neural machine translation. *arXiv preprint arXiv:1701.02810*.

Philipp Koehn, Hieu Hoang, Alexandra Birch, Chris Callison-Burch, Marcello Federico, Nicola Bertoldi, Brooke Cowan, Wade Shen, Christine Moran, Richard Zens, et al. 2007. Moses: Open source toolkit for statistical machine translation. In *Proceedings of the 45th annual meeting of the ACL on interactive poster and demonstration sessions*, pages 177–180. Association for Computational Linguistics.

Lung-Hao Lee, RAO Gaoqi, Liang-Chih Yu, XUN Endong, Baolin Zhang, and Li-Ping Chang. 2016. Overview of nlp-tea 2016 shared task for Chinese grammatical error diagnosis. In *Proceedings of the 3rd Workshop on Natural Language Processing Techniques for Educational Applications (NLPTEA2016)*, pages 40–48.

Lung-Hao Lee, Liang-Chih Yu, and Liping Chang. 2015. Overview of the nlp-tea 2015 shared task for Chinese grammatical error diagnosis.

Minh-Thang Luong, Hieu Pham, and Christopher D Manning. 2015. Effective approaches to attention-based neural machine translation. *arXiv preprint arXiv:1508.04025*.

Nitin Madnani, Joel Tetreault, and Martin Chodorow. 2012. Exploring grammatical error correction with not-so-crummy machine translation. In *Proceedings of the Seventh Workshop on Building Educational Applications Using NLP*, pages 44–53. Association for Computational Linguistics.

Courtney Napoles and Chris Callison-Burch. 2017. Systematically adapting machine translation for grammatical error correction. In *Proceedings of the 12th Workshop on Innovative Use of NLP for Building Educational Applications*, pages 345–356.

Hwee Tou Ng, Siew Mei Wu, Ted Briscoe, Christian Hadiwinoto, Raymond Hendy Susanto, and Christopher Bryant. 2014. The conll-2014 shared task on grammatical error correction. In *Proceedings of the Eighteenth Conference on Computational Natural Language Learning: Shared Task*, pages 1–14.

Hwee Tou Ng, Siew Mei Wu, Yuanbin Wu, Christian Hadiwinoto, and Joel Tetreault. 2013. The conll-2013 shared task on grammatical error correction.

Alla Rozovskaya, Kai-Wei Chang, Mark Sammons, and Dan Roth. 2013. The university of illinois system in the conll-2013 shared task. In *Proceedings of the Seventeenth Conference on Computational Natural Language Learning: Shared Task*, pages 13–19.

Alla Rozovskaya and Dan Roth. 2011. Algorithm selection and model adaptation for esl correction tasks. In *Proceedings of the 49th Annual Meeting of the Association for Computational Linguistics: Human Language Technologies-Volume 1*, pages 924–933. Association for Computational Linguistics.

Mike Schuster and Kuldip K Paliwal. 1997. Bidirectional recurrent neural networks. *IEEE Transactions on Signal Processing*, 45(11):2673–2681.

Chengjie Sun, Xiaoqiang Jin, Lei Lin, Yuming Zhao, and Xiaolong Wang. 2015. Convolutional neural networks for correcting english article errors. In *Natural Language Processing and Chinese Computing*, pages 102–110. Springer.

Ilya Sutskever, Oriol Vinyals, and Quoc V Le. 2014. Sequence to sequence learning with neural networks. In *Advances in neural information processing systems*, pages 3104–3112.

Xiupeng Wu, Peijie Huang, Jundong Wang, Qingwen Guo, Yuhong Xu, and Chuping Chen. 2015. Chinese grammatical error diagnosis system based on hybrid model. In *Proceedings of the 2nd Workshop on Natural Language Processing Techniques for Educational Applications*, pages 117–125.

Pengjun Xie et al. 2017. Alibaba at ijcnlp-2017 task 1: Embedding grammatical features into lstms for Chinese grammatical error diagnosis task. *Proceedings of the IJCNLP 2017, Shared Tasks*, pages 41–46.

Liang-Chih Yu, Lung-Hao Lee, and Li-Ping Chang. 2014. Overview of grammatical error diagnosis for learning Chinese as a foreign language. In *Proceedings of the 1st Workshop on Natural Language Processing Techniques for Educational Applications*, pages 42–47.

Zheng Yuan and Ted Briscoe. 2016. Grammatical error correction using neural machine translation. In *Proceedings of the 2016 Conference of the North American Chapter of the Association for Computational Linguistics: Human Language Technologies*, pages 380–386.

Zheng Yuan and Mariano Felice. 2013. Constrained grammatical error correction using statistical machine translation. In *Proceedings of the Seventeenth Conference on Computational Natural Language Learning: Shared Task*, pages 52–61.

Ling@CASS Solution to the NLP-TEA CGED Shared Task 2018

Qinan Hu[12], Yongwei Zhang[12], Fang Liu[32], Yueguo Gu[2]
[1]Institute of Linguistics, Chinese Academy of Social Sciences
[2]China Multilingual and Multimodal Corpora and Big Data Research Centre
[3]School of Software & Microelectronics, Peking University
qinan.hu@qq.com, zhangyw@cass.org.cn, liu_fang@pku.edu.cn, gyg@beiwaionline.com

Abstract

In this study, we employ the sequence to sequence learning to model the task of grammar error correction. The system takes potentially erroneous sentences as inputs, and outputs correct sentences. To breakthrough the bottlenecks of very limited size of manually labeled data, we adopt a semi-supervised approach. Specifically, we adapt correct sentences written by native Chinese speakers to generate pseudo grammatical errors made by learners of Chinese as a second language. We use the pseudo data to pre-train the model, and the CGED data to fine-tune it. Being aware of the significance of precision in a grammar error correction system in real scenarios, we use ensembles to boost precision. When using inputs as simple as Chinese characters, the ensembled system achieves a precision at 86.56% in the detection of erroneous sentences, and a precision at 51.53% in the correction of errors of Selection and Missing types.

1 Introduction

An inter-language is an idiolect developed by a learner of a second language (or L2). It is characteristic that it preserves some features of the first language (or L1), and can overgeneralize some L2 linguistic rules. An investigation on the grammatical errors made by L2 learners will disclose the error patterns, which are beneficial to the teaching and learning process. On the other hand, it will promote the development of systems which can correct grammatical errors made by L2 learners automati-

cally.

The rest of this paper is organized as follows: Section 2 briefly introduces the definition of the NLP-TEA CGED Shared Task 2018. Section 3 gives a quick review on previous studies. Section 4 describes the generation of pseudo data in detail. Section 5 introduces the modeling of the correction task using sequence to sequence learning. Section 6 analyses the experimental results. Finally, conclusions and prospects are drawn in Section 7.

2 NLP-TEA CGED Shared Task 2018

The goal of Chinese Grammar Error Diagnosis (CGED) Shared Task in NLP Tech for Education Application (NLP-TEA) is to develop NLP techniques to automatically correct grammatical errors in Chinese sentences written by L2 learners. The shared task facilitate researchers using different linguistic knowledges and computational techniques to compare their results on the basis of common datasets and evaluation frameworks.

Grammatical errors made by speakers as a second language consist of different types. In CGED, the errors are defined as four types: Missing words ("M"), Redundant words ("R"), word Selection errors ("S"), and Word ordering errors ("W"). It is noticeable that this categorization is different from that of a traditional linguistic point of view, in which the errors are typically categorized into mis-usages of determiners, prepositions, noun forms, verb forms and subject-verb agreement etc. The categorization of errors in CGED tasks correspond to the four operations, i.e. insertions, deletions, substitutions, and transpositions, as defined in Damerau–Levenshtein dis-

Proceedings of the 5th Workshop on Natural Language Processing Techniques for Educational Applications, pages 70–76
Melbourne, Australia, July 19, 2018. ©2018 Association for Computational Linguistics

tance (Bard, 2006), respectively. These operations are used to edit a sequence into another.

A developed system should indicate types and positions of the errors, and propose corrections for the errors of S and M types. A system is to be evaluated using four tasks, including the detection of errors, the identification of error types, the identification of positions, and the corrections.

3 Previous Solutions: A Quick Review

Lee et al. (2013) employed handcrafted linguistic rules to detect grammatical errors made by learners of Chinese as a second language. Their system is further integrated with N-gram models to detect the errors (Lee et al., 2014). Most previous studies take the diagnosis of grammatical errors as a sequence labeling problem. They generally assign a B/I/O tag to each word in an input sentence, or each character in a word, to detect the errors. Yu and Chen (2012) proposed to use Conditional Random Field (CRF) (Lafferty et al., 2001) to detect Chinese word ordering errors. In 2014, Cheng et al. (2014) adopted a Support Vector Machine (SVM) (Hearst et al., 1998) to identify Chinese word ordering errors. In recent years, Long-short Term Memory (LSTM) (Hochreiter and Schmidhuber, 1997) has been a popular neural network model used for this task (Zheng et al., 2016; Yang et al., 2017).

Various features have been taken as the inputs into sequence labeling models, including characters, words, Part-of-Speech (POS) tags (Zheng et al., 2016), dependency information, and Point-wise Mutual Information (Yang et al., 2017), among many others.

4 Pseudo Labeling

The manually labeled dataset for the task of grammar error correction is of very limited size. Since manual labeling is both labor and time consuming, the size of the data set has been a bottleneck for the performances of automatic error correction systems. There have been several approaches to tackling this problem. Cahill et al. (2013) and Grundkiewicz and Junczys-Dowmunt (2014) use the error corrections extracted from Wikipedia revision history as training corpora. Further-

more, many studies adopt a semi-supervised approach to automatically generating a large scale pseudo data set and have reported promising results (Foster and Andersen, 2009; Rozovskaya and Roth, 2010; Dickinson, 2010; Imamura et al., 2012; Felice and Yuan, 2014; Rozovskaya et al., 2017).

4.1 Error Types

In our study, the pseudo data are generated based on a close observation on the errors collected from the manually labeled dataset.

4.1.1 Missing

It is observed that missing words are often functional words. As shown in Sentence 1, in which a particle and a preposition are missing. (The erroneous sentence is represented with E; and the correct sentence, C. The erroneous phrases are in bold.) Sentences 2 and 3 show another type of missing errors, which are caused by improper uses of ellipses.

(1-E) 认识到结婚 Ø 过程不满六个月，也可以说 Ø 我的故事中我是主动的。

(1-C) 认识到结婚的过程不满六个月，也可以说在我的故事中我是主动的。

(2-E) 所以家长会在孩子很小的时候就让其接受各种各样的学校教育，使 Ø 还很脆弱的心理和生理都受到很多压力。

(2-C) 所以家长会在孩子很小的时候就让其接受各种各样的学校教育，使孩子还很脆弱的心理和生理都受到很多压力。

(3-E) 在韩国最近很流行不允许 Ø 的电视节目，这节目说公共场所抽烟是不道德的行为。

(3-C) 在韩国最近不允许抽烟的电视节目很流行，这些节目说在公共场所抽烟是不道德的行为。

4.1.2 Redundant

Of all the redundant errors in CGED data set, functional words are among the most frequent. For instance, the particle and the conjunction in Sentences 4-5 are redundant.

(4-E) 如何处理现在在**做**香烟**的**工厂的人的以后的生活。

(4-C) 如何处理现在在香烟工厂工作的人的以后的生活。

(5-E) 大家在手术间里，合作无间**而**救了那位病人。

(5-C) 大家在手术间里，合作无间救了那位病人。

4.1.3 Selection

Selection errors often occur when near-synonyms are misused, as shown in Sentences 6-7. The differences of the usages between these near-synonyms are subtle.

(6-E) 他们知不道吸烟对未成年年的影响会造成的各种**害处**。

(6-C) 他们不知道吸烟对未成年人会造成的各种**伤害**。

(7-E) 从此，父母亲就会教**咱们**爬行、走路、叫爸爸妈妈。

(7-C) 从此，父母亲就会教**我们**爬行、走路、叫爸爸妈妈。

4.1.4 Word Order

Word ordering errors are typically related to the modification of verbs. For instance, the modifiers of the verbs, the auxiliary verb and the adverbs, are misplaced in Sentences 8-10.

(8-E) **采取几种方法应该**帮助他们。

(8-C) **应该采取几种方法**帮助他们。

(9-E) ……但**还是年轻的学生**需要大人的支持和指导……

(9-C) ……但**年轻的学生还是**需要大人的支持和指导……

(10-E) 我走路时常常想抽烟，可能另外抽烟者也**想这样**。

(10-C) 我走路时常常想抽烟，可能别的抽烟者也**这样想**。

4.2 Data Generation

Based on the above observations, we adapt the sentences written by native Chinese speakers to generate ungrammatical sentences. The canonical sentences come from 12 serials of textbooks for students learning Chinese as a second language, 7 serials of textbooks for native Chinese students, and People's Daily newspapers. The sentences are filtered with a length threshold and the controlled vocabularies for teaching Chinese as a second language (Hanban, 2001, 2010). These sentences are tokenized using LTP (Che et al., 2010). And then, the errors of redundant words, missing words, word selection errors and word ordering errors are generated using the operations of insertions, deletions, substitutions, and transpositions, respectively. All adaptations are done in terms of words. 2 millions sentences are adapted in this way.

4.2.1 Missing

(1) To make erroneous sentences with missing words, we randomly select a position in the input sentence. (2) If the word in that position is a functional word, or it is a content word with an antecedent in that sentence, drop this word. Example sentences are shown below.

(11-E) 一天，庙里来 Ø 一个瘦和尚。

(11-C) 一天，庙里来**了**一个瘦和尚。

(12-E) 他不仅爱收集动植物标本，还阅读了许多描写 Ø 的书。

(12-C) 他不仅爱收集动植物标本，还阅读了许多描写**动植物**的书。

4.2.2 Redundant

(1) Randomly select a position in the input sentence. (2) Randomly select a word according to word frequencies. (3) Insert the word into that position.

(13-E) 达尔文妈妈喜欢种花**的**。

(13-C) 达尔文妈妈喜欢种花。

4.2.3 Selection

(1) Randomly select a position in the input sentence. (2) Select a near-synonym of the word in that position based on their similarities computed using word embeddings. (3) Replace the word in that position with the near-synonym.

(14-E) 老鼠又去咬蜡烛，蜡烛倒了，庙里**爆炸**了。

(14-C) 老鼠又去咬蜡烛，蜡烛倒了，庙里**着火**了。

4.2.4 Word Order

(1) Randomly select a position in the input sentence. (2) Swap the word in that position with its neighbor.

(15-E) 这些剪纸的技艺，都是人们世代一代手把手**地下来传**的。

(15-C) 这些剪纸的技艺，都是人们世代一代手把手**地传下来**的。

5 Ling@CASS Solution: Methodology and System Development

A new task, the corrections of the errors of missing and selection types, has been introduced to CGED 2018. We accordingly need a reconsideration of the appropriateness of using sequence labeling models (Sakaguchi et al., 2017). Unlike the B/I/O tag set which is close, the corrections of the missing, and selection types of errors form an open set. In addition, the corrections generally give rise to output sentences with lengths different from input ones. Therefore, the correction task has gone beyond the capabilities of sequence labeling models.

Sequence to sequence learning (seq2seq) maps an input sequence to an output sequence of varying lengths. It has been the mainstream model for machine translation nowadays (Klein et al., 2017). The correction task can be modeled as a translation task, in which the ungrammatical sentences are from an original language, and the corrections are from a target language. The translation model has been used in several previous studies on grammar error corrections (Schmaltz et al., 2016; Chaitanya, 2017; Yuan and Felice, 2013).

The state-of-the-art performances on machine translation are presented by FairSeq in terms of both accuracy and speed (Gehring et al., 2017). FariSeq significantly differs from previous seq2seq models in that its architecture is based entirely on Convolutional Neural Networks (CNN), instead of the prevalent Recurrent Neural Networks (RNN), so that computations can be fully parallelized during training and optimization.

In our study, we employ the FairSeq model. The Fairseq models are pre-trained with the pseudo labeled data, and fine-tuned with the manually labeled data delivered in CGED. The inputs to Fairseq models are as simple as Chinese characters and POS tags of characters. The POS are tagged using LTP (Che et al., 2010). We use the default settings of FairSeq, except that we use 512 dimensions of character embeddings. The embeddings are randomly initialized and we do NOT use any other resources.

6 Ling@CASS Solution: the Outcome

6.1 Evaluation on Corrections

As shown in Table 1, we have four basic system configurations. These configurations are different in the use of pseudo corpus and POS tags. The evaluation in Table 1 reveals that the use of pseudo data has improved both precision and recall in the correction task of the word selection errors and missing errors, while that of POS tags does not make a significant contribution.

In real scenarios of grammar error diagnoses, the evaluation metrics of precision, recall and F1 are not of the same importance. A teacher would always prefers a grammar error correction system with high precision, even if it has a low recall, than a system returns lots of noises. Being aware of the significance of precision in a grammar error correction system in practice, we further use ensembles to boost precisions. The tag "(>1)" indicates that the correction has been confirmed by at least two basic systems; and "(>2)", at least three. The ensembled systems steadily achieve a precision greater than 50%, with a recall greater than 8%. These performances are much higher than the best in CGED 2018 submissions, where the precision is 29.32%, and recall is 1.58%.

The official submission of our team to CGED 2018 is the result of an ensemble of the systems 3 and 4, where the results are simply merged.

6.2 Evaluation on Detections, Identifications of Error Types, and Positions

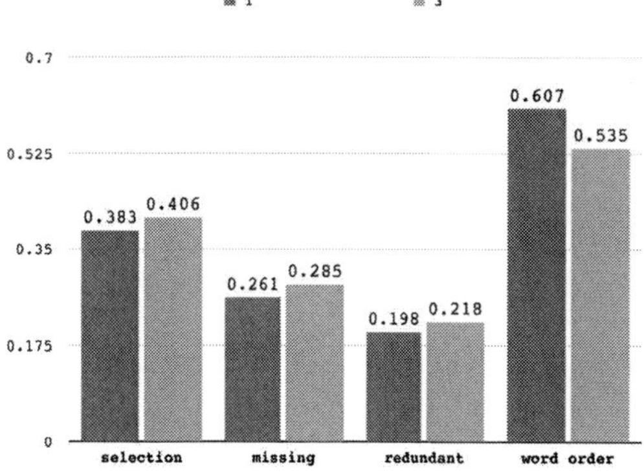

Figure 1: Impacts of Pseudo Data

We also evaluated the systems on the detections, and the identifications of error types and positions. Figure 2 shows a detailed analysis on the precision of the identification of error positions for all four types of errors. It reveals

ID	Pseudo corpus	CGED corpus	Character	POS	P	R	F1
1		Y	Y		0.2678	0.0984	0.1439
2		Y	Y	Y	0.2657	0.1060	0.1515
3	Y	Y	Y		0.2830	0.1153	0.1638
4	Y	Y	Y	Y	0.2672	0.1139	0.1597
1+3 (>0)					0.2149	0.1313	0.1631
3+4 (>0) Submission					0.2126	0.1395	0.1685
1+2 (>1)					**0.5153**	0.0806	0.1394
3+4 (>1)					0.5056	0.0896	0.1523
1+3 (>1)					0.5105	0.0823	0.1417
1+2+3+4 (>2)					0.5080	0.0896	0.1524

Table 1: Performances on Corrections

	FPR	Detection				Identification			Position		
		Acc.	P	R	F1	P	R	F1	P	R	F1
3+4 (>0) Submission	0.3470	0.6630	0.7109	0.6709	0.6903	0.4853	0.4096	0.4442	0.2482	0.1814	0.2096
1+2 (>1)	0.064	0.5342	0.8127	0.2184	0.3443	0.6653	0.1436	0.2362	0.4861	0.0906	0.1528
3+4 (>1)	0.0512	0.5599	0.8632	0.2542	0.3927	0.7015	0.1663	0.2688	0.5024	0.1006	0.168
1+3 (>1)	**0.0448**	0.5475	**0.8656**	0.227	0.3596	0.6853	0.1463	0.2411	0.5104	0.0932	0.1577
1+2+3+4 (>2)	0.0544	0.5545	0.8524	0.2471	0.3831	0.6819	0.1600	0.2592	0.5030	0.0996	0.1663

Table 2: Performances on Detections, Identifications of Error Types & Positions

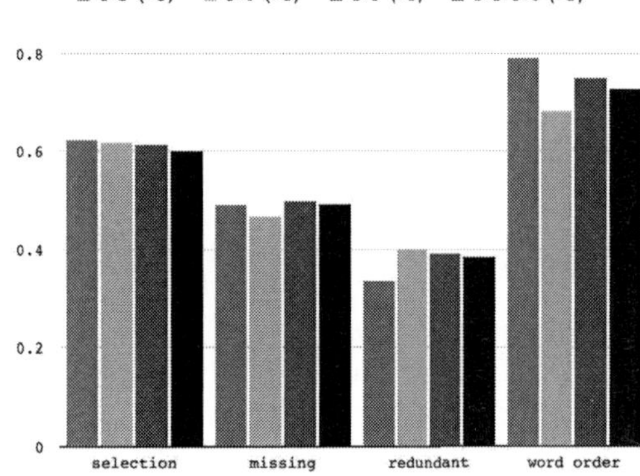

Figure 2: Difficulties of Error Types

that the current pseudo data has a positive impact on the precision of all error types, except for the word ordering errors. It indicates the word ordering pseudo data has much room for improvements.

Figure 1 shows that the identification of the positions of these errors is of different difficulties to the systems. While the ensembled systems are proficient in handling word ordering errors, they have the most difficulties in handling redundant errors.

Table 2 shows the ensembled system 1+3 (>1) achieves a False Positive Rate (FPR) at 4.48% and a precision of 86.56% the detection of erroneous sentences, which are better than the best FPR 4.99% and the best precision 82.76% in CGED 2018 submissions, respectively.

7 Conclusion and Future Work

In CGED 2018, we employ the sequence to sequence learning to model the task of grammar error correction. We adopt a semi-supervised approach to breakthrough the bottlenecks of very limited size of manually labeled data. Specifically, we adapt correct sentences written by native Chinese speakers to generate pseudo grammatical errors made by learners of Chinese as a second language. The pseudo data is used to pre-train the model and gives rise to improvements in both precision and recall. Being aware of the significance of precision in a grammar error correction system in real scenarios, we use ensembles to boost precision. The use of pseudo data has a positive impact on the identification of missing errors, redundant errors, and word selection errors.

In the future work, we will use multi-task to jointly optimize the four tasks all together (Luong et al., 2015). In addition, we will investigate more sophisticated techniques for the generation of pseudo data.

References

Gregory V. Bard. 2006. Spelling-error tolerant, order-independent pass-phrases via the damerau-levenshtein string-edit distance metric. In *Australasian Symposium on Acsw Frontiers*, pages 117–124.

Aoife Cahill, Nitin Madnani, Joel Tetreault, and Diane Napolitano. 2013. Robust systems for preposition error correction using wikipedia revisions. In *Proceedings of the 2013 Conference of the North American Chapter of the Association for Computational Linguistics: Human Language Technologies*, pages 507–517.

G Krishna Chaitanya. 2017. *GRAMMATICAL ERROR CORRECTION*. Ph.D. thesis, Indian Institute of Technology Bombay Mumbai 400076 (India) 14.

Wanxiang Che, Zhenghua Li, and Ting Liu. 2010. Ltp: a chinese language technology platform. In *International Conference on Computational Linguistics: Demonstrations*, pages 13–16.

Shuk-Man Cheng, Chi-Hsin Yu, and Hsin-Hsi Chen. 2014. Chinese word ordering errors detection and correction for non-native chinese language learners. In *Proceedings of COLING 2014, the 25th International Conference on Computational Linguistics: Technical Papers*, pages 279–289.

Markus Dickinson. 2010. Generating learner-like morphological errors in russian. In *Proceedings of the 23rd International Conference on Computational Linguistics*, pages 259–267. Association for Computational Linguistics.

Mariano Felice and Zheng Yuan. 2014. Generating artificial errors for grammatical error correction. In *Proceedings of the Student Research Workshop at the 14th Conference of the European Chapter of the Association for Computational Linguistics*, pages 116–126.

Jennifer Foster and Øistein E Andersen. 2009. Generrate: generating errors for use in grammatical error detection. In *Proceedings of the fourth workshop on innovative use of nlp for building educational applications*, pages 82–90. Association for Computational Linguistics.

Jonas Gehring, Michael Auli, David Grangier, Denis Yarats, and Yann N Dauphin. 2017. Convolutional sequence to sequence learning.

Roman Grundkiewicz and Marcin Junczys-Dowmunt. 2014. The wiked error corpus: A corpus of corrective wikipedia edits and its application to grammatical error correction. In *International Conference on Natural Language Processing*, pages 478–490. Springer.

Hanban. 2001. 汉语水平词汇与汉字等级大纲 *The Syllabus of the Graded Words and Characters for Chinese Proficiency Test*. 经济科学出版社 Economic Science Press.

Hanban. 2010. 新汉语水平考试大纲 *New Chinese Proficiency Test Syllabus*. 商务印书馆 The Commercial Press, China.

Marti A. Hearst, Susan T Dumais, Edgar Osuna, John Platt, and Bernhard Scholkopf. 1998. Support vector machines. *IEEE Intelligent Systems and their applications*, 13(4):18–28.

Sepp Hochreiter and Jürgen Schmidhuber. 1997. Long short-term memory. *Neural computation*, 9(8):1735–1780.

Kenji Imamura, Kuniko Saito, Kugatsu Sadamitsu, and Hitoshi Nishikawa. 2012. Grammar error correction using pseudo-error sentences and domain adaptation. In *Proceedings of the 50th Annual Meeting of the Association for Computational Linguistics: Short Papers-Volume 2*, pages 388–392. Association for Computational Linguistics.

Guillaume Klein, Yoon Kim, Yuntian Deng, Jean Senellart, and Alexander M. Rush. 2017. Opennmt: Open-source toolkit for neural machine translation.

John Lafferty, Andrew McCallum, and Fernando CN Pereira. 2001. Conditional random fields: Probabilistic models for segmenting and labeling sequence data.

Lung-Hao Lee, Li-Ping Chang, Kuei-Ching Lee, Yuen-Hsien Tseng, and Hsin-Hsi Chen. 2013. Linguistic rules based chinese error detection for second language learning. In *Work-in-Progress Poster Proceedings of the 21st International Conference on Computers in Education (ICCE-13)*, pages 27–29.

Lung-Hao Lee, Liang-Chih Yu, Kuei-Ching Lee, Yuen-Hsien Tseng, Li-Ping Chang, and Hsin-Hsi Chen. 2014. A sentence judgment system for grammatical error detection. In *Proceedings of COLING 2014, the 25th International Conference on Computational Linguistics: System Demonstrations*, pages 67–70.

Minh Thang Luong, Quoc V. Le, Ilya Sutskever, Oriol Vinyals, and Lukasz Kaiser. 2015. Multitask sequence to sequence learning. *Computer Science*.

Alla Rozovskaya and Dan Roth. 2010. Training paradigms for correcting errors in grammar and usage. In *Human language technologies: The 2010 annual conference of the north american chapter of the association for computational linguistics*, pages 154–162. Association for Computational Linguistics.

Alla Rozovskaya, Dan Roth, and Mark Sammons. 2017. Adapting to learner errors with minimal supervision. *Computational Linguistics*, 43(4):723–760.

Keisuke Sakaguchi, Kevin Duh, Matt Post, and Benjamin Van Durme. 2017. Robsut wrod reocginiton via semi-character recurrent neural network.

Allen Schmaltz, Yoon Kim, Alexander M Rush, and Stuart M Shieber. 2016. Sentence-level grammatical error identification as sequence-to-sequence correction. *arXiv preprint arXiv:1604.04677*.

Yi Yang, Pengjun Xie, Jun Tao, Guangwei Xu, Linlin Li, and Si Luo. 2017. Alibaba at IJCNLP-2017 task 1: Embedding grammatical features into lstms for chinese grammatical error diagnosis task. In *Proceedings of the IJCNLP 2017, Shared Tasks, Taipei, Taiwan, November 27 - December 1, 2017, Shared Tasks*, pages 41–46.

Chi-Hsin Yu and Hsin-Hsi Chen. 2012. Detecting word ordering errors in chinese sentences for learning chinese as a foreign language. *Proceedings of COLING 2012*, pages 3003–3018.

Zheng Yuan and Mariano Felice. 2013. Constrained grammatical error correction using statistical machine translation. In *Proceedings of the Seventeenth Conference on Computational Natural Language Learning: Shared Task*, pages 52–61.

Bo Zheng, Wanxiang Che, Jiang Guo, and Ting Liu. 2016. Chinese grammatical error diagnosis with long short-term memory networks. In *Proceedings of the 3rd Workshop on Natural Language Processing Techniques for Educational Applications (NLPTEA2016)*, pages 49–56, Osaka, Japan. The COLING 2016 Organizing Committee.

Chinese Grammatical Error Diagnosis Based on Policy Gradient LSTM Model

Changliang Li
Kingsoft
lichangliang@kingsoft.com

Ji Qi
Communication University of China
ji.qi@cuc.edu.cn

Abstract

Chinese Grammatical Error Diagnosis (CGED) is a natural language processing task for the NLPTEA2018 workshop held during ACL2018. The goal of this task is to diagnose Chinese sentences containing four kinds of grammatical errors through the model and find out the sentence errors. Chinese grammatical error diagnosis system is a very important tool, which can help Chinese learners automatically diagnose grammatical errors in many scenarios. However, due to the limitations of the Chinese language's own characteristics and datasets, the traditional model faces the problem of extreme imbalances in the positive and negative samples and the disappearance of gradients. In this paper, we propose a sequence labeling method based on the Policy Gradient LSTM model and apply it to this task to solve the above problems. The results show that our model can achieve higher precision scores in the case of lower False positive rate (FPR) and it is convenient to optimize the model on-line.

1 Introduction

In English and many other languages , the space is a good approximation of a word divider (word delimiter), a sentence separated by spaces into multiple words. Unlike the English, Chinese does not have a separator on the written scripts, a sentence consists of Chinese characters that are next to each other, where sentences but not words are delimited. This is very difficult for the machine or learner without a Chinese foundation to analyze Chinese grammar, because it first has to face the problem of Chinese word segmentation (Xue, 2003). Compared to English, Chinese has neither singular/plural change, nor the tense changes of the verb, and it uses more short sentences but less clauses. In addition, the same word may express different meanings in different contexts, namely ambiguity. All these problems make learning Chinese very difficult. Most non-native Chinese language learners usually need professional Chinese teachers to guide them and correct grammatical errors. However, online teaching has recently become the main channel for language learning, which requires the system to automatically diagnose and give advice to a large number of learners' grammatical errors. Therefore, the study of Chinese grammatical error automatic diagnosis system is very important. The goal of Chinese Grammatical Error Diagnosis (CGED) is to build a system that can automatically diagnose errors in Chinese sentences. Such errors are defined as redundant words (denoted as a capital "R"), missing words ("M"), word selection errors ("S"), and word ordering errors ("W"). Evaluation includes three levels, which are detection level, identification level and position level.

At present, most methods regard the Chinese grammatical error diagnosis task as a sequence labeling task (Settles and Craven, 2008), such as using a conditional random field construction sequence labeling model (Lafferty et al., 2001) and a sequence labeling model constructed using LSTM (Hochreiter and Schmidhuber, 1997). However, the characteristics of Chinese language leads to a obvious problem in constructing Chinese grammatical error diagnosis model, which is the imbalance between positive and negative samples. For example, a sentence to be labeling is: "人战胜了饥饿，才努力为了下一代作更好的、更健康的东西。"，The correct labeling result should be: "NNNNNNNNNPNNNNNNNPNNNNNNNNNNNN",

Proceedings of the 5th Workshop on Natural Language Processing Techniques for Educational Applications, pages 77–82
Melbourne, Australia, July 19, 2018. ©2018 Association for Computational Linguistics

where N denotes a negative label, ie there is no wrong label, P denotes a positive label, ie there is a wrong label. We can see that the proportion of positive and negative sample labels in a not very long sentence is seriously unbalanced, in the above example, the ratio is 2:27, which is a serious problem faced by the Chinese grammatical error diagnosis model. In order to solve the above problems, we propose a Policy Gradient-based model to tag Chinese sentences. Similar to the recent work, we also use the LSTM model to handle this task as a sequence labeling problem (Zheng et al., 2016). Moreover, we use the Policy Gradient method to deal with the imbalance of positive and negative samples. The results show that our method can achieve better results.

This paper is organized as follows. Section 2 introduces some related work . Section 3 briefly describes the CGED Shared Task. Section 4 illustrates our methodology, including data preparation, model description and the details of policy gradient method. Section 5 shows the experiment settings and results. And finally, section 6 concludes the paper and presents future work.

2 Related works

The English Grammatical Error Correction task has been held for two consecutive years as one of the natural language processing tasks of the Conference on Computational Natural Language Learning (CoNLL). The researchers used many different methods to study the task and achieved good results (Tou et al., 2017). where (Junczys-Dowmunt and Grundkiewicz, 2014) usesd phrase-based translation optimized for F-score using a combination of kb-MIRA and MERT with augmented language models and task-specific features, and got a good result. As a universal language model, the Long Short-Term Memory network (LSTM) (Hochreiter and Schmidhuber, 1997) has achieved good results in many tasks in natural language processing in recent years, including text classification tasks, machine translation tasks, and sequence annotation tasks. (Yuan and Briscoe, 2016) used the Encoder-Decoder model similar to neural machine translation to process the English Grammatical error correction Task and achieved good results. Compared with English, the research time of Chinese grammatical error diagnosis system is short, the data sets and effective methods are lacking. (Yu and Chen,

2012) uses the CRF-based model to construct a Chinese word ordering error detection model and obtains a higher accuracy on the experimental data set. In recent years, Chinese grammatical error diagnosis has been cited as a shared task of NLPTEA CGED. Many researchers in the field of natural language processing have researched and proposed several effective methods (Yu et al., 2014; Lee et al., 2015, 2016). HIT propose a CRF+BiLSTM model based on character embedding on bigram embedding, on the CGED-HSK dataset of NLP-TEA-3 shared task, their system presents the best F1-scores in all the three levels (Zheng et al., 2016).

3 CGED Task Description

The goal of The NLPTEA CGED task is to use a model to perform a grammar diagnosis on a data set containing Chinese sentences, these datasets are written by Chinese Foreign Language (CFL) leaner. These datasets contain the following four errors, such errors are defined as redundant words (denoted as a capital "R"), missing words ("M"), word selection errors ("S"), and word ordering errors ("W"). The input sentence may contain one or more such errors, and there may also be no errors. The developed system should indicate which error types are embedded in the given sentence and the position at which they occur. Some typical examples are shown in Table 1:

Sentence	人战胜了饥饿，才努力为了下一代作更好的、更健康的东西。
Correction	人战胜了饥饿，才能努力为了下一代做更好的、更健康的东西。
Errors	9, 9, M, 能 16, 16, S, 做

Table 1: Typical Error Examples

Table1 shows the CGED shared task input data and output data samples. Each sentence contains a single id, each output error contains the sentence id, and the number in Errors indicates the index of the error location. The criteria for judging correctness are determined at three levels as detection level, identification level and position level.

4 Methodology

In this section, we will introduce our entire process of the CGED task, including data preprocessing, model construction, and the construction of objective functions based on the Policy Gradient. Same as previous work, we treat the CGED task as a sequence labeling problem. Such as given a sentence x, our model generates a corresponding label sequence y. Each label in y is a token from a specific tag set. We use "O" to indicate the correct character's tag, 'B-X' indicating the beginning positions for errors of type 'X' and 'I-X' as middle and ending positions for errors of type 'X'.

First, we will introduce our CGED task data preprocessing process, including Bigram feature construction, POS data annotation, and data label settings. Second, we will introduce the construction of the ensemble model that combines Bigram feature, POS feature, and character embedding. Finally, we will introduce the idea and mathematical formula of the objective function based on the Policy Gradient.

4.1 Data Preparation

First, we use the Word2vec tool to train the Bigrams of all Chinese sentences in the data set into word vectors. These word vectors will be used to generate input sentence features during model building. we first convert the original character sequence to a bigram sequence. Then we can train bigram embeddings readily using word2vec (Mikolov et al., 2013) on the resulting bigram sequences.

We use the Part-of-speech (POS) feature to improve the performance of the system. Therefore, we use the part-of-speech (POS) feature to generate a corresponding POS tag sequence for each Chinese sentence sequence of the data set, B-pos indicating the beginning character's POS tag while I-pos indicating the middle and end characters'.

We define each character in the sentence as a separate tag that contains the character's position in the word. We use "O" to indicate the correct character's tag, 'B-X' indicating the beginning positions for errors of type 'X' and 'I-X' as middle and ending positions for errors of type 'X'. In the CGED task, we will get 8 labels: B-W, I-R, B-R, B-M, I-S, I-W, B-S, O. After the data is preprocessed, each sample can be represented as the structure shown by Table 2. The input of each sample during training is composed of three parts as shown in the inputs features of Table 2, and the label sequence of each sample is composed of 8 pre-defined labels.

4.2 Model Description

We regard the Chinese grammatical error diagnosis task as a sequence labeling task, and first use LSTM to construct a sequence labeling model. LSTM network is a variant of recurrent neural network (RNN) and have better ability to capture long term dependencies. Given a sequence of input vectors $X = x_1, x_2, \ldots, x_T = \{x_t\}_1^T$, a recurrent unit $\mathcal{H}$ computes a sequence of hidden vectors $h = h_1, h_2, \ldots, h_T = \{h_t\}_1^T$ and a sequence of output symbols $\hat{Y} = \hat{y}_1, \hat{y}_2, \ldots, \hat{y}_T = \{\hat{y}_t\}_1^T$ by iterating the following equations,

$$h_t = \mathcal{H}(x_t, h_{t-1}) \tag{1}$$
$$\hat{y}_t = argmax(softmax(W_{hy}h_t)) \tag{2}$$

where $softmax(z_m) = e^{z_m} / \sum_i e^{z_i}$, The LSTM recurrent unit $\mathcal{H}$ represents the calculation process of the LSTM network. A typical LSTM network consists of input gates, oblivion gates, output gates, and memory cells. Which input gate controls the current time step which information will be input into the memory cell, the forgotten gate controls the current time step which history information will be forgotten by the memory cell, and the output gate controls which information will be output as h_t according to the current memory cell state. Each gate consists of a sigmoid neural net layer and a point-wise multiplication operation.

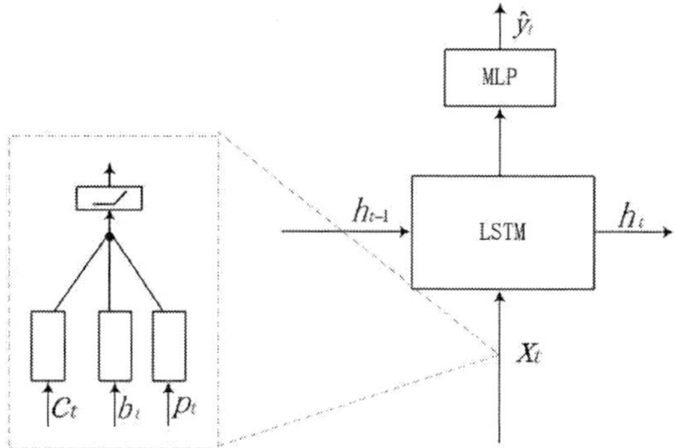

Figure 1: An illustration of LSTM model

In this work, we denote the input of the time step i as:

$$x_t = \sigma(W_x(c_t, b_t, p_t)) \tag{3}$$

Where σ represents the nonlinear activation function, c_t is the character embeddings that are initialized immediately, b_t represents the bigram

Sentence	我根本不能了解这妇女辞职回家的现象。		
Char	我 根 本 不 能 了 解 这 妇 女 辞 职 回 家 的 现 象 。		
Bigram	<s>我 我根 根本 本不 不能 能了 了解 解这 这妇 妇女 女辞 辞职 职回 回家 家的 的现 现象 象。 。</s>		
POS	B-r B-d I-d B-d B-v B-v I-v B-r B-n I-n B-v I-v B-v I-v B-u B-n I-n B-wp		
Label	O O O O O B-S I-S B-R O O O O O O O O O O		

Table 2: A snapshot of our training data after the pre-processing

vector of the current time step, and p_t represents the POS discrete feature. These three simple features are combined as the input vector for the time step t. The ensemble model is shown in Figure 1.

4.3 Policy Gradient

Deep Reinforcement Learning (DRL) is divided into Value-Based Deep RL (Mnih et al., 2015) and Policy-Based Deep RL (Lillicrap et al., 2015) in terms of implementation[16]. Value-Based Deep RL is a Neural Network usually used as a Q function to estimate the return of an action which can be obtained in the current environment, namely Deep Q-network (DQN). Such as (Mnih et al., 2013) present the first deep learning model to successfully learn control policies directly from high-dimensional sensory input using reinforcement learning, model is a convolutional neural network, trained with a variant of Q-learning. The Policy-Based Deep RL is Represent policy by deep network with weights u, as shown below:

$$a = \pi(a|s, u) \quad or \quad a = \pi(s, u) \tag{4}$$

Where π is the policy expressed by the neural network and u is the network learning parameter. Define objective function as total discounted reward:

$$L(u) = \mathbb{E}[r_1 + \gamma r_2 + \gamma^2 r_3 + ... | \pi(\cdot, u)] \tag{5}$$

$L(\mathbf{u})$ denotes the objective function, $r_1, r_2, ...$ denotes the returns obtained in each step. In this paper, the value of the return of the tagged result of each token is indicated. $\gamma \in [0, 1]$ is the discount factor, which indicates the importance of future returns. In this article we set $\gamma = 0.9$. To make high-value actions more likely, the gradient of a stochastic policy $\pi(a|s, u)$ is given by:

$$\frac{\partial L(u)}{\partial u} = \mathbb{E}[\frac{\partial \log \pi(a|s, u)}{\partial u} Q^\pi(s, a)] \tag{6}$$

Where Q^π is a function value that measures the return of each action. In this article, we define that the return value of the tag "O" is successfully marked as 1, and the return value of the failed tag is -1. Defining all other error labels "B-W, I-W, B-M, I-W ..." is marked with a score of 10 for a successful return, and a return of -10 for a failed tag. Finally, update parameters u by stochastic gradient ascent. Our ensemble model is shown in Figure 2.

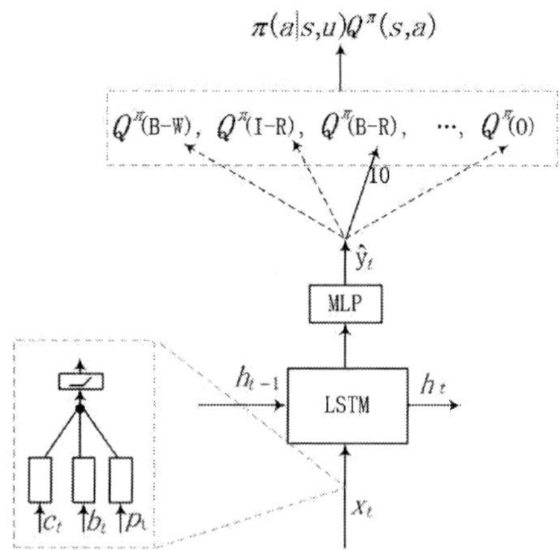

Figure 2: An illustration of Policy Gradient-based LSTM model

Where $Q^\pi(X)$ represents the reward after label "X" was tagged, for example, the "X" is "B-R", $\hat{y}_t$ represents the policy obtained by the network. Finally, the final output $\pi(a|s, u)Q^\pi(s, a)$ of the network is obtained with the policy π and reward Q known. This output is used to calculate the policy gradient $\frac{\partial L(u)}{\partial u}$, and then the gradient is used to update the network parameters.

5 Experiments

In this section, we introduce the entire process of the experiment. First of all, we introduce the use of data sets and division, and then briefly introduce the CGED experimental results evaluation method. Finally, we introduce the results on the validation dataset and the results from the evaluation dataset based on our proposed model.

5.1 Dataset and criteria

During the training of the model, we use the collection of training set of CGED2017 and training set of CGED2018 as the training dataset. In CGED2017 training set, provide 10,449 training units with a total of 26,448 grammatical errors, categorized as redundant (5,852 instances), missing (7,010), word selection (11,591) and word ordering(1,995). In the CGED2018 training set, contain total of 1,067 grammatical errors, categorized as redundant (208 instances), missing (298), word selection (87) and word ordering(474). In addition, use CGED2017's test set as the validation set during training, it's contain total of 4,871 grammatical errors, categorized as redundant (1,060 instances), missing (1,269), word selection (2,156) and word ordering(386). Table 3 shows the data distribution in the training data.

	R error	M error	S error	W error
Train	6060	7308	11678	2469
Validation	1060	1269	2156	386

Table 3: Data statistics

The criteria for judging correctness are determined at three levels, (1)Detection-level: Binary classification of a given sentence, that is, correct or incorrect, should be completely identical with the gold standard. All error types will be regarded as incorrect. (2)Identification-level: This level could be considered as a multi-class categorization problem. All error types should be clearly identified. A correct case should be completely identical with the gold standard of the given error type. (3)Position-level: In addition to identifying the error types, this level also judges the occurrence range of the grammatical error. That is to say, the system results should be perfectly identical with the quadruples of the gold standard. The False Positive Rate(FPR), Accuracy (Acc), Precision (Pre), Recall (Rec) and F1 score(F1) are measured at all levels with the help of the confusion matrix.

5.2 Experiment results

We use the above data partitioning to train and converge the training set based on our proposed Policy Gradient-based model, the trained model was tested on the validation set and evaluation set.

5.2.1 Results on Validation Dataset

We refer to the model's results on the validation dataset and select the best hyper-parameters model. Table 4 shows the results.

5.2.2 Results on evaluation Dataset

We testing on the final evaluation dataset for CGED2018 test set, the result showing with table 5. As we can see, our model can obtain better identification score and position score while obtaining a better detection level score.

Our model obtains good results at three levels, and the Policy Gradient-based model can be easily applied to online tasks to optimize the network structure through continuous interaction and attempting to obtain maximum rewards.

5.3 Conclusion and Future Work

This paper proposes a method based on policy gradient applied to NLPTEA 2018 CGED shared task. We use the value function method of deep reinforcement learning to map the labeling results to rewards to solve the problem of imbalanced positive and negative samples in Chinese grammatical error diagnosis. Moreover, our system can be applied to online optimization as easily as a depth-enhanced model. In this paper, we verify the effectiveness of the Policy Gradient through experiments on the validation dataset and the evaluation dataset.

In the future, we hope to betterly solve the problem of serial labeling with imbalanced positive and negative samples in Chinese grammatical error diagnosis through deep reinforcement learning strategies. In terms of Policy Gradients, we hope to be able to define reward functions that are more in line with the mission requirements and optimize the entire network. In addition, we hope to optimize the network through multiple rounds of online annotation results and further conduct relevant online experiments. Ultimately, the network can achieve good labeling results while also being able to cope with the challenges posed by online data changes.

References

Sepp Hochreiter and Jürgen Schmidhuber. 1997. Long short-term memory. *Neural computation*, 9(8):1735–1780.

Model runs	Detection Level			Identification Level			Position Level		
	Pre	Rec	F1	Pre	Rec	F1	Pre	Rec	F1
1	0.64	0.26	0.37	0.45	0.28	0.35	0.17	0.02	0.03
2	0.71	0.47	0.52	0.48	0.17	0.25	0.21	0.01	0.02

Table 4: Results on Validation Dataset

Model runs	Detection Level			Identification Level			Position Level		
	Pre	Rec	F1	Pre	Rec	F1	Pre	Rec	F1
1	0.6349	0.4232	0.5079	0.4792	0.1995	0.2817	0.1185	0.0442	0.0644
2	0.6698	0.2494	0.3634	0.5139	0.1323	0.2105	0.1585	0.0331	0.0547
3	0.6346	0.5426	0.5850	0.4735	0.2646	0.3395	0.1129	0.0609	0.0792

Table 5: Results on Evaluation Dataset

Marcin Junczys-Dowmunt and Roman Grundkiewicz. 2014. The amu system in the conll-2014 shared task: Grammatical error correction by data-intensive and feature-rich statistical machine translation. In *Proceedings of the Eighteenth Conference on Computational Natural Language Learning: Shared Task*, pages 25–33.

John Lafferty, Andrew McCallum, and Fernando CN Pereira. 2001. Conditional random fields: Probabilistic models for segmenting and labeling sequence data.

Lung-Hao Lee, RAO Gaoqi, Liang-Chih Yu, XUN Endong, Baolin Zhang, and Li-Ping Chang. 2016. Overview of nlp-tea 2016 shared task for chinese grammatical error diagnosis. In *Proceedings of the 3rd Workshop on Natural Language Processing Techniques for Educational Applications (NLPTEA2016)*, pages 40–48.

Lung-Hao Lee, Liang-Chih Yu, and Li-Ping Chang. 2015. Guest editoral: Special issue on chinese as a foreign language. *International Journal of Computational Linguistics & Chinese Language Processing, Volume 20, Number 1, June 2015-Special Issue on Chinese as a Foreign Language*, 20(1).

Timothy P Lillicrap, Jonathan J Hunt, Alexander Pritzel, Nicolas Heess, Tom Erez, Yuval Tassa, David Silver, and Daan Wierstra. 2015. Continuous control with deep reinforcement learning. *arXiv preprint arXiv:1509.02971*.

Tomas Mikolov, Kai Chen, Greg Corrado, and Jeffrey Dean. 2013. Efficient estimation of word representations in vector space. *arXiv preprint arXiv:1301.3781*.

Volodymyr Mnih, Koray Kavukcuoglu, David Silver, Alex Graves, Ioannis Antonoglou, Daan Wierstra, and Martin Riedmiller. 2013. Playing atari with deep reinforcement learning. *arXiv preprint arXiv:1312.5602*.

Volodymyr Mnih, Koray Kavukcuoglu, David Silver, Andrei A Rusu, Joel Veness, Marc G Bellemare,

Alex Graves, Martin Riedmiller, Andreas K Fidjeland, Georg Ostrovski, et al. 2015. Human-level control through deep reinforcement learning. *Nature*, 518(7540):529.

Burr Settles and Mark Craven. 2008. An analysis of active learning strategies for sequence labeling tasks. In *Proceedings of the conference on empirical methods in natural language processing*, pages 1070–1079. Association for Computational Linguistics.

Ng Hwee Tou, Wu Siew Mei, Ted Briscoe, Christian Hadiwinoto, Raymond Hendy Susanto, and Christopher Bryant. 2017. Conll-2014 shared task: Grammatical error correction.

Nianwen Xue. 2003. Chinese word segmentation as character tagging. *International Journal of Computational Linguistics & Chinese Language Processing, Volume 8, Number 1, February 2003: Special Issue on Word Formation and Chinese Language Processing*, 8(1):29–48.

Chi-Hsin Yu and Hsin-Hsi Chen. 2012. Detecting word ordering errors in chinese sentences for learning chinese as a foreign language. *Proceedings of COLING 2012*, pages 3003–3018.

Liang-Chih Yu, Lung-Hao Lee, and Li-Ping Chang. 2014. Overview of grammatical error diagnosis for learning chinese as a foreign language. In *Proceedings of the 1st Workshop on Natural Language Processing Techniques for Educational Applications*, pages 42–47.

Zheng Yuan and Ted Briscoe. 2016. Grammatical error correction using neural machine translation. In *Proceedings of the 2016 Conference of the North American Chapter of the Association for Computational Linguistics: Human Language Technologies*, pages 380–386.

Bo Zheng, Wanxiang Che, Jiang Guo, and Ting Liu. 2016. Chinese grammatical error diagnosis with long short-term memory networks. In *Proceedings of the 3rd Workshop on Natural Language Processing Techniques for Educational Applications (NLPTEA2016)*, pages 49–56.

The Importance of Recommender and Feedback Features in a Pronunciation Learning Aid

Dzikri Rahadian Fudholi

The Australian National University / Canberra, ACT, Australia
Universitas Gadjah Mada / D.I.Yogyakarta, Indonesia
u5857432@alumni.anu.edu.au

Hanna Suominen

The Australian National University / Canberra, ACT, Australia
Data61, The Commonwealth Scientific and
Industrial Research Organisation / Canberra, ACT, Australia
University of Canberra / Canberra, ACT, Australia
University of Turku / Turku, Finland
hanna.suominen@anu.edu.au

Abstract

Verbal communication — and pronunciation as its part — is a core skill that can be developed through guided learning. An artificial intelligence system can take a role in these guided learning approaches as an enabler of an application for pronunciation learning with a recommender system to guide language learners through exercises and feedback system to correct their pronunciation. In this paper, we report on a user study on language learners' perceived usefulness of the application. 16 international students who spoke non-native English and lived in Australia participated. 13 of them said they need to improve their pronunciation skills in English because of their foreign accent. The feedback system with features for pronunciation scoring, speech replay, and giving a pronunciation example was deemed essential by most of the respondents. In contrast, a clear dichotomy between the recommender system perceived as useful or useless existed; the system had features to prompt new common words or old poorly-scored words. These results can be used to target research and development from information retrieval and reinforcement learning for better and better recommendations to speech recognition and speech analytics for accent acquisition.

1 Introduction

Pronunciation Learning Aid (PLA) is a system for learning to pronounce better. Pronunciation learning is needed because speaking is a hard task for the human brain (Levelt, 1993). In the process of learning, a person uses another person, a book, or another resource to get the knowledge they need. PLA is one of those facilities that enables a learning experience by giving a practice module.

A number of use cases for PLA exist in real life. They encompass the entire spectrum from supporting teachers' work flow in classrooms to computer-assisted virtual learning environments (Figure 1). That is, more and more learning can happen from home and teachers' time can be used more sparingly.

In this short paper, we are introducing an English PLA prototype with a *Recommender System* (RS) and *Feedback System* (FS). RSs are commonly used to recommend movies, books, music, or similar items (Lü et al., 2012), but their applications to language learning are only emerging. On the contrary, FSs for language learning are more established (e.g., using visual feedback (Wen et al., 2006) or *Speech Recognition* applied to pronunciation evaluation (Abdou et al., 2006)). These two systems could work together to facilitate a language learner to do self-practicing as follows: The RS can give specialized guidance to the language learner (Adomavicius and Tuzhilin, 2005) which in our case translates to the PLA users being guided through a series of exercises that are fit for them. After this, the user can practice by reading and pronouncing these recommended

83

Proceedings of the 5th Workshop on Natural Language Processing Techniques for Educational Applications, pages 83–87
Melbourne, Australia, July 19, 2018. ©2018 Association for Computational Linguistics

Figure 1: Illustration of replacing teaching role to PLA

word/phrases. One of the best options to learn pronunciation is by listening to an example (Leather, 1983). Consequently, providing an audio example is one of the feedback features in our FS.

The focus of the paper is on the result of our user study regarding the importance of each system feature in our PLA. Instead of assuming that both the RS and the FS are needed, we need actual evaluation data to inform our judgment and decision-making regarding the features to include.

The rest of the paper is organized as follows: First, in Section 2, we describe our materials and methods. Then, in Sections 3 and 4, we present and discuss our results, respectively. Finally, in Section 5, we conclude the paper.

2 Materials and Methods

The PLA prototype had the following two main data elements: *item* and *user*. *Item* [word] was the recommended option, which was populated by using the *Ogden's basic word list* (Ogden and Halász, 1935). Each word was also associated with a commonness status by counting its occurrences in the *Europarl* corpus (Koehn, 2005). *User* referred to a specific language learner and *user data* to this person's recorded pronunciation history (i.e., the past learning experience while using the system) and demographic data (e.g., first language, nationality, and age). These recordings were enriched by comparisons to other users' data.

The prototype included the following features. The RS produced the recommendation choices of 1) a *New Common Word*, 2) an *Old Poorly-Scored Word*, and 3) a *New Word from Others' Poorly-*

scored Words. The FS had the feedback features of 1) a *Speech Replay*, 2) a *Pronunciation Example*, and 3) a *Pronunciation Score*. Each of the six features was implemented using a different processing method but based on the same data available in the system.

2.1 Processing Methods

Some of the methods were as simple as reading or counting the data such as counting word frequency whilst others used more advanced machine learning algorithms. In the RS, the New Common Word feature combined the word commonness and the user history to find the most common word that the user has not seen yet. For the Old Poorly-Scored Word feature, it only used the user history to recommend a word with the poorest pronunciation score by the FS. The last feature (i.e., New Word from Others' Poorly-scored Words) analyzed all users' history and demographic data: First, using the *K-Nearest Neighbors* algorithm (Bobadilla et al., 2013), it found similar users to the current user, followed by applying two equally weighted spaces as follows: users' history space with each word score as a dimension and demographic space with demographics as dimensions. Second, the RS built a list of words that were poorly scored in other similar users' histories but not yet seen by the current user. Each of the three RS methods ran once to initialize interaction with the user and again every time the user finished an exercise.

In FS, once one of the three recommendation options was chosen, the system generated three feedback features for that specific word option.

Table 1: Kano conclusion table

		Response to a negative question				
		I like it that way	It must be that way	I am neutral	I can live with it that way	I dislike it that way
Response to a positive question	I like it that way	Questionable	Delighting	Delighting	Delighting	Satisfier
	It must be that way	Reverse	Indifferent	Indifferent	Indifferent	Basic
	I am neutral	Reverse	Indifferent	Indifferent	Indifferent	Basic
	I can live with it that way	Reverse	Indifferent	Indifferent	Indifferent	Basic
	I dislike it that way	Reverse	Reverse	Reverse	Reverse	Questionable

The *Pronunciation Example* feature worked by playing a stored example (i.e., sound file) for the word. Both the *Speech Replay* and *Pronunciation Score* feedback were available after the user had recorded their own speech: The *Speech Replay* feature simply replayed the recording. The *Pronunciation Score* feature was similar to *Automatic Pronunciation Scoring* (Kim et al., 1997). However, due to the time constraint of our research, we had to use random scoring instead in the user study.

2.2 Evaluation Methods

After obtaining the proper ethics approvals and research permissions, we evaluated the importance of each feature in our prototype by conducting a user study. We asked 16 international students to complete our questionnaire after they had tried using the prototype. We used a scenario for each feature so that every respondent had the same experience but with freedom to continue practicing as they wished.

For our questions, we used the *Kano Model* (Yadav, 2016) that built a positive and negative question for each feature to allow concluding whether the user likes a given feature or not. For example, a positive question was "How do you feel if the system is able to replay your recorded speech?" and a negative question was "How do you feel if the system cannot replay your recorded speech?".

To make conclusions from the question pairs for each feature, we used Table 1 (Yadav, 2016). One example of the conclusion was *Delighting*, which meant that the existence of the feature is good. The conclusion of *Reverse* meant that the system is better without the feature.

At the end of the questionnaire, we also asked open questions as follows: "Do you need help to learn pronunciation?", "What difficulties are you having?", "What do you think about the PLA?", "What improvements would you like to see?".

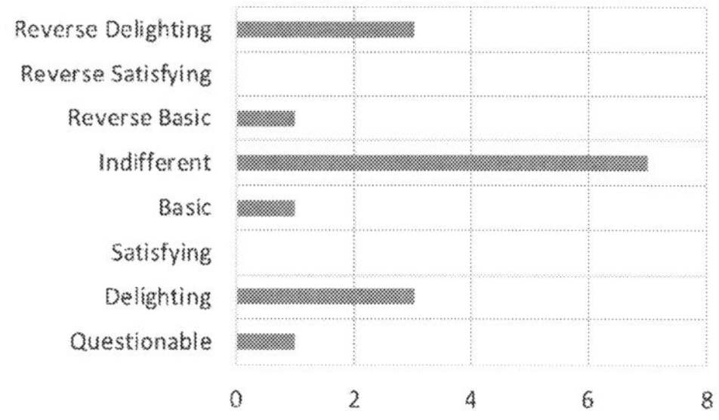

Figure 2: The importance of the RS as a whole

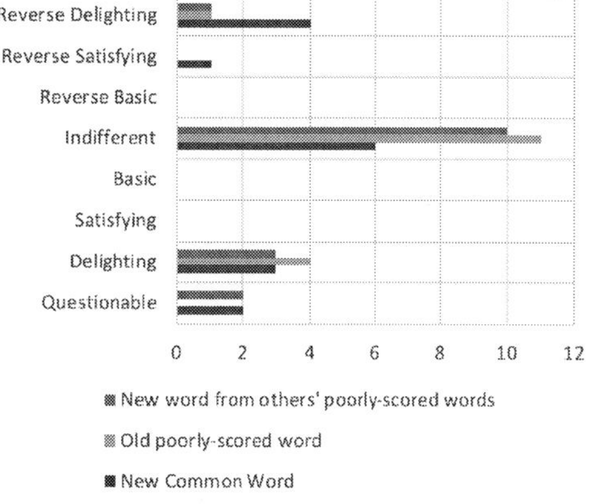

Figure 3: The importance of each RS feature

3 Results

In order to have a realistic case where the language learners are using their own personal computers or laptops, we used an online questionnaire in the user study. Alongside the questionnaire link, we provided the respondents a link to download the prototype. The prototype was built in *Java* and each respondent had to install it on their device.

Before assessing the importance of each feature, we addressed the importance of the RS and FS. Most of the respondents were feeling indifferent about the existence of RS (Figure 2). The same number of respondents were feeling delighted and

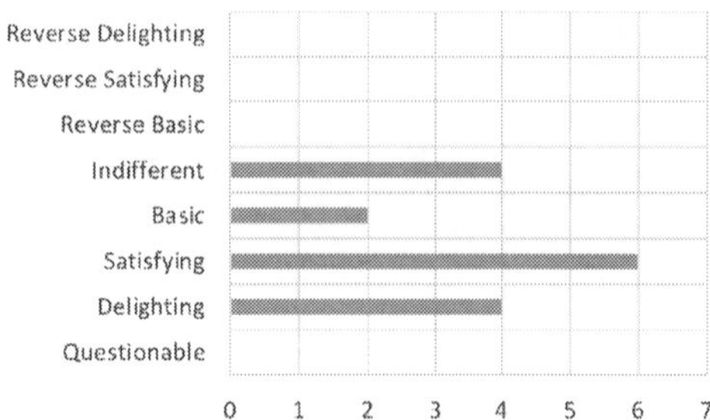

Figure 4: The importance of the FS as a whole

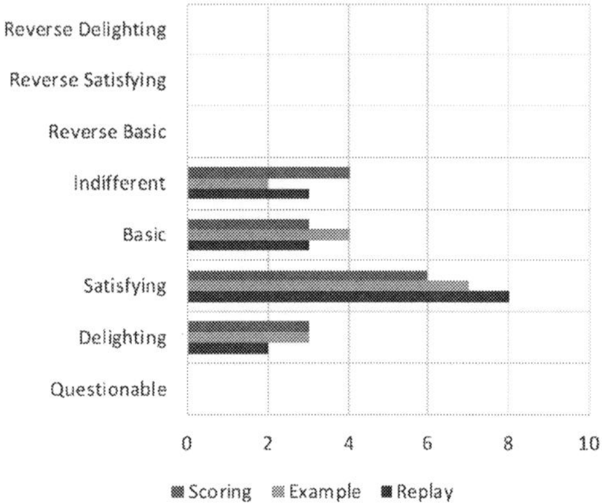

Figure 5: The importance of each FS feature

4 Discussion

From the result we can see that most respondents were having difficulties with their pronunciation learning, mainly because their foreign accent. They welcomed help from any source, including PLA, to correct their pronunciation.

The role of RS in PLA was somewhat unclear. The results diverged between the RS being needed or not needed with the same number of respondents in both sides while most of them felt indifferent. Some respondents did not know how to begin the exercises and needed the guide to do so. Otherwise, some respondents felt the system recommendation was not the best for them to learn and they know better what they should learn.

For each recommendation options, a new common word was not preferred. The respondents preferred to choose on their own because they did not want to just learn common words. Possibilities to practicing poorly-scored words were requested for.

Including the FS in the PLA was crucial but the RS features could be optional. None of the respondents said that the PLA would be better without the entire FS or any of its features. Their key expectation was to receive feedback. Having examples and replay options was also expected but having correctness scoring as a pronunciation feedback functionality was not an expectation but rather a bonus.

5 Conclusion

As expected, our technology-assisted approach for pronunciation learning was perceived as useful but surprisingly, recommendations were not a key feature for a good system. Instead, receiving feedback was essential in a PLA. However, sixteen respondents is a small sample, and this limits the generalizability of these conclusions.

Acknowledgments

LPDP is an Indonesian state agency who manage scholarship that is funded by the Indonesia Endowment Fund for Education. LPDP scholarships are for postgraduate level and open to any Indonesian residence including fresh graduates. We acknowledge Greg Cassagne for his contribution.

reverse delighted, and the same conclusion held for the basic and reverse basic. The trends for the features in RS and FS were similar (Figure 3). Most respondents were feeling indifferent and the numbers of respondents feeling delighted and reversely delighted were approximately the same.

We asked the importance of FS in PLA and got the result that a clear majority of respondents were feeling satisfied without anyone feeling the reverse (Figure 4). A similar trend also occurred in the result of each FS feature (Figure 5); most respondents felt satisfied without any reverse feeling.

Based on the answers to the open questions, thirteen respondents needed help to learn pronunciation with the main reason of their accent. Most respondents felt the usefulness of PLA and especially the FS features were desirable. The respondents were keen to use a PLA not only for English but also for Mandarin and French.

References

Sherif Mahdy Abdou, Salah Eldeen Hamid, Mohsen Rashwan, Abdurrahman Samir, Ossama Abdel-Hamid, Mostafa Shahin, and Waleed Nazih. 2006. Computer aided pronunciation learning system using speech recognition techniques. In *Ninth International Conference on Spoken Language Processing*.

Gediminas Adomavicius and Alexander Tuzhilin. 2005. Toward the next generation of recommender systems: A survey of the state-of-the-art and possible extensions. *IEEE transactions on knowledge and data engineering*, 17(6):734–749.

Jesús Bobadilla, Fernando Ortega, Antonio Hernando, and Abraham Gutiérrez. 2013. Recommender systems survey. *Knowledge-Based Systems*, 46:109–132.

Yoon Kim, Horacio Franco, and Leonardo Neumeyer. 1997. Automatic pronunciation scoring of specific phone segments for language instruction. In *Eurospeech*.

Philipp Koehn. 2005. Europarl: A parallel corpus for statistical machine translation. In *MT summit*, volume 5, pages 79–86.

Jonathan Leather. 1983. Second-language pronunciation learning and teaching. *Language Teaching*, 16(3):198–219.

Willem JM Levelt. 1993. *Speaking: From Intention to Articulation*, volume 1. MIT press, Cambridge, MA, USA.

Linyuan Lü, Matúš Medo, Chi Ho Yeung, Yi-Cheng Zhang, Zi-Ke Zhang, and Tao Zhou. 2012. Recommender systems. *Physics Reports*, 519(1):1–49.

Charles Kay Ogden and Gyula Halász. 1935. *Basic English*. Kegan Paul, Trench Trubner & Co., Ltd., London, UK.

Sayling Wen, Zechary Chang, and Pinky Ma. 2006. Language learning system and method with a visualized pronunciation suggestion. US Patent 7,153,139.

Sachendra Yadav. 2016. The Kano model — a tool to prioritize the user's wants and desires. Last Accessed: 16 October 2017.

Selecting NLP Techniques to Evaluate Learning Design Objectives in Collaborative Multi-perspective Elaboration Activities

Aneesha Bakharia
Institute of Teaching and Learning Innovation
The University of Queensland
Brisbane, Australia
aneesha.bakharia@gmai.com

Abstract

PerspectivesX is a multi-perspective elaboration tool designed to encourage learner submission and curation across a range of collaborative learning activities. In this paper, it is shown that the learning design objectives of collaborative learning activities can be evaluated using NLP techniques, but that careful analysis of learner impact and pedagogical intent are required in order to select appropriate techniques. In particular, this paper focuses on the NLP techniques required to deliver an instructor dashboard, personalized learner feedback and content recommendation within multi-perspective elaboration activities. Key NLP techniques considered for inclusion include summarization, topic modeling, paraphrase detection and diversified content recommendation.

1 Introduction

PerspectivesX is a multi-perspective elaboration tool that allows instructors to create grid activities where students are able to both submit their own ideas and curate diverse ideas from other learners (i.e., add ideas submitted by other learners to their own list) using a declarative user interface. PerspectivesX allows instructors to either select a multi-perspective elaboration template such as Strengths Weaknesses Threats and Opportunities (SWOT) analysis, Six Thinking Hats (De Bono and Pandolfo, 1999) or define a custom template. PerspectivesX incorporates ideas from Computer Supported Collaborative Learning (CSCL) and the Knowledge Community of Inquiry (KCI) model (Slotta and Najafi, 2013). The tool adheres to the key principles of KCI by providing a knowledge base of student perspective submissions (Principle

1), including curation mechanics (Principle 2&3) and facilitating instructor moderation (Principle 4) (Slotta and Najafi, 2013). The tool development has been directed by clear design guidelines (Bakharia and Lindley, 2018).

NLP techniques have the potential to play an important role in collaborative learning activities, particularly at scale when a large number of learners are participating (i.e., in MOOCs or within large on-campus courses with enrollments exceeding a thousand students). In this paper, the domain of multi-perspective elaboration is used to illustrate that while Natural Language Processing (NLP) techniques are able to aid in the evaluation and implementation of key tool learning design objectives, that principled and critical analysis of learner impact is required in order to select appropriate techniques.

2 PerspectivesX Functionality

The PerspectivesX learner interface is shown in Figure 1. Each perspective is displayed as a grid element. Learners are able to submit new items and specify whether the item is shared with other learners, submitted as an anonymous submission or not shared. Learners are also able to view a full list of submissions for a perspective from all other learners and are able to curate items for inclusion in their own grid (i.e., perspective). On each perspective grid, the items that a learner has submitted are clearly distinguished from their list of curated items. PerspectivesX encourages active participation, idea sharing and learner knowledge growth. In particular curation, should lead to learner knowledge diversification.

The PerspectivesX tool has been implemented using React and the Django web application framework. PerspectivesX is open source and integrates with edX and other learning management

Proceedings of the 5th Workshop on Natural Language Processing Techniques for Educational Applications, pages 88–92
Melbourne, Australia, July 19, 2018. ©2018 Association for Computational Linguistics

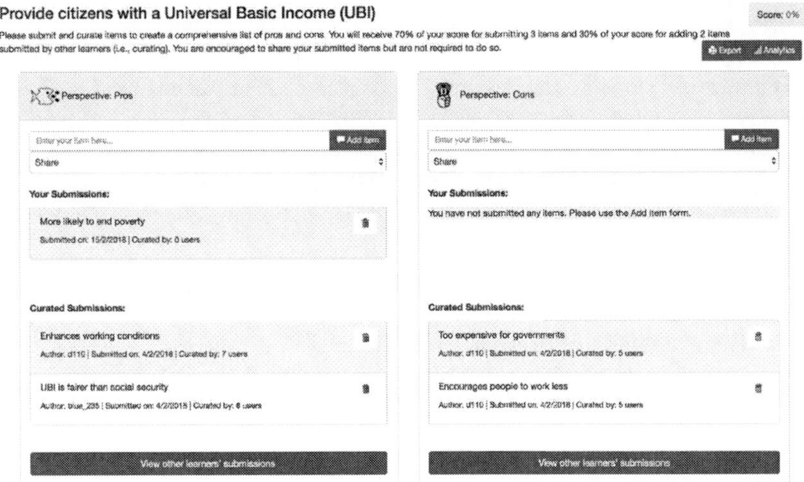

Figure 1: The learner multi-perspective activity submission interface.

systems via the LTI specification (LTI, 2015).

3   Learning Design Objectives

Learning design objectives are targeted statements about the expected student performance when participating in a learning activity. In the case of multi-perspective elaboration, the learning design objectives define the pedagogical intent of learner interaction within the PerspectivesX tool. The aim of the PerspectivesX tool is to support the following learning design objectives:

1. Encourage students to submit ideas across all perspectives

2. Encourage students to curate a list of diverse ideas within and across perspectives

3. Trigger discussion among learners in a post-activity forum

4. Encourage students to start sharing ideas (even if they initially submit ideas as anonymous or choose not to share ideas)

At scale when hundreds of learners are participating in a learning activity, it becomes difficult for instructors and learning designers to evaluate whether more complex learning design objectives are being met. NLP techniques may therefore be required to serve as computational aids. Learning Design Objectives 1, 3 and 4 are clearly able to be evaluated using simple statistical clickstream analysis. The evaluation of Learning Design Objective 2, however, requires the use of NLP techniques. In the sections that follow, NLP techniques will be discussed and selected to assist both instructors in evaluating learning design objectives and learners in meeting the desired learning design objectives.

4   Learner Item Recommendation

The curation of diverse, original and innovative items is an intrinsic requirement of learner participation in a multi-perspective elaboration activity. NLP techniques are required to help the learner navigate the knowledge base consisting of ideas submitted by other learners.

Multiple learners may submit the same ideas but use slightly different phrases. Within the MOOC context where a cohort may reach sizes exceeding 100,000, the submission of similar items presents an information retrieval issue. The learner may need to read multiple pages of similar learner submissions. Either paraphrase detection (Socher et al., 2011) or clustering algorithms can be used in PerspectivesX. Similar student responses can be grouped together, with only the centroid submission shown to learners.

While the activity is progressing, if a learner is unable to curate a diverse list of items within and across perspectives, one of the techniques considered was diversified item recommendation. Numerous techniques and algorithms exist to find a diversified and novelty list of items in a corpus. Simply suggesting items for inclusion in the learner's curation list, however, would make the activity too easy and not require any effort from the learner. The activity only becomes beneficial to learners if they are able to view others submissions and actively decide on the items that need to be curated. Curation in itself is a key 21st-century literacy that depends on critical inquiry and exploration (Mihailidis and Cohen, 2013).

The use of a new algorithm that uses the output of a topic modeling algorithm provides a good solution to suggest a topic that a learner needs to curate items on, without suggesting the exact item. Topic modeling algorithms such as Latent Dirichlet Allocation (Blei et al., 2003) and Non Negative Matrix Factorization (Xu et al., 2003) are able to find the topics within a document collection. An item to word matrix needs to be created from student submissions and passed to the topic modeling algorithm. The output of the topic modeling algorithm is a topic defined by the top words and top documents that belong to the topic.

The algorithm implemented in PerspectivesX, matches a learners submissions to topics and suggests topics that the learner has not submitted or curated items on. As only a few top words in a topic are shown to the learner, the learner is still required to explore the knowledge base. For a future release, a topic labeling technique (Mei et al., 2007) will be included as some topics can be hard to interpret from only the top words.

5 The Instructor Dashboard

Submission count distributions are included for each perspective to support the evaluation of Learning Design Objective 1. The instructor dashboard currently includes a timeline chart with a series for each sharing option (i.e., shared with other learners, shared anonymously or not shared). The timeline gives the instructor an indication of learner sharing behavior over time to support the evaluation of Learning Design Objective 4. NLP techniques are however required to aid in the evaluation of Learning Design Objective 2 (i.e., "Encourage students to curate a list of diverse ideas within and across perspectives"). In order to evaluate Learning Design Objective 2, instructors require the ability to gain a high-level overview of student submissions.

Summarization, either abstractive (Luo et al., 2016) or subtractive (Rush et al., 2015), was initially considered to provide a high-level overview of learner contributions and curated items. Sum-

marization techniques were however found to be inappropriate because usually only a top sentence is returned. Instructors need an indication of how learners as a group are contributing and the topics that are being covered. Topic modeling was selected as the high-level overview of topics was found to be more conducive to the aims of instructors.

Topic modeling algorithms, by returning the key topics in a collection of documents, provide a high-level overview of the topics encapsulating the items submitted by learners to a perspective. As topic modeling algorithms return both the top words and top documents (i.e., items) in a topic, the instructor is given an indication of the number of learner submissions per topic. As the top words in a topic may be hard for the instructor to interpret, the top n items are displayed where n can be specified.

While providing a high-level overview of the topics covered by learner submissions, the topic modeling algorithms (both NMF and LDA) are not able to directly return the number of students that have contributed to a topic. This is, however, determined by linking the top documents in a topic to the author (i.e., learner) of the item. Once the topics that a learner has contributed to has been determined, a distribution of the number of topics learners have contributed to, can be calculated. The distribution of learner submissions to topics provides useful insight to the instructor on whether a diverse range of topics is being addressed by learners for each perspective.

Topic modeling can also be applied to curated items as well. In particular, the topics of submitted items can be compared to the topics that are being curated. The comparison of topics gives a good indication of the level of originality in learner submissions and how ideas have diversified after curation.

6 Instructor Provided Feedback

The high-level overview of topics, generated by a topic modeling algorithm provides a good foundation for providing personalized feedback for learners. As learner submissions can be mapped to a topic, the instructor is able to identify common topics that learners have not been addressing. An interface for instructors to filter learners based upon submissions to a topic and send personalised feedback to learners is provided. Feedback can either be displayed on the learner's submission grid or sent via email.

Instructor feedback also needs to address misconceptions. Topic modeling algorithms, however, will include both the correct and incorrect items in the same topic if they use similar words. Providing keyword-in-context functionality will help the instructor to inspect word usage. The inclusion of keyword-in-context functionality has been shown to aid in the interpretation of topic models and allow the user to gather supporting evidence (Bakharia, 2018). Instructors are able to view and click on top words in a topic with the top words highlighted within the text of student submitted items. Paraphrase detection and clustering can also be used to group similar learner submitted items within a topic, making it easier for instructors to gain an overview of the range of items that are placed in the topic. Once misconceptions are identified, they can be linked back to contributing or curating learners, with appropriate feedback provided.

Instructor feedback can either direct learners to submit additional items for a perspective or provide guidance on the types of items that must be curated.

7 Discussion

While NLP techniques are able to support key learning design objectives, critical analysis of pedagogical intent must be conducted. The examples presented in this paper have shown that content (i.e., item) recommendation distracts from the purpose of curation (i.e., critical inquiry and exploration) and that a hybrid topic modeling and recommendation algorithm is instead able to meet pedagogical intent.

Both abstractive and subjective summarization were also considered as NLP options to provide instructors with a high-level overview of learner submissions per perspective. Summarization algorithms, however, produce a single sentence which would not provide the instructor with an overview of all topics being discussed and a count of learner contributions across topics. Topic modeling algorithms were selected for inclusion on the instructor dashboard but required enhancements. The output of topic modeling algorithms in particular, need to link items (i.e., documents) back to their authors (i.e., learners) to enable learner contribution and curation distribution counts per perspective to be calculated.

Topic modeling was also found to be useful in helping the instructor identify student misconceptions but only if the keyword-in-context functionality was included.

8 Conclusion

In this paper, the rationale underpinning the selection of NLP techniques for PerspectivesX, a collaborative multi-perspective elaboration and curation tool were discussed. NLP techniques were required to support and aid in the evaluation of a key learning design objective ("Encourage students to curate a list of diverse ideas within and across perspectives"). NLP techniques were considered for inclusion in an instructor dashboard, to help the instructor provide feedback and to recommend content items for learners to curate. Paraphrase detection and clustering were able to be used to help group together similar student submissions. A hybrid topic modeling algorithm was found to provide a viable solution for providing a high level overview of the topics learners were contributing to within a perspective for instructors. Diversified content recommendation algorithms were found to detract from the pedagogical intent of curation by making the selection of items too simplistic for learners. A hybrid topic modeling and recommendation algorithm was selected instead to recommend topics that the learner had to curate item on rather than the actual items to curate. Summarization algorithms were not selected as their single sentence output did not provide instructors with an appropriate high-level overview for analysing student contributions.

References

Aneesha Bakharia. 2018. Designing interactive topic discovery systems for research and decision making. In *Intelligent Decision Technologies*.

Aneesha Bakharia and Marco Lindley. 2018. Perspectivesx: A collaborative multi-perspective elaboration learning tool. In *Smart Education and eLearning Conference Proceedings*.

David M Blei, Andrew Y Ng, and Michael I Jordan. 2003. Latent dirichlet allocation. *Journal of machine Learning research*, 3(Jan):993–1022.

Edward De Bono and Marcela Pandolfo. 1999. *Six thinking hats*, volume 192. Back Bay Books New York.

IMS LTI. 2015. Learning tools interoperability specification. *IMS Global Learning Consortium*.

Wencan Luo, Fei Liu, Zitao Liu, and Diane Litman. 2016. Automatic summarization of student course feedback. In *Proceedings of the 2016 Conference of the North American Chapter of the Association for Computational Linguistics: Human Language Technologies*, pages 80–85.

Qiaozhu Mei, Xuehua Shen, and ChengXiang Zhai. 2007. Automatic labeling of multinomial topic models. In *Proceedings of the 13th ACM SIGKDD international conference on Knowledge discovery and data mining*, pages 490–499. ACM.

Paul Mihailidis and James Cohen. 2013. Exploring curation as a core competency in digital and media literacy education. *Journal of Interactive Media in Education*, 2013(1).

Alexander M Rush, Sumit Chopra, and Jason Weston. 2015. A neural attention model for abstractive sentence summarization. *arXiv preprint arXiv:1509.00685*.

James D. Slotta and Hedieh Najafi. 2013. *Supporting Collaborative Knowledge Construction with Web 2.0 Technologies*. Springer New York, New York, NY.

Richard Socher, Eric H Huang, Jeffrey Pennin, Christopher D Manning, and Andrew Y Ng. 2011. Dynamic pooling and unfolding recursive autoencoders for paraphrase detection. In *Advances in neural information processing systems*, pages 801–809.

Wei Xu, Xin Liu, and Yihong Gong. 2003. Document clustering based on non-negative matrix factorization. In *Proceedings of the 26th annual international ACM SIGIR conference on Research and development in informaion retrieval*, pages 267–273. ACM.

Augmenting Textual Qualitative Features in Deep Convolution Recurrent Neural Network for Automatic Essay Scoring

Tirthankar Dasgupta, **Abir Naskar**, **Rupsa Saha** and **Lipika Dey**

TCS Innovation Lab, India
(dasgupta.tirthankar, abir.naskar, rupsa.s, lipika.dey)@tcs.com

Abstract

In this paper we present a qualitatively enhanced deep convolution recurrent neural network for computing the quality of a text in an automatic essay scoring task. The novelty of the work lies in the fact that instead of considering only the word and sentence representation of a text, we try to augment the different complex linguistic, cognitive and psychological features associated within a text document along with a hierarchical convolution recurrent neural network framework. Our preliminary investigation shows that incorporation of such qualitative feature vectors along with standard word/sentence embeddings can give us better understanding about improving the overall evaluation of the input essays.

1 Introduction

The quality of text depends upon a number of linguistic factors, corresponding to different textual properties, such as grammar, vocabulary, style, topic relevance, clarity, comprehensibility, informativeness, lexical diversity, discourse coherence, and cohesion (Crossley et al., 2008)(McNamara et al., 2002). In addition, there are deep cognitive and psychological features, such as types of syntactic constructions, grammatical relations and measures of sentence complexity, that make automatic analysis of text quality a non-trivial task.

Developing tools for automatic text quality analysis have become extremely important to organizations that need to assess writing skills among adults and students on a regular basis. Because of the high participation in such assessments, the amount of time and effort required to grade the large volume of textual data generated is too high to be feasible by a human evaluator.

Manual evaluation processes by multiple evaluators may also be prone to erroneous judgments due to mutual disagreements between the evaluators. Therefore, developing a means through which such essays can be automatically scored, with minimum human interference, seem to be the best way forward to meet the growing demands of the education world, while keeping inter-evaluator disagreements to a minimum. Automatic Essay Scoring (AES) systems have thus been in the research focus of multiple organizations to counter the above issues (Landauer, 2003).

A typical AES system takes as input an essay written on a specific topic. The system then assigns a numeric score to the essay reflecting its quality, based on its content, grammar, organization and other factors discussed above.

A plethora of research have been done to develop AES systems on various languages (Taghipour and Ng, 2016; Dong et al., 2017; Alikaniotis et al., 2016; Attali and Burstein, 2004; Chen and He, 2013; Chen et al., 2010; Cummins et al., 2016). Most of these tools are based on regression methods applied to a set of carefully designed complex linguistic and cognitive features. Knowledge of such complex features have been shown to achieve performance that is indistinguishable from that of human examiners. However, since it is difficult to exhaustively enumerate all the multiple factors that influence the quality of texts, the challenge of automatically assigning a satisfactory score to an essay still remains.

Recent advancement in deep learning techniques have influenced researchers to apply them for AES tasks. The deep multi-layer neural networks can automatically learn useful features from data, with lower layers learning basic feature detectors and upper levels learning more high-level abstract features. Deep neural network models, however, do not allow us to identify and extract those properties of text that the network identi-

93

Proceedings of the 5th Workshop on Natural Language Processing Techniques for Educational Applications, pages 93–102
Melbourne, Australia, July 19, 2018. ©2018 Association for Computational Linguistics

fies as discriminative (Alikaniotis et al., 2016). In particular, deep network models fail to take into account integral linguistic and cognitive factors present in text, which play an important role in an essay score assigned by experts. Such models emphasizes a simple uniform paradigm for NLP: *"language is just sequences of words"*. While this approach has rapidly found enormous popularity and success, its limitations are now becoming more apparent. Gradually researchers stressing towards the importance of linguistic structure and the fact that it reduces the search space of possible outputs, making it easier to generate well-formed output (Lapata, 2017). Dyer (Dyer, 2017) also argued for the importance of incorporating linguistic structure into deep learning. He drew attention to the inductive biases inherent in the sequential approach, arguing that RNNs have an inductive bias towards sequential recency, while syntax-guided hierarchical architectures have an inductive bias towards syntactic recency. Several papers noted the apparent inability of RNNs to capture long-range dependencies, and obtained improvements using recursive models instead (Chen et al., 2017).

In order to overcome the aforementioned issues, in this paper we propose a qualitatively enhanced deep convolution recurrent neural network architecture for automatic scoring of essays. Our model takes into account both the word-level and sentence-level representations, as well as linguistic and psychological feature embeddings. To the best of our knowledge, no other prior work in this field has investigated the effectiveness of combining word and sentence embeddings with linguistic features for AES tasks. Our preliminary investigation shows that incorporation of linguistic feature vectors along with standard word/sentence embeddings do improve the overall scoring of the input essays.

The rest of the paper is organized as follows: Section 2 describes the recent state of art in AES systems. Our proposed Linguistically informed Convolution LSTM model architecture is discussed in Section 3, while section 4 has further details on generation of linguistic feature vectors. In section 5, we cover the experimentation and evaluation technique, reporting the obtained results in section 6, and finally concluding the paper in section 7.

2   Related Works

A plethora of attempts have been taken to develop AES systems over the years. A detailed overview of the early works on AES is reported in (Valenti et al., 2003). An Intelligent Essay Assessor (Foltz et al., 1999) was proposed more recently that uses Latent Semantic Analysis to compute the semantic similarity between texts. Lonsdale and Strong-Krause (Lonsdale and Strong-Krause, 2003) used the Link Grammar parser (Sleator and Temperley, 1995) to score texts based on average sentence-level scores calculated from the parser's cost vector. In Rudner and Liang's Bayesian Essay Test Scoring System (Rudner and Liang, 2002), stylistic features in a text are classified using a Naive Bayes classifier. Attali and Burstein's e-Rater (Attali and Burstein, 2004), includes aspects of grammar, vocabulary and style among other linguistic features, whose weights are fitted by regression. A weakly supervised bag-of-word approach was proposed by Chen et al. (Chen et al., 2010). A discriminative learning based approach was proposed by Yannakoudakis et al. (Yannakoudakis and Cummins, 2015) that extracts deep linguistic features and employs a discriminative learning-to-rank model that out-performs regression. Recently, Farra et al. (Farra et al., 2015) utilized variants of logistic and linear regression and developed scoring models. McNamara et al.'s hierarchical classification approach (McNamara et al., 2015) uses linguistic, semantic and rhetorical features. Despite the existing body of work, attempts to incorporate more diverse features to text scoring models are ongoing. (Klebanov and Flor, 2013) demonstrated improved performance by adding information about levels of association among word pairs in a given text. (Somasundaran et al., 2014) used the interaction of lexical chains with discourse elements for evaluating the quality of essays. Crossley et al. (Crossley et al., 2015) identified student attributes, such as standardized test scores, and used them in conjunction with textual features to develop essay scoring models. Readability features (Zesch et al., 2015) and text coherence have also been proposed as a source of information to assess the flow of information and argumentation of an essay (Chen and He, 2013). A detailed overview of the features used in AES systems can be found in (Zesch et al., 2015). Some attempts have been made to address different aspects of essay writing, like argument strength and organization, independently, through designing task-specific features for each aspect (Persing et al., 2010; Persing and Ng, 2015). There has been a lot of recent work in deep neural network models based on continuous-space representation of the input and non-linear functions. Recently, deep learning techniques have been applied to text analysis problems including AES systems (Alikaniotis et al., 2016; Dong and Zhang, 2016; Dong et al., 2017; Taghipour and Ng, 2016), giving better results compared to statistical models with handcrafted features (Dong and Zhang, 2016). Both recurrent neural networks (Williams and Zipser, 1989; Mikolov et al., 2010) and convolution neural networks (LeCun et al., 1998; Kim, 2014) have been used to automatically score input essays. In comparison to the work of Alikaniotis et al. (Alikaniotis et al., 2016) and Taghipour and Ng (Taghipour and Ng, 2016) that uses single-layer LSTM (Hochreiter and Schmidhuber, 1997) over the word embeddings for essay scoring, and Dong and Zhang (Dong and Zhang, 2016) used a two-level hierarchical CNN structure to model sentences and documents separately. More recently, (Dong et al., 2017) et al. proposed a hierarchical attention based CNN-LSTM model for automatic essay scoring.

Although the deep learning based approaches are reported to be performing better than the previous approaches, the performance may yet be bettered by the use of the complex linguistic and cognitive features that are important in modeling such texts. Our proposed system, takes into account both word and sentence level embeddings, as well as deep linguistic features available within the given text document and together learns the model. The detail architecture and working of the model is depicted in the following sections.

3 The Qualitatively Enhanced Convolution Recurrent Neural Network

As mentioned earlier, neural network based models are capable of modeling complex patterns in data and do not depend on manual engineering of features, but they do not consider the latent linguistic characteristics of a text. In this section, we will present a deep neural network based model that takes into account different complex linguistic, cognitive and psychological features associated within a text document along with a hierarchical convolution network connected with a bidirectional long-short term memory (LSTM) model (Hochreiter and Schmidhuber, 1997) (Schmidhuber et al., 2006). We will begin the model architecture by first explaining about generating the linguistic and psychological feature embeddings that will in turn be used by the neural network architecture.

3.1 Generating Linguistic and Psychological Feature Embeddings

We have used different linguistic and psychological features available within a text to augment them with the deep neural architecture.

The **psychological features** used in this work are mostly derived from Linguistic Information and Word Count (LIWC) tool (Tausczik and Pennebaker, 2010). The rapid development of AI, Internet technologies, social network, and elegant new statistical strategies have helped usher in a new age of the psychological study of language. By drawing on massive amounts of text, it is indeed possible to link everyday language use with behavioral and self-reported measures of personality, social behavior, and cognitive styles (Tausczik and Pennebaker, 2010). LIWC is a text analysis tool that counts words in psychologically meaningful categories. Empirical results using LIWC already demonstrated its ability to detect meaning in a wide variety of experimental settings, such as to show attentional focus, emotionality, social relationships, thinking styles, and individual differences.

The linguistic features we use to make our model linguistically informed are: *Part of Speech(POS)* (Manning et al., 2014), *Universal Dependency relations* (De Marneffe et al., 2006) , *Structural Well-formedness, Lexical Diversity, Sentence Cohesion, Causality* and *Informativeness of the text.*

The **lexical diversity** of a given text is defined as the ratio of different unique word stems (types) to the total number of words (tokens). According to Jarvis's model (Jarvis, 2002), lexical diversity includes six properties that are measured by the indices discussed in Table 1.

We device a novel algorithm to determine **cohesion** between sentences in a document. The algorithm follows the following steps: a) identify the GloVe word embeddings(Pennington et al., 2014) of each constituent word of two sentences $S_1, /S_2$.

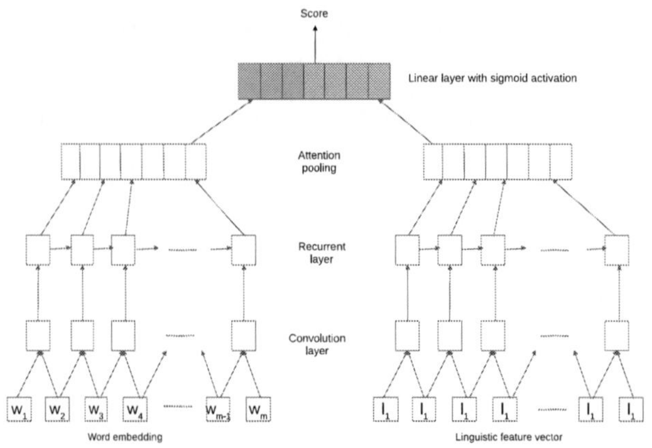

Figure 1: Overview of the qualitatively enhanced convolution recurrent neural network for AES.

Table 1: Lexical Diversity Indices

Property	Measure
Variability	Measure of Textual Lexical Diversity (MTLD)
Volume	Total number of words in the text
Evenness	Standard deviation of tokens per type
Rarity	Mean BNC rank
Dispersion	Mean distance between tokens of type
Disparity	Mean number of words per sense

b) create sentence embeddings by computing a tensor product between the individual word embeddings. For example, given two sentences S_1 and S_2 $S_1 = w_1, w_2..., w_i$ and $S_2 = w'_1, w'_2, ...w'_j$, where $w_1, w_2, ...w_k$ and $w'_1, w'_2...w'_k$ are the word embeddings of S_1 and S_2. Sentence embedding $SE(S_1)$ is $(w_1 \otimes w_2) \otimes w_3)...\otimes w_k)$. Where $\otimes$ refers to the tensor product of each adjacent word embedding pairs in S_1. Similarly for sentence S_2. c) define A and B as the number of word embeddings in S_1 $and S_2$ respectively. d) the cohesion score between S_1 and S_2 can be computed as $coh(S_1, S_2) = \frac{(S' + Sim(p_1, p_2))}{N_1 + 1}$ The expression N_1 represents $A \cup B$. S' and S'' are computed as: $S' = \sum_{\forall w_i \in C_1} S_{w_i}$ Where, $S_{w_i} = \max_{\forall w'_j \in C_2}(Sim(w_i, w'_j))$ p_1 and p_2 are sentence embeddings of S_1 and S_2 respectively, and $Sim(x, y)$ is the cosine similarity between two vector V_i and V_j.

To indicate presence of **causality**, we use the semantic features as identified by Girju (Girju, 2003) - nine noun hierarchies (H(1) to H(9)) in WordNet, namely, *entity, psychological feature, abstraction, state, event, act, group, possession, and phenomenon*. A single feature Primary Causal

Class (PCC) is defined for a word w_i. If $w_i \in H_i$ where H_i is as defined, $PCC = H_i$, else $PCC = null$. Another feature, Secondary Causal Class(SCC) is also defined. This takes value $H(i)$ if any WordNet synonym of the word belongs to $H(i)$, and is $Null$ otherwise.

The **informativeness of a text** refers to how much information is present in a text with respect to a given collection. We have introduced an information theoretic approach towards determining such informativeness in text. We consider each document d, represented by a bag-of-word as, $< (q_1, w_1), (q_2, w_2), ..., (q_n, w_n) >$ where q_i is the ith unique term in document d and w_i is the corresponding weight computed with respect to a collection of documents C. The Informativeness score $NS(d, C)$ of each new text document d, is computed with respect to the collection C, indicating the informativeness of d amongst C. In the described context, we declare a document d_i as informative when the corresponding $NS(d_i, C)$ is higher than a threshold θ. We have defined the informativeness of d in terms of its information content (IC). Information content is a heuristic measure for term specificity and is a function of term use. Our idea is to therefore use it as an estimator of informativeness *an informative document is more likely to use unique vocabulary than other documents*. We compute the information content of a document in terms of its Entropy. We define the entropy of a text T, with N words out of which n are unique, as: $E_T(p_1, p_2, ..., p_n) = \frac{1}{N} \sum_{i=1}^{n}(p_i * (\log_{10} N - \log_{10} p_i))$. $p_i(i = 1...n)$ is the probabilistic measure of the specificity of the ith word in the T. The technique to compute term specificity is discussed below. In order to avoid the problem of zero probabilities, we have used linear interpolation smoothing, where document weights are smoothed against the set of the documents in the corpus. Then the probabilities are defined as: $\theta_{d_n}(q) = \lambda * \theta_d(q) + (1-\lambda) * \theta_{d_1}...\theta_{d_n}(q)$. Where, $\lambda \in [0,1]$ is the smoothing parameter and is the probability of term q in the corpus C. In our experiments, λ was set to 0.9.

As discussed earlier, the cornerstone of our informativeness prediction engine is to compute the rarity of a document, which can, in turn, be computed by determining the rarity of individual terms. Accordingly, we have applied the principle of Inverse Document Frequency (IDF) (Karkali et al., 2014). Aggregating all the IDF of the terms of a given document may led us to a better estimator of the documents Informativeness. IDF is originally defined as, $IDF(q, C) = \log(\frac{N}{df_q})$ where, q is the term in hand, df_q is the document frequency of the term q across the corpus C and N is the total number of documents in the collection. On the other hand, in probabilistic terms IDF can be computed as: $IDF_p(q, c) = \log(\frac{N-df_q}{df_q})$.

3.2 Model architecture

The proposed linguistically informed convolution recurrent neural network architecture that we have used in this paper is illustrated in Figure 1. In the next few subsections, we describe each layer in detail.

Generating Embeddings: Pre-trained GloVe word vector representations of dimension 300 have been used for this work (Pennington et al., 2014) for the word embeddings. Similarly we have constructed a pre-trained sentence vectors. The Sentence vectors from each input essay is appended with the vector formed from the linguistic features identified for that particular sentence.

Convolution Layer: Since convolution networks works best in determining local features from texts, it is important to feed each of the generated word embeddings to a convolution layer. Accordingly, the convolution layer applies a linear transformation to all K windows in the given sequence of vectors. We perform a zero padding to ensure the same dimensionality between the input and output vectors. Therefore, given a word representations $X_1, X_2, ...X_l$, the convolution layer

first concatenates these vectors to form a vector $\bar{x}$ of length $l.d_{LT}$ and then uses $Conv(\bar{x}) = W.(x) + b$ to calculate the output vector of length d_c. Where, **W** and **b** are the weights that the network learns.

Long short-term memory In AES systems, the surrounding context is of paramount information. While typical LSTMs allow the preceding elements to be considered as context for an element under scrutiny, we prefer to use bidirectional LSTMs (Bi-LSTM) networks (Graves et al., 2012) that are connected so that both future and past sequence context (i.e. both preceding and succeeding elements) can be examined. Corresponding to each input text, we determine the word embedding representation (W_e) of each word of the text and the different linguistic feature embeddings (W_l). The input to the Bi-LSTM unit is an embedding vector E which is the composition of W_e and W_l, i.e. $\overrightarrow{E} = \overrightarrow{W_e} \otimes \overrightarrow{W_l}$

Activation layer: After obtaining the intermediate hidden layers from the Bi-LSTM layer $h_1, h_2, ..., h_T$, we use an attention pooling layer over the sentence representations. The attention pooling helps to acquire the weights of sentence contribution to final quality of the text. The attention pooling over sentences is represented as: $a_i = \tanh(W_a.h_i + b_a)$, $\alpha_i = \frac{e^{w_\alpha.a_i}}{\sum e^{w_\alpha.a_i}}$, $O = \sum(\alpha_i.h_i)$. Where W_a, w_α are weight matrix and vector respectively, b_a is the bias vector, a_i is attention vector for i-th sentence, and α_i is the attention weight of i-th sentence. O is the final text representation, which is the weighted sum of all the sentence vectors.

The Sigmoid Activation Function: The linear layer performs a linear transformation of the input vector that maps it to a continuous scalar value. We apply a sigmoid function to limit the possible scores to the range $[0, 1]$. The mapping of the linear layer after applying the sigmoid activation function is given by $s(x) = sigmoid(w.x + b)$. Where, x is the input vector, w is the weight vector, and b is bias value. We normalize all gold-standard scores to $[0, 1]$ and use them to train the network. However, during testing, we rescale the output of the network to the original score range and use the rescaled scores to evaluate the system.

Table 2: Statistics of the Kaggle dataset; Range:score range and Med: median scores.

Set	#Essays	Genere	Avg. Len.	Range	Med.
1	1783	ARG	350	2-12	8
2	1800	ARG	350	1-6	3
3	1726	RES	150	0-3	1
4	1772	RES	150	0-3	1
5	1805	RES	150	0-4	2
6	1800	RES	150	0-4	2
7	1569	NAR	250	0-30	16
8	723	NAR	650	0-60	36

Table 3: Hyper-parameters

Layer	Parameter Name	Parameter Value
Lookup	Word embedding dim	50
CNN	Window size	5
	No. of filters	100
Bi-LSTM	Hidden units	100
Dropout	Dropout rate	1.0
	Epochs	200
	Batch size	10
	Initial learning rate η	0.001
	Momentum	0.9

4 Experiments

4.1 Dataset

An Automated Student Assessment Prize (ASAP) contest was hosted at Kaggle in 2012. It was supported by the Hewlett Foundation, aiming to explore the capabilities of automated text scoring systems (Shermis and Burstein, 2013). The dataset released consists of around twenty thousand texts (60% of which are marked), produced by middle-school English-speaking students, which we use as part of our experiments to develop our models. In order to train and test the proposed models, we have used the same dataset as published at the Kaggle challenge. Table 2 reports some of the basic statistics about the dataset. Due to the unavailability of the testing set, we have performed a 7-fold cross validation to evaluate our proposed models. In each fold, 80% of the data is used for training, 10% as the development set, and 10% as the test set. We train the model for a fixed number of epochs (around 8000) and then choose the best model based on the development set. We have used the NLTK toolkit to perform various NLP tasks over the given dataset. For ease of experimentation, we have further normalized the expert scores (gold-standard scores) to the range of $[0, 1]$. During testing, we rescale the system-generated normalized scores to the original range of scores and measure the performance.

4.2 Training and parameter estimation

For a given learning function our goal is to minimize the mean squared error (MSE) rate. Accordingly, we have used the RMSProp optimization algorithm (Dauphin et al., 2015) to minimize the mean squared error (MSE) loss function over the training data. This is represented as: $MSE(s^*, s) = \frac{1}{N} * \sum_{i=1}^{N} (s_i - s_i^*)^2$. Therefore, given N training samples and their corresponding expert generated scores p_i^* normalized within a range of $[0.1]$, the model computes the predicted scores p_i for all training essays and then updates the network parameters such that the mean squared error is minimized.

The 10% data kept for development is used to identify the different hyper-parameters for the models. There are several hyper-parameters that need to be set. We use the RMSProp optimizer with decay rate (ρ) set to 0.9 to train the network and we set the base learning rate to 0.001. The mini-batch size is 64 in our experiments and we train the network for 400 epochs. We have also make use of dropout regularization (Srivastava et al., 2014) to avoid over-fitting. We also clip the gradient if the norm of the gradient is larger than a threshold. We do not use any early stopping methods, instead, we train the neural network model for a fixed number of epochs and monitor the performance of the model on the development set after each epoch. Once training is finished, we select the model with the best QWK score on the development set. During training, the norm of the gradient is clipped to a maximum value of 10. We set the word embedding dimension ($d_L T$) to 50 and the output dimension of the recurrent layer (d_r) to 300. For the convolution layer, the window size (l) is set to 5 and the output dimension of this layer (d_c) is set to 50. The details of the hyper-parameters are summarized in Table 3.

4.3 Evaluation

In past literature, a number of techniques were used to measure the quality of AES systems. This includes Pearson's correlation r, Spearman's ranking correlation ρ, Kendall's Tau and kappa, and quadratic weighted kappa (QWK). (Alikaniotis et al., 2016) proposed to evaluate their model in terms of the first three parameters, whereas works of (Taghipour and Ng, 2016; Dong and Zhang, 2016; Dong et al., 2017) uses QWK as the evaluation criteria. This is primarily due to the fact that

Table 4: Comparing the performance of the present system with that of the state-of-the-art

Models/Prompts	1	2	3	4	5	6	7	8	AVG QWK
EASE (BLRR)	0.761	0.606	0.621	0.742	0.784	0.775	0.730	0.617	0.705
CNN	0.797	0.634	0.646	0.767	0.746	0.757	0.746	0.687	0.722
LSTM	0.775	0.687	0.683	0.795	0.818	0.813	0.805	0.594	0.746
LSTM-CNN	0.821	0.688	0.694	0.805	0.807	0.819	0.808	0.644	0.761
LSTM-MoT	0.818	0.688	0.679	0.805	0.808	0.817	0.797	0.527	0.742
CNN-CNN-MoT	0.805	0.613	0.662	0.778	0.800	0.809	0.758	0.644	0.734
LSTM-CNN-att	0.822	0.682	0.672	0.814	0.803	0.811	0.801	0.705	0.764
Qe-C-LSTM	0.799	0.631	0.712	0.711	0.801	0.831	0.815	0.695	0.786

Table 5: Comparing performance of the proposed model taking all the prompts together with that of the existing models

Models	Pearson's r	Spearman's ρ	RMSE	Cohen's κ
doc2vec	0.63	0.62	4.43	0.85
SVM	0.77	0.78	8.85	0.75
LSTM	0.60	0.59	6.80	0.54
Bi-LSTM	0.5	0.70	7.32	0.36
word2vec + Bi-LSTM	0.86	0.75	4.34	0.85
SSWE+ Bi-LSTM	0.92	0.80	3.21	0.95
SSWE+ Two-layer Bi-LSTM	0.96	0.91	2.40	0.96
Qe-C-LSTM	0.97	0.94	2.1	0.97

the Automated Student Assessment Prize (ASAP) competition official criteria takes QWK as evaluation metric.

The QWK statistics or its other variants are widely used to measure inter-rater agreement of the annotators or experts. In our case inter-raters refer to the human rater and the system predicted ratings. QWK is modified from kappa which takes quadratic weights. The quadratic weight matrix in QWK is defined as: $W_{i,j} = \frac{(i-j)^2}{(R-1)^2}$, where i and j are the reference rating (assigned by a human rater) and the system rating (assigned by an AES system), respectively, and R is the number of possible ratings.

An observed agreement score O is calculated such that $O_{i,j}$ refers to the number of essays that receive a rating i by the human rater and a rating j by the AES system. An expected score E is calculated as the outer product of the two ratings. Finally, given the three matrices W, O, and E, the QWK value is calculated as: $\kappa = 1 - \frac{\sum(W_{i,j} * O_{i,j})}{\sum(W_{i,j} * E_{i,j})}$

5 Results

We evaluate the performance of our proposed model by comparing it with some of the well known state-of-the-art models. These models are: a) the publicly available 'Enhanced AI Scoring Engine' (EASE[1]). EASE is based on hand-crafted linguistic features and regression methods including support vector regression (SVR) and Bayesian linear ridge regression (BLRR). In the present paper we have used only the BLRR model as our baseline systems due to its improved performance in comparison to the SVR model. b) The LSTM-MoT models proposed by (Taghipour and Ng, 2016). c) the Attention-based Recurrent Convolution Neural Network model proposed by (Dong et al., 2017). d) The hierarchical CNN (CNN-CNN-MoT)(Dong and Zhang, 2016) and e) the hierarchical CNN layer with LSTM along with an additional attention layer (CNN-LSTM-att) (Dong and Zhang, 2016) (Dong et al., 2017) as our baselines.

The LSTM-MoT uses one layer of LSTM over the word embeddings, and takes the average pooling over all time-step states as the final text representation, which is called Mean-over-Time (MoT) pooling (Taghipour and Ng, 2016). Next, a linear layer with sigmoid function follows the MoT

---

[1] https://github.com/edx/ease

layer to predict the score of an essay script. On the other hand, CNN-CNN-MoT uses two layers of CNN, in which one layer operates over each sentence to obtain representation for each sentence and the other CNN is stacked above, followed by mean-over-time pooling to get the final text representation. Similarly, the CNN-LSTM-att model uses hierarchical architecture with the CNN layer followed by an LSTM layer attached with an attention layer instead of the MoT layer(Dong et al., 2017).

Table 4 reports the comparison of the performance of our system and the existing baselines by taking the eight prompts from the Kaggle ASAP dataset individually. In general we can observe that our proposed performance of the proposed Qe-CLSTM model is comparable to that of the existing baseline systems. However, in certain cases it outperforms all the base-line models. For example, in prompt 3, 6 and 7 we have achieved an QWK of 0.712, 0.831 and 0.815 respectively as compared to the best reported average QWK score of 0.694, 0.827 and .0.811 respectively for the 10 fold run of CNN-LSTM and LSTM only.

It is worth mentioning here that all these models are compared with respect to the QWK score. On the other hand, we have also used evaluation matrices like, Pearson's correlation r, Spearman's ranking correlation ρ, RMSE scores in order to compare our model with systems proposed by (Alikaniotis et al., 2016).

Table 5 shows the comparison of the performance of our system and the existing baselines by taking all the prompts together. We have compared the systems with respect to the different models as discussed in 5. We found that that in terms of all these parameters our system performs better than the existing, LSTM, Bi-LSTM and EASE models. We have achieved a Pearson's and Spearman's correlation of 0.94 and 0.97 respectively as compared to that of 0.91 and 0.96 in (Alikaniotis et al., 2016). We also achieved and RMSE score of 2.09. We also compute a pair wise Cohen's κ value of 0.97.

Apart from scoring each of the individual essays, we also tried to analyze some of the typical cases where our model fails to predict the desired output. Figure 2 shows the general distribution of difference in average expert score and the system predicted score. We observe a minimum difference of 0 and maximum difference of 20 with me-

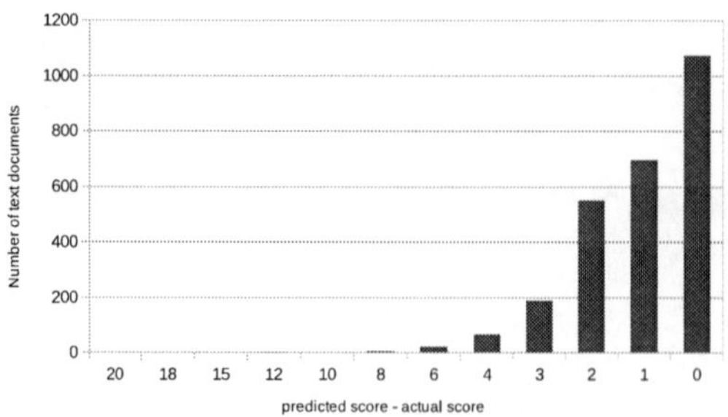

Figure 2: Distribution of difference in predicted scores with respect to the actual score

dian of 1 and average of 1.08. In 82% cases the difference lies between the range of [0,1].

6   Conclusion

In this paper, we have proposed a novel technique that uses deep neural network model to perform Automatic Essay Assessment task. The traditional way of applying deep neural nets like CNN, LSTM or their other forms fails to identify the interconnection between the different factors involved in assessing the quality of a text. To address this issue, our method not only rely upon the pre-trained word or sentence representations of text, but also takes into account qualitatively enhanced features such as, lexical diversity, informativeness, cohesion, well-formedness etc., that have proved to be important in determining text quality. Further, we have explored a variety of neural network model architectures for automated essay scoring and have achieved significant improvements over baseline in certain cases. We would like to conclude that it is indeed possible to enhance the performance of such AES system by intelligently incorporating the supporting linguistic features into the model. One of the limitations of the present approach is that all the linguistic and qualitative features used in this work are computed off-line and then fed into the deep learning architecture. However, in principle deep learning models are supposed to learn these features apriori and perform accordingly. Therefore, one possible future directions of this work is to develop or modify the existing intermediate scores in such a way that the task specific models can automatically learn these features.

References

Dimitrios Alikaniotis, Helen Yannakoudakis, and Marek Rei. 2016. Automatic text scoring using neural networks. *arXiv preprint arXiv:1606.04289*.

Yigal Attali and Jill Burstein. 2004. Automated essay scoring with e-rater® v. 2.0. *ETS Research Report Series*, 2004(2).

Hongbo Chen and Ben He. 2013. Automated essay scoring by maximizing human-machine agreement. In *Proceedings of the 2013 Conference on Empirical Methods in Natural Language Processing*, pages 1741–1752.

Huadong Chen, Shujian Huang, David Chiang, and Jiajun Chen. 2017. Improved neural machine translation with a syntax-aware encoder and decoder. *arXiv preprint arXiv:1707.05436*.

Yen-Yu Chen, Chien-Liang Liu, Chia-Hoang Lee, Tao-Hsing Chang, et al. 2010. An unsupervised automated essay scoring system. *IEEE Intelligent systems*, 25(5):61–67.

Scott Crossley, Laura K Allen, Erica L Snow, and Danielle S McNamara. 2015. Pssst... textual features... there is more to automatic essay scoring than just you! In *Proceedings of the Fifth International Conference on Learning Analytics And Knowledge*, pages 203–207. ACM.

Scott A Crossley, Jerry Greenfield, and Danielle S McNamara. 2008. Assessing text readability using cognitively based indices. *Tesol Quarterly*, 42(3):475–493.

Ronan Cummins, Meng Zhang, and Ted Briscoe. 2016. Constrained multi-task learning for automated essay scoring. Association for Computational Linguistics.

Yann Dauphin, Harm de Vries, and Yoshua Bengio. 2015. Equilibrated adaptive learning rates for nonconvex optimization. In *Advances in neural information processing systems*, pages 1504–1512.

Marie De Marneffe, Bill MacCartney, Christopher Manning, et al. 2006. Generating typed dependency parses from phrase structure parses. In *Proceedings of LREC*, volume 6.

Fei Dong and Yue Zhang. 2016. Automatic features for essay scoring–an empirical study. In *Proceedings of the 2016 Conference on Empirical Methods in Natural Language Processing*, pages 1072–1077.

Fei Dong, Yue Zhang, and Jie Yang. 2017. Attention-based recurrent convolutional neural network for automatic essay scoring. In *Proceedings of the 21st Conference on Computational Natural Language Learning (CoNLL 2017)*, pages 153–162.

Chris Dyer. 2017. Should neural network architecture reflect linguistic structure? *CoNLL 2017*, page 1.

Noura Farra, Swapna Somasundaran, and Jill Burstein. 2015. Scoring persuasive essays using opinions and their targets. In *Proceedings of the Tenth Workshop on Innovative Use of NLP for Building Educational Applications*, pages 64–74.

Peter W Foltz, Darrell Laham, and Thomas K Landauer. 1999. Automated essay scoring: Applications to educational technology. In *EdMedia: World Conference on Educational Media and Technology*, pages 939–944. Association for the Advancement of Computing in Education (AACE).

Roxana Girju. 2003. Automatic detection of causal relations for question answering. In *Proceedings of the ACL 2003 workshop on Multilingual summarization and question answering-Volume 12*. Association for Computational Linguistics.

Alex Graves et al. 2012. *Supervised sequence labelling with recurrent neural networks*, volume 385. Springer.

Sepp Hochreiter and Jürgen Schmidhuber. 1997. Long short-term memory. *Neural computation*, 9(8):1735–1780.

Scott Jarvis. 2002. Short texts, best-fitting curves and new measures of lexical diversity. *Language Testing*, 19(1):57–84.

Margarita Karkali, François Rousseau, Alexandros Ntoulas, and Michalis Vazirgiannis. 2014. Using temporal idf for efficient novelty detection in text streams. *arXiv preprint arXiv:1401.1456*.

Yoon Kim. 2014. Convolutional neural networks for sentence classification. *arXiv preprint arXiv:1408.5882*.

Beata Beigman Klebanov and Michael Flor. 2013. Word association profiles and their use for automated scoring of essays. In *Proceedings of the 51st Annual Meeting of the Association for Computational Linguistics (Volume 1: Long Papers)*, volume 1, pages 1148–1158.

Thomas K Landauer. 2003. Automatic essay assessment. *Assessment in education: Principles, policy & practice*, 10(3):295–308.

Mirella Lapata. 2017. Translating from multiple modalities to text and back. *ACL 2017*, page 1.

Yann LeCun, Léon Bottou, Yoshua Bengio, and Patrick Haffner. 1998. Gradient-based learning applied to document recognition. *Proceedings of the IEEE*, 86(11):2278–2324.

Deryle Lonsdale and Diane Strong-Krause. 2003. Automated rating of esl essays. In *Proceedings of the HLT-NAACL 03 workshop on Building educational applications using natural language processing-Volume 2*, pages 61–67. Association for Computational Linguistics.

Christopher Manning, Bauer Surdeanu, Mihai, Finkel John, Bethard Jenny, J. Steven, and David. Mc-Closky. 2014. The stanford corenlp natural language processing toolkit. In *52nd Annual Meeting of the Association for Computational Linguistics: System Demonstrations*.

Danielle S McNamara, Scott A Crossley, Rod D Roscoe, Laura K Allen, and Jianmin Dai. 2015. A hierarchical classification approach to automated essay scoring. *Assessing Writing*, 23:35–59.

Danielle S McNamara, Max M Louwerse, and Arthur C Graesser. 2002. Coh-metrix: Automated cohesion and coherence scores to predict text readability and facilitate comprehension. Technical report, Technical report, Institute for Intelligent Systems, University of Memphis, Memphis, TN.

Tomáš Mikolov, Martin Karafiát, Lukáš Burget, Jan Černockỳ, and Sanjeev Khudanpur. 2010. Recurrent neural network based language model. In *Eleventh Annual Conference of the International Speech Communication Association*.

Jeffrey Pennington, Richard Socher, and Christopher Manning. 2014. Glove: Global vectors for word representation. In *Empirical Methods in Natural Language Processing (EMNLP)*.

Isaac Persing, Alan Davis, and Vincent Ng. 2010. Modeling organization in student essays. In *Proceedings of the 2010 Conference on Empirical Methods in Natural Language Processing*, pages 229–239. Association for Computational Linguistics.

Isaac Persing and Vincent Ng. 2015. Modeling argument strength in student essays. In *Proceedings of the 53rd Annual Meeting of the Association for Computational Linguistics and the 7th International Joint Conference on Natural Language Processing (Volume 1: Long Papers)*, volume 1, pages 543–552.

Lawrence M Rudner and Tahung Liang. 2002. Automated essay scoring using bayes' theorem. *The Journal of Technology, Learning and Assessment*, 1(2).

Jürgen Schmidhuber, F Gers, and Douglas Eck. 2006. Learning nonregular languages: A comparison of simple recurrent networks and lstm. *Learning*, 14(9).

Mark D Shermis and Jill Burstein. 2013. *Handbook of automated essay evaluation: Current applications and new directions*. Routledge.

Daniel DK Sleator and Davy Temperley. 1995. Parsing english with a link grammar. *arXiv preprint cmp-lg/9508004*.

Swapna Somasundaran, Jill Burstein, and Martin Chodorow. 2014. Lexical chaining for measuring discourse coherence quality in test-taker essays. In *Proceedings of COLING 2014, the 25th International Conference on Computational Linguistics: Technical Papers*, pages 950–961.

Nitish Srivastava, Geoffrey E Hinton, Alex Krizhevsky, Ilya Sutskever, and Ruslan Salakhutdinov. 2014. Dropout: a simple way to prevent neural networks from overfitting. *Journal of machine learning research*, 15(1):1929–1958.

Kaveh Taghipour and Hwee Tou Ng. 2016. A neural approach to automated essay scoring. In *Proceedings of the 2016 Conference on Empirical Methods in Natural Language Processing*, pages 1882–1891.

Yla R Tausczik and James W Pennebaker. 2010. The psychological meaning of words: Liwc and computerized text analysis methods. *Journal of language and social psychology*, 29(1):24–54.

Salvatore Valenti, Francesca Neri, and Alessandro Cucchiarelli. 2003. An overview of current research on automated essay grading. *Journal of Information Technology Education: Research*, 2:319–330.

Ronald J Williams and David Zipser. 1989. A learning algorithm for continually running fully recurrent neural networks. *Neural computation*, 1(2):270–280.

Helen Yannakoudakis and Ronan Cummins. 2015. Evaluating the performance of automated text scoring systems. In *Proceedings of the Tenth Workshop on Innovative Use of NLP for Building Educational Applications*, pages 213–223.

Torsten Zesch, Michael Wojatzki, and Dirk Scholten-Akoun. 2015. Task-independent features for automated essay grading. In *Proceedings of the Tenth Workshop on Innovative Use of NLP for Building Educational Applications*, pages 224–232.

Joint learning of frequency and word embeddings
for multilingual readability assessment

Dieu-Thu Le
Institute for Natural
Language Processing (IMS)
University of Stuttgart
thu@ims.uni-stuttgart.de

Cam-Tu Nguyen
National Key Laboratory for
Novel Software Technology
Nanjing University
ncamtu@nju.edu.cn

Xiaoliang Wang
National Key Laboratory for
Novel Software Technology
Nanjing University
waxili@nju.edu.cn

Abstract

This paper describes two models that employ word frequency embeddings to deal with the problem of readability assessment in multiple languages. The task is to determine the difficulty level of a given document, i.e., how hard it is for a reader to fully comprehend the text. The proposed models show how frequency information can be integrated to improve the readability assessment. The experimental results testing on both English and Chinese datasets show that the proposed models improve the results notably when comparing to those using only traditional word embeddings.

1 Introduction

Readability assessment is the task of determining how difficult a given document is to understand. It is useful in many applications such as selecting learning material for children of different grade levels, for language learners, for comprehension tests, skills training, text summarisation, simplification systems and so on. Readability assessment has a long research history, and many methods have been developed in the last couple of decades (Dale and Chall, 1948; Mc Laughlin, 1969; Kincaid et al., 1975; Chall and Dale, 1995; Si and Callan, 2001; Heilman et al., 2007; Jiang et al., 2015; Wang and Andersen, 2016). These approaches, however, rely on hand-crafted features that depend heavily on the languages and require adjustment when applying to a new language. Our aim is to develop a universal method that can be used in a multilingual setting, which involve little effort when extending to other languages.

Recent machine learning techniques, such as convolutional neural networks (CNN) (Collobert et al., 2011) typically do not have to be supplied with hand-crafted features. These models often use pre-trained word embeddings for NLP tasks and have been proven to achieve good results on multiple benchmarks (Mikolov et al., 2013b; Pennington et al., 2014; Mikolov et al., 2013a). The pre-trained word embeddings are generally designed in a way that they can capture word meaning and topics. Though they are useful since topics are good indications of whether a document is difficult to comprehend, word embeddings do not directly reflect the frequency levels of words.

In our scenario, it is desirable that the system can take into account the frequency level of words rather purely focusing on their meanings. It is based on the assumption that more frequent words are supposed to be easier to understand. We therefore propose two models that jointly represent words based on their meanings with traditional word embeddings and their frequency levels with the so-called frequency embeddings. These two embedding layers are employed in a CNN architecture to determine the readability level of a given document. Since this model does not depend on hand-crafted features, it can be easily adapted to multiple languages.

2 Related Work

Readability assessment methods can be classified into two categories, the traditional approach and data driven approach. The traditional approach include (Dale and Chall, 1948), FOG Index (Gunning, 1952), SMOG (Mc Laughlin, 1969) and Flesch-Kincaid Index (Kincaid et al., 1975), (Chall and Dale, 1995). These early studies evaluated text difficulty based on shallow features such as word difficulty levels, the average sentence length, the average number of syllables. Though considered quick and easy to compute, these tra-

Proceedings of the 5th Workshop on Natural Language Processing Techniques for Educational Applications, pages 103–107
Melbourne, Australia, July 19, 2018. ©2018 Association for Computational Linguistics

ditional metrics/formulae are designed with some specific language in mind, and thus they may not work well when applying to other languages.

The data driven approach treats readability assessment as a machine learning problem, that is to automatically learn the mapping from documents to difficulty levels based on training examples (Si and Callan, 2001; Heilman et al., 2007; Jiang et al., 2015; Wang and Andersen, 2016). In these studies, documents are represented by different types of features such as bag of words, lexical and grammatical features extracted from parse trees (Heilman et al., 2007), grammatical templates (Wang and Andersen, 2016), word frequency smoothed by correlation information (Jiang et al., 2015). Most of these studies however require hand-crafted, language-dependent features, and not readily applicable to multilingual setting.

3   Our method

While traditional methods are simple to implement, they focus mostly on Latin languages such as English. These methods are not easily transferred to other languages especially Asian. Motivated by the recent success of Convolutional Neural Network (CNN) models in many text classification tasks, we employ the models for learning and classifying a given text to its difficulty level.

Word embeddings are used transferrably in many general NLP tasks. They take into account the context in which a word appears to learn the representation of words. Although they can reflect word meaning and topics, they do not take directly frequency information of a word into account. In the readability assessment scenario, frequency information is important in deciding whether a document is hard to read or not (Jiang et al., 2015).

From this observation, we propose a model that takes into account also word frequency information besides word embeddings. Our hypothesis is that the model can learn better from knowing words' difficulty levels besides their meanings. Word embeddings help associating the topics of documents, which are important to assess the readability levels (e.g., there are topics that are more difficult to understand than others from their natures). In addition, frequency information plays the role of pointing out which words are more difficult to understand[1].

---

[1]We have not taken into account rare words that are easy to understand, for examples names, locations

The three common metrics representing word frequency information are raw counts (number of times a word appears in the whole corpus), ranking (i.e., rank 0 for the most common word) and frequency classes. We take these metrics directly as an embedding vector represents words in the corpus. Among these metrics, the word frequency class information is the most generalised one.

In particular, the frequency class $\text{FC}(w)$ of a word w describes the frequency $\text{freq}(w)$ of the word in relation to the frequency freq_{max} of the most frequent word, i.e., the word with ranking 0 (Sabine Fiedler and Quasthoff, 2012):

$$\text{FC}(w) = \log_2 \frac{\text{freq}_{max}}{\text{freq}_w} \qquad (1)$$

Our architecture is slightly different from the CNN architecture presented in (Kim, 2014). In particular, we propose two models (Figure 1) WFE-COM (left) and WFE-SEP (right).

WFE-COM Model. In this model, the filters are applied to the concatenated embeddings of word and frequency. The network learns these filters' weights that activate features extracted from the these embeddings.

Let $x_i^w \in \mathbb{R}^{k_w}$ and $x_i^f \in \mathbb{R}^{k_f}$, where x_i is a word in a sentence of length n, k_w is the word embedding dimension and k_f is the frequency embedding dimension. x_i^w represents the word embeddings of word w_i while x_i^f represents its frequency embeddings.

Note that in the frequency embeddings, instead of randomly assigning values to unknown words as in word embeddings, we set them to the highest frequency class adopted from the training corpus. The sentence with length n is then represented by a matrix:

$$[x_1^w \oplus x_1^f, ..., x_i^w \oplus x_i^f, ..., x_n^w \oplus x_n^f] \qquad (2)$$

and $x_i^E = x_i^w \oplus x_i^f$ represents the final embedding of word x_i, which is a concatenation of word and frequency embeddings. A feature map is generated using filters of window size h to the sentence matrix in Eq. 2, where a feature c_i is obtained using a non-linear activation function f:

$$c_i = f(w \cdot x_{i:i+h-1}^E + b) \qquad (3)$$

where $x_{i:i+h-1}$ represents the matrix which composes of vectors from x_i to x_{i+h-1}. This convolution operation in Eq. 4 is applied on the window size h from x_i to x_{i+h-1}, and the weights $w \in \mathbb{R}^{hk_e}$ where $k_e = k_w + k_f$ and b is the bias.

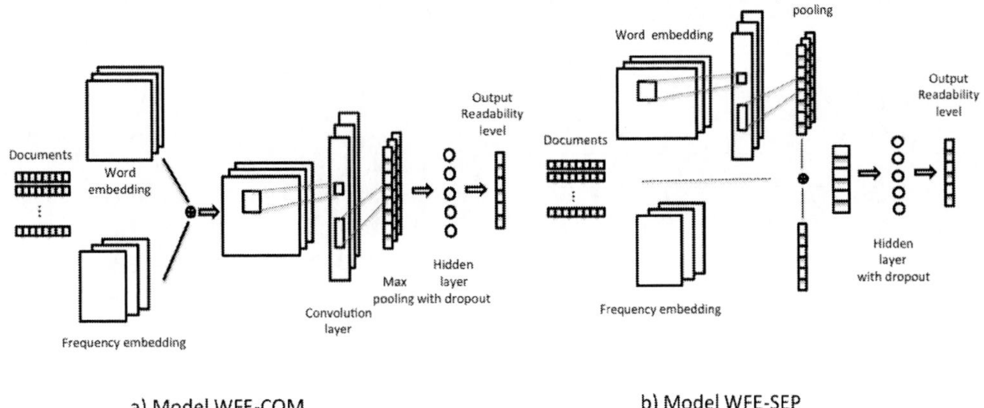

Figure 1: Convolutional Neural Network architecture with word frequency embedding

We then apply max-over-time pooling operations in the feature map.

WFE-SEP Model. In this model, word embeddings and frequency embeddings are learned separately before being fetched into a fully connected layer. Convolutional layers and max poolings are applied to the word embeddings as these layers help finding and representing features of interests, while these layers are omitted for frequency embeddings.

The feature map extracted from applying the filters on word embeddings is then computed as:

$$c_i = f(w \cdot x^w_{i:i+h-1} + b) \qquad (4)$$

Finally this feature map is concatenated with the frequency embeddings, and then use dropout for regularisation similar to the architecture described in (Kim, 2014) (see section 4.2).

4 Evaluation

4.1 Dataset

We evaluate our methods for English and Chinese readability assessment on two datasets collected by (Jiang et al., 2015). The first dataset, ENCT, was built with four reading levels from English New Concept textbook. The second dataset, CPT, was collected from Chinese primary textbook and contains six difficulty levels. In total, there are 279 documents with 4671 sentences in ENCT and 637 documents with 16145 sentences in CPT. In both datasets, the difficulty levels were assigned by human experts. We split randomly the dataset 70% for training, 27% for testing and 3% for a development set.

4.2 Experiment setup

NDC-Level. The New Dale-Chall Readability level (Chall and Dale, 1995) is a traditional readability test. $\mathbb{P}^{DW}$ is the percentage of difficult words in a document, calculated as the number of difficult words divided by the total number of words in the document. Raw score Φ is calculated as: $\Phi = 0.1579 \times \mathbb{P}^{DW} + 0.0496 \times \dfrac{n_w}{n_s}$ where n_w is the number of words and n_s is the number of sentences in the whole corpus, hence $\dfrac{n_w}{n_s}$ represents the average sentence length in the corpus. Finally, if $\mathbb{P}^{DW}$ is above 5%, then add 3.6365 to the raw score Φ to get the adjusted score.

We implemented the New Dale-Chall Readability level (NDC) and converted the raw score Φ to corresponding readability levels as follows:

Φ	Dale-Chall Notes	English	Chinese
$\leq$4.9	Grade 4 and Below	level 1	level 1
5.0 to 5.9	Grades 5 - 6	level 1	level 2
6.0 to 6.9	Grades 7 - 8	level 2	level 3
7.0 to 7.9	Grades 9 - 10	level 3	level 4
8.0 to 8.9	Grades 11 - 12	level 3	level 5
9.0 to 9.9	College	level 4	level 6
$\geq$10	College Graduate	level 4	level 6

Word embeddings (WE). For English, we used the pre-trained word2vec by (Mikolov et al., 2013b) on Google News. For Chinese, we collected a dataset consisting of news ($\approx$ 320K documents) and Wikipedia, tokenised and trained the word embeddings on it.

Frequency embeddings. We used the pre-trained frequency lists for English obtained from (Sabine Fiedler and Quasthoff, 2012), and created our own Chinese frequency lists using the same

Model	English	Chinese
NDC-Level	55	17
Random-WE	64	32
Static-WE	80	41
Non-Static-WE	74	37
Multichannel-WE	76	37
Static-FE-class	75	39
Static-WFE-COM	77	40
Static-WFE-class-COM	**83**	**42**
Static-WFE-class-SEP	**93**	**49**

Table 1: Accuracy of readability assessment with different settings

dataset used for Chinese word embeddings.

CNN architecture. We followed the setting as suggested in (Kim, 2014). The filter windows' sizes are 3, 4, 5 with 100 feature maps each. We used rectified linear units as activation functions for the convolutional layers, dropout rate of 0.5 and mini-batch size of 50.

Static and non-static WE. These two settings followed the method in (Kim, 2014), where all words are kept either static (in static setting) or updated (in non-static setting) including the unknown ones while others parameters are learned.

Random-WE. All words are randomly initialised and modified while training.

Multichannel-WE. Each static and non-static WE is treated as one channel while gradients are back-propagated only through one of the channels.

Static-FE. Only frequency embeddings are used in this setting (without word embeddings).

Word Frequency Embeddings (WFE). We concatenate the pre-trained word embeddings and the frequency embeddings as explained in section 3. In the **WFE** setting, we use the three frequency metrics: raw counts, ranking and frequency class, while in the **WFE-class** setting, we use only the frequency class metric. In both settings, the frequency embeddings are kept static during training.

4.3 Result and discussion

The result shows that the traditional method NDC works much better for English dataset (50%) than for Chinese (17%), which is probably explained by the fact that the formulae was originally designed for English language. Their results are still much lower than the CNN methods using pre-trained frequency and word embeddings.

The random-WE method works better for English and much better for Chinese in compared

to the NDC, but lower than when using pre-trained frequency and word embeddings. It shows that pre-trained embeddings play an important role in determining the difficulty levels. Among three WE methods (using pre-trained word embeddings), the static model achieves the best results. Non-static model is supposed to fine-tune to the specific given task. However, in our case, it does not work as well as when keeping the embedding vectors static for both English and Chinese.

When using all frequency levels, word ranks and number of occurrences together for frequency embedding, the results are better than other models. This model is however worse than when using only frequency class information. Since frequency class information is more representative than word counts and word ranks, it perhaps helps the model learn to classify the difficulty levels better in more general cases.

The result suggests that model WFE-SEP works better than WFE-COM. It means that it is not necessary to apply filters and max poolings on the frequency embeddings and the frequency and word embeddings can be learned separated and finally concatenate before going to the fully connected layer. Finally, it shows that the frequency embeddings help improving the results in both English (to 93%) and Chinese (to 49%) when we concatenate the frequency embeddings and word embeddings, using the frequency class information. It proves our hypothesis that frequency information is useful in judging the difficulty level of a document. This method is extensible and can easily be applied to different languages without prior knowledge about these languages.

5 Conclusion

In this paper, we have proposed two models that employ both word and frequency embeddings for the readability assessment task. The experimental results show that (1) using frequency class metric can represent frequency information better than using other common metrics such as raw counts or ranking; (2) the model that integrates the frequency embeddings directly to the fully-connected layer performs better than applying filters on the concatenated word frequency embeddings and (3) both proposed models outperform the baseline (the traditional NDC method) and the CNN models without using frequency information in both English and Chinese datasets.

References

Jeanne S Chall and Edgar Dale. 1995. Readability revisited. *The New Dale-Chall Readability Formula. Brookline: Brookline Books.*

Ronan Collobert, Jason Weston, Léon Bottou, Michael Karlen, Koray Kavukcuoglu, and Pavel Kuksa. 2011. Natural language processing (almost) from scratch. *J. Mach. Learn. Res.*, 12:2493–2537.

Edgar Dale and Jeanne S Chall. 1948. A formula for predicting readability: Instructions. *Educational research bulletin*, pages 37–54.

Robert Gunning. 1952. The technique of clear writing.

Michael Heilman, Kevyn Collins-Thompson, Jamie Callan, and Maxine Eskenazi. 2007. Combining lexical and grammatical features to improve readability measures for first and second language texts. In *Human Language Technologies 2007: The Conference of the North American*, pages 460–467.

Zhiwei Jiang, Gang Sun, Qing Gu, Tao Bai, and Daoxu Chen. 2015. A graph-based readability assessment method using word coupling. In *Proceedings of the 2015 Conference on Empirical Methods in Natural Language Processing*, pages 411–420.

Yoon Kim. 2014. Convolutional neural networks for sentence classification. In *Proceedings of the 2014 Conference on Empirical Methods in Natural Language Processing (EMNLP)*, pages 1746–1751.

J Peter Kincaid, Robert P Fishburne Jr, Richard L Rogers, and Brad S Chissom. 1975. Derivation of new readability formulas (automated readability index, fog count and flesch reading ease formula) for navy enlisted personnel. Technical report, Naval Technical Training Command Millington TN Research Branch.

G Harry Mc Laughlin. 1969. Smog grading-a new readability formula. *Journal of reading*, 12(8):639–646.

Tomas Mikolov, Kai Chen, Greg Corrado, and Jeffrey Dean. 2013a. Efficient estimation of word representations in vector space. *CoRR*, abs/1301.3781.

Tomas Mikolov, Ilya Sutskever, Kai Chen, Greg Corrado, and Jeffrey Dean. 2013b. Distributed representations of words and phrases and their compositionality. In *Proceedings of the 26th International Conference on Neural Information Processing Systems - Volume 2*, NIPS'13, pages 3111–3119, USA. Curran Associates Inc.

Jeffrey Pennington, Richard Socher, and Christopher D. Manning. 2014. Glove: Global vectors for word representation. In *Empirical Methods in Natural Language Processing (EMNLP)*, pages 1532–1543.

Dirk Goldhahn Sabine Fiedler and Uwe Quasthoff. 2012. *Frequency Dictionary English.* Uwe Quasthoff, Sabine Fiedler and Erla Hallsteindttir (eds.). Leipziger UniversitŁtsverlag.

Luo Si and Jamie Callan. 2001. A statistical model for scientific readability. In *Proceedings of the tenth international conference on Information and knowledge management*, pages 574–576. ACM.

Shuhan Wang and Erik Andersen. 2016. Grammatical templates: Improving text difficulty evaluation for language learners. In *Proceedings of the 26th International Conference on Computational Linguistics*, pages 1692–1702.

MULLE: A grammar-based Latin language learning tool to supplement the classroom setting

Herbert Lange and **Peter Ljunglöf**
Computer Science and Engineering
University of Gothenburg and Chalmers University of Technology
`herbert.lange@cse.gu.se`   `peter.ljunglof@cse.gu.se`

Abstract

MULLE is a tool for language learning that focuses on teaching Latin as a foreign language. It is aimed for easy integration into the traditional classroom setting and syllabus, which makes it distinct from other language learning tools that provide standalone learning experience. It uses grammar-based lessons and embraces methods of gamification to improve the learner motivation. The main type of exercise provided by our application is to practice translation, but it is also possible to shift the focus to vocabulary or morphology training.

1 Introduction

Computer-assisted language learning is a growing field that is also more and more in the focus of the general public thanks to popular tools such as Duolingo[1] or Rosetta Stone.[2] In combination with the rise of the smartphone it has become possible to learn languages almost any time and anywhere in an entertaining way.

Text input on mobile devices equiped with touch screens as the primary input device can be difficult, but is relevant to language learning tasks. This general problem led to the development of several alternative input methods (Ward et al., 2002; Kumar et al., 2012; Felzer et al., 2014; Shibata et al., 2016) including Ljunglöf's method of grammar-backed word-based text editing (2011).

We present the MUSTE[3] Language Learning Environment (MULLE)[4], an application for lan-

guage learning that combines several techniques: tree-based sentence modification, controlled natural language grammars for the exercise creation as well as concepts of gamification.

The goal of our system is to provide a tool that enriches the traditional language learning setting in an enjoyable way and helps to avoid problems with learner motivation that can be encountered in language classes.

2 Previous and related work

MULLE is based on an underlying theory of word-based grammatical text editing by Ljunglöf (2011).

The software used to translate between the surface text and the syntax trees is the Grammatical Framework (GF) (Ranta, 2009b, 2011). It is a grammar formalism and parsing framework based on type theory. On top of this formalism, a multilingual library of grammars is build, the so-called Resource Grammar Library (RGL) (Ranta, 2009a) which covers more than 30 languages including Latin (Lange, 2017). It provides an interface that can be used to implement more application-specific grammars similar to an Application Programming Interface (API) in computer programming.

An important aspect of CALL is the factor of both long and short-term motivation for which the concept of gamification is relevant (Deterding et al., 2011). Several approaches are possible, of which we focus on GameFlow by Sweeter and Wyeth (2005) and MICE by Lafourcade (described in Fort et al. (2014, section 4)). GameFlow translates the more general Flow approach (Csikszentmihalyi, 1990) to computer games.

Finally, comparison to other language systems is relevant for our work. Most language systems share common features, especially translation ex-

---

[1]`https://www.duolingo.com/`

[2]`http://www.rosettastone.eu/`

[3]`http://www.cse.chalmers.se/~peb/muste.html`

[4]`https://github.com/MUSTE-Project/MULLE`

Proceedings of the 5th Workshop on Natural Language Processing Techniques for Educational Applications, pages 108–112
Melbourne, Australia, July 19, 2018. ©2018 Association for Computational Linguistics

ercises seem quite similar across different systems. Still there are major differences in the way these systems work and the use cases they are developed for. Duolingo for example heavily relies on text input created by the user, uses a mixture of user-generated content and machine learning techniques (Horie, 2017) and is meant for open independent online learning mostly for modern languages. MULLE on the other hand uses resources created by experts, does not require text input created by the user, and is intended for, but not restricted to, accompanying language classes in a closed classroom setting.

3 Creation of interactive exercises from a Latin textbook

The idea of grammar-based text modification led us to the creation of MULLE. It is game-like and the player solves language learning exercises focusing on translation. Each exercise consists of two sentences in different languages, one language that the user already knows (i.e. the metalanguage), and the language to be learned (i.e. the object language). Both sentences differ in some respect, depending on the grammatical features that the lesson is focusing on.

Using GF together with the RGL helps us to create domain-specific grammars in a straightforward way. Such grammars can be designed to catch exactly the complexity of the lessons in a classic textbook. That way we can mirror the same lesson structure in MULLE, at the same time adding more flexibility and giving the possibility of generating a large supply of interactive exercises with plenty of variation using vocabulary and concepts familiar from class and textbook.

A textbook for language learning is usually split into a sequence of lessons with texts and exercises of growing syntactical complexity. This is the case for textbooks both at high-school and university levels (e.g. Lindauer et al. (2000); Ehrling (2015)). Typically, each chapter consists of a text part, a vocabulary list, some grammatical explanation and additional exercises. The growing vocabulary and increase in complexity helps the student learn the whole of a language in a slow pace. This approach is also common in language learning applications and can readily be implemented in MULLE.

Each grammar lesson in MULLE covers a set of interactive exercises. So we need lesson-specific grammars that use the same lexicon and grammatical constructions as the corresponding parts of the textbook. For that we can use the RGL, when writing a new grammar for a lesson we already have access to an extensive description of the languages we want to cover and only have to select the concepts we want to include.

First a lexicon is created that covers exactly the vocabulary of a lesson. Extensive lexical resources are already available for GF and they can easily be extended by the author of the grammar relying on the morphological component of the grammar to generate the correct word forms.

Next the grammatical constructions that will be used in this lesson are selected by exposing only the parts that are relevant to the planned learning outcomes. The RGL can be seen as a collection of grammatical constructions, and each lesson uses a subset of these concepts. So by only providing a restricted subset together with the selected vocabulary it is possible control the complexity of the lessons.

Finally every grammar we create needs to be multilingual for at least two languages: the metalanguage (e.g. Swedish), and the object language (e.g. Latin). Since the RGL is inherently multilingual it is straightforward to provide the lessons in multiple languages; With only minimal adjustments we can cover as many languages as we want as long as they are already included in the RGL.

The usual size of the lesson grammars we encountered so far was between 50 and 100 lexical items and about 20 syntax rules.

The main focus of our work is on one form of translation exercises but other forms of exercises are also useful in the context of language learning. That usually includes explicit vocabulary exercises and, in the case of languages with a strong morphology like Latin, some exercise for practicing word forms.

Practicing vocabulary is possible either by using lexical categories as top-level categories of the syntax trees or by using sentences that are almost correct except for a lexical mismatch in one position.

Exercises for morphology involve slightly more work since our grammar formalism by default only creates grammatical sentences including correct word agreement. So to be able to practice morphology in our setup have to relax these morphological constraints in the grammars. That gives

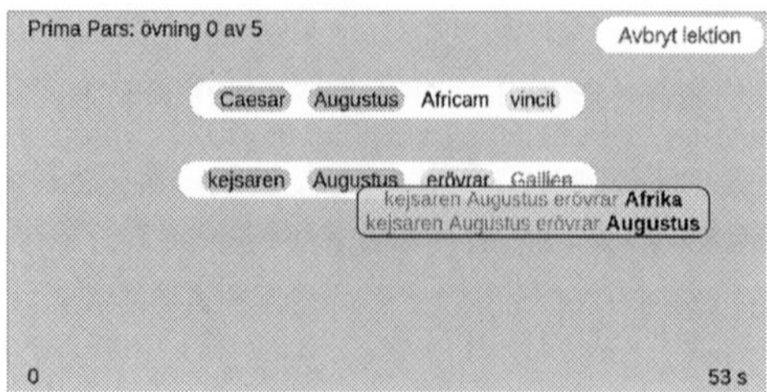

Figure 1: Screenshot of the exercise view

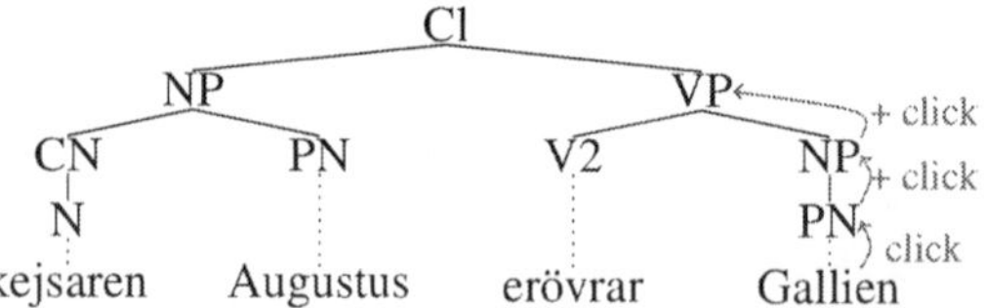

Figure 2: Syntax tree including the path through the tree after several clicks on the word "Gallien"

us a way to create exercises where the user has to both identify wrong morphological forms in a sentence and find the right form to replace them with.

4 Implementation

Based on these ideas we have implemented MULLE which can already be used in language classes. In order to be independent of certain kinds of devices and operating systems we provide the whole application as a browser-based online application.

The application is developed independent of the grammars that can be used. That means that the whole system can be set up by providing the application with a set of lesson grammars and a fully usable language learning environment is available.

4.1 User interface

The user interface is kept minimalist, as can be seen in Figure 1, and only provides the user with the most essential information, including the current score count, the sample sentence in the metalanguage and the modifiable sentence in the object language that has to be altered to match the sample, and the time elapsed since starting the exercise as well as clicks spent on the exercise.

Colours are an important aspect of the interface because they indicate progress in solving the exercise. The background colours of the words highlight which parts of the two sentences already match up with each other. In the example "kejsaren" is a proper translation of "Caesar" which is shown by highlighting them in the same colour. The same is the case for both occurrences of "Augustus" as well as the pair "vincit" and "erövrar". The meaning of the colours is that phrases in the same colour are are translations of each other. Only one pair of words, "Africam" and "Gallien", is not highlighted, so here some user intervention is needed.

This current design reduces the possible distractions while supporting the learner. Depending on the target age group a more elaborate graphics design could have a more positive effect on the acceptance of the system.

4.2 Gamification

We presented two approaches for gamification in Section 2, based on which we selected certain aspects to be included in our application. For our application the following features of GameFlow seem most relevant: *Concentration*, i.e., minimising the distraction from the task, *Challenge* by giving a scoring schema, *Control* by providing an intuitive way to modify the sentence, *Clear goals* by providing a lesson structure, and *Immediate feedback* with the colour schema.

The concept of lessons and exercises is essential for this kind of language learning because it makes the learning progress explicit. The completed lessons are presented to the student together with the scores, so that they can see their own progress on the way to reaching their final goal of learning the language.

By applying methods from GameFlow, we positively influence the motivation while learning a new language. Adding more features of gamification, especially involving social aspects, is a possible extension for the future.

5 User interaction

After logging into the system the user is presented with a list of lessons and the current status, i.e. the number of finished exercises for each lesson and the current score. Some lessons might be disabled because they require previous lessons to be completed first. Now the user can choose one of the enabled lessons to start the exercises.

As soon as a user starts a lesson a set of exercises is selected. These exercises are chosen from a list of exercises in a database. The exercises consist of two syntax trees that different in certain grammatical aspects. Associated with each syntax tree is one sentence, one in the metalanguage and one in the object language. The syntax trees are hidden from the user and only implicitly influence the user experience.

The exercises are presented in the form shown in Figure 1. The background colours of the words show the state of the translation. When the user clicks on one of the words in the bottom sentence, they are presented with a list of potential replacements. This selection is based on where in the tree the word is introduced. In the example the user clicked on the word "Gallien", which is a proper name, so all proper names contained in the grammar are presented. By clicking several times on the same word the focus can be expanded to cover larger phrases, e.g. from proper name to noun phrase, and so on, by traversing upwards through the tree (Figure 2). The menu contains all phrases of the syntactic category selected by clicking on words. That means that suggestions can contain more or less words than currently in focus. So for example if a noun phrase is in focus, both noun phrases with and without adjectives appear in the list. Selecting a longer phrase is the same as inserting words in the sentence and selecting shorter phrases corresponds to deleting words from the phrase.

With these operations, i.e. substitution, insertion, and deletion, the user can modify the sentence to finish their task. When the two sentences are proper translation of each other, i.e. the two syntax trees are similar, the user is congratulated on the success and presented the final score.

Lessons can be interrupted and resumed at any time as well as repeated to improve the score.

6 Evaluation

For the evaluation of our approach we have designed an experiment setup. The full setup includes a basic placement test in the beginning that is repeated at the end of the test period to provide information about the learning outcome. The placement test consists of a fixed set of exercises from all lessons that will be covered during the experiment period. Both error rate and completion time are measured. A questionnaire controls for factors like learner background, previous knowledge, etc. It also gives insight into the learner motivation in the beginning so it can be repeated in the end to see any development in this relevant aspect. Then over the span of the experiment the students can use the software independently online. The lessons are kept in sync with the syllabus of the course that is accompanied by the experiment. In the end the collected data consists of changes in learning outcome and learner motivation as well as activity of the student in the system.

In a pilot experiment we tried aspects of this experimental evaluation. The results were not yet statistical significant because the course size was very small and the dropout rate was high. From the initial 10 Students only 4 finished the course so we only received complete feedback from two students out of initially 6 participants. Anyways, the general interest, both by teachers and students, in this kind of application is strong.

A larger scale follow-up experiment will focus on the change in the learner attitude, which is relevant for showing that our tool is suited for tackling potential anxiety in learners, a problem Latin teachers have pointed out (Dimitrijevic, 2017). With more participants different kinds of control and test conditions can be introduced.

7 Discussion

One challenge with the user interface is the semantics of clicks, especially concerning word insertion. Clicking on a gap between two words to insert words seems more intuitive than clicking on a word. But where to click might also depend on the languages involved.

Another important question for the current application is the influence of the grammar design both on the learning experience and the learning outcome. It is possible to vary the design of the grammar to change the behaviour of our system.

Related is the role of semantics in the lesson grammars. The lessons and exercises are meant for learning the syntax of a language but nonsensical semantics can be an obstacle for the learning process. For example the famous sentence "Colorless green ideas sleep furiously" (Chomsky, 1957, p. 15) is considered grammatical but would probably distract the learner.

8 Future work

This project is work in progress and we plan to extend the system in several ways. First, we will repeat the experiment from Section 6 on a larger scale. Furthermore we plan to extend our implementation to become more feature-rich with a special focus on investigating the points addressed in the discussion section. Finally we want to continue collaborating both with teachers and students to improve the system in order to enrich teaching and learning Latin.

References

Noam Chomsky. 1957. *Syntactic Structures*. Mouton de Gruyter, Berlin New York. Reprint 2002.

Mihaly Csikszentmihalyi. 1990. *Flow: The Psychology of Optimal Experience*. HarperCollins.

Sebastian Deterding, Dan Dixon, Rilla Khaled, and Lennart Nacke. 2011. From Game Design Elements to Gamefulness: Defining "Gamification". In *Proceedings of the 15th International Academic MindTrek Conference: Envisioning Future Media Environments*, pages 9–15, New York, NY, USA. ACM.

Dragana Dimitrijevic. 2017. Latin Curricula, Attitudes and Achievement: An Empirical Investigation. In *Proceedings of the 19th International Colloquium on Latin Linguistics*.

Sara Ehrling. 2015. *Lingua Latina novo modo – En nybörjarbok i latin för universitetsbruk*. University of Gothenburg.

Torsten Felzer, Ian Scott MacKenzie, and Stephan Rinderknecht. 2014. Efficient computer operation for users with a neuromuscular disease with On-ScreenDualScribe. *Journal of Interaction Science*, 2(2).

Karën Fort, Bruno Guillaume, and Hadrien Chastant. 2014. Creating Zombilingo, a Game with a Purpose for Dependency Syntax Annotation. In *Proceedings of the First International Workshop on Gamification for Information Retrieval*, GamifIR '14, pages 2–6, New York, NY, USA. ACM.

André Kenji Horie. 2017. Rewriting Duolingo's engine in Scala. `http://making.duolingo.com/rewriting-duolingos-engine-in-scala`. Accessed 04.04.2018.

Anuj Kumar, Tim Paek, and Bongshin Lee. 2012. Voice typing: A new speech interaction model for dictation on touchscreen devices. In *Proceedings of CHI 2012, SIGCHI Conference on Human Factors in Computing Systems*, Austin, Texas, USA.

Herbert Lange. 2017. Implementation of a Latin Grammar in Grammatical Framework. In *DATeCH2017*, Göttingen, Germany.

Josef Lindauer, Klaus Westphalen, and Bernd Kreiler. 2000. *Roma, Ausgabe C für Bayern, Bd.1*. C.C. Buchner.

Peter Ljunglöf. 2011. Editing Syntax Trees on the Surface. In *Nodalida'11: 18th Nordic Conference of Computational Linguistics*, Rīga, Latvia.

Aarne Ranta. 2009a. The GF Resource Grammar Library. *Linguistic Issues in Language Technology*, 2(2).

Aarne Ranta. 2009b. Grammatical Framework: A Multilingual Grammar Formalism. *Language and Linguistics Compass*, 3(5):1242–1265.

Aarne Ranta. 2011. *Grammatical Framework: Programming with Multilingual Grammars*. CSLI Publications, Stanford.

Tomoki Shibata, Daniel Afergan, Danielle Kong, Beste F. Yuksel, I. Scott MacKenzie, and Robert J.K. Jacob. 2016. Text Entry for Ultra-Small Touchscreens Using a Fixed Cursor and Movable Keyboard. In *Proceedings of CHI 2016: The ACM SIGCHI Conference Extended Abstracts on Human Factors in Computing Systems*, Santa Clara, California.

Penelope Sweetser and Peta Wyeth. 2005. GameFlow: A Model for Evaluating Player Enjoyment in Games. *Comput. Entertain.*, 3(3):3–3.

David J. Ward, Alan F. Blackwell Y, and David J. C. Mackay Z. 2002. Dasher: A Gesture-Driven Data Entry Interface for Mobile Computing Human-Computer Interaction. *Human-Computer Interaction*, page 228.

Textual Features Indicative of Writing Proficiency in Elementary School Spanish Documents

Diana Yazmín Dueñas Chávez **Gemma Bel-Enguix**
Universidad Nacional Autónoma de México
Grupo de Ingeniería Lingüística
{DDuenasC,GBelE}@iingen.unam.mx

Arturo Curiel
CONACYT-Universidad Veracruzana
me@arturocuriel.com

Abstract

Childhood acquisition of written language is not straightforward. Writing skills evolve differently depending on external factors, such as the conditions in which children practice their productions and the quality of their instructors' guidance. This can be challenging in low-income areas, where schools may struggle to ensure ideal acquisition conditions. Developing computational tools to support the learning process may counterweight negative environmental influences; however, few work exists on the use of information technologies to improve childhood literacy.

This work centers around the computational study of Spanish word and syllable structure in documents written by 2nd and 3rd year elementary school students. The studied texts were compared against a corpus of short stories aimed at the same age group, so as to observe whether the children tend to produce similar written patterns as the ones they are expected to interpret at their literacy level. The obtained results show some significant differences between the two kinds of texts, pointing towards possible strategies for the implementation of new education software in support of written language acquisition.

1 Introduction

Acquiring literacy is not an easy process. Educators have to consider many different variables that may affect student performance, such as their psychological and linguistic development (Flower and Hayes, 1981; McDonald Connor et al., 2011; De-

fior and Tudela, 1994). The latter is specially relevant when considering that writing isn't the mere transcription of vocal sounds, but an abstract endeavor of language representation. Thus, teachers have to assume that an important cognitive effort is required from the students to understand the nuances of a symbolic encoding, which may be influenced by a myriad of environmental factors (Bissex, 1980; Menn and Bernstein Ratner, 1999).

In this sense, finding an optimal strategy to ensure that a group of students will acquire literacy at the same pace is not straightforward (Bradley, 1988; Anthony and Lonigan, 2004): the learning conditions of each individual are likely different, which may prove challenging for the design of generalized pedagogic approaches (Piaget, 1971; Rogoff, 1984). This situation can complicate critical tasks for the teaching process, such as evaluating the acquisition progress of a group of students. In this regard, data-driven analyses may provide new automatic evaluation tools for teachers, making it possible to dynamically adapt their teaching strategies based on data to improve the learning conditions of specific groups or individuals.

This work presents an exploratory approach to the computational study of written language, oriented towards improving literacy acquisition in school-age children. The idea is to explore whether written productions made by children contain patterns that may be indicative of proficiency, in an effort to pursue novel research on the automatic monitoring of the students' writing skills. To this end, some seminal quantitative analyses were performed over two independent Spanish corpora of child productions. The obtained results were compared against a control corpus, representative of the level of literacy expected from children in the same age group. Early results show

Proceedings of the 5th Workshop on Natural Language Processing Techniques for Educational Applications, pages 113–118
Melbourne, Australia, July 19, 2018. ©2018 Association for Computational Linguistics

that some regularities exist in the texts produced by the children, which contrast with the expected outcome inferred from the control corpus. Identifying these and other possible proficiency indicators may the first step towards the training of robust written acquisition evaluation models.

2   Related work

Research on the written acquisition of Spanish by Zamudio Mesa (2008), Flores Hernández (2012) and Ferreiro & Teberosky (1991) has shown that, starting the acquisition process, children systematically try to codify the words they hear into a simple interleaving of consonants (C) and vowels (V). This translates into a disproportionate use of simple syllabic patters such as CV, VC or CVC, which tends to decrease as the student progresses.

In an ideal learning environment, as the children gain proficiency they should start using more complex patterns such as VCC, CVCC or CCVC (Bowey, 2002; Ferroni et al., 2016). However, some authors claim that, without the proper conditions, children aren't able to perform this transition, which affects their overall academic performance in the future (Ardila and Rosselli, 2014).

Nonetheless, even though some data exists on the evolution of the complexity of children writing in Spanish, as of the authors' knowledge no previous work has explored how it can be assessed automatically by way of a computational method.

Some data on the evolution of reading ability – Bradley (1988), Ferroni and Diuk (2016), Anthony and Lonigan (2004) Bowey (2002) – showed how teachers can prevent future reading and writing children's failures. However, they focused only on speech and not on the complexity of children's writing (Casillas and Goikoetxea, 2007; Levy and Ransdell, 2013).

This paper presents some results obtained with experiments performed over well-known corpora of children writing in Spanish. These results directly contradict the theories of researchers who have previously approached the problem. We show how this contradiction between our data and the language of children as it has been described in the literature is caused by the way the complexity of the texts was measured. In general, the perspicuity tests used to classify the texts assume that writers have a regular proficiency in the use of written language. However, children's writing display phenomena such as lack of punctuation marks and other conventions that have had an impact in the results, as it will be discussed below.

3   Methodology

To identify candidate characteristics that may be indicative of written proficiency, two children-produced corpora were analyzed:

- CEELE[1]: Corpus of 300 documents in Spanish written by children from 7 to 8 years old. The corpus was elicited by asking the subjects to describe their school after showing them an example through a story. Roughly, this prompted the children to write about their daily commute and their usual activities in a normal school day.

- EXCALE[2]: Corpus of 286 documents in Spanish written by children from 7 to 13 years old. It was elicited by showing the students a series of related images and asking them to turn them into a short story (Zamudio Mesa, 2016). Originally, the corpus contains only document scans with no transcriptions, which had to be created for the experiments. In that regard, all documents that were unreadable, incomplete or that didn't hold a story structure (*e.g.* introduction, plot and conclusion) were discarded.

A third corpus of short stories was collected to serve as a control. It served to compare how the children productions fared against adult-written texts for elementary school literacy level:

- Short Stories: 70 texts of between 200 and 250 words written in Spanish, collected from public websites oriented to literacy acquisition in grade school children.

The documents in the three corpora were classified into seven *readability* levels as given by the Sigriszt-Pazos (1993) readability index ($\mathcal{P}$): an adaptation of the Flesch-Kincaid (1948) readability tests for the Spanish language. Equation 1 shows how $\mathcal{P}$ is calculated:

$$\mathcal{P} = 206.835 - 62.3 \cdot \frac{S}{P} - \frac{P}{F} \tag{1}$$

where:

---

[1] http://www.corpus.unam.mx:8080/
unificado/index.jsp?c=ceele
[2] http://www.inee.edu.mx/index.php/
proyectos/excale/corpus-excale

- P corresponds to the total number of words in the document;

- S denotes the total number of syllables; and,

- F is the total number of sentences.

Table 1 shows how documents are classified into seven readability levels according their P value. An interpretation of each level is provided as well.

$\mathcal{P}$	LEVEL	INTERPRETATION
86-100	1	very easy to read
76-85	2	easy to read
66-75	3	fairly easy to read
51-65	4	plain
36-50	5	fairly difficult to read
16-35	6	difficult to read
0-15	7	very difficult to read

Table 1: Readability level as given by the Sigriszt-Pazos readability index ($\mathcal{P}$).

Once every document in the three corpora was assigned to a level in Table 1, the following measures were calculated for every individual level:

- The average number of words per sentence.

- The average number of syllables per word.

- The average word length.

- The frequency of the syllables per level.

- The frequency of the syllabic patterns appearing in the level.

4 Results

Figure 1 shows three graphs depicting the values calculated for the average number of words per sentence (1a); the average number of syllables per word (1b) and the average word length (1c), for all seven levels in each corpora.

Each graph in Figure 1 shows groups of side-by-side bars for the three corpora, in each of the seven readability levels.

Figure 1a shows that both children produced corpora—CEELE and EXCALE—tend to hold more words per sentence in average than the Short Stories control. Furthermore, the averages per level in both EXCALE and CEELE always surpass the ones from the Short Stories corpus. In general,

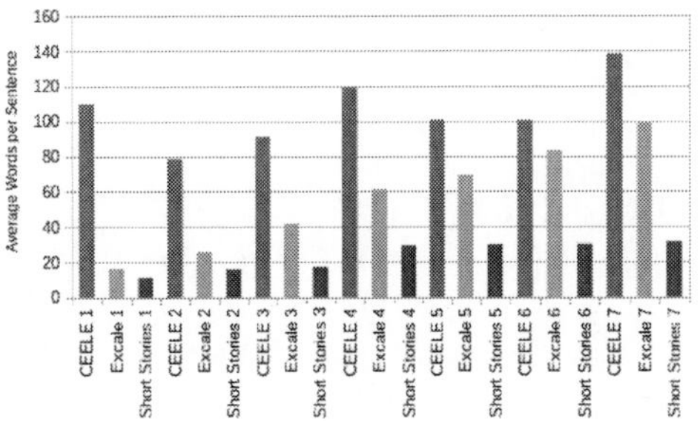

(a) Average Words per Sentence

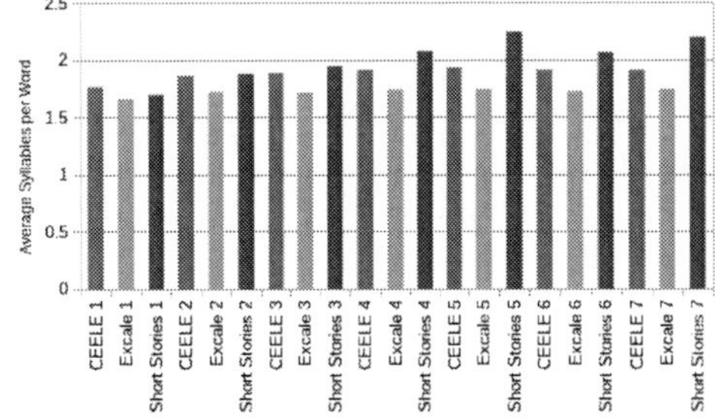

(b) Average Syllables per Word

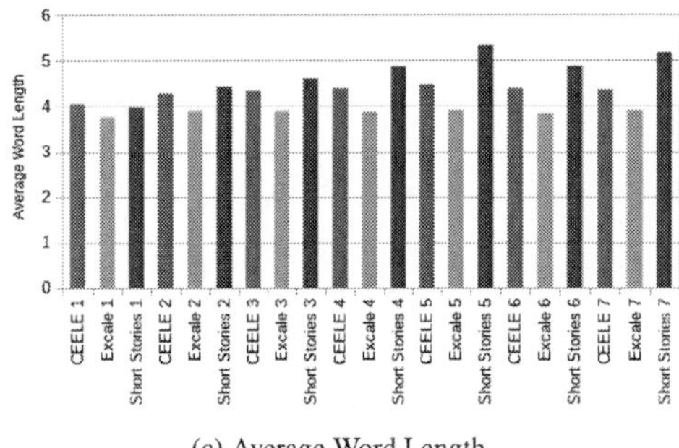

(c) Average Word Length

Figure 1: Word statistics for the three corpora.

a strict order between the averages per level is respected: Short Stories < EXCALE < CEELE.

The generally high number of words per sentence is explained by the lack of punctuation marks in the children corpora. In general, almost no instances of full stops nor semi-colons are to be found in the children's texts; they tended to write the entire document into a single phrase. In itself, this also affected how the documents themselves were classified by the Sigriszt-Pazos formula, as it takes into account the number of words per sentence to calculate the difficulty level. The latter would also help to explain why the correlation between this value and the readability level seems so strong.

Table 2 shows the Pearson (ρ) correlation values between the average number of words per sentence and the readability level for each corpus.

CORPUS	PEARSON CORRELATION (ρ)
CEELE	0.5456
EXCALE	0.9965
Short Stories	0.8958

Table 2: Correlation between the average number of words per sentence and readability level.

From Table 2 it can be observed that both ρ(Short Stories) and ρ(EXCALE) denote stronger correlation values between the aforementioned variables than ρ(CEELE).

Figures 1b and 1c show that there are no remarkable differences across the three corpora in terms of the average word length (between four and five characters) or the number of syllables per word (around two).

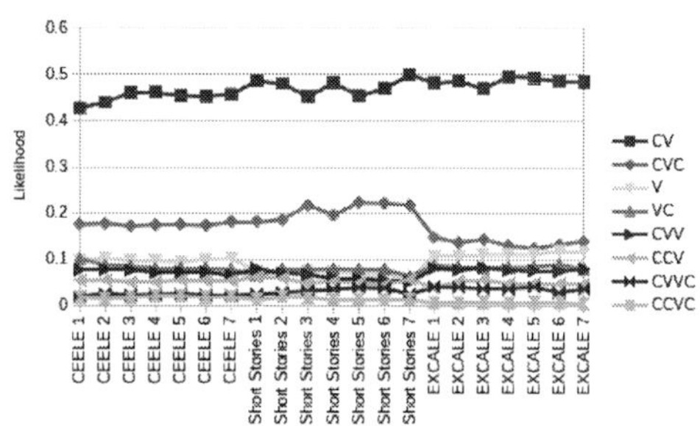

(a) Likelihood normalized to one of the 10 most common syllabic patterns occurring in the corpora.

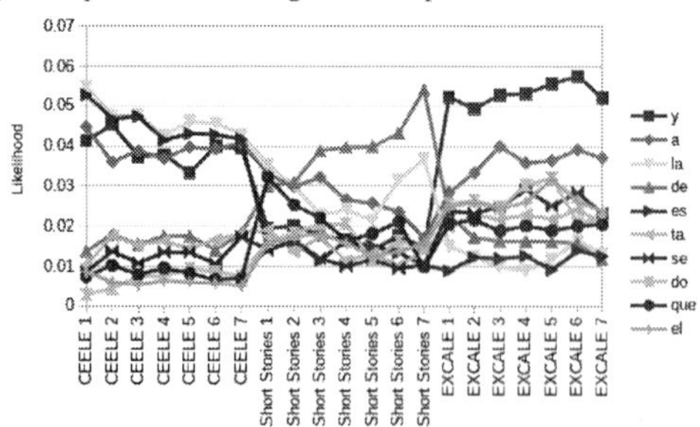

(b) Likelihood normalized to one of the 10 more common syllables in the corpora.

Figure 2: Likelihood of occurrence of syllabic patterns and syllables.

Figure 2 shows the likelihood of occurrence of the 10 most common syllabic patterns (2a) and syllables (2b) in each readability level of the three corpora. In particular, Figure 2a shows that syllabic patterns tend to occur with similar probability across every readability level and corpus.

Simple patterns such as CV and CVC are the most likely to appear with surprisingly regular frequency across corpora. In contrast, Figure 2b shows that the specific syllable realizations of the patterns display a higher level of variability: overall, the relative probabilities for even the 10 most common realizations fall below ten percent. This would indicate that proficient writing skills don't necessarily entail the use of complex syllabic patterns; rather, proficiency would lie on the specific vocabulary used by the speaker, maybe because it contains more words or because it is perceived to be more specialized.

Figure 3 shows the likelihoods of occurrence of the specific realizations for the most frequent patterns: CV (3a), CVC (3b) and V (3c).

Globally, the figure shows that the children in CEELE tend to favor specific syllables in some readability levels for the CV and CVC patterns, such as "mi" and "los" in levels 4 and 7. The EXCALE documents show a similar behavior with syllables "su" and "por". Also, Figure 3c shows that CEELE documents tend to disproportionately favor the use of "e", "u" and "i" as one-character syllables, contrasting with the lower variability shown by both the EXCALE and the control corpus. The results are discussed in the next section.

5   Discussion and Conclusions

The data shows that there might be several characteristics that could help to automatically measure written proficiency. According to the ideas of (Zamudio Mesa, 2008; Flores Hernández and Ramírez Hernández, 2012; Ferreiro and Teberosky, 1991), we expected that children between 7 and 12 years old would already have know how to use punctuation marks and blank spaces between words—particularly, full stops. Clearly, these capabilities had not been acquired by the children whose writing was reported in the corpora, causing very unexpected results.

The more notable deviation corresponds to the average number of words per sentence, which seems to be an strong indicator of literacy; in the CEELE documents, which are expected to show a lower literacy level than the remaining two, the number of average words per sentence explodes. As previously mentioned, the explanation for this is that the children did not use punctuation marks throughout the writings, causing the algorithm to perceive documents as containing only one

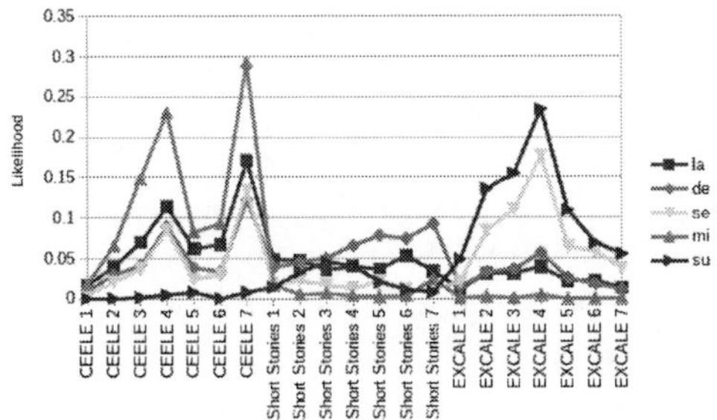

(a) Likelihoods normalized to one of the 5 most common CV realizations.

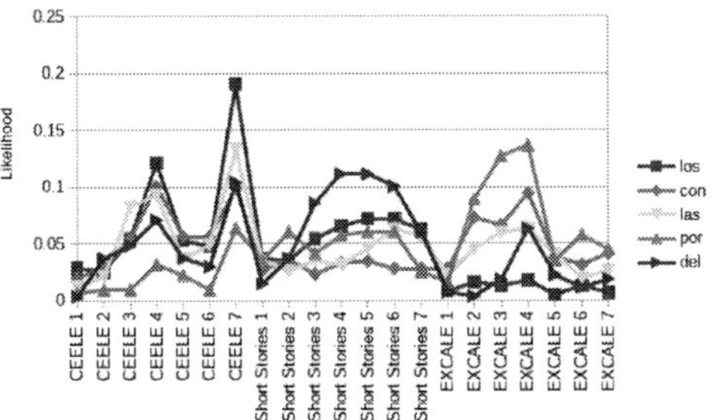

(b) Likelihoods normalized to one of the 5 most common CVC realizations.

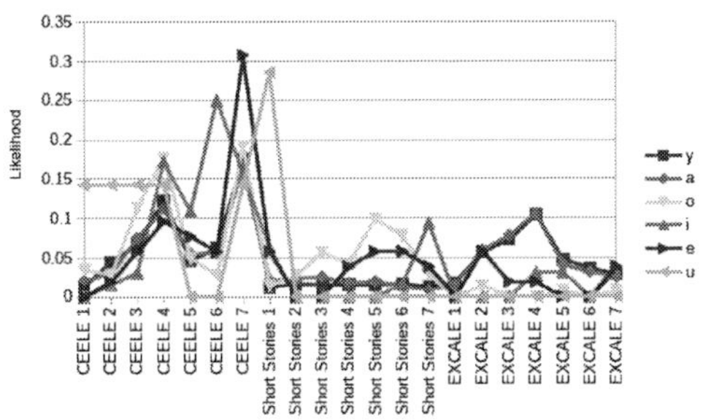

(c) Likelihoods normalized to one of the 6 most common V realizations.

Figure 3: Likelihoods of CV, CVC and V pattern realizations.

or two sentences. This happens even with the occurrence of unnaturally long words such as **"CuantosañostienescomoSellamaendondebibes"**, product of the erroneous use of whitespace; intuitively this should shorten sentences, however the overall average remained high. More analyses are needed to observe how this variable correlates with others, such as the use of punctuation marks, which might be what is pulling the averages up.

Regarding the use of syllables, the corpora presented instances of invalid Spanish syllabic patterns like strings of consonants without vowels. These irregularities could credibly be indicators of a lack of proficiency; however, the observed prob-

abilities are so low (near zero) that few conclusions can be obtained, as they could correspond to transcription mistakes or else.

For the rest of the patterns, their likelihoods of occurrence remain consistent across all levels on every corpora, meaning that their realizations might give more meaningful information, as explained by the hypothesis of a specialized or more diverse vocabulary. In this regard, Figure 3 provides some evidence that the overuse of simple words and common syllables might be indicative of lack of writing skills. Thus, further exploration is needed on larger corpora, covering written productions by persons with different literacy levels and even learners of Spanish as L2.

Results show that Sigriszt-Pazos readability formula tests productions for expert Spanish writers. Although it measures the complexity of texts written especifically for children, such texts are carefully composed for adapting to the capablities of the readers. However, a child does not have an idea of the parameters that should be used in order to make the text easier. Is it clear, then, that student's productions need different parameters witch calculate their writing proficiency.

In general, more experiments are needed to reach stronger conclusions. Future work will explore how syllabic patterns and syllables combine inside of words, and how this correlates with writing proficiency. This might provide more useful information about the literacy level of the students, rather than just looking at single syllables as it has been done until now.

Finally, it is expected that these studies will lead to the creation of *writability* formulas, which will measure not how readable a text can be, but how difficult it is to write. Moreover, we suggest the creation of a method to measure students' writing skills based on these formulas.

References

Jason Anthony and Christopher J Lonigan. 2004. The nature of phonological awareness: Converging evidence from four studies of preschool and early grade school children. *Journal of educational psychology*, 96(1):43.

Alfredo Ardila and Mónica Rosselli. 2014. Spanish and the characteristics of acquired disorders in reading and writing. *Estudios de Psicología*, 35(3):502–518.

Glenda L Bissex. 1980. *GNYS AT WRK: A child learns to write and read*. Harvard University Press.

Judith A Bowey. 2002. Reflections on onset-rime and phoneme sensitivity as predictors of beginning word reading. *Journal of Experimental Child Psychology*, 82(1):29–40.

Lynette Bradley. 1988. Rhyme recognition and reading and spelling in young children.

Angela Casillas and Edurne Goikoetxea. 2007. Syllable, onset-rhyme, and phoneme as predictors of early reading and spelling. *Infancia y Aprendizaje*, 30(2):245–259.

Sylvia Defior and Pio Tudela. 1994. Effect of phonological training on reading and writing acquisition. *Reading and Writing*, 6(3):299–320.

Emilia Ferreiro and Ana Teberosky. 1991. *Los sistemas de escritura en el desarrollo del niño*. siglo XXI.

Marina Ferroni, Beatriz Diuk, and Milagros Mena. 2016. Acquisition of orthographic knowledge: orthographic representations and context sensitive rules. *Psicología desde el Caribe*, 33(3):237–249.

Rudolph Flesch. 1948. A new readability yardstick. *Journal of applied psychology*, 32(3):221.

Ana Abigahil Flores Hernández and Esthela Ramírez Hernández. 2012. Jakobsons universalist theory and order of acquisition of consonants in mexican spanish: A case study.

Linda Flower and John R Hayes. 1981. A cognitive process theory of writing. *College composition and communication*, 32(4):365–387.

C Michael Levy and Sarah Ransdell. 2013. *The science of writing: Theories, methods, individual differences and applications*. Routledge.

Fredrick J McDonald Connor, Carol, Barry Fishman, Sarah Giuliani, Melissa Luck, Phyllis S Underwood, Aysegul Bayraktar, Elizabeth C Crowe, and Christopher Schatschneider. 2011. Testing the impact of child characteristics instruction interactions on third graders' reading comprehension by differentiating literacy instruction. *Reading Research Quarterly*, 46(3):189–221.

Lise Menn and Nan Bernstein Ratner. 1999. *Methods for studying language production*. Psychology Press.

Francisco Szigriszt Pazos. 1993. *Sistemas predictivos de legibilidad del mensaje escrito: fórmula de perspicuidad*. Universidad Complutense de Madrid, Servicio de Reprografía.

Jean Piaget. 1971. The theory of stages in cognitive development.

Barbara Rogoff. 1984. *Children's learning in the" zone of proximal development"*. 23. Jossey-Bass Inc Pub.

Celia Zamudio Mesa. 2008. Influencia de la escritura alfabética en la segmentación de sonidos vocálicos y consonánticos. *Lectura y vida*, pages 10–21.

Celia Zamudio Mesa. 2016. Evaluación del corpus excale de escritura.

Assessment of an Index for Measuring Pronunciation Difficulty

Katsunori Kotani
Kansai Gaidai University
`kkotani@kansaigaidai.ac.jp`

Takehiko Yoshimi
Ryukoku University
`yoshimi@rins.ryukoku.ac.jp`

Abstract

This study assesses an index for measuring the pronunciation difficulty of sentences (henceforth, pronounceability) based on the normalized edit distance from a reference sentence to a transcription of learners' pronunciation. Pronounceability should be examined when language teachers use a computer-assisted language learning system for pronunciation learning to maintain the motivation of learners. However, unlike the evaluation of learners' pronunciation performance, previous research did not focus on pronounceability not only for English but also for Asian languages. This study found that the normalized edit distance was reliable but not valid. The lack of validity appeared to be because of an English test used for determining the proficiency of learners.

1 Introduction

Research on computer-assisted language learning (CALL) has been carried out for learning the pronunciation of European languages as a foreign language such as English (Witt & Young 2002, Mak et al. 2004, Ai & Xu 2015, Liu & Hung 2016) and Swedish (Koniaris 2014). CALL research on Asian languages has considered Japanese as a foreign language (Hirata 2004) and Chinese as a foreign language (Zhao et al. 2012). The primary goal of CALL systems for the learning of foreign language pronunciation is to resolve interference from the first language of learners. For instance, a CALL system can analyze the speech in which a learner reads English sentences aloud and presents pronunciation errors that a learner must read aloud again for reducing the errors.

Even though the methods of evaluating learners' pronunciation performance have received considerable attention in previous research, the pronunciation difficulty of sentences (henceforth, pronounceability) has not been examined extensively. Given that readability and the difficulty of listening influence learners' motivation and outcomes (Hwang 2005, Lai 2015, Yoon et al. 2016), we consider that CALL for pronunciation learning should consider pronounceability in evaluating learners' pronunciation.

Pronounceability can be represented as the phonetic edit distance from reference pronunciation to a learner's expected pronunciation based on the proficiency. Phonetic edit distance can be measured using a modified version of the Levenshtein edit distance (Wieling et al. 2014) or a deep-neural-network-based classifier (Li et al. 2016).

This study measured normalized edit distance (NED) using the orthographical transcription of learners' pronunciation of reference sentences. An advantage of the NED based on orthographic transcription is the availability of data. This is because language teachers can obtain orthographical transcription without being trained for phonetic transcription.

This study measures pronounceability using multiple regression analysis considering orthographic NED as a dependent variable and the features of a sentence and a learner as independent variables. First, a corpus for multiple regression analysis is developed. This corpus includes the data for NED and the proficiency data in a score-based scale of Test of English for International Communication (TOEIC). TOEIC is a widely used English test in Asian countries, and its test score ranges from 10 to 990. In previous research (Grahma et al. 2015, Delais-Roussarie 2015, Gósy et al. 2015), proficiency was demonstrated using a point-scale such as the Common European Framework of Reference for Languages (six levels from A1 to C2).

This study assessed our phonetic learner corpus data by answering the following research questions:

Proceedings of the 5th Workshop on Natural Language Processing Techniques for Educational Applications, pages 119–124
Melbourne, Australia, July 19, 2018. ©2018 Association for Computational Linguistics

- How stable is NED as a pronounceability index?

- To what extent does NED classify learners depending on their proficiency?

- How strongly does NED correlate with a learner's proficiency?

- How accurately is NED measurable based on linguistic and learner features for pronounceability measurement?

2 Compilation of Phonetic Learner Corpus

2.1 Collection of Pronunciation Data

Our phonetic learner corpus was compiled by recording pronunciation data for English texts that learners read aloud sentence by sentence. In addition, after reading a sentence aloud, learners subjectively determined the pronounceability of sentences on a five-point Likert scale (1: easy; 2: somewhat easy; 3: average; 4: somewhat difficult; 5: difficult) (henceforth, SBJ).

The texts for reading aloud (the title of Text I is the North Wind and the Sun and that of Text II is the Boy who Cried Wolf) were selected from the texts distributed by the International Phonetic Association (International Phonetic Association 1999). Even though these texts contain only 15 sentences, they cover the basic sounds of English (International Phonetic Association 1999, Deterding 2006). This enables us to analyze which types of English sounds influence learners' pronunciation. Deterding (2006) reported that Text I failed to cover certain sounds, such as initial and medial /z/ and syllable-initial /θ/, and then developed material that covered the English pronunciation for these sounds by rewriting a well-known fable by Aesop (Text II).

The corpus data were compiled from 50 learners of English as a foreign language at university (28 males, 22 females; mean age: 20.8 years (standard deviation, SD, 1.3)). The learners were compensated for their participation. In our sample, the mean TOEIC score was 607.7 (SD, 186.2). The minimum and maximum scores were 295 and 900, respectively.

2.2 Annotation of Pronunciation Data

Our phonetic learner corpus includes NED, the linguistic features of sentences, and learner features.

NED was derived as the Levenshtein edit distance normalized by sentence length. It reflected the differences from the reference sentences to the transcription of learners' pronunciation due to the substitution, deletion, or insertion of letters. Before measuring the edit distance, symbols such as commas and periods were deleted and expressions were uncapitalized in the transcription and reference data.

The pronunciation was manually transcribed by a transcriber who was a native speaker of English and trained to replicate interviews and meetings but was unaccustomed to the English spoken by learners. The transcriber examined the texts before starting the transcription task. The transcriber was required to replicate learners' pronunciation without adding, deleting, and substituting any expressions for improving grammaticality and/or acceptability (except the addition of symbols such as commas and periods).

Linguistic features were automatically derived from a sentence as follows: Sentence length was derived as the number of words in a sentence. Word length was derived as the number of syllables in a word. The number of multiple-syllable words in a sentence were derived by calculating $\sum_{i=1}^{N}(S_i - 1)$, where n was the number of words in a sentence, and S_i was the number of syllables in the i-th word (Fang 1966). This derivation eliminated the presence of single-syllable words. Word difficulty was derived as the rate of words not listed in a basic vocabulary list (Kiyokawa 1990) relative to the total number of words in a sentence. Table 1 summarizes the linguistic features of the texts that learners read aloud, i.e., text length and

	Text I	Text II
Text length (sentences)	5	10
Text length (words)	113	216
Sentence length (words)	22.6 (8.3)	21.6 (7.6)
Word length (syllables)	1.3 (0.1)	1.2 (0.1)
Multiple syllable word (syllables)	6.4 (2.8)	5.7 (3.0)
Word difficulty	0.3 (0.1)	0.2 (0.1)

Table 1: Linguistic features of the texts that learners read aloud.

the mean (standard deviation, *SD*) values of sentence length, word length, multiple-syllable words, and word difficulty.

Learner features were determined using the scores of TOEIC for the current or previous year. Even though TOEIC consists of listening and reading tests, it is strongly correlated with the Language Proficiency Interview, which is a well-established direct assessment of oral language proficiency developed by the Foreign Service Institute of the U.S. Department of State (Chauncey Group International 1998).

3 Properties of Phonetic Learner Corpus

Our phonetic learner corpus was compiled using the method described in Section 2, and this corpus included 750 instances (15 sentences read aloud by 50 learners). Table 2 shows the descriptive statistics for NED and SBJ in the phonetic learner corpus.

	NED	SBJ
Minimum	0.01	1
Maximum	0.78	5
Mean	0.15	3.03
SD	0.22	0.91
n	750	750

Table 2: Descriptive statistics of NED and SBJ.

The relative frequency distributions of NED and SBJ, in which NED was classified into five levels based on SBJ, are shown in Figure 1. The distributions are dissimilar, as the peak of NED appears at pronounceability level 2 ("somewhat easy") while that of SBJ appears at pronounceability level 3 ("average"). If NED appropriately accounts for learners' pronounceability, learners

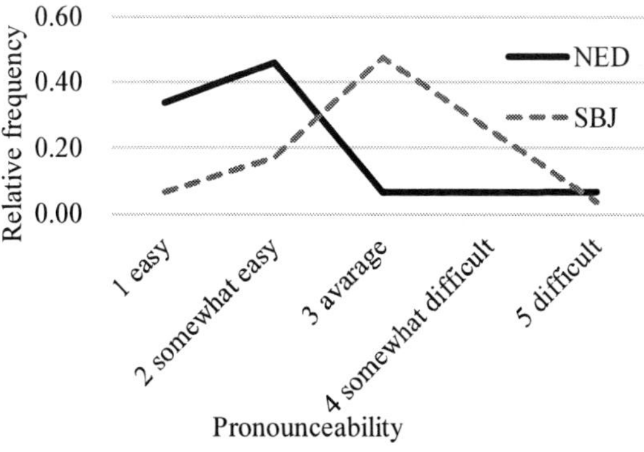

Figure 1: Distribution of NED and SBJ.

appear to overvalue pronounceability. On the contrary, if NED fails to explain pronounceability, learners appear to undervalue pronounceability. This provides a solution for the improvement of NED.

4 Assessment of NED as a Pronounceability Index

In Sections 4.1, 4.2, and 4.3, research questions 1–3 are assessed using the classical test theory (Brown 1996). The fourth question is answered in Section 4.4.

4.1 Reliability of NED

The reliability of NED was examined through internal consistency in terms of Cronbach's α (Cronbach 1970). Internal consistency refers to whether NED demonstrates similar results for sentences with similar pronounceability. Cronbach's α is a reliability coefficient defined by the following equation: $\alpha = \frac{k}{k-1}\left(1 - \sum_{i=1}^{k} \frac{S_i^2}{S_T^2}\right)$, where k is the number of items (sentences in this study), S_i^2 is the variance associated with item i, and S_T^2 is the variance associated with the sum of all k item values. Cronbach's α reliability coefficient ranges from 0 (absence of reliability) to 1 (absolute reliability), and empirical satisfaction is achieved with values above 0.8.

As reliability depends on the number of items, the reliability coefficients were derived individually for each text (Text I containing 5 sentences and Text II containing 10 sentences) and jointly for both texts. The reliability coefficients of NED and SBJ are shown in Table 3.

	NED	SBJ
Text I	0.72	0.80
Text II	0.82	0.91
Text I & II	0.86	0.92

Table 3: Cronbach α coefficient of NED and SBJ.

The reliability coefficient of NED exceeded the value required for empirical satisfaction ($\alpha = 0.8$) in Text II and Texts I & II. Hence, NED is partially reliable as a pronounceability index. However, NED demonstrated lower reliability compared to SBJ. This suggests that NED should be improved through modification.

4.2 Construct Validity of NED

Construct validity was examined from the viewpoint of distinctiveness. If NED appropriately reflects learners' proficiency, NED should demonstrate a statistically significant difference ($p < 0.01$) among learners at different proficiency levels. Our phonetic learner corpus data were classified into three levels based on the TOEIC scores below 490 (beginner level) ($n = 240$), below 730 (intermediate level) ($n = 240$), and 730 or above (advanced level) ($n = 270$).

Table 4 shows the mean (SD) values of NED and SBJ for the three levels. The distinctiveness of NED was investigated using ANOVA. ANOVA showed statistically significant differences between the three levels of learners for SBJ (F (2, 747) = 10.13, $p < 0.01$) but not for NED (F (2, 747) = 0.55, $p > 0.01$). NED failed to demonstrate construct validity depending on TOEIC-based proficiency.

	Beginner level	Intermediate level	Advanced level
NED	0.13 (0.21)	0.12 (0.22)	0.11 (0.21)
SBJ	3.15 (0.95)	3.13 (0.92)	2.83(0.83)

Table 4: Descriptive statistics of NED and SBJ

4.3 Criterion-related Validity of NED

Criterion-related validity was examined from the viewpoint of the correlation with learners' proficiency in terms of TOEIC scores. NED should reflect learners' proficiency because pronounceability should depend on learners' proficiency. Then, the correlation between NED and TOEIC scores and between SBJ and TOEIC scores was examined.

NED exhibited weaker correlation with TOEIC scores ($r = -0.04$) compared to SBJ ($r = -0.20$). Owing to this, NED failed to demonstrate criterion-related validity depending on TOEIC-based proficiency.

4.4 Pronounceability Measurement

Pronounceability was measured through multiple regression analysis. NED was the dependent variable, and the linguistic and learner features described in Section 2 were the independent variables. However, multiple-syllable words were not used owing to the variance inflation factor ($VIF = 12.3$) (Kutner et al. 2002). A significant regression equation was found (F (4, 745) = 124.15, $p < 0.01$) with an adjusted squared correlation coefficient (R^2) of 0.40, which indicates that the equation measured approximately 40% of the pronounceability.

The contribution of linguistic and learner features can be observed using standardized particle regression coefficients; the contribution increases with the absolute value of the coefficients. The standardized partial regression coefficients are summarized in Table 5. Significant contribution is observed in word difficulty but not in the other features. This result contradicts the finding of previous research, which reported the significant contribution of sentence length and word length in other modes such as readability (Crossley et al. 2017) and listening difficulty (Messerklinger 2006).

Variable	Coefficient	$*p < 0.01$
Sentence length	-0.07	
Word length	0.06	
Word difficulty	0.61*	
TOEIC score	-0.04	

Table 5: Standardized partial regression coefficients.

The pronounceability measurement method was examined n times ($n = 750$) using a leave-one-out cross validation test, considering one instance as test data and $n - 1$ instances as training data. The measured NED exhibited moderate correlation with the observed NED ($r = 0.63$). NED demonstrated a low coefficient of determination and low predictability.

5 Conclusion

This study assessed whether NED appropriately demonstrated pronounceability for learning the pronunciation of English as a foreign language. The assessment suggests that NED is reliable (Section 4.1) but not valid (Sections 4.2 and 4.3). The results of pronounceability measurement (Section 4.4) suggest that NED was appropriately explained by the word difficulty.

In future, we will work on the improvement of pronounceability measurement in English based on NED and investigate pronounceability measurement in Asian languages as a foreign language.

Acknowledgments

This work was supported by JSPS KAKENHI Grant Numbers, 22300299, 15H02940, 17K18679.

References

Renlong Ai and Feiyu Xu. 2015. A system demonstration of a framework for computer assisted pronunciation training. In *Proceedings of the ACL-IJCNLP 2015 System Demonstrations*. Association for Computational Linguistics and the Asian Federation of Natural Language Processing, pages 1–6. https://doi.org/10.3115/v1/P15-4001.

James Dean Brown. 1996. *Testing in Language Programs*. Prentice-Hall, Englewood Cliffs, NJ.

Chauncey Group International. 1998. *TOEIC Technical Manual*. Chauncey Group International, Princeton, NJ.

Lee Joseph Cronbach. 1970. *Essentials of Psychological Testing 3rd edition*. Harper & Row, New York.

Scott A. Crossley, Stephen Skalicky, Mihai Dascalu, Danielle S. McNamara, and Kristopher Kyle. 2017. Predicting text comprehension, processing, and familiarity in adult readers: New approaches to readability formulas. *Discourse Processes*, 54(5-6), pages 340–359. http://dx.doi.org/10.1080/0163853X.2017.1296264.

Elisabeth Delais-Roussarie, Fabián Santiago, and Hi-Yon Yoo. 2015. The extended COREIL corpus: First outcomes and methodological issues. In *Proceedings of Workshop on Phonetic Learner Corpora*. Individualized Feedback for Computer-Assisted Spoken Language Learning Project, pages 57–59.

Irving E. Fang. 1966. The "Easy listening formula." *Journal of Broadcasting* 11(1), pages 63–68. https://doi.org/10.1080/08838156609363529.

Mária Gósy, Dorottya Gyarmathy, and András Beke. 2015. The development of a Hungarian-English learner speech database and a related analysis of filled pauses. In *Proceedings of Workshop on Phonetic Learner Corpora*. Individualized Feedback for Computer-Assisted Spoken Language Learning Project, pages 61–63.

Calbert Graham. 2015. Phonetic and prosodic features in automated spoken language assessment. In *Proceedings of Workshop on Phonetic Learner Corpora*. Individualized Feedback for Computer-Assisted Spoken Language Learning Project, pages 37–40.

Yukari Hirata. 2004. Computer assisted pronunciation training for native English speakers learning Japanese pitch and durational contrasts. *Computer Assisted Language Learning* 17(3–4), pages 357–376. https://doi.org/10.1080/0958822042000319629.

Myung-Hee Hwang. 2005. How strategies are used to solve listening difficulties: Listening proficiency and text level effect. *English Teaching* 60(1), pages 207–226. https://doi.org/10.3968/7538.

International Phonetic Association. 1999. *Handbook of the International Phonetic Association: A Guide to the Use of the International Phonetic Alphabet*. Cambridge University Press, Cambridge, UK. https://doi.org/10.1017/S0952675700003894.

Hideo Kiyokawa. 1990. A formula for predicting listenability: the listenability of English language materials 2. *Wayo Women's University Language and Literature* 24, pages 57–74.

Christos Koniaris. 2014. An approach to measure pronunciation similiarity in second language learning using Radial Basis Function Kernel. In *Proceedings of the Third Workshop on NLP for Computer-assisted Language Learning*. The Fifth Swedish Language Technology Conference, pages 74–86.

Michael H. Kutner, Christopher J. Nachtsheim, John Neter, and William Li. 2002. *Applied Linear Statistical Models* (5th ed.), McGrawHill/Irwin, New York.

Degang Lai. 2015. A study on the influencing factors of online learners' learning motivation. *Higher Education of Social Science* 9(4), pages 26–30. https://doi.org/10.3968/7538.

Wei Li, Sabato Marco Siniscalchi, Nancy F. Chen, and Chin-Hui Lee. 2016. Improving non-native mispronunciation detection and enriching diagnostic feedback with DNN-based speech attribute modeling. In *Proceedings of 2016 IEEE International Conference on Acoustics, Speech and Signal Processing*. The Institute of Electrical and Electronics Engineers, pages 6135–6139. https://doi.org/10.1109/ICASSP.2016.7472856.

Sze-Chu Liu and Po-Yi Hung. 2016. Teaching pronunciation with computer assisted pronunciation instruction in a technological university. *Universal Journal of Educational Research* 4(9), pages 1939–1943. https://doi.org/10.1016/S0167-6393(99)00044-8.

Brian Mak, Manhung Siu, Mimi Ng, Yik-Cheung Tam, Yu-Chung Chan, Kin-Wah Chan, Ka-Yee Leung, Simon Ho, Fong-Ho Chong, Jimmy Wong, and Jacqueline Lo. 2004. PLASER: Pronunciation learning via automatic speech recognition. In *Proceedings of HLT-NAACL Workshop on Building Educational Applications using Natural Language Processing*. Association for Computational Linguistics, pages 1–8. https://doi.org/10.3115/1118894.1118898.

Josef Messerklinger. 2006. Listenability. *Center for English Language Education Journal* 14, pages 56–70.

Martijn Wieling, Jelke Bloem, Kaitlin Mignella, Mona Timmerneister, and John Nerbonne. 2014. Measuring foreign accent strength in English: Validating Levenshtein distance as a measure. *Language Dynamics and Change* 4, pages 253–269. https://doi.org/10.1163/22105832-00402001.

Silke Maren Witt and Steve Young. 2000. Phone-level pronunciation scoring and assessment for interactive language learning. *Speech Communication* 30(2–3), pages 95–108. https://doi.org/10.1016/S0167-6393(99)00044-8.

Su-Youn Yoon, Yeonsuk Cho, and Diane Napolitano. 2016. Spoken text difficulty estimation using linguistic features. In *Proceedings of the 11th Workshop on Innovative Use of NLP for Building Educational Applications*. Association for Computational Linguistics and the Asian Federation of Natural Language Processing, pages 1–6. https://doi.org/10.18653/v1/W16-0531.

Tongmu Zhao, Akemi Hoshino, Masayuki Suzuki, Nobuaki Minematsu, and Keikichi Hirose. 2012. Automatic Chinese pronunciation error detection using SVM trained with structural features. In *Proceedings of Spoken Language Technology Workshop*. The Institute of Electrical and Electronics Engineers, pages 473–478. https://doi.org/10.1109/SLT.2012.6424270.

A Short Answer Grading System in Chinese by Support Vector Approach

Shih-Hung Wu, Wen-Feng Shih
Dept. of CSIE, Chaoyang University of Technology
168, Jifeng E.Rd. Wufeng District,
Taichung, 41349, Taiwan (R.O.C)
shwu@cyut.edu.tw, wu0fu491@gmail.com

Abstract

In this paper, we report a short answer grading system in Chinese. We build a system based on standard machine learning approaches and test it with translated corpus from two publicly available corpus in English. The experiment results show similar results on two different corpus as in English.

1 Introduction

To assess the learning outcomes of students with tests in various question types and grading methods, short answer question is one type of test that can test the level of students' understanding of specific concepts in a subject domain. Since grading short answer question requires natural language understanding, the test was manually graded by teachers.

Although technically similar to automatic essay grading, automatic short answer grading is not as mature as automatic essay grading. (Burrows et al., 2015) gives a survey on how the automatic short answer grading is dealt by various researchers. The traditional approach is string matching, which could be very efficient but not very effective.

Early work relied on regular expression patterns which were manually extracted from reference answers (Mitchell et al., 2002). The patterns included keywords in the reference answers. Patterns could also be learnt from the reference answers (Ramachandran et al., 2015). (Sultan et al., 2016) adopted the simpler notion of semantic alignment to avoid explicitly generating complicated patterns.

Semantic matching had also been proposed in early work (Leacock and Chodorow, 2003). This approach was also used by many researchers (Mohler et al., 2009; Mohler et al., 2011; Heilman and Madnani, 2013) in supervised learning machine learning. A large set of similarity measures is defined as features for a supervised learning model. Features range from word level n-gram overlap to deeper semantic similarity measures based on dictionary and distributional methods.

The short-text grading in SemEval Semantic Textual Similarity (STS) task (Agirre et al., 2012; Agirre et al., 2013; Agirre et al., 2014; Agirre et al., 2015) drew the attention of many researchers and provided an evaluation platform. Since then, several systems have been proposed for short answer grading based on the semantic similarity with given reference answers (Mohler and Mihalcea, 2009; Mohler et al., 2011; Heilman and Madnani, 2013; Ramachandran et al., 2015). (Sultan et al., 2016) presented a simple short answer grading system for short answer in English. Given a question and its reference answers, a system measures the correctness of a student answer by calculating the similarity with the correct answers.

Comparing to the field in English, there are very little research projects on short answer grading in Chinese, and there is no publicly available corpus for short answering grading in Chinese.

In this paper we report how we build a system and how to test it with a translated corpus from two publicly available English corpus.

The system first extracts the text similarity features, and the features are used in a support vector model. In the first corpus, answers are graded from 0 to 5; we use support vector regression (SVR) model to learn the grading. In the second corpus, answers are graded as correct/incorrect; we use a support vector machine (SVM) classifier approach to deal with it. In the following sections, we will show the system architecture and experimental results.

Proceedings of the 5th Workshop on Natural Language Processing Techniques for Educational Applications, pages 125–129
Melbourne, Australia, July 19, 2018. ©2018 Association for Computational Linguistics

2 System Architecture

We adopt the previous works on the textual entailment (TE) as our prototype to tackle the short answer grading problem in Chinese. TE can be briefly defined as: "Given a pair of sentences (Student Answer, Reference answer), a program has to decide whether the information in Reference answer can be inferred by the Student answer". TE can be used in various applications, such as question answering system, information extraction, information retrieval, and machine translation. Once a system is able to decide whether T1 entails T2 or not, it can be regarded as an information filter to help users find useful information. Traditional approaches to TE are based on the semantic and syntactic similarities of the words in the sentences.

2.1 Support Vector Machines

Support vector machines (SVM) is a supervised machine learning classification algorithm, which can be used for classifying problem in n-dimension space. It is used widely in various natural language processing research projects and generally generates good results. Comparing to other classification algorithms, SVM algorithm usually has better result when the number of features is quite large and the data is sparse.

SVM uses $g(x) = w^T \emptyset(x) + b$ as the linear separation hyperplane, where w is the weight vector, b is the bias, $\emptyset(\cdot)$ is a set of high dimensional non-linear transformation function, where w and b is determined by training data that optimizes the following formulas:

$$\min \frac{1}{2} W^t W + C \sum_{i=1}^{N} \xi_i \qquad (1)$$

$$\text{s.t.} \begin{cases} y_i g(x_i) \geq 1 - \xi_i \\ \xi_i \geq 0, i = 1 \cdots N \end{cases}$$

where ξ_I is the slack variables, and C is the penalty coefficient for all the training samples (x_i, y_i).

2.2 Support Vector Regression

Support Vector Regression (SVR) is using the SVM algorithm on regression problem. The goal of SVM is to find the separation hyperplane, and the goal of SVR is to find the regression hyperplane. For the given training set:

$$\{(x_1, z_1), \dots, (x_1, z_1)\}$$

where $x_i \in R^n$ is a feature vector, and $z_i \in R^1$ is the target output. In order to find the hyperplane, two parameters C > 0, and ε > 0 must be given and the support vector regression can be defined:

$$\min_{w,b,\xi,\xi^*} \frac{1}{2} w^T w + C \sum_{i=1}^{l} \xi_i + \sum_{i=1}^{l} \xi_i^* \qquad (2)$$

$$\text{Subject to} \quad w^T \phi(x_i) + b - z_i \leq \epsilon + \xi_i,$$
$$z_i - w^T \phi(x_i) - b \leq \epsilon + \xi_i^*,$$
$$\xi_i, \xi_i^* \geq 0, i = 1, \dots, l$$

In our experiment, we use a free SVM toolkit, LIBSVM, to train the SVR model.[1] (Chang and Lin, 2011)

2.3 Feature extraction

In this section, we briefly introduce the features used in SVM, which are the same as those used in previous work. Table 1 shows the ten features used in the experiments. The first three features are the numbers of common terms both in T1 and T2. The next three features are the BLEU scores. The rest four features are the numbers and differ-

No	Feature
1	unigram_recall
2	unigram_precision
3	unigram_F_measure
4	log_bleu_recall
5	log_bleu_precision
6	log_bleu_F_measure
7	difference in sentence length (character)
8	absolute difference in sentence length (character)
9	difference in sentence length (term)
10	absolute difference in sentence length (term)

Table 1: Features used in the system

ences of sentence length of T1 and T2.

3 Data Sets

3.1 Data Sets in English

SciEntBank:
This data set was used in SemEval-2013 and available via github[2]. The data set assigns one of five labels to a student response: correct, partially

---

[1] https://www.csie.ntu.edu.tw/~cjlin/libsvm/

[2] https://github.com/leocomelli/score-freetext-answer/archive/master.zip

correct/incomplete, contradictory, irrelevant, and non-domain.

SciEntBank corpus in English contains 9,804 answers to 197 questions in 15 scientific domains. There is one reference answer for each question.

Data Structure Data Set:[3]

The data set is provided by (Mohler and Mihalcea, 2009), which is Data Structure questions and student responses graded by two judges. The data set assigns one of two labels to a student response: correct or incorrect. The questions are collected from ten assignments and two tests, and each one has a topic such as programming basics or sorting algorithms. A reference answer is also provided for each question. The interannotator agreement is 0.586 (Pearson's r) and .659 (RMSE on a 5-point scale). Average score of the two judges is used as the final gold score for each student answer.

3.2 Chinese Corpus Translation

Since there is no publicly available data set in Chinese, our experiments are conducted on the translated corpus. With the help of machine translation, we translate the two data set into Chinese and use them in our experiments. The sentences are then segmented into words by the Jieba[4] word segmentation toolkit. The quality of machine translation is not perfect, 12% of the sentences have to be corrected manually. The major error types are synonyms with improper usage in the context for both nouns and adjectives. There are also sentences with bad grammar.

4 Experiments

Since the SciEntBank data set has 5 way labelling, we use regression model to predict the scores of the student responses. And the Data Structure Data Set has 2 way labelling, we use the classification model to predict the scores of the student responses.

4.1 Metrics

For a regression result evaluation, we adopt the squared correlation coefficient and mean squared error. For a classification result evaluation, we adopt the accuracy.

Squared correlation coefficient, R^2

R^2 is the square of the Pearson correlation coefficient between the observed x and modeled (pre-

Features	Accuracy(%)
all features	59.569
only bleu	59.568

Table 3: Performance on the Chinse version of the SemEval-2013 datasets.

dicted) y data values of the score. Pearson's correlation coefficient is commonly represented by the letter r. So if we have one dataset $\{x_1,...,x_n\}$ containing n values and the prediction of the dataset $\{y_1,...,y_n\}$ containing n values, then that formula for r is:

$$r = \frac{\sum_{i=1}^{n}(x_i-\bar{x})(y_i-\bar{y})}{\sqrt{\sum_{i=1}^{n}(x_i-\bar{x})^2}\sqrt{\sum_{i=1}^{n}(y_i-\bar{y})^2}}$$

where n is the sample size, x_i is the sample indexed with i, y_i is the correspondent system prediction, and $\bar{x}$, $\bar{y}$ are the means of x_i, and y_i, respectively.

Root mean squared error (RMSE)

Features	R^2	RMSE
all features	0.083041	1.173427
only bleu	0.127850	1.102370

Table 2: Performance on the Chinse version of the Mohler et al. (2011) dataset with in-domain training.

RMSE is defined as

$$\text{RMSE} = \sqrt{\frac{1}{n}\sum_{i=1}^{n}(x_i - y_i)^2}$$

4.2 Results

Features	R^2	RMSE
all features	0.083041	1.173427
only bleu	0.127850	1.102370

Table 2 shows the regression results on the Chinese version of the Mohler et al. (2011) dataset. Where all features means the system uses all the features listed in Table 1, and only bleu means the system uses only the bleu features. The experiment result shows that more features can improve the performance.

Table 3 shows the classification result on the Chinese version of the SemEval-2013 dataset, where all features means the system uses all the features listed in Table 1, and only bleu means

---

[3] http://web.eecs.umich.edu/~mihalcea/downloads/ShortAnswerGrading_v1.0.tar.gz

[4] https://github.com/fxsjy/jieba

the system uses only the bleu features. In this experiment, the accuracy is almost the same. The result shows that more features do not improve the performance.

4.3 Discussions

Since the data sets are translated ones, it is not suitable to compare the results to the original ones. However, comparing to the result in English (Sultan et al., 2016), we find that the performance is similar.

5 Conclusion and Future Works

In this paper, we report a short answer grading system in Chinese based on a machine learning approach. We test it with translated corpus from two publicly available corpus in English. The experiment result shows that the results on the two different corpus is promising.

In the future, we will further develop the system with deep learning models. First at all, we will use distributed word embedding technique, such as word2vec, to improve the representation of the text. Then a recurrent neural network with long short term memory neuron is desired to replace the SVM model. Also curate corpus from native Chinese students is also important. Word segmentation is also important; instead of Jieba, we might use CKIP word segmentation service (Ma and Chen, 2003).

Most research projects require reference answers, and unsupervised automatic short answer grading is an interesting way to bypass the requirement (Adams et al., 2016)

6 Acknowledgment

This study is supported by the Ministry of Science under the grant numbers MOST106-2221-E-324-021-MY2.

References

Oliver Adams, Shourya Roy, Raghuram Krishnapuram. 2016. Distributed Vector Representations for Unsupervised Automatic Short Answer Grading, in Proceedings of The 3rd Workshop on Natural Language Processing Techniques for Educational Applications, Osaka, Japan.

Eneko Agirre, Daniel Cer, Mona Diab, and Aitor Gonzalez-Agirre. 2012. SemEval-2012 task 6: A Pilot on Semantic Textual Similarity. In SemEval.

Eneko Agirre, Daniel Cer, Mona Diab, Aitor Gonzalez-Agirre, and Weiwei Guo. 2013. *SEM 2013 Shared Task: Semantic Textual Similarity. In Second Joint Conference on Lexical and Computational Semantics (*SEM).

Eneko Agirre, Carmen Banea, Claire Cardie, Daniel Cer, Mona Diab, Aitor Gonzalez-Agirre, Weiwei Guo, Rada Mihalcea, German Rigau, and Janyce Wiebe. 2014. SemEval-2014 Task 10: Multilingual Semantic Textual Similarity. In SemEval.

Eneko Agirre, Carmen Banea, Claire Cardie, Daniel Cer, Mona Diab, Aitor Gonzalez-Agirre, Weiwei Guo, I˜nigo Lopez-Gazpio, Montse Maritxalar, Rada Mihalcea, German Rigau, Larraitz Uria, and Janyce Wiebe. 2015. SemEval-2015 Task 2: Semantic Textual Similarity, English, Spanish and Pilot on Interpretability. In SemEval.

Steven Burrows, Iryna Gurevych, and Benno Stein. 2015. The Eras and Trends of Automatic Short Answer Grading. International Journal of Artificial Intelligence in Education 25: 60. https://doi.org/10.1007/s40593-014-0026-8

Chih-Chung Chang and Chih-Jen Lin. 2011. LIBSVM : a library for support vector machines. ACM Transactions on Intelligent Systems and Technology, 2:27:1--27:27.

Michael Heilman and Nitin Madnani. 2013. ETS: Domain Adaptation and Stacking for Short Answer Scoring. In SemEval.

Claudia Leacock and Martin Chodorow. 2003. C-rater: Automated Scoring of Short-Answer Questions. Computers and the Humanities, 37(04).

Ma, Wei-Yun and Keh-Jiann Chen, 2003, "Introduction to CKIP Chinese Word Segmentation System for the First International Chinese Word Segmentation Bakeoff", Proceedings of ACL, Second SIGHAN Workshop on Chinese Language Processing, pp168-171.

Tom Mitchell, Terry Russell, Peter Broomhead, and Nicola Aldridge. 2002. Towards Robust Computerised Marking of Free-Text Responses. In Proceedings of the 6th International Computer Assisted Assessment (CAA) Conference.

Michael Mohler and Rada Mihalcea. 2009. Text-to-text Semantic Similarity for Automatic Short Answer Grading, in Proceedings of the European Chapter of the Association for Computational Linguistics (EACL 2009), Athens, Greece.

Michael Mohler, Razvan Bunescu, and Rada Mihalcea. 2011. Learning to Grade Short Answer Questions Using Semantic Similarity Measures and Dependency Graph Alignments. In ACL.

Lakshmi Ramachandran, Jian Cheng, and Peter Foltz. 2015. Identifying Patterns For Short Answer Scoring using Graph-based Lexico-Semantic Text Matching. In SemEval.

Md Arafat Sultan, Cristobal Salazar, and Tamara Sumner. 2016. Fast and Easy Short Answer Grading with High Accuracy. Proceedings of NAACL-HLT 2016, pages 1070–1075, San Diego, California, June 12-17, 2016.

From Fidelity to Fluency:
Natural Language Processing for Translator Training

Oi Yee Kwong

Department of Translation

The Chinese University of Hong Kong

`oykwong@arts.cuhk.edu.hk`

Abstract

This study explores the use of natural language processing techniques to enhance bilingual lexical access beyond simple equivalents, to enable translators to navigate along a wider cross-lingual lexical space and more examples showing different translation strategies, which is essential for them to learn to produce not only faithful but also fluent translations.

1 Introduction

Online dictionaries are important computer-aided tools for translators today (Bowker, 2015), while parallel corpora, despite their relative scarcity, have become useful resources for translation teaching (Olohan, 2004). The two kinds of reference provide what lexicographers like Atkins and Rundell (2008) would distinguish as context-free and context-sensitive translations respectively. The current work, as a prelude to a larger project, discusses the limitations of existing bilingual lexical resources and proposes natural language processing approaches for enhancing their navigational means for better usability in translator training and computer-aided translation.

Consider the translation of the English sentence "I still have <u>vivid</u> <u>memories</u> of that evening" into Chinese. The Online Cambridge English-Chinese Dictionary[1] shows two senses of "vivid", and quite straightforwardly the word can be disambiguated between the first sense (Vivid descriptions, memories, etc. produce very clear, powerful, and detailed images in the mind) and the second sense (very brightly coloured). Hence, notwithstanding the normal associative strengths between words, when "vivid" has been properly disambiguated, its associations with "colour", "bright",

etc. are down-weighted compared with its associations with "recollection", "memory", "clear", etc.

Once the decoding purpose is fulfilled, with the appropriate senses identified ("vivid" as above and "memory" as "something that you remember from the past"), one can then refer to the Chinese "equivalents" provided by the dictionary: 栩栩如生的, 鮮活的, and 生動的 for "vivid", and 記憶 and 回憶 for "memory". But the encoding purpose is not achieved yet, because none of the combinations between these lexical items could be considered satisfactory. They are only conceptually close to what we need, but not exactly appropriate for the context. It will only be helpful if we can depart from them and navigate further along their associations. The ability to do so is essentially what translator training would need to foreground, especially for novice translators to produce not only faithful but also fluent translations.

In the rest of this paper, we will first illustrate, in Section 2, the limitations of existing bilingual resources from the cognitive perspective, especially with reference to word associations. We will discuss in Section 3 the implications on the need for enhanced access of those resources to facilitate translator training. Section 4 outlines the natural language processing techniques employed in our ongoing work in this regard.

2 Word Association for Lexical Access

Word association has been deemed an important element in the mental lexicon (e.g. Collins and Loftus, 1975; Aitchison, 2003) as well as many lexical resources employed in a variety of natural language processing tasks (e.g. Fellbaum, 1998; Navigli and Ponzetto, 2012), and is believed to be able to provide useful navigational means to address the search problem in lexical access in dictionaries (Zock et al., 2010).

---

[1] http://dictionary.cambridge.org

Proceedings of the 5th Workshop on Natural Language Processing Techniques for Educational Applications, pages 130–134
Melbourne, Australia, July 19, 2018. ©2018 Association for Computational Linguistics

While there are various ways to model different associative relations from large corpora (e.g. Church and Hanks, 1990; Wettler and Rapp, 1993; Biemann et al., 2004; Kilgarriff et al., 2004; Hill et al., 2015), certain knots remain to be untied for them to be better utilised in language applications. First, corpus-based modelling of associations often focuses on specific relations (e.g. similarity, hierarchical relations, collocations, etc.), but in real-life lexical access, a combination of relations is often retrieved, as shown in human word association norms (e.g. Moss and Older, 1996). Moreover, some associations are bound to be more relevant than others in a given context, and they are readily activated regardless of their normal associative strengths. Second, for tasks requiring bilingual lexical access, care must be taken especially when onsidering the non-identical conceptual and linguistic structures across languages. Given the scarcity of complete equivalence and different linguistic properties, bilingual (or multilingual) word associations based entirely on bi- or multi-lingual concept lexicalisations (equivalents) may not be adequate for representing the cross-lingual word association patterns.

Existing bilingual dictionaries nevertheless generally presume the existence of lexical translation equivalents. Analysis of human association responses, as in Kwong (2013; 2016), suggests an alternative view. On the one hand, very different association types are found for different word classes (e.g. more taxonomic associations for nouns and more collocational associations for verbs), and across English and Chinese (e.g. more paradigmatic responses for English but clear preference for syntagmatic associations for Chinese). On the other hand, free associations may be modelled from large corpora, but the results vary considerably for individual words, some even counter-intuitive. Less frequent associations are normally disadvantaged, but humans readily retrieve them when prompted by a certain context. Hence, modelling of associations should be task-driven.

In addition, the equivalents given in bilingual lexicons are basically decontextualized, and they often do not appear in the example bilingual sentences in the dictionaries. Thus, an association found in the source language may not hold for the equivalents found in a target language. When using word associations in a bilingual context, other than associative strengths, cross-lingual correspondence of the associations is also worth investigation.

One conventional issue in psycholinguistics regarding models of bilingual lexicon is whether the conceptual stores for two languages are shared or separated (Keatley, 1992), and many studies suggest that the store is mostly shared (e.g. Kroll and Sunderman, 2003). Another issue is what is shared and what is separated in particular lexical concepts (Jarvis and Pavlenko, 2008). Pavlenko (2009) suggested, in contrast to the conclusions by many, that weaker connections failing to show a semantic priming effect may not necessarily indicate the lack of shared meaning, as conceptual equivalence can range from complete equivalence to partial and even non-equivalence, and the bilingual mental lexicon undergoes conceptual restructuring during language learning when cross-linguistic differences are encountered. Such cognitive aspects may not have been sufficiently modelled in static bilingual linguistic lexicons, especially between two very different languages like English and Chinese.

In the following we will compare the word associations obtained from various resources, and evaluate them against the information need in our earlier example situated in the translation context.

2.1 Word Association Norms

Table 1 shows the non-single responses in descending order of frequency in the University of South Florida (USF) Association Norms (Nelson et al., 1998), for the stimuli "vivid" and "memories". Apparently, should "vivid" and "memories" be associated, they are linked by "dream". In fact, "memory" was among the 33 single responses for "vivid", while "vivid" was not among any of the responses for "memories" or "memory".

vivid	memories	
clear	past	album
color	thoughts	cats
bright	happy	**good**
imagination	pictures	love
real	**dreams**	photos
alive	mind	tears
dream	**bad**	boyfriends
read	childhood	fond
unclear	friends	high school
natural	remember	recollections
strong	songs	sad

Table 1: Responses from USF Association Norms

The equivalents in the Online Cambridge Dictionary for "vivid" (栩栩如生(的), 鮮活(的), and

清晰 (clear)	印象 (impression)
可見 (visible)	深刻 (deep)
目標 (objective)	印象派 (impressionism)
指引 (guideline)	**良好 (good)**
模糊 (unclear)	**差 (bad)**
清楚 (clear)	人 (person)
影像 (image)	第一印象 (first impression)
明白 (understand)	派 (-ism)

Table 2: Responses from HKC Association Norms

生動(的)) and for "memory" (記憶 and 回憶) are not found in the Hong Kong Chinese (HKC) association norms (Kwong, 2013), so instead we look at the responses for two similar items, 清晰 (clear/vivid) and 印象 (impression/memory), respectively[2]. The non-single responses for these stimuli are shown in Table 2. For 清晰, the responses 清楚 (clear) and 模糊 (unclear) can be said to match the English responses for "vivid", but other than that the response patterns differ considerably across languages. The only response related to "memory" is 印象 which appeared only once. Similarly, the stimulus 印象 has its own cluster of associations and the most typical adjective associated with it (深刻) is not one expected in English for "memories", although more general ones like "good" and "bad" are found in common.

2.2 Dictionary Text

Based on the content words gathered from the definitions in the Online Cambridge English-Chinese Dictionary (Table 3), it seems that "vivid" and "memories" are closely associated, with the latter appearing in the definition of the former. But as mentioned above, one cannot really take the given Chinese equivalents and combine them for the translation. None of the combinations would sound idiomatic to a native Chinese speaker.

vivid	memory
descriptions	something
memories	remember
produce	past
clear	
powerful	
detailed	
images	
mind	

Table 3: Associations from Dictionary Definitions

[2]The former is among the equivalents for "vivid" in iCIBA (http://www.iciba.com/) and the latter is a near-synonym for 記憶 in a Chinese dictionary (http://dict.revised.moe.edu.tw).

2.3 Large Corpora

Making use of the Word Sketch function for selected *gramrel* collocations and the Thesaurus function in the Sketch Engine (Kilgarriff et al., 2004; Rychlý and Kilgarriff, 2007) on the ukWaC corpus and twWaC corpus, Tables 4 and 5 show the top 10 results for our target words.

vivid		memory	
modifies	thesaurus	modifier	thesaurus
recollection	compelling	fond	image
imagination	vibrant	loving	thought
evocation	evocative	childhood	knowledge
imagery	poignant	short-term	picture
depiction	colourful	distant	feeling
memory	imaginative	**vivid**	sense
portrayal	striking	collective	vision
dream	fascinating	episodic	experience
color	dramatic	flash	character
portrait	memorable	happy	idea

Table 4: Associations from ukWaC

清晰		回憶	
noun_right	thesaurus	adj_left	thesaurus
影像	清楚	美好	美好
照片	模糊	共同	記憶
概念	完整	老	童年
畫面	生動	許多	回想
聲音	深刻	深刻	時光
條理	流暢	難忘	快樂
輪廓	鮮明	浪漫	故事
認識	明確	永久	感動
文字	簡單	不愉快	往事
方向	呈現	永生	難忘

Table 5: Associations from twWaC

The following are noted from the results. First, in English, "vivid" and "memory" are strongly collocated, as the same collocation pops up from both directions (what does "vivid" modify / what modifies "memory"). But to a certain extent, whether an expected association can be extracted depends on individual corpora. For instance, with thesaurus function on ukWaC, "recollection" (synonym of "memory") is not even found, and the near-synonym "impression" ranked after the 450th place. Second, very little overlap is found between the English and Chinese associations extracted (even if based on partial equivalents). Arguably we started with partial equivalents anyway (but that is inevitable), and it shows that the word association patterns may not be the same across translation equivalents.

3   Implications

Realising that Adj-N constructions in English are not necessarily rendered as Adj-(的de)-N in Chinese, one must go beyond the context-free equivalents given in bilingual dictionaries to look for potential target expressions which may sometimes be found from the context-sensitive translations shown in the example sentences. While one might faithfully combine the bilingual lexicalisations of "vivid" and "memory" to give 生動/鮮活/逼真/清晰的記憶, other more idiomatic and fluent ways of expressing the same meaning in Chinese should be accessible for reference, including word-class shifts like 清楚記得/記得清清楚楚 (remember vividly), use of four-character expressions like 記憶猶新, as well as other appropriate expressions depending on context, such as 印象深刻 and 歷歷在目, to name a few examples.

The process of determining the appropriate target expression from the partial equivalents can sometimes be tricky especially considering the word formation, polysemy, and collocation patterns across the two languages (e.g. even for the same sense, "clear" appropriately corresponds to 清晰/清楚 when collocated with image/explanation respectively, and 清澈/透明 with river/glass respectively). The challenge is even more pronounced when no correspondence can be spotted from the examples, or for generally weakly associated words (e.g. strongendorsement). Thus, natural language processing techniques are adopted to enhance bilingual access beyond lexical equivalents for translators.

4   Work in Progress

It is not simply lexical transfer but a transfer of the whole relevant semantic space that is needed in translation. With this in mind, we are pursuing two routes using natural language processing approaches to enhance bilingual lexical access beyond simple translation equivalents, for reference in the translation process.

The first involves chaining up collocation information in a cross-lingual manner. Many have realised that there are often conceptual gaps across languages, but in addition to the bilingual correspondences of individual lexicalised concepts, it is necessary to consider the cross-lingual difference in terms of not only conceptual structure but also collocation patterns. As McKeown and Radev (2000) pointed out, a concept expressed by way of a collocation in one language may not have a corresponding collocation in another language.

Hence, ideally one should be able to start from a certain collocation or cluster of collocation in one language (e.g. vivid-memory) and, through some translation equivalents as seed words (e.g. memory-回憶), extend into the relevant semantic space in the other language (e.g. 往事/歷歷/印象/深刻) which is otherwise unretrievable from bilingual lexicons alone, as Figure 1 shows. For experiments, the Bilingual Word Sketch function in the Sketch Engine (Baisa et al., 2014) is taken as a starting point, upon which strategic application of word sense disambiguation, clustering, and word embedding techniques is tested for their effects on re-prioritising word associations with respect to specific collocations for a given context.

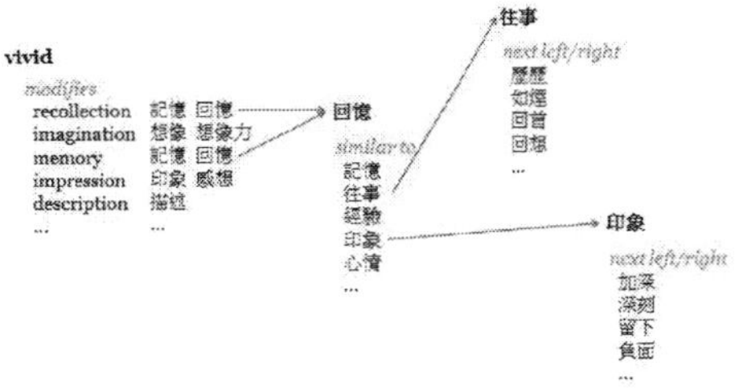

Figure 1: A Glimpse of a Cross-lingual Collocation Chain

The second makes use of neural machine translation (NMT) to obtain paraphrase sentence pairs. While most machine translation research focuses primarily on the fidelity of the target text, other possible and perhaps more fluent renditions are either ranked very low or completely ignored. They may exist in parallel corpora but with so low a frequency that often leaves NMT models to consider them noise. Thus we propose to identify paraphrase (that is, non-literal translation) cases from NMT with the attention mechanism (Bahdanau et al., 2014). While most work would pay attention to the more strongly correlated parts in the resulting word alignments which often indicate very faithful and literal translation, we assume that the less correlated parts would correspond to free yet more fluent translation, provided that the bilingual parallel corpus is of good quality. Preliminary experiments are underway, and there are certainly technical issues to overcome, including threshold setting, noise filtering, and properly making use of the less strongly aligned parts. Evaluation would also need to be considered.

Acknowledgements

The work described in this paper was fully supported by a grant from the Research Grants Council of the Hong Kong Special Administrative Region, China (Project No. CUHK 14616317).

References

J. Aitchison. 2003. *Words in the Mind: An Introduction to the Mental Lexicon.* Blackwell Publishers.

B.T.S. Atkins and M. Rundell. 2008. *The Oxford Guide to Practical Lexicography.* Oxford University Press.

D. Bahdanau, K. Cho, and Y. Bengio. 2014. Neural machine translation by jointly learning to align and translate. In *arXiv e-prints, abs/1409.0473.*

V. Baisa, M. Jakubíček, A. Kilgarriff, V. Kovář, and P. Rychlý. 2014. Bilingual Word Sketches: the translate button. In *Proceedings of the 16th EURALEX International Congress,* pages 505–513, Bolzano, Italy.

C. Biemann, S. Bordag, and U. Quasthoff. 2004. Automatic acquisition of paradigmatic relations using iterated co-occurrences. In *Proceedings of 4th International Conference on Language Resources and Evaluation (LREC 2004),* pages 967–970, Lisbon, Portugal.

L. Bowker. 2015. Computer-aided translation: Translator training. In S-W. Chan, editor, *The Routledge Encyclopedia of Translation Technology.* Routledge.

K.W. Church and P. Hanks. 1990. Word association norms, mutual information, and lexicography. *Computational Linguistics,* 16(1):22–29.

A.M. Collins and E.F. Loftus. 1975. A spreading-activation theory of semantic processing. *Psychological Review,* 82(6):407–428.

C. Fellbaum. 1998. *WordNet: An Electronic Lexical Database.* MIT Press.

F. Hill, R. Reichart, and A. Korhonen. 2015. Simlex-999: Evaluating semantic models with (genuine) similarity estimation. *Computational Linguistics,* 41(4):665–695.

S. Jarvis and A. Pavlenko. 2008. *Crosslinguistic Influence in Language and Cognition.* Routledge, New York.

C. Keatley. 1992. History of bilingualism research in cognitive psychology. In R. Harris, editor, *Cognitive Processing in Bilinguals,* pages 15–49. North-Holland, Amsterdam.

A. Kilgarriff, P. Rychlý, P. Smrz, and D.Tugwell. 2004. The Sketch Engine. In *Proceedings of EURALEX 2004,* Lorient, France.

J. Kroll and G. Sunderman. 2003. Cognitive processes in second language learners and bilinguals: The development of lexical and conceptual representations. In C. Doughty and M. Long, editors, *The Handbook of Second Language Acquisition,* pages 104–129. Blackwell, Malden, MA.

O.Y. Kwong. 2013. Exploring the Chinese mental lexicon with word association norms. In *Proceedings of the 27th Pacific Asia Conference on Language, Information and Computation (PACLIC 27),* pages 153–162, Taipei.

O.Y. Kwong. 2016. Strong associations can be weak: Some thoughts on cross-lingual word webs for translation. In *Proceedings of the 30th Pacific Asia Conference on Language, Information and Computation (PACLIC 30),* pages 249–257, Seoul, Korea.

K.R. McKeown and D.R. Radev. 2000. Collocations. In R. Dale, H. Moisl, and H. Somers, editors, *A Handbook of Natural Language Processing.* Marcel Dekker.

H. Moss and L. Older. 1996. *Birkbeck Word Association Norms.* Psychology Press, Hove, UK.

R. Navigli and S. Ponzetto. 2012. Babelnet: The automatic construction, evaluation and application of a wide-coverage multilingual semantic network. *Artificial Intelligence,* 193:217–250.

D.L. Nelson, C.L. McEvoy, and T.A. Schreiber. 1998. *The University of South Florida word association, rhyme, and word fragment norms.* http://w3.usf.edu/FreeAssociation/.

M. Olohan. 2004. *Introducing Corpora in Translation Studies.* Routledge.

A. Pavlenko. 2009. Conceptual representation in the bilingual lexicon and second language vocabulary learning. In A. Pavlenko, editor, *The Bilingual Mental Lexicon: Interdisciplinary Approaches,* pages 125–160. Multilingual Matters, Bristol, UK.

P. Rychlý and A. Kilgarriff. 2007. An efficient algorithm for building a distributional thesaurus (and other Sketch Engine developments). In *Proceedings of the 45th Annual Meeting of the ACL on Interactive Poster and Demonstration Sessions,* pages 41–44, Czech Republic.

M. Wettler and R. Rapp. 1993. Computation of word associations based on the co-occurrences of words in large corpora. In *Proceedings of the 1st Workshop on Very Large Corpora: Academic and Industrial Perspectives,* pages 84–93, Columbus, Ohio.

M. Zock, O. Ferret, and D. Schwab. 2010. Deliberate word access: an intuition, a roadmap and some preliminary empirical results. *International Journal of Speech Technology,* 13(4):201–218.

Countering Position Bias in Instructor Interventions in MOOC Discussion Forums

Muthu Kumar Chandrasekaran[1], Min-Yen Kan[1,2]
[1]Department of Computer Science, School of Computing, National University of Singapore
[2]Institute for Application of Learning Science and Educational Technology (ALSET)
National University of Singapore
{muthu.chandra, kanmy}@comp.nus.edu.sg

Abstract

We systematically confirm that instructors are strongly influenced by the user interface presentation of Massive Online Open Course (MOOC) discussion forums. In a large scale dataset, we conclusively show that instructor interventions exhibit strong position bias, as measured by the position where the thread appeared on the user interface at the time of intervention. We measure and remove this bias, enabling unbiased statistical modelling and evaluation. We show that our de-biased classifier improves predicting interventions over the state-of-the-art on courses with sufficient number of interventions by 8.2% in F_1 and 24.4% in recall on average.

1 Introduction

Massive Open Online Course (MOOC) platforms continue to evolve towards facilitating a better online learning experience. A key component of this effort is in platforms' ability to facilitate communication well, in part emulating the physical, face-to-face synchronous classroom experience. Despite debate on their effectiveness (Onah et al., 2014; Mak et al., 2010), MOOC discussion forums are still the primary communication medium for students to reach instructors.

In MOOCs, certain elements of traditional teaching are challenged by the scale of the class enabled by technology. The bandwidth of the MOOC instructor is especially strained given the high student-to-instructor ratio. Early research to address this gap proposed the problem of predicting instructor's intervention (Chaturvedi et al., 2014) in MOOC forums, as a means of aiding instructors in prioritizing their time towards productive intervention. That is, given historical account

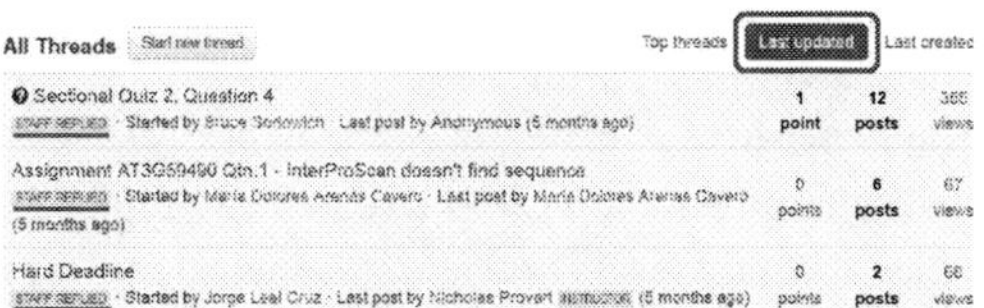

Figure 1: Coursera's forum user interface used by both instructors and students lists threads sorted by "last updated time" by default. "top threads" and "last created" are other available sort options.

of discussion threads that were intervened by instructors, can a model learn to predict future interventions?

However, in this and follow-on studies on the same problem (Chandrasekaran et al., 2015b), there is a tacit assumption that what instructors actually intervene on is an optimal pattern of intervention. An underlying issue remains: Is there a difference between what instructors should intervene on and what they actually intervene on? Might there be systematic biases that influence the decision to intervene? While suspected, to date there has been no systematic study that proves that such bias exists.

Our study definitively shows that the answer is **yes**: instructors are biased and show suboptimality in their intervention patterns. Specifically, we show that instructor interventions in MOOC forums are influenced by position bias, akin to users of web search engines whose clicks on search results are biased by the order in which the results are presented (Joachims et al., 2005). Instructors view the list of threads being discussed on MOOC forums most often sorted by their "last update time" such as in Figure 1. We find that the distribution of instructor interventions over the positions of the sorted list of threads – the *positional*

135

Proceedings of the 5th Workshop on Natural Language Processing Techniques for Educational Applications, pages 135–142
Melbourne, Australia, July 19, 2018. ©2018 Association for Computational Linguistics

rank – follows a log-normal distribution (see Figure 2). This implies that threads appearing at the top of the list are more likely to be intervened than those lower down. Given these defaults, observed ordering of items is time-dependent: the threads observed at one time can significantly differ between the different time points in which an instructor visits the forum. This effect, in turn, contributes to possible arbitrariness in an instructor's decision to intervene.

The impact of this biased intervention is two-fold. First, the training and evaluation of statistical models that use the biased intervention data as in the previous work, is inaccurate. Second, the biased intervention decision may cause other intervention-worthy threads that appear further down the list to not be intervened at all. While previous work such as (Wise et al., 2012) propose alternative discussion forum designs to address the second problem the first problem deserves attention since large volumes of MOOC research data (e.g., the Stanford MOOC posts dataset (Agrawal and Paepcke, 2014))) has been collected from existing interfaces. In this paper, we propose methods to measure the bias and systematically remove its effects from a statistical model that learns the instructor's intervention decision.

2 Preliminaries

Our corpus consists of discussion forum threads from 14 MOOC instances across different subject areas hosted by various universities across the world and taught by instructor teams of varying sizes on Coursera[1]. In partnership with Coursera and in line with its Terms of Service, we obtained the data for use in our academic research[2]. Table 1 shows our corpus' demographics.

A discussion thread consists of posts by students, instructors, teaching assistants (TA) and community teaching assistants (CTA). Following prior work, we consider threads that are initiated by a student and replied to at least once by an instructor, TA or a CTA as an intervened thread. Threads started by an instructor are omitted since they are not interventions in a student discussion. Our problem is to predict interventions at a thread level, that is, the first post an instructor makes on a thread. So, we truncate intervened threads

Course (–Iteration)	# of threads intervened	# of non–interventions	I. Ratio
BIOELEC TRICITY-002	187	62	3.01
BIOINFO METHODS1-001	129	105	1.23
CALC1-003	577	378	1.52
MATHTHINK-004	240	254	0.94
ML-005	883	1090	0.81
RPROG-003	359	738	0.49
SMAC-001	106	512	0.21
CASEBASED BIOSTAT-002	25	96	0.26
GAME THEORY2-001	22	100	0.22
MEDICAL NEURO-002	29	294	0.09
COMPILERS-004	15	601	0.02
MUSICPROD UCTION-006	2	228	0.01
COMPARCH-002	61	71	0.86
BIOSTATS-005	0	55	0.00
Total	**2635**	**4584**	

Table 1: Thread counts over the four main sub-forums of (*Errata*, *Exam*, *Lecture* and *Homework*) of each course iteration, with their intervention ratio (I. Ratio), defined as the ratio of # of intervened to non-intervened threads.

by removing posts after the first instructor post. We treat the problem of intervention prediction as a binary classification problem where intervened threads are positive samples and non-intervened threads are negative samples. We report the predictive performance of the classifier as F_1 score of the positive class.

We study threads gathered from Coursera sub-forums that are either self-identified or easily identifiable as contributing to the categories of *Technical Issues*, *Exam*, *Errata*, *Lecture* and *Homework* sub-forums. We omit others (e.g., *General*) as they are noisy with social discussions, or other reports on course logistics, irrelevant to the subject matter. To facilitate feature extraction we remove stopwords and replace occurrences of equations, URLs and video lecture timestamps with tokens <EQU>, <URL> and <TIMEREF>, respectively.

2.1 Baseline Classifier to Predict Interventions

We choose (Chandrasekaran et al., 2015b) as a state-of-the-art baseline system, hereafter referred to as EDM, for comparison. This system bettered the original (Chaturvedi et al., 2014) system in performance, and conducted work over a wider

<hr>

[1]Coursera is a commercial MOOC platform accessible at https://www.coursera.org

[2]However, we are unable to release the data for research without consent to release from the participating universities.

Id	Thread Title	Last Update Time
971	In-video quizzes cannot be submitted	2014-03-24 20:46
968	Submit button does not work in one ...	2014-03-24 19:36
967	There is a typo or error	2014-03-24 19:35
966	When I click on Quiz submit button ...	2014-03-24 19:33
963	Duplicate lecture content ...	2014-03-24 19:15
957	Broken hyperlink in email	2014-03-24 19:12
902	**Mistake in Q1 HW2**	2014-03-23 18:17

Table 2: An intervened thread (ID 971) which was the last updated thread in this snapshot, taken at the time of its intervention. The forum user interface lists threads sorted by "last updated time" by default, introducing a position bias in instructor interventions. Note that thread with ID 962 is relegated to the bottom is perhaps a more important thread needing intervention.

range of MOOC instances.

EDM consists of a maximum entropy classifier, a type of linear classifier that handles feature spaces typical in text data, with several content-based features extracted from student posts in each thread. The features include unigrams (several thousands of features) from student posts weighted by its $tf.idf$ score, the sub-forum type in which the thread appears, the length of the discussion thread in terms of number of posts, average length of posts, number of comments per post, discourse cues to the original post conveying affirmations, non-lexical references such as URLs to learner resources such as lecture materials, Wikipedia pages and timestamps in lecture video. The ratio of intervened (positive class) to non-intervened threads (negative class) is low (see Table 1). This class imbalance leads to poor prediction performance. To correct for this imbalance, they used class weights on examples, estimated as the ratio of intervened to non-intervened threads.

3 Measuring Position Bias in Interventions

To quantify the observed position bias on interventions we fit the data from a larger corpus of 61 different MOOCs, inclusive of the 14 MOOCs listed in Table 1 to different statistical distributions. For each intervened thread we obtain the snapshots of the list of threads ordered by their last modified time at the time of intervention. Using the snapshots, we count the number of interventions at each positional rank over all the courses, and fit this distribution of interventions over positional ranks against the power law and log-normal distri-

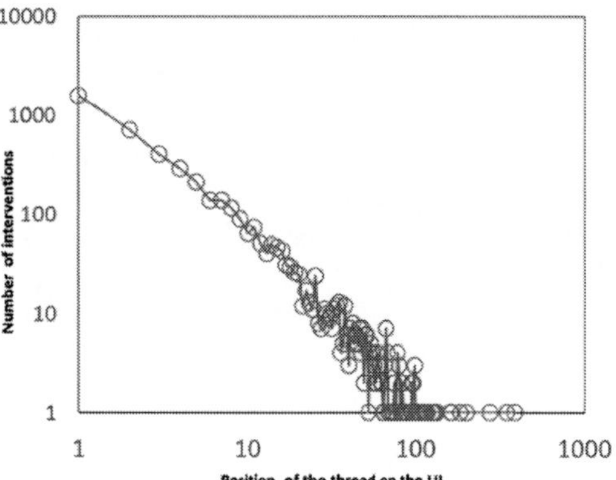

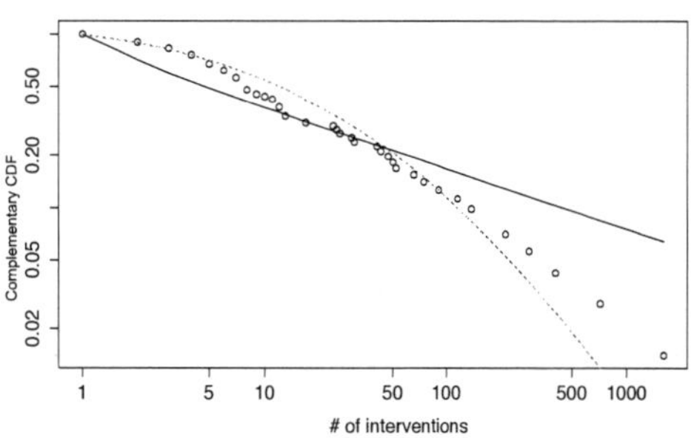

Figure 2: Log–log plots of (top) positional rank of threads vs. the # of interventions it received (bottom) the complementary cumulative distribution function (CCDFs) of the empirical distribution (circles) of interventions fit over a power law (grey line) and log–normal (red dashed line) distributions. Plots show interventions are clearly position biased and the log–normal (red dashed line) curve fits the distribution better.

butions.

We obtained the best fit for the log-normal distribution with parameters $\mu = 2.054; \sigma = 1.652$. (0.196) (0.139) Since our dataset is discrete we calculated the Kolmogorov-Smirnov (KS) goodness-of-fit statistic, $D = 0.143$, as prescribed by (D'Agostino and Stephens, 1986). Log-normal distributions are driven by multiplicative growth mechanism. It is typical in UI user log data where the attention (e.g., clicks) an object (e.g., search engine result) receives is proportional to the attention it already has. We did a model selection procedure to compare the goodness of fit of the log-normal distribution versus a power law distribution. We used the Likelihood ratio test (Clauset et al., 2009), where a positive sign on the log likelihood ratio with a $p < 0.1$ on the one-sided p-value rules out a better fit to the competing distribution. Our results indicate that the log-normal distribution is a significantly better fit than a power law distribution ($-3.36; p < 0.001$; see Figure 2). The parameters of the distribution, μ and σ and the goodness-of-fit statistics, together quantify the position bias on interventions.

The above analysis shows that position is strongly correlated with intervention. This is not surprising; if instructors intervene often or if they can predict periods when intervention might be warranted (say, when an assignment is due), we should expect high correlation. To show that the position correlation leads to unwanted bias, we need to demonstrate that instructors intervene suboptimally and favor intervening on results at the top at the cost of other, possibly more productive threads.

4 Does Position Bias Predict Intervention?

We ask if the signal from the position bias is strong enough to improve intervention prediction over the state-of-the-art (EDM). To test this hypothesis we model position bias as a simple, binary-valued feature set to 1 for a thread with a positional rank 1, and 0 otherwise. We augment this single feature to the feature set of EDM to create a new EDM+PB system. We compare the performance of EDM and EDM+PB individually over each of the 14 courses in Table 1. The models are trained on a random sample of 80% of the threads of a course and tested on the remaining 20%.

Table 3 shows the results from this experiment. On average, even this simple, position-augmented classifier improves EDM by a large margin of 13.7% in weighted macro average and 17.6% in simple macro average. CALC1-003 and BIOELECTRICITY-002 are notable exceptions where EDM+PB performs significantly worse than EDM. The intervention ratio of both these courses are above 1.0 (*cf* Table 1). We did not observe any decay in the numbers of interventions by position for these courses. Looking in depth, the instructors of these two courses may have monitored the forums continuously and tried to intervene on every thread, or may have also intervened without bias, based on the content.

The improvement on average and in the remaining courses is mainly due to increase in precision. This further indicates that the interventions are

Course	EDM			EDM+PB		
	P	R	F_1	P	R	F_1
BIOELEC TRICITY-002	76.9	60.6	**67.8**	100.0	24.2	39.0
CALC1-003	65.4	88.5	**75.2**	100.0	49.6	66.3
BIOINFOR METHODS1-001	35.3	26.1	30.0	100.0	56.5	**72.2**
MATHTHINK-004	36.8	17.1	23.3	100.0	48.8	**65.6**
ML-005	81.1	46.5	59.1	92.8	55.7	**69.6**
RPROG-003	47.2	50.0	48.6	67.3	51.5	**58.3**
SMAC-001	23.5	15.4	18.6	100.0	73.1	**84.4**
CASEBASED BIOSTAT-002	8.3	50.0	14.3	20.0	50.0	**28.6**
GAME THEORY2-001	25.0	14.3	18.2	100.0	57.1	**72.7**
MEDICAL NEURO-002	83.3	83.3	83.3	100.0	100.0	**100.0**
COMPILERS-004	33.3	50.0	40.0	33.3	50.0	40.0
COMPARCH-002	42.9	60.0	**50.0**	100.0	30.0	46.2
Macro Avg.	43.0	43.2	43.1	78.0	49.7	**60.7**

Table 3: Prediction performance of the position-augmented system EDM+PB showing significant improvement, over the baseline line EDM. Scores on musicproduction-006, biostats-005 are 0 due to low I. Ratio and are omitted.

strongly correlated with the position bias feature. Strikingly, on 8 out of the 14 courses, EDM+PB achieves a 100% precision. Examining the predictions in these courses, we found that the position bias feature was turned on in every correct intervention prediction, accounting for the improved performance.

5 De-biased Classifier

The EDM baseline does not account for the biased (non-) interventions. Due to the presence of position bias, thread instances thus vary in their *propensity* to be intervened. We need to counter the bias at the instance level. To implement this, we perform per-instance weighing with an appropriate classifier. We use SVM (Joachims, 1999)[3], with the default linear kernel. We compute the per instance weights, w_{inst}, of intervened (positive) and non-intervened (negative) threads from two implicit signals respectively. They are (i) instructor's propensity to intervene due to thread's positional rank (ii) instructor's confidence in discarding a thread from intervention.

Instance Weight Estimation. We estimate the propensity of a thread to be intervened from its observed positional rank. To discover an intervened thread's positional rank at its intervention time t_i,

---

[3]We use the SVM implementation SVM^{light} (`http://svmlight.joachims.org/`)

| | Biased | | | De-biased | | |
Course	P	R	F_1	P	R	F_1
ML-005	56.7	61.6	59.1	55.1	79.0	**64.9**
RPROG-003	67.5	33.8	45.1	36.2	75.0	**48.0**
CALC1-003	63.5	93.8	**75.7**	61.5	92.0	73.8
MATHTHINK-004	39.3	26.8	31.9	47.4	65.9	**55.1**
BIOELEC TRICITY-002	77.8	63.6	70.0	77.5	94.0	**84.9**
BIOINFOR METHODS1-001	40	34.8	37.2	51.61	69.6	**59.3**
COMPARCH-002	43.8	70.0	53.9	44.4	80.0	**57.1**
Macro Avg.	55.5	54.9	55.2	53.4	79.3	**63.4**

Table 4: Model performance of the de-biased classifier Vs. a biased (SVM with class weights) classifier. I. Ratio on these courses are between 0.49 and 3.01. Best performance is bolded.

we reconstruct the snapshot of the thread (see Figure 2) listing at t_i. The number of interventions at each positional rank over all interventions was counted and normalised into probabilities. We then use the propensity of a thread to be intervened given its positional rank, $p(i = 1|r)$ to derive its weight, $w_{inst} = 1 - p(i = 1|r)$. That is, we weigh interventions that happen on threads with high positional ranks (i.e., towards the bottom of the user interface) as more significant and higher than those that occur on low positional ranks (i.e., towards the top of the user interface).

We also weigh non-intervened threads. We count the number of times a thread is skipped in favour of a different thread to intervene (# of snapshots where a non-intervened thread had appeared).

The resultant de-biased classifier (denoted EDM+DB) uses the same feature set used by the state-of-the-art-baseline, EDM. We compare its performance against a biased classifier, a system with the same feature set as EDM but without any instance weights. The biased classifier is equivalent to the EDM baseline.

6   Results and Discussion

The EDM+DB classifier varies in its performance in removing bias across different courses. To better understand its varied improvement, we examine its performance through three related questions.

1. How well does the de-biased classifier perform? Our de-biased classifier improves over the biased classifier on courses with sufficient number of interventions by 8.2% in F_1 and 24.4% in recall on average (see Table 4). We observe that the performance of the de-biased classifier is sensitive to the number of interventions in the course. This is because the propensity score estimation (and the per-instance weights) are dependant on the number of times we can observe the state of the forum. De-biasing improves the F_1 on the high ratio courses in Table 4 (I. Ratio between 0.49 and 3.01), but does not improve F_1 performance for the 7 courses listed in Table 5, which all have low intervention ratios (less than 0.20).

2. Can the de-biased classifier recover interventions that are missed by the biased classifier? To be concrete, here we examine instances that were intervened by the instructor (positive), and identified correctly by our EDM+DB classifier (positive) but not by the biased classifier (negative). We randomly sampled 25 of 81 such instances that covered the courses in Table 3. The first author examined each of these threads and their instructor intervention using a taxonomy for interventions proposed by (Chandrasekaran et al., 2015a). This taxonomy grounded in pedagogy deems certain intervention types (e.g., justification request) are effectively made exclusively by instructors whereas certain other types (e.g., clarification) are optional for an instructor to make as peers can do them well enough. On this basis, the first author classified the 25 samples into those that warrant an instructor intervention and those that are optional. It was found that on 11 (44%) out of the 25 threads, instructor intervention was warranted. In the remaining 13, peers were actively answering the query, so we deemed these cases as optional for intervention. None of the threads were found to be solved or closed before the instructor intervened. We interpret this as a win for the EDM+DB classifier.

3. Can the de-biased classifier identify thread instances that were not intervened due to the position bias? Here, we examine instances that were not intervened by an instructor (negative), but were predicted to need intervention (positive) by EDM+DB. Again, we randomly sampled 25 of 42 such instances. As before we judged 9 (36%) instances as needing instructor intervention; *i.e.,* we believe that instructors should have intervened, even though they did not. Two such instances are shown in Fig. 3. Another 8 (32%) instances had peer answers, which we deem as being optional. The remaining 8 were either solved or had social chatter that did not require instructor intervention;

Example 1: Thread Title: There is a mistake at 6:00 in the Week 3 Regularization - Cost Function lecture
Original Poster:The error can be seen and heard in the Week 3, Regularization, Cost Function lecture at the 6 min mark (image attached). The newly added regularization summation term in pink is written as the summation over variable i, but theta is subscripted with j. The summation should be over variable j. Andrew Ng also orally refers to "summation over i" of that term, which again should be summation over j. The next slide shows a typeset version of the formula with the correct subscripts. Screenshot:
Example 2: Thread Title: PS6 #2
Original Poster: I missed this one so I thought I'd seek clarification. If a nonempty finite set X has n elements, then X has exactly 2^n distinct subsets. In the proof, the validation of $n = 1$ used the two subsets and itself. But I thought this was contrary to the statement "if a nonempty finite set"... Can someone help me understand this because set theory is definitely a weakness of mine.
(various student answers follow ...)
Original Poster: I understand the empty set is a subset of every set, and i agree that the the Theorem is true, but in the proof, when element a is added to each subset, isn't it also added to the emtpy set, which would then create the situation of not having an empty set now? Just confused about how the proof handles the empty set situation with the 'union U' procedure in the middle of the proof story.

Figure 3: Two threads that should have been intervened by instructors, where EDM+DB correctly identifies as needing intervention. Example 1 shows a thread that should be identified as an erratum report; Example 2 shows a thread where the original student poster expresses confusion that has not been clarified by any of the student answers.

but we note that such threads can easily be identified. Solved threads could be easily identified by attending to the last post made by the original poster, or the overall last post, both which typically provide the final answer to the original poster's query and solves the thread. In one instance, the solved status of the thread was later indicated in the (updated) title of the thread, which could be easily captured.

We interpret this as major win for the de-biased classifier, as it can reliably pick out threads that have been overlooked by instructors that need intervention, with the false negative cases largely easy to correct using simple heuristics.

7 Related Work on Modelling Position Bias

Position bias due to the user interface and its effects on user behaviour has been observed in many domains. Much research on modelling or debiasing position exist, mainly in the context of web search engines (Joachims et al., 2005; Pan et al., 2007; Craswell et al., 2008; Wang et al., 2016; Joachims et al., 2017) and recommendation systems (Schnabel et al., 2016; Liang et al., 2016). Joachims *et al.* (2005) and Pan *et al.* (2007) conducted eye-tracking experiments to confirm that users gaze at search results at top of the page and are, therefore, more likely to click them more often than the rest of the results. They observed that click behavior was biased, and does not always correlate with the relevance of the search result. Craswell *et al.* (2008) found that a cascade model – which posits that users examine results from top to bottom – best explained the bias. This examination pattern has been revisited by others (e.g., Liu *et al.* (2014)). In our study, we are interested in modeling user behavior and debiasing and correcting for it. Similar work has also been pioneered in the Web context. To model such observed user behaviour, improved ranking and click models were proposed. Joachims *et al.* (2005) proposed strategies to learn the relative preference between search results which are unbiased estimates of relevance. More recently, Schnabel *et al.* (2016) provided a generic framework to remove noise from biased training and evaluation data for recommender systems. Their algorithm learns disproportionately from items in recommendation systems according to their propensity to be clicked.

All the above works had access to reliable surrogate signals such as mouse cursor movements and clicks. In our MOOC scenario, we have only interventions (or lack of), recorded as instructor posts. Further, ranking frameworks assume a query to which retrieved items are listed in relevance order. In contrast, the default view of discussion forums are not ordered by relevance. While we cannot directly apply existing work to our setting, we draw from their inspiration and use the preferential judgement of the instructor to de-bias interventions.

8 Conclusion

We confirm the existence of *position bias* in instructor interventions in MOOC discussion forums and provide for a way to statistically quantify the bias. To enable accurate modelling and analysis we further proposed a de-biased classifier to counter for the bias and learn from biased instructor interventions. We show that the de-biased clas-

Course	Biased			De-biased		
	P	R	F_1	P	R	F_1
MEDICAL NEURO-002	100	83.33	**90.9**	66.7	33.3	44.4
SMAC-001	71.4	19.2	**30.3**	66.7	7.7	13.8
CASEBASED BIOSTAT-002	10.0	50.0	**16.7**	9.1	50.0	15.4
GAME THEORY2-001	50.0	14.3	**22.2**	16.7	14.3	15.4
Macro Avg.	33.1	**23.9**	**27.7**	22.7	15.0	18.1

Table 5: EDM+DB performance on low intervention (I. Ratio 0.0 to 0.2) courses compared against a SVM classifier with class weights, where each MOOC is evaluated individually. Best performance is bolded. Scores on compilers-004, musicproduction-006, biostats-005 are 0 due to low I.Ratio and are omitted.

sifier improves prediction when the training data consists of sufficient interventions. Importantly, the classifier can also identify clear cases where intervention is warranted but were overlooked by instructors.

We confirm earlier findings (Wise et al., 2012; Marbouti and Wise, 2016) on the bias induced by UI/UX. Since the effect of position bias, when extrapolated, can diminish students' learning gains by compromising the instructor's ability to judiciously intervene, we also call attention to the community to be mindful of the bias that UI/UX design can induce in MOOC platforms, intelligent tutoring systems and learning management systems, and to make design choices to mitigate this bias.

Acknowledgements

This research is funded in part by NUS Learning Innovation Fund – Technology grant #C-252-000-123-001, and by the Singapore National Research Foundation under its International Research Centre @ Singapore Funding Initiative and administered by the IDM Programme Office. We thank NUS Centre for Instructional Technology, Andreina Parisi-Amon from Coursera and Prof. Bernard Tan for helping us acquire legal permission to use Coursera's data for our academic research.

References

Akshay Agrawal and Andreas Paepcke. 2014. The stanford moocposts data set.

Muthu Chandrasekaran, Kiruthika Ragupathi, Min-Yen Kan, and Bernard Tan. 2015a. Towards feasible instructor intervention in mooc discussion forums. In *The Thirty Sixth International Conference on Information Systems (ICIS 2015), Fort Worth, TX, USA,* Research-in-Progress.

Muthu Kumar Chandrasekaran, Min-Yen Kan, Bernard CY Tan, and Kiruthika Ragupathi. 2015b. Learning instructor intervention from mooc forums: Early results and issues. In *Proc. of EDM*, pages 218–225. IEDM.

Snigdha Chaturvedi, Dan Goldwasser, and Hal Daumé III. 2014. Predicting instructor's intervention in mooc forums. In *Proc. of the ACL (1)*, pages 1501–1511. ACL.

Aaron Clauset, Cosma Rohilla Shalizi, and Mark EJ Newman. 2009. Power-law distributions in empirical data. *SIAM review*, 51(4):661–703.

Nick Craswell, Onno Zoeter, Michael Taylor, and Bill Ramsey. 2008. An experimental comparison of click position-bias models. In *Proc. of WSDM*, pages 87–94. ACM.

Ralph B D'Agostino and Michael A Stephens. 1986. Goodness-of-fit techniques. *Statistics: Textbooks and Monographs, New York: Dekker, 1986, edited by D'Agostino, Ralph B.; Stephens, Michael A.*, 1.

Thorsten Joachims. 1999. Svmlight: Support vector machine. *SVM-Light Support Vector Machine http://svmlight. joachims. org/, University of Dortmund*, 19(4).

Thorsten Joachims, Laura Granka, Bing Pan, Helene Hembrooke, and Geri Gay. 2005. Accurately interpreting clickthrough data as implicit feedback. In *Proc. of SIGIR*, pages 154–161. ACM.

Thorsten Joachims, Adith Swaminathan, and Tobias Schnabel. 2017. Unbiased learning-to-rank with biased feedback. In *Proc. of WSDM*, pages 781–789.

Dawen Liang, Laurent Charlin, James McInerney, and David M Blei. 2016. Modeling user exposure in recommendation. In *Proceedings of the 25th International Conference on World Wide Web*, pages 951–961. Proc. of WWW.

Yiqun Liu, Chao Wang, Ke Zhou, Jianyun Nie, Min Zhang, and Shaoping Ma. 2014. From skimming to reading: A two-stage examination model for web search. In *Proc. of CIKM*, pages 849–858. ACM.

Sui Mak, Roy Williams, and Jenny Mackness. 2010. Blogs and forums as communication and learning tools in a mooc.

Farshid Marbouti and Alyssa Friend Wise. 2016. Starburst: a new graphical interface to support purposeful attention to others posts in online discussions. *Educational Technology Research and Development*, 64(1):87–113.

Daniel FO Onah, Jane Sinclair, and Russell Boyatt. 2014. Exploring the use of MOOC discussion forums. In *Proc. of London International Conference on Education*, pages 1–4. LICE.

Bing Pan, Helene Hembrooke, Thorsten Joachims, Lori Lorigo, Geri Gay, and Laura Granka. 2007. In google we trust: Users' decisions on rank, position, and relevance. *Journal of Computer-Mediated Communication*, 12(3):801–823.

Tobias Schnabel, Adith Swaminathan, Ashudeep Singh, Navin Chandak, and Thorsten Joachims. 2016. Recommendations as Treatments: Debiasing Learning and Evaluation. In *Proc.of ICML*.

Xuanhui Wang, Michael Bendersky, Donald Metzler, and Marc Najork. 2016. Learning to rank with selection bias in personal search. In *Proc.of SIGIR*, pages 115–124. ACM.

Alyssa Friend Wise, Farshid Marbouti, Ying-Ting Hsiao, and Simone Hausknecht. 2012. A survey of factors contributing to learners'listening behaviors in asynchronous online discussions. *Journal of Educational Computing Research*, 47(4):461–480.

Measuring Beginner Friendliness of Japanese Web Pages explaining Academic Concepts by Integrating Neural Image Feature and Text Features

Hayato Shiokawa, Kota Kawaguchi, Bingcai Han, Takehito Utsuro
Graduate School of Systems and Information Engineering,
University of Tsukuba, Tsukuba, 305-8573, JAPAN

Yasuhide Kawada	**Masaharu Yoshioka**	**Noriko Kando**
Logworks Co., Ltd.	Hokkaido University	National Institute of Informatics
Tokyo, 151-0051, JAPAN	Sapporo, 060-0808, JAPAN	Tokyo, 101-8430, JAPAN

Abstract

Search engine is an important tool of modern academic study, but the results are lack of measurement of beginner friendliness. In order to improve the efficiency of using search engine for academic study, it is necessary to invent a technique of measuring the beginner friendliness of a Web page explaining academic concepts and to build an automatic measurement system. This paper studies how to integrate heterogeneous features such as a neural image feature generated from the image of the Web page by a variant of CNN (convolutional neural network) as well as text features extracted from the body text of the HTML file of the Web page. Integration is performed through the framework of the SVM classifier learning. Evaluation results show that heterogeneous features perform better than each individual type of features.

1 Introduction

Search engine is a quite important tool for obtaining fundamental as well as practical knowledge when it comes to the study of academic concepts. However, when we intend to find beginner friendly Web pages through search engine, it is necessary to compare many pages by manual work. The reason of ineffective manual comparison is that there is no systematic criterion on measuring beginner friendliness of Web pages in the results of search engine. Therefore, it comes up with us to invent a technique of measuring beginner friendliness of Web pages explaining academic concepts automatically, and finally build a whole assisting system for promoting academic study using search engine, which would improve the efficiency of Web learning.

More specifically, this paper proposes how to automatically measure beginner friendliness of Web pages explaining academic concepts. Before we formalize the framework of automatic measurement of beginner friendliness of Web pages explaining academic concepts, we examine how we manually measure beginner friendliness of those Web pages. The upper half of Figure 1 lists each individual factor that are supposed to be consulted when we judge the overall beginner friendliness of those Web pages. This paper, namely, considers that those individual factors include a) whether or not to contain definition of academic concepts, b) whether or not to contain formulas, c) whether or not to contain figures, d) whether or not to contain examples, e) beginner friendliness of the text of the Web page, and f) visual intelligibility of the Web page layout.

Figure 2(a) shows an example of beginner friendly Web page explaining an academic concept ("probability density function") of the field of statistics. The Web page of Figure 2(a) can be judged as beginner friendly since it has a visually intelligible layout of the title of the page, the formula, the text of its explanation, and its figure. The text of its explanation is simple but easy to understand, while it has a reference for further studies in the bottom of the page. Figure 2(b), on the other hand, illustrates typical cases of Web pages explaining academic concepts that are not beginner friendly. The case 1 contains a sufficient definition of the academic concept, a figure, a formula, and an example, while its layout is not visually intelligible and its explanation text is not easy to understand. The case 2 is an opposite case, which has a visually intelligible layout as well as the explanation text which is easy to understand, while it lacks a figure nor an example, and having an insufficient definition of the academic concept.

Proceedings of the 5th Workshop on Natural Language Processing Techniques for Educational Applications, pages 143–151
Melbourne, Australia, July 19, 2018. ©2018 Association for Computational Linguistics

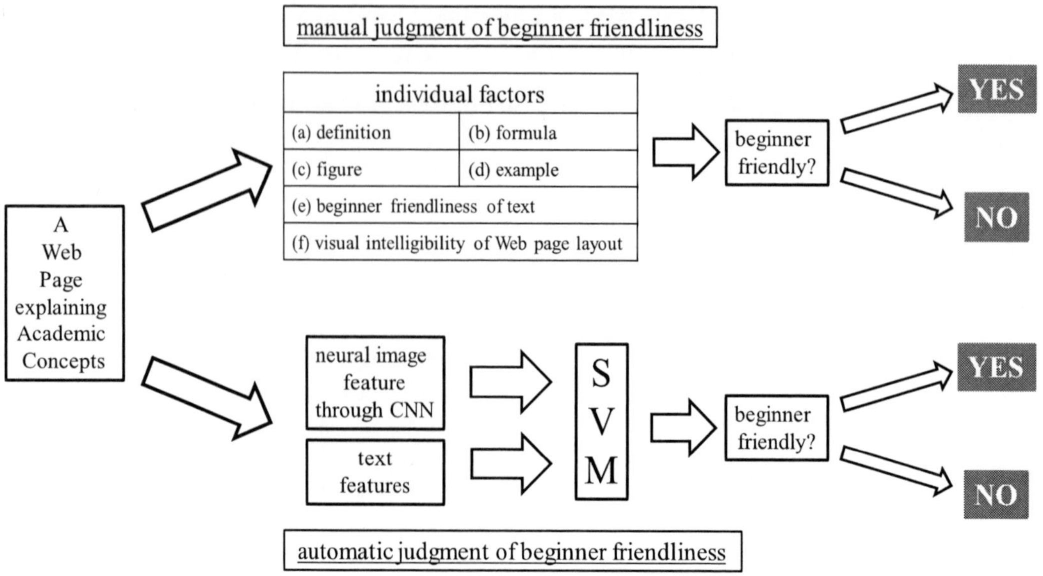

Figure 1: Beginner Friendliness of Web Pages explaining Academic Concepts: Manual Judgment vs. Automatic Judgment by SVM

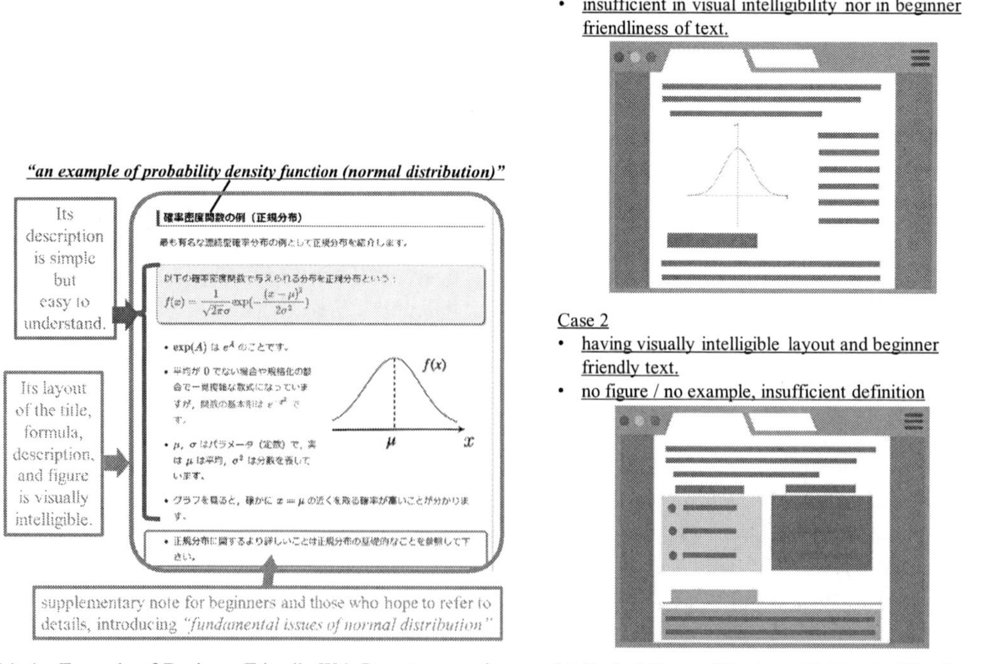

(a) An Example of Beginner Friendly Web Page (excerpt from https://mathtrain.jp/pmitsudo)

(b) Typical Cases of Beginner Unfriendly Web Pages

Figure 2: Beginner Friendly/Unfriendly Web Pages explaining Academic Concepts

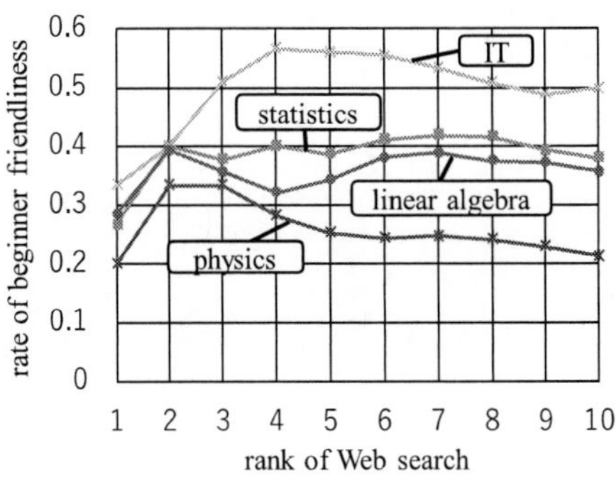
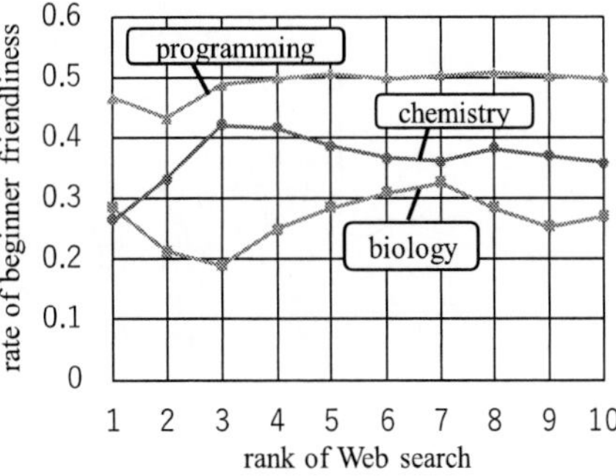

(a) linear algebra, physics, IT, and statistics   (b) biology, programming, and chemistry

Figure 3: Rate of Beginner Friendly Web Pages explaining Academic Concepts ranked at 10th or Higher in the Results of Search Engine

More importantly, when we intend to find beginner friendly Web pages explaining academic concepts through search engine, it is necessary to compare many pages by manual work. The reason of ineffective manual comparison is that there is no systematic criterion on measuring beginner friendliness of Web pages in the results of search engine. Figure 3 shows an evidence of non-existence of such systematic criterion on measuring beginner friendliness of Web pages ranked at 10th or higher by Google search engine in the case of the overall 96 queries of academic terms from the seven academic fields of linear algebra, physics, biology, programming, IT, statistics, and chemistry. The figure plots the rates of the beginner friendly Web pages among those ranked at N-th or higher ($N = 1, \ldots, 10$), among which are mostly those explaining academic concepts of the query academic terms. This evidence supports the claim that there is no systematic criterion on measuring beginner friendliness of Web pages explaining academic concepts in the results of Google search engine.

Based on such observation as well as the motivation of finding beginner friendly Web pages explaining academic concepts, this paper studies how to automatically measure beginner friendliness of Web pages explaining academic concepts. As we formalize in the lower half of Figure 1, we integrate heterogeneous features such as a neural image feature generated from the image of the Web page by a variant of CNN (convolutional neural network) as well as text features extracted from the body text of the HTML file of the Web page. Among those individual factors above, the neural image feature is mostly intended to cover f) visual intelligibility of the Web page layout, while it also partially covers a) definition of academic concepts, b) formulas, c) figures, and d) examples. The text features, on the other hand, are intended to cover d) examples, and e) beginner friendliness of the text of the Web page.

This paper formalizes to integrate those heterogeneous features through the framework of the SVM classifier learning. Evaluation results show that heterogeneous features perform better than each individual type of features.

2 Factors of Beginner Friendliness of Web Pages explaining Academic Concepts

This section describes details of individual factors of beginner friendliness of Web pages explaining academic concepts, as well as their correlations to the overall judgment of beginner friendliness of Web pages.

2.1 Individual Factors

As we describe in the previous section as well as in the upper half of Figure 1, we abstract six individual factors including definition, formula, figure, example, beginner friendliness of text and Web page layout. For each factor, the followings illustrate rough rules on how we manually measure each factor.

(a) Definition: with this factor, it is examined whether the Web page contains correct and precise definition of the explained academic concept.

Table 1: Query Academic Terms

academic fields	# of queries	academic terms
linear algebra	14	階数 (rank), 共役勾配 (conjugate gradient), 行列式 (determinant), クラメルの公式 (Cramer's rule), クロネッカーのデルタ (Kronecker delta), 三角行列 (triangular matrix), 正規直交基底 (orthonormal basis), 対角化 (diagonalization), 直交行列 (orthogonal matrix), 特性多項式 (characteristic polynomial), 二次形式 (quadratic form), ノルム (norm), メネラウスの定理 (Menelaus' theorem), ヤコビ行列 (Jacobian matrix)
physics	15	電気力線 (line of electric force), 張力 (tension), 慣性の法則 (Newton's first law), 遠心力 (centrifugal force), 電波 (radio wave), 電流 (electric current), 万有引力 (universal gravitation), 交流 (alternating current), 音波 (acoustic wave), ホイートストンブリッジ (Wheatstone bridge), 反発係数 (coefficient of restitution), 相互誘導 (mutual induction), 正電荷 (positive electric charge), 速度 (velocity), 変圧器 (transformer)
biology	7	DNA, ショウジョウバエ (Drosophilidae), 原核生物 (Prokaryote), 減数分裂 (meiosis), 光合成 (photosynthesis), 細胞 (cell), 葉緑体 (Chloroplast)
programming	15	C 言語 (C), Java, エスケープシーケンス (escape sequence), コマンドライン引数 (command line arguments), スコープ (scope), フィールド値 (field value), ポインタ (pointer), メソッド (method), 繰り返し処理 (repetitive processing), 構造体 (structure), 算術演算子 (arithmetic operator), 条件分岐 (branch), 配列変数 (array variable), 文字列 (string), 論理演算 (logical operation)
IT	15	API, DBMS, HTML, IP アドレス (IP address), JDBC, RDB, SDK, SQL, Unicode, URL, スコープマネジメント (scope management), ステークホルダーマネジメント (stakeholder management), タイムマネジメント (time management), ナレッジマネジメント (knowledge management), リスクマネジメント (risk management)
statistics	15	事後分布 (posterior distribution), 確率 (probability), 相関係数 (correlation coefficient), 信頼区間 (confidence interval), k 平均法 (k-means clustering), 回帰分析 (regression), 十分統計量 (sufficient statistic), 確率密度関数 (probability density function), ガンマ分布 (gamma distribution), 事前分布 (prior distribution), 主成分分析 (principal component analysis), コーシー分布 (Cauchy distribution), f 分布 (F distribution), 自己回帰モデル (autoregressive model), 自己回帰 (autoregressive)
chemistry	15	イオン結合 (ionic bond), エステル (ester), カルボン酸 (carboxylic acid), ケトン (ketone), 化学反応式 (chemical equation), 化学平衡 (chemical equilibrium), 共有結合 (covalent bond), 合成高分子 (synthetic polymer), 酸化還元 (redox), 遷移元素 (transition elements), 典型元素 (main-group element), 天然高分子 (natural polymer), 燃料電池 (fuel cell), 物質の三態 (three states of matter), 芳香族有機化合物 (aromatic compounds)
total	96	—

(b) Formula: with this factor, it is examined whether the Web page contains formula within its text or figures. The formulas should be relevant to the academic concept explained in the Web page.

(c) Figure: with this factor, it is examined whether the Web page contains figures or pictures relevant to the academic concept explained in the Web page, except when the figure shows formula(s) only.

(d) Example: with this factor, it is examined whether the Web page contains examples relevant to the academic concept explained in the Web page, including examples of application, proof, explanation and so on. When the examples are shown in figures, it is considered as positive for both of the factors figure and example.

(e) Beginner friendliness of text: with this factor, it is examined whether the text of the Web page is beginner friendly. More specifically, the amount of information of the text content needs to be within a certain range. The beginner friendliness of the text is violated when too many occurrences of technical terms are observed in the text. It is also required that if too little or too much academic information is included in the text, then that is regarded as violating beginner friendliness of the text. Another criterion is to avoid that the text is to be too stiff.

(f) Visual intelligibility of Web page layout: with this factor, it is examined whether the layout of the Web page is visually intelligible. More specifically, the topmost part of the Web page should not be only in text, but should also include figures. Also, the rate of of the area of advertisements should be less than a certain upper bound. Furthermore, the background of the Web page should not be in dark color. It is recommended that the top

146

page has a menu bar as well as a table of contents.

2.2 Overall Measurement considering Individual Factors

When we manually judge the overall beginner friendliness of Web pages explaining academic concepts, there exist certain rules and each individual factor has a certain correlation to the overall judgment. Out of the a) to f) individual factors, the three factors a) definition, e) beginner friendliness of text, as well as f) visual intelligibility of Web page layout, are primary factors compared to the remaining other three factors. All the three two factors should be satisfied in order for the overall beginner friendliness to be satisfied. When all the three factors are satisfied, the overall beginner friendliness tends to be satisfied if at least one of the remaining three factors is satisfied. Out of the remaining other three factors, the more of them are satisfied, the more the overall beginner friendliness is satisfied.

3 Reference Data Set of Web Pages Explaining Academic Concepts

This section describes the details of how we collect the reference data set of Web pages explaining academic concepts as well as the procedure before we judge the overall beginner friendliness of each collected Web page explaining academic concepts according to the criterion discussed in the previous section.

3.1 Academic Fields and Concepts for Study

As for the academic fields for which we collect academic terms to be used as queries, we focus on those within science and technology academic fields, mainly because science and technology academic fields tend to have similar criterion on judging the beginner friendliness of text, the visual intelligibility of the Web page layout, and the overall beginner friendliness of the Web page itself. Out of those science and technology academic fields, we select the following seven for study: linear algebra, physics, biology, programming, IT, statistics, and chemistry. For each filed, we select 15 or less academic terms as queries for academic concepts that are around the level of high school or university education, as listed in Table 1. Those query academic terms are selected under the criterion that certain number of Web pages ranked at

10th or higher by Google search engine are those explaining academic concepts.

3.2 Reference Data Set

For each academic term collected in the previous section, we collect the highest 10 Web pages ranked by the Google search engine when each academic term used as the query. In this procedure of collecting Web pages, we ignore Web pages whose HTML files can not be accessed. Then, the first author of this paper[1] judged the overall beginner friendliness as well as the visual intelligibility of the Web page layout of each collected Web page explaining academic concepts according to the criterion discussed in Section 2. Finally, in the procedure of fine-tuning the VGG16 model for judging visual intelligibility of the layout of the Web pages explaining academic concepts, we consider those Web pages which satisfy the visual intelligibility as positive samples while those which do not satisfy the visual intelligibility as negative samples, where their numbers are as shown in Table 2. Similarly, in the procedure of training the SVM classifier for judging the overall beginner friendliness of the Web pages explaining academic concepts, we consider those Web pages which satisfy the overall beginner friendliness as positive samples while those which do not satisfy the overall beginner friendliness as negative samples, where their numbers are also as shown in Table 2. Out of the total seven academic fields, we use the Web pages from five academic fields as training samples, while those from the remaining two as test samples.

4 Neural Image Feature

This section describes the procedure of transforming each Web page explaining academic concepts into its Web page layout image, and then of generating the neural image feature expression from each Web page layout image.

---

[1] In the preliminary study where two authors of this paper worked on developing reference data set and analyzed their agreement rate, it is discovered that the results of the task of judging the overall beginner friendliness of Web pages explaining academic concepts as well as the visual intelligibility of their Web page layout may vary according to the annotators' knowledge level as well as preferences. Thus, in this paper, in the procedure of developing reference data set, we prefer the consistency of the reference data and we decided to develop reference data set with only one annotator.

Table 2: Numbers of Positive/Negative Samples of Manual Judgment of Visual Intelligibility of Page Layout and Overall Beginner Friendliness of the Web Page

		visual intelligibility		overall beginner friendliness		
	academic fields	positive	negative	positive	negative	total
training	linear algebra	31	58	36	53	89
	physics	34	93	26	101	127
	biology	12	52	17	47	64
	programming	58	84	70	72	142
	IT	37	52	39	50	89
	total	172	339	188	323	511
test	statistics	58	53	49	62	111
	chemistry	50	83	49	84	133
	total	108	136	98	146	244
	total	280	475	286	469	755

4.1 VGG16 (Simonyan and Zisserman, 2015)

It has been well known that deep learning techniques have been applied to a number of tasks in a broad range of research fields and have achieved remarkable improvement over the state of the art baselines. In the domain of pattern recognition such as image recognition, especially, it is noted that convolutional neural networks (CNN) as well as a large scale image data set such as ImageNet (Russakovsky et al., 2014) greatly contribute to achieving high performance in various image recognition tasks. Furthermore, parameters of CNN pre-trained using a large scale general purpose data set of images (e.g. natural images) have been proved to be quite useful for extracting universal features that can be easily fine-tuned to image recognition tasks of certain specific domains such as the medical domain (Shin et al., 2016; Tajbakhsh et al., 2016).

Following those successes of the approach of fine-tuning of pre-trained general purpose CNN parameters for image recognition, this paper applies the approach to the task of automatic judgment of visual intelligibility of the layout of the Web pages explaining academic concepts. More specifically, we employ VGG16 model (Simonyan and Zisserman, 2015) as the general purpose CNN for extracting universal features. VGG16 model won second prize in the image classification task and first prize in the single-object localization task in the ImageNet Large Scale Visual Recognition Challenge (ILSVRC) 2014 (Russakovsky et al., 2014). Its neural net architecture consists of a stack of 13 convolutional layers with 5 intermediate max-pooling layers, followed by three fully-connected layers, among which the third layer performs 1000-way ILSVRC classification with 1000 channels (one for each class). The final layer is the soft-max layer. The VGG16 model is pre-trained for the task of 1000-way ILSVRC classification with the ImageNet 2014 data set and is publicly available. It is also known that the pre-trained VGG16 model is widely transferable to other image recognition tasks through fine-tuning. In this paper, as one of the available versions of VGG16 model, we employ the one[2] available as a model within Keras[3], an open source neural network library written in Python.

4.2 Feature of Visual Intelligibility of Web Pages explaining Academic Concepts

This section describes how to generate the neural image feature expression from the layout each Web page explaining academic concepts.

First, each Web page is transformed into its Web page layout image, to which the fine-tuned VGG16 model is applied so as to automatically judge the visual intelligibility of the Web page layout image.

Next, in the fine-tuning of the VGG16 model, its three fully-connected layers of 1000-way ILSVRC classification as well as the soft-max layer are replaced with another three fully-connected layers of binary classification (of judging visual intelligibility of the Web page layout image) as well as the soft-max layer. Throughout the fine-tuning, out of the overall 13 convolutional layers with 5 intermediate max-pooling layers, pre-trained parameters of 10 convolutional layers with 4 intermediate max-pooling layers are

---

[2] https://github.com/keras-team/keras/blob/master/keras/applications/vgg16.py
[3] https://keras.io/ja/

kept unchanged, while the remaining three convolutional layers, one max-pooling layer, and the subsequent three fully-connected layers are fine-tuned with the reference training data set (i.e., from the five academic fields of linear algebra, physics, biology, programming, and IT) developed in Section 3.2. Those Web pages from the two remaining academic fields of statistics and chemistry are the reference test samples.

The actual feature values utilized in the subsequent classifier learning of judging the overall beginner friendliness of the Web page explaining academic concepts are the score of the softmax function, ranging within the interval of [0,1], which can be regarded as the confidence of judging the visual intelligibility of the Web page layout.

More specifically, for the five training academic fields, each Web page is annotated with the neural image feature according to the following procedure: i.e., we fine-tune the VGG16 model with four training academic fields out of the total five, then, each Web page of the remaining one training academic field is annotated with the visual intelligibility judged by the VGG16 model fine-tuned with the other four training academic fields.

For the two test academic fields, on the other hand, first we fine-tune five VGG16 models each of which is fine-tuned with four out of five training academic fields. Then, for each test Web page explaining academic concepts, out of those five fine-tuned VGG16 models, one model is randomly selected and applied to the test Web page, where the test Web page is annotated with the visual intelligibility judged by the selected fine-tuned VGG16 model.

5 Text Features

Within the scope of this paper, as the text features for judging the beginner friendliness of the text of explaining academic concepts, almost low level features such as frequencies of character types, words/strings, and HTML tags for pagination functions are employed. The number of specific features among those three types of text features employed in this paper is ten in total. With a preliminary evaluation procedure, we examined much larger candidates list of text features including those ten features[4], and then, we decided to

---

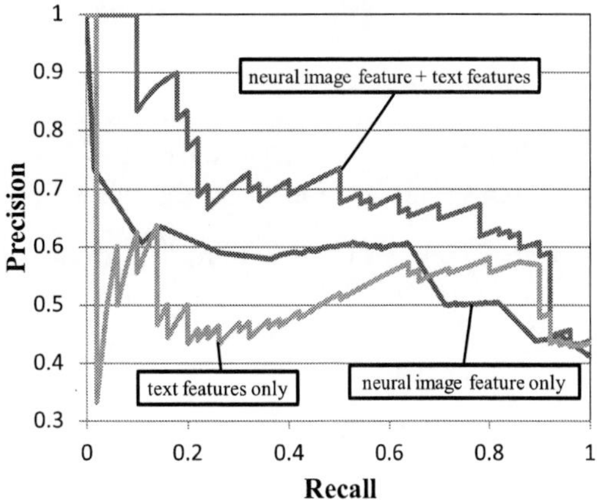

Figure 4: Evaluation Results

employ only those ten features.

5.1 Character Type Features

Japanese sentences are composed mostly of three types of characters, kanji, hiragana, and katakana. Kanji is Chinese characters. Hiragana and katakana are original Japanese characters, where hiragana character is used for Japanese words not covered by kanji and for grammatical inflections, while katakana character is used for transcription of foreign language words into Japanese and the writing of loan words, for emphasis, for onomatopoeia, for technical and scientific terms, and for names of plants, animals, minerals, and often Japanese companies. Following those situations of character types of Japanese sentences, as character type features, we use frequencies of those three character types, kanji, hiragana, and katakana.

5.2 Word/String Features

In this paper, we examined various words/strings as candidates of word/string features, where we finally decided to employ the following six Japanese words/strings and use the frequencies of those words/strings as word/string features.

- "利用規約"(terms of use)

- "相談"(consultation)

- "ノウハウ"(know-how)

- "法"(a constituent character of words such as "方法"(expedient) and "手法"(method))

---

[4] Actually, we examined in total 26 features, i.e., eight character type features, 16 word/string features, HTML tag features for pagination, and HTML tag features for images, out of which ten is selected as an optimal feature combination.

- "困"(a constituent character of a verb "困る" (get into a situation where one needs assistance), where it is intended to count the frequency of a phrase such as "こんな困ったことありませんか?" (Do you have any experience of having a trouble like this?))

- Total frequencies of a word "例"(example) and symbols "Q0", ..., "Q9", which are intended to count the frequencies of examples and questions.

5.3 Pagination Feature

This feature is introduced to detect paginated Web pages, where a Web page content is divided into a sequence of paginated numbered Web pages. More specifically, any digit sequence immediately after the HTML tag ">" and immediately before the HTML tag "<" is detected and their frequency is counted and used as the pagination feature.

6 Evaluation

6.1 Evaluation Procedure

In this paper, we apply the sklearn.SVM.SVC tool of scikit-learn (Pedregosa et al., 2011) package to the task of judging the overall beginner friendliness of the Web page explaining academic concepts. Here, for each Web page, the overall beginner friendliness of the Web page explaining academic concepts is used as the class value. We examined the following two approaches to binarizing features which take more than two discrete values or continuous values;

(a) Dividing the range of discrete values or the continuous values into a certain number of disjoint sub-ranges each of which is exclusive of other sub-ranges.

(b) Dividing the range of discrete values or the continuous values into a certain number of overlapping sub-ranges which share their lower bounds, i.e., those sub-ranges have exactly the same lower bound.

Through the preliminary evaluation, we employed the approach (b), where the ranges of discrete feature values or the continuous feature values are divided into 20 to 40 overlapping sub-ranges. As the kernel function of the SVM, we used the Radial Basis Function (RBF) kernel. A cost parameter (1 or 10) and a gamma parameter (0.01, 0.001, and 0.0001) of RBF kernel were set by grid search where the area of the ROC curve is optimized.

6.2 Evaluation Results

In the evaluation, we plot recall-precision curves by changing the lower bound of the confidence score of the SVM judgment. Figure 4 compares the performance the following three combinations of features:

(i) Both the neural image feature and the text features are used.

(ii) Only the neural image feature is used.

(iii) Only the text features are used.

The evaluation results clearly show that integrating the two types of features as in (i) outperform each individual feature(s) (ii) and (iii).

7 Related Work

No existing work studied the task of judging beginner friendliness of Web pages explaining academic concepts. As one of the related tasks, that of estimating presentation skills based on slides and audio features has been studied. For example, Luzard et al. (2014) applied machine learning methods, where the most relevant slide-based features are number of words, images, and tables as well as the maximum font size, while the most significant audio-based features are pitch and filled pauses related ones. Another related task is to evaluate community QA answers (e.g., Wang et al. (2009) and Sakai et al. (2011)). For example, Wang et al. (2009) studied how to rank community answers and evaluated the method using user-labeled "best answers" of Yahoo!Answers Web site as the gold standard positive examples. Compared to the task of ranking community answers, the current task of judging beginner friendliness of Web pages explaining academic concepts is different in that we examine neural image feature, while, in the community answer ranking task, they usually do not consider any image feature when ranking community answers. Also, approaches to text readability judgment (e.g., (Pitler and Nenkova, 2004; González-Garduño and Søgaard, 2017)) are closely related to the task of beginner friendliness of the text of the Web page and the features studied in those previous work need to be studied also in this paper.

8 Conclusion

This paper studied how to integrate heterogeneous features such as a neural image feature generated from the image of the Web page by a variant of CNN as well as text features extracted from the body text of the HTML file of the Web page. Integration was performed through the framework of the SVM classifier learning. Evaluation results showed that heterogeneous features perform better than each individual type of features. We are now working on developing a reference data set where several annotators participate in the task of developing a reference data set, and then the inter-annotator agreement rate is examined.

Future work include introducing more sophisticated techniques of measuring beginner friendliness of text contents, where it is expected that features that are more semantics-based than frequencies of character types as well as words/strings frequencies contribute to measuring beginner friendliness. Another future work is to incorporate much more detailed list of HTML tags as features of SVM. Preliminary evaluation results indicate that those HTML tag features also contribute to judging beginner friendliness of Web pages explaining academic concepts. This is mainly because one who is capable of developing beginner friendly Web pages explaining academic concepts tends to use certain types of HTML tags frequently and this tendency helps judging beginner friendliness of those Web pages. We plan to report those results in other conferences.

References

A. V. González-Garduño and A. Søgaard. 2017. Using gaze to predict text readability. In *Proc. 12th BEA*, pages 438–443.

G. Luzard, B. Guamán, K. Chiluiza, G. Castells, and X. Ochoa. 2014. Estimation of presentations skills based on slides and audio features. In *Proc. MLA*, pages 37–44.

F. Pedregosa, G. Varoquaux, A. Gramfort, V. Michel, B. Thirion, O. Grisel, M. Blondel, P. Prettenhofer, R. Weiss, V. Dubourg, J. Vanderplas, A. Passos, D. Cournapeau, M. Brucher, M. Perrot, and E. Duchesnay. 2011. Scikit-learn: Machine learning in Python. *Journal of Machine Learning Research*, 12:2825–2830.

E. Pitler and A. Nenkova. 2004. Revisiting readability: A unified framework for predicting text quality. In *Proc. EMNLP*, pages 186–195.

O. Russakovsky, J. Deng, H. Su, J. Krause, S. Satheesh, S. Ma, Z. Huang, A. Karpathy, A. Khosla, M. S. Bernstein, A. C. Berg, and F.-F. Li. 2014. ImageNet large scale visual recognition challenge. *CoRR*, abs/1409.0575.

T. Sakai, D. Ishikawa, N. Kando, Y. Seki, K. Kuriyama, and C.-Y. Lin. 2011. Using graded-relevance metrics for evaluating community QA answer selection. In *Proc. 4th WSDM*, pages 187–196.

H.-C. Shin, H. R. Roth, M. Gao, L.. Lu, Z. Xu, I. Nogues, J. Yao, D. Mollura, and R. M. Summers. 2016. Deep convolutional neural networks for computer-aided detection: CNN architectures, dataset characteristics and transfer learning. *IEEE Transactions on Medical Imaging*, 35(5):1285–1298.

K. Simonyan and A. Zisserman. 2015. Very deep convolutional networks for large-scale image recognition. In *Proc. 3rd ICLR*.

N. Tajbakhsh, J. Y. Shin, S. R. Gurudu, R. T. Hurst, C. B. Kendall, M. B. Gotway, and J. Liang. 2016. Convolutional neural networks for medical image analysis: Full training or fine tuning? *IEEE Transactions on Medical Imaging*, 35(5):1299–1312.

X.-J. Wang, X. Tu, D. Feng, and L. Zhang. 2009. Ranking community answers by modeling question-answer relationships via analogical reasoning. In *Proc. 32nd SIGIR*, pages 179–186.

Learning to Automatically Generate Fill-In-The-Blank Quizzes

Edison Marrese-Taylor, Ai Nakajima, Yutaka Matsuo
Graduate School of Engineering
The University of Tokyo
`emarrese,ainakajima,matsuo@weblab.t.u-tokyo.ac.jp`

Ono Yuichi
Center for Education of Global Communication
University of Tsukuba
`ono.yuichi.ga@u.tsukuba.ac.jp`

Abstract

In this paper we formalize the problem automatic fill-in-the-blank question generation using two standard NLP machine learning schemes, proposing concrete deep learning models for each. We present an empirical study based on data obtained from a language learning platform showing that both of our proposed settings offer promising results.

1 Introduction

With the advent of the Web 2.0, regular users were able to share, remix and distribute content very easily. As a result of this process, the Web became a rich interconnected set of heterogeneous data sources. Being in a standard format, it is suitable for many tasks involving knowledge extraction and representation. For example, efforts have been made to design games with the purpose of semi-automating a wide range of knowledge transfer tasks, such as educational quizzes, by leveraging on this kind of data.

In particular, quizzes based on multiple choice questions (MCQs) have been proved efficient to judge students knowledge. However, manual construction of such questions often results a time-consuming and labor-intensive task.

Fill-in-the-blank questions, where a sentence is given with one or more blanks in it, either with or without alternatives to fill in those blanks, have gained research attention recently. In this kind of question, as opposed to MCQs, there is no need to generate a WH style question derived from text. This means that the target sentence could simply be picked from a document on a corresponding topic of interest which results easier to automate.

Fill-in-the-blank questions in its multiple-choice answer version, often referred to as cloze questions (CQ), are commonly used for evaluating proficiency of language learners, including official tests such as TOEIC and TOEFL (Sakaguchi et al., 2013). They have also been used to test students knowledge of English in using the correct verbs (Sumita et al., 2005), prepositions (Lee and Seneff, 2007) and adjectives (Lin et al., 2007). Pino et al. (2008) and Smith et al. (2010) generated questions to evaluate students vocabulary.

The main problem in CQ generation is that it is generally not easy to come up with appropriate distractors —incorrect options— without rich experience. Existing approaches are mostly based on domain-specific templates, whose elaboration relies on experts. Lately, approaches based on discriminative methods, which rely on annotated training data, have also appeared. Ultimately, these settings prevent end-users from participating in the elaboration process, limiting the diversity and variation of quizzes that the system may offer.

In this work we formalize the problem of automatic fill-in-the-blank question generation and present an empirical study using deep learning models for it in the context of language learning. Our study is based on data obtained from our language learning platform (Nakajima and Tomimatsu, 2013; Ono and Nakajima; Ono et al., 2017) where users can create their own quizzes by utilizing freely available and open-licensed video content on the Web. In the platform, the automatic quiz creation currently relies on hand-crafted features and rules, making the process difficult to adapt. Our goal is to effectively provide an adaptive learning experience in terms of style and difficulty, and thus better serve users' needs (Lin et al., 2015). In this context, we study the ability of our proposed architectures in learning to generate quizzes based on data derived of the interaction of users with the platform.

Proceedings of the 5th Workshop on Natural Language Processing Techniques for Educational Applications, pages 152–156
Melbourne, Australia, July 19, 2018. ©2018 Association for Computational Linguistics

2 Related Work

The problem of fill-in-the-blank question generation has been studied in the past by several authors.
Perhaps the earlies approach is by Sumita et al.
(2005), who proposed a cloze question generation
system which focuses on distractor generation using search engines to automatically measure English proficiency. In the same research line, we
also find the work of Lee and Seneff (2007), Lin
et al. (2007) and Pino et al. (2008). In this context,
the work of Goto et al. (2009) probably represents
the first effort in applying machine learning techniques for multiple-choice cloze question generation. The authors propose an approach that uses
conditional random fields (Lafferty et al., 2001)
based on hand-crafted features such as word POS
tags.

More recent approaches also focus on the problem of distractor selection or generation but apply
it to different domains. For example, Narendra and
Agarwal (2013), present a system which adopts
a semi-structured approach to generate CQs by
making use of a knowledge base extracted from a
Cricket portal. On the other hand, Lin et al. (2015)
present a generic semi-automatic system for quiz
generation using linked data and textual descriptions of RDF resources. The system seems to be
the first that can be controlled by difficulty level.
Authors tested it using an on-line dataset about
wildlife provided by the BBC. Kumar et al. (2015)
present an approach automatic for CQs generation
for student self-assessment.

Finally, the work of Sakaguchi et al. (2013)
presents a discriminative approach based on SVM
classifiers for distractor generation and selection
using a large-scale language learners corpus. The
SVM classifier works at the word level and takes a
sentence in which the target word appears, choosing a verb as the best distractor given the context.
Again, the SVM is based on human-engineered
features such as n-grams, lemmas and dependency
tags.

Compared to approaches above, our take is different since we work on fill-in-the-blank question generation without multiple-choice answers.
Therefore, our problem focuses on word selection
—the word to blank— given a sentence, rather
than on distractor generation. To the best of our
knowledge, our system is also the first to use representation learning for this task.

3 Proposed Approach

We formalize the problem of automatic fill-on-the-
blanks quiz generation using two different perspectives. These are designed to match with
specific machine learning schemes that are well-
defined in the literature. In both cases. we consider a training corpus of N pairs (S_n, C_n), $n =
1 \ldots N$ where $S_n = s_1, \ldots, s_{L(S_n)}$ is a sequence
of $L(S_n)$ tokens and $C_n \in [1, L(S_n)]$ is an index
that indicates the position that should be blanked
inside S_n.

This setting allows us to train from examples
of single blank-annotated sentences. In this way,
in order to obtain a sentence with several blanks,
multiple passes over the model are required. This
approach works in a way analogous to humans,
where blanks are provided one at a time.

3.1 AQG as Sequence Labeling

Firstly, we model the AQG as a sequence labeling problem. Formally, for an embedded input
sequence $S_n = s_1, \ldots, s_{L(n)}$ we build the corresponding label sequence by simply creating a one-
hot vector of size $L(S_n)$ for the given class C_n.
This vector can be seen as a sequence of binary
classes, $Y_n = y_1, \ldots, y_{L(n)}$, where only one item
(the one in position C_n) belongs to the positive
class. Given this setting, the conditional probability of an output label is modeled as follows:

$$p(y \mid s) \propto \prod_{i=1}^{n} \hat{y}_i \qquad (1)$$

$$\hat{y}_i = H(y_{i-1}, y_i, s_i) \qquad (2)$$

Where, in our, case, function H is modeled using
a bidirectional LSTM (Hochreiter and Schmidhuber, 1997). Each predicted label distribution $\hat{y}_t$ is
then calculated using the following formulas.

$$\vec{h}_i = LSTM_{fw}(\vec{h}_{i-1}, x_i) \qquad (3)$$

$$\overleftarrow{h}_i = LSTM_{bw}(\overleftarrow{h}_{i+1}, x_i) \qquad (4)$$

$$\hat{y}_i = \text{softmax}([\vec{h}_i; \overleftarrow{h}_i]) \qquad (5)$$

The loss function is the average cross entropy
for the mini-batch. Figure 1 summarizes the proposed model.

$$L(\theta) = -\frac{1}{n} \sum_{i=1}^{n} y_i \log \hat{y}_i + (1 - y_i) \log(1 - \hat{y}_i)$$

$$(6)$$

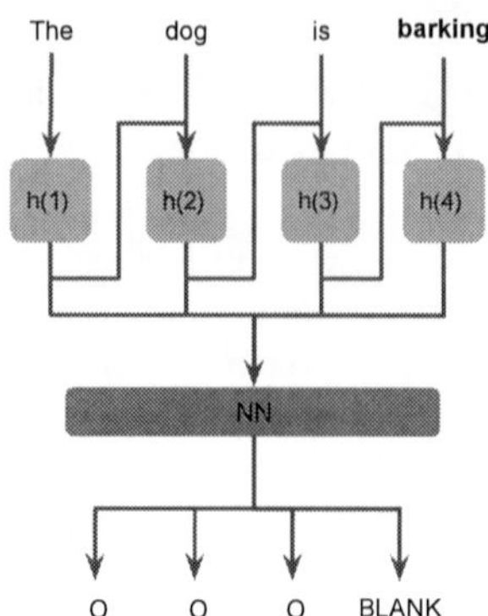

Figure 1: Our sequence labeling model based on an LSTM for AQG.

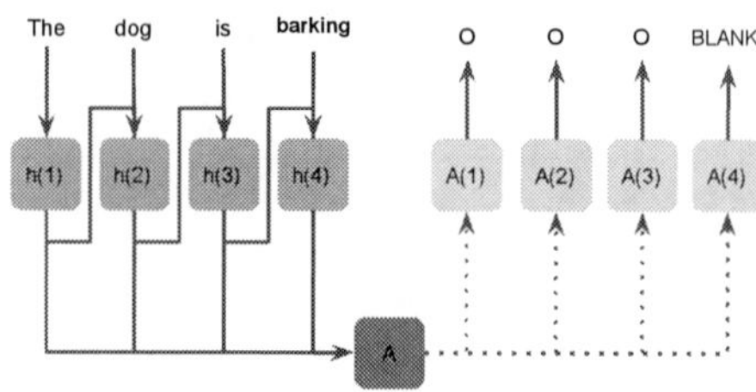

Figure 2: Our sequence classification model, based on an LSTM for AQG.

3.2 AQG as Sequence Classification

In this case, since the output of the model is a position in the input sequence S_n, the size of output dictionary for C_n is variable and depends on S_n. Regular sequence classification models use a softmax distribution over a fixed output dictionary to compute $p(C_n|S_n)$ and therefore are not suitable for our case. Therefore, we propose to use an attention-based approach that allows us to have a variable size dictionary for the output softmax, in a way akin to Pointer Networks (Vinyals et al., 2015). More formally, given an embedded input vector sequence $S_n = s_1, ..., s_{L(n)}$, we use a bidirectional LSTM to first obtain a dense representation of each input token.

$$\vec{h}_i = LSTM_{fw}(\vec{h}_{i-1}, x_i) \tag{7}$$

$$\overleftarrow{h}_i = \overleftarrow{LSTM}_{bw}(\overleftarrow{h}_{i+1}, x_i) \tag{8}$$

$$h_i = [\vec{h}_i; \overleftarrow{h}_i] \tag{9}$$

We later use pooling techniques including max and $mean$ to obtain a summarized representation $\bar{h}$ of the input sequence, or simply take the $last$ hidden state as a drop-in replacement to do so. After this, we add a global content-based attention layer, which we use to to compare that summarized vector to each hidden state h_i. Concretely,

$$u = v^\mathsf{T} W[h_i; \bar{h}] \tag{10}$$

$$p(C_n|P_n) = softmax(u) \tag{11}$$

Where W and v are learnable parameters of the model, and the softmax normalizes the vector u to be an output distribution over a dictionary of size $L(S_n)$. Figure 2 summarizes the proposed

model graphically. Then, for a given sentence C_k, the goal of our model is to predict the most likely position $C^\star \in [1, L(S_n)]$ of the next word to be blanked.

4 Empirical Study

Although the hand-crafted rule-based system currently used in our language learning platform offers us good results in general, we are interested in developing a more flexible approach that is easier to tailor depending on the case. In particular, in an adaptive learning setting where the goal is resource allocation according to the unique needs of each learner, rule-based methods for AQG appear to have insufficient flexibility and adaptability to accurately model the features of each learner or teacher.

With this point in mind, this section presents an empirical study using state-of-the-art Deep Learning approaches for the problem of AQG. In particular, the objective is to test to what extent our prosed models are able to encode the behavior of the rule-based system. Ultimately, we hope that these can be used for a smooth transition from the current human-engineered feature-based system to a fully user-experience-based regime.

In Natural Language Processing, deep models have succeeded in large part because they learn and use their own continuous numeric representational systems for words and sentences. In particular, distributed representations (Hinton, 1984) applied to words (Mikolov et al., 2013) have meant a major breakthrough. All our models start with random word embeddings, we leave the usage of other pre-trained vectors for future work.

Using our platform, we extracted anonymized user interaction data in the manner of real quizzes generated for a collection of several input video sources. We obtained a corpus of approximately

300,000 sentences, from which roughly 1.5 million single-quiz question training examples were derived. We split this dataset using the regular 70/10/20 partition for training, validation and testing.

As the system required the input sentences to be tokenized and makes use of features such as word pos-tags and such, the sentences in our dataset are processed using CoreNLP (Manning et al., 2014). We also extract user-specific and quiz-specific information, including word-level learning records of the user, such as the number of times the learner made a mistake on that word, or whether the learner looked up the word in the dictionary. In this study, however, we restrain our model to only look at word embeddings as input.

We use the same data pre-processing for all of our models. We build the vocabulary using the train partition of our dataset with a minimum frequency of 1. We do not keep cases and obtain an unknown vocabulary of size 2,029, and a total vocabulary size of 66,431 tokens.

4.1 Sequence Labeling

We use a 2-layer bidirectional LSTM, which we train using Adam Kingma and Ba (2014) with a learning rate of 0.001, clipping the gradient of our parameters to a maximum norm of 5. We use a word embedding size and hidden state size of 300 and add dropout (Srivastava et al., 2014) before and after the LSTM, using a drop probability of 0.2. We train our model for up to 10 epochs. Training lasts for about 3 hours.

For evaluation, as accuracy would be extremely unbalanced given the nature of the blanking scheme —there is only one positive-class example on each sentence— we use Precision, Recall and F1-Score over the positive class for development and evaluation. Table 1 summarizes our obtained results.

Set	Loss	Prec.	Recall	F1-Score
Valid	0.0037	88.35	88.81	88.58
Test	0.0037	88.56	88.34	88.80

Table 1: Results of the seq. labeling approach.

4.2 Sequence Classification

In this case, we again use use a 2-layer bidirectional LSTM, which we train using Adam with a learning rate of 0.001, also clipping the gradient

of our parameters to a maximum norm of 5. Even with these limits, convergence is faster than in the previous model, so we only trained the the classifier for up to 5 epochs. Again we use a word embedding and hidden state of 300, and add dropout with drop probability of 0.2 before and after the LSTM. Our results for different pooling strategies showed no noticeable performance difference in preliminary experiments, so we report results using the last hidden state.

For development and evaluation we used accuracy over the validation and test set, respectively. Table 2 below summarizes our obtained result, we can see that model was able to obtain a maximum accuracy of approximately 89% on the validation and testing sets.

Set	Loss	Accuracy
Valid	101.80	89.17
Test	102.30	89.31

Table 2: Results of the seq. classification approach.

5 Conclusions

In this paper we have formalized the problem of automatic fill-on-the-blanks quiz generation using two well-defined learning schemes: sequence classification and sequence labeling. We have also proposed concrete architectures based on LSTMs to tackle the problem in both cases.

We have presented an empirical study in which we test the proposed architectures in the context of a language learning platform. Our results show that both the0 proposed training schemes seem to offer fairly good results, with an Accuracy/F1-score of nearly 90%. We think this sets a clear future research direction, showing that it is possible to transition from a heavily hand-crafted approach for AQG to a learning-based approach on the base of examples derived from the platform on unlabeled data. This is specially important in the context of adaptive learning, where the goal is to effectively provide an tailored and flexible experience in terms of style and difficulty

For future work, we would like to use different pre-trained word embeddings as well as other features derived from the input sentence to further improve our results. We would also like to test the power of the models in capturing different quiz styles from real questions created by professors.

References

Takuya Goto, Tomoko Kojiri, Toyohide Watanabe, Tomoharu Iwata, and Takeshi Yamada. 2009. An automatic generation of multiple-choice cloze questions based on statistical learning. In *Proceedings of the 17th International Conference on Computers in Education*, pages 415–422. Asia-Pacific Society for Computers in Education.

Geoffrey E Hinton. 1984. Distributed representations.

Sepp Hochreiter and Jürgen Schmidhuber. 1997. Long short-term memory. *Neural computation*, 9(8):1735–1780.

Diederik P. Kingma and Jimmy Ba. 2014. Adam: A method for stochastic optimization. *CoRR*.

G. Kumar, R. E. Banchs, and L. F. D'Haro. 2015. Automatic fill-the-blank question generator for student self-assessment. In *2015 IEEE Frontiers in Education Conference (FIE)*, pages 1–3.

John D. Lafferty, Andrew McCallum, and Fernando C. N. Pereira. 2001. Conditional Random Fields: Probabilistic Models for Segmenting and Labeling Sequence Data. In *Proceedings of the Eighteenth International Conference on Machine Learning*, ICML '01, pages 282–289, San Francisco, CA, USA. Morgan Kaufmann Publishers Inc.

John Lee and Stephanie Seneff. 2007. Automatic generation of cloze items for prepositions. In *Eighth Annual Conference of the International Speech Communication Association*.

Chenghua Lin, Dong Liu, Wei Pang, and Zhe Wang. 2015. Sherlock: A Semi-automatic Framework for Quiz Generation Using a Hybrid Semantic Similarity Measure. *Cognitive Computation*, 7(6):667–679.

Yi-Chien Lin, Li-Chun Sung, and Meng Chang Chen. 2007. An automatic multiple-choice question generation scheme for english adjective understanding. In *Workshop on Modeling, Management and Generation of Problems/Questions in eLearning, the 15th International Conference on Computers in Education (ICCE 2007)*, pages 137–142.

Christopher D. Manning, Mihai Surdeanu, John Bauer, Jenny Finkel, Steven J. Bethard, and David McClosky. 2014. The Stanford CoreNLP natural language processing toolkit. In *Association for Computational Linguistics (ACL) System Demonstrations*.

Tomas Mikolov, Ilya Sutskever, Kai Chen, Greg S Corrado, and Jeff Dean. 2013. Distributed Representations of Words and Phrases and their Compositionality. In *Advances in Neural Information Processing Systems 26*. Curran Associates, Inc.

Ai Nakajima and Kiyoshi Tomimatsu. 2013. New potential of e-learning by re-utilizing open content online. In *International Conference on Human Interface and the Management of Information*.

Annamaneni Narendra and Manish Agarwal. 2013. Automatic cloze-questions generation. In *Proceedings of the International Conference Recent Advances in Natural Language Processing RANLP 2013*, pages 511–515.

Yuichi Ono and Ai Nakajima. Automatic quiz generator and use of open educational web videos for english as general academic purpose. In *Proceedings of the 23rd International Conference on Computers in Education*, pages 559–568. Asia-Pacific Society for Computers in Education.

Yuichi Ono, Ai Nakajima, and Manabu Ishihara. 2017. Motivational effects of a game-based automatic quiz generator using online educational resources for japanese efl learners. In *Society for Information Technology and Teacher Education International Conference*.

Juan Pino, Michael Heilman, and Maxine Eskenazi. 2008. A selection strategy to improve cloze question quality. In *Proceedings of the Workshop on Intelligent Tutoring Systems for Ill-Defined Domains. 9th International Conference on Intelligent Tutoring Systems, Montreal, Canada*, pages 22–32.

Keisuke Sakaguchi, Yuki Arase, and Mamoru Komachi. 2013. Discriminative approach to fill-in-the-blank quiz generation for language learners. In *Proceedings of the 51st Annual Meeting of the Association for Computational Linguistics (Volume 2: Short Papers)*, volume 2, pages 238–242.

Simon Smith, P. V. S. Avinesh, and Adam Kilgarriff. 2010. *Gap-fill Tests for Language Learners: Corpus-Driven Item Generation*.

Nitish Srivastava, Geoffrey Hinton, Alex Krizhevsky, Ilya Sutskever, and Ruslan Salakhutdinov. 2014. Dropout: A simple way to prevent neural networks from overfitting. *The Journal of Machine Learning Research*, 15(1):1929–1958.

Eiichiro Sumita, Fumiaki Sugaya, and Seiichi Yamamoto. 2005. Measuring Non-native Speakers' Proficiency of English by Using a Test with Automatically-generated Fill-in-the-blank Questions. In *Proceedings of the Second Workshop on Building Educational Applications Using NLP*, EdAppsNLP 05, pages 61–68, Stroudsburg, PA, USA. Association for Computational Linguistics.

Oriol Vinyals, Meire Fortunato, and Navdeep Jaitly. 2015. Pointer networks. In *Advances in Neural Information Processing Systems*, pages 2692–2700.

Multilingual Short Text Responses Clustering for Mobile Educational Activities: a Preliminary Exploration

Yuen-Hsien Tseng[1], Lung-Hao Lee[1,2], Yu-Ta Chien[3], Chun-Yen Chang[4], Tsung-Yen Li[4]
[1]Graduate Institute of Library and Information Studies, National Taiwan Normal University
[2]MOST Joint Research Center for AI Technology and All Vista Healthcare, NTU
[3]Institute of Education, National Taiwan Ocean University
[4]Science Education Center, National Taiwan Normal University
{samtseng, changcy, yan}@ntnu.edu.tw
lhlee@ntu.edu.tw, ytchien@ntou.edu.tw

Abstract

Text clustering is a powerful technique to detect topics from document corpora, so as to provide information browsing, analysis, and organization. On the other hand, the Instant Response System (IRS) has been widely used in recent years to enhance student engagement in class and thus improve their learning effectiveness. However, the lack of functions to process short text responses from the IRS prevents the further application of IRS in classes. Therefore, this study aims to propose a proper short text clustering module for the IRS, and demonstrate our implemented techniques through real-world examples, so as to provide experiences and insights for further study. In particular, we have compared three clustering methods and the result shows that theoretically better methods need not lead to better results, as there are various factors that may affect the final performance.

1 Introduction

The development of Natural Language Processing (NLP) has advanced to a level that affects the research landscape of academic domains and has practical applications in various industrial sectors. On the other hand, educational environment has also been improved to impact the world society, such as the emergence of MOOCs (Massive Open Online Courses), and new learning tools or teaching paradigms have also change the way of class interactions, such as the use of Classroom Response Systems (CRS) (Siau et al., 2006). The advance of these two fields has converged to support some of the online or on-site course activities that are previously infeasible, such as real-time understanding of student's responses (Beatty and Gerace, 2009) and mobile language learning (Cardoso, 2010).

Research issues in this direction have gained more and more attention (Hearst, 2015). Examples include the workshops on Innovative Use of NLP for Building Educational Applications (BEA) since 2003[1] and the workshops on Natural Language Processing Techniques for Educational Applications (NLPTEA) since 2014[2], where the former was held in North America mainly for English or western languages, while the latter was held in Asia mainly for Chinese or oriental languages.

NLP for educational applications not only concerns the academic community, but also has great potential in the educational market. Systems for online writing evaluation service (or automated essay scoring) like ETS's Criterion[3] and for plagiarism identification like Turnitin[4] have established their market share. However, these successful services are built upon mature educational activities and deal with relatively long articles or complete sentences for reliable performance. In contrast, processing of short texts (or sub-sentences, non-sentences, or even a few terms) is under-developed for novel educational applications.

---

[1] https://ekaterinakochmar.wixsite.com/sig-edu
[2] https://www.sigcall.org/
[3] http://www.criterion.com.tw/
[4] http://turnitin.com/zh_tw/

Proceedings of the 5th Workshop on Natural Language Processing Techniques for Educational Applications, pages 157–164
Melbourne, Australia, July 19, 2018. ©2018 Association for Computational Linguistics

Electronic classroom response systems (CRS), also called instant response systems (IRS) or clickers, have been tested and used in higher education classrooms since the 1960's (Deal, 2007). According to a CNET report (Gilbert, 2005), schools and universities, most in the United States, bought nearly a million clickers in year 2004 alone, using infrared or radio frequency technology for students' transmitters. This number accumulated to nearly nine million units in under a decade by just two of many companies that make clickers (Hoffman, 2012). Recently, IRS has gained even greater popularity in class interaction (Bartsch and Murphy, 2011; Chen et al., 2013; Han, 2014; Morais et al., 2015) due to the ubiquitous availability of mobile devices for each individual and cloud-based technology for ease of data collection and integration. IRS services in Taiwan like Zuvio (http://www.zuvio.com.tw/) have attracted local university users in a short term because of its easier use than traditional transmitter-required IRS and LMS (Learning Management System) such as Moodle App. For example, over the course of year 2014, Zuvio usage in National Taiwan University (NTU) increased from 61 to 263 instructors, 68 to 384 courses, and 2,037 to 11,172 students (Lee and Shih, 2015).

By broadcasting a question to all students' mobile devices and getting responses instantly, such systems help teachers know the learning status of each student better and also help students maintain their attention during the class due to the instant feedback from the teachers and/or their classmates (Bartsch and Murphy, 2011; Beatty and Gerace, 2009). However, the potential of such IRS may still be under-explored (Chien and Chang, 2015a). In the above NTU case, although the majority (54%) of questions deployed in Zuvio were multiple choices, many instructors also used open-ended questions (20%) and composite questions (21%) to promote deeper engagement and reflection (J. W.-S. Lee and Shih, 2015). Previous studies even indicated that multiple-choice examinations pose an obstacle for higher-level thinking in science classes (Stanger-Hall, 2012) and constructed response (e.g. free text writing) assessments are widely viewed as providing greater insight into student thinking than closed form (e.g. multiple-choice) assessments (Birenbaum and Tatsuoka, 1987).

However, no IRS system has yet provided analysis of these open-ended text responses in real time, to our best knowledge. By applying NLP techniques to the IRS or similar mobile interaction systems where only short text interaction is feasible, more information for the students could be provided and therefore more meaningful engagement and efficient learning could be achieved (Chien and Chang, 2015b).

Based on the above trends and observations, this study aims at developing related NLP techniques applicable to the current and future educational environment. More specifically, this paper focuses on the short text response processing in the situation where some forms of instant response systems (IRS) are used in and after the class.

2 Short Text Response Clustering

As our purpose is to support IRS-related educational activities, an existing IRS would be used for integrating the techniques to be developed so that we can focus on the required new functions without re-inventing the wheel. We choose CloudClassRoom (CCR, http://ccr.tw/) because it is developed by the team of our collaborators (Chien and Chang, 2015a) and because it supports at least 12 languages for international use. This choice would facilitate our testing and evaluation of the developed techniques. However, we keep in mind that the techniques to be developed should be independent of the CCR system, such that they can be ported to another IRS instantly. In fact, CCR is developed in JQuery and PHP language, while the NLP techniques to be developed mainly use Python as our programming language.

Once we have an IRS platform, we can package the required techniques into one of the IRS's module to meet the research purposes. Figure 1 shows a series of processing step packaged into a Semantic Processing Module (SPM), where each rectangular box denotes a processing sub-module and each cylinder denotes a set of language knowledge, corpora, resources, or technical options.

The first-row in the figure mainly deals with refining the terms from the response texts, which heavily depends on the language knowledge and resources. The second-row deals with the sematic processing of the texts, which is basically language independent, except the term expansion step. This pipeline structure is inevitable as there are many options in processing texts for a certain

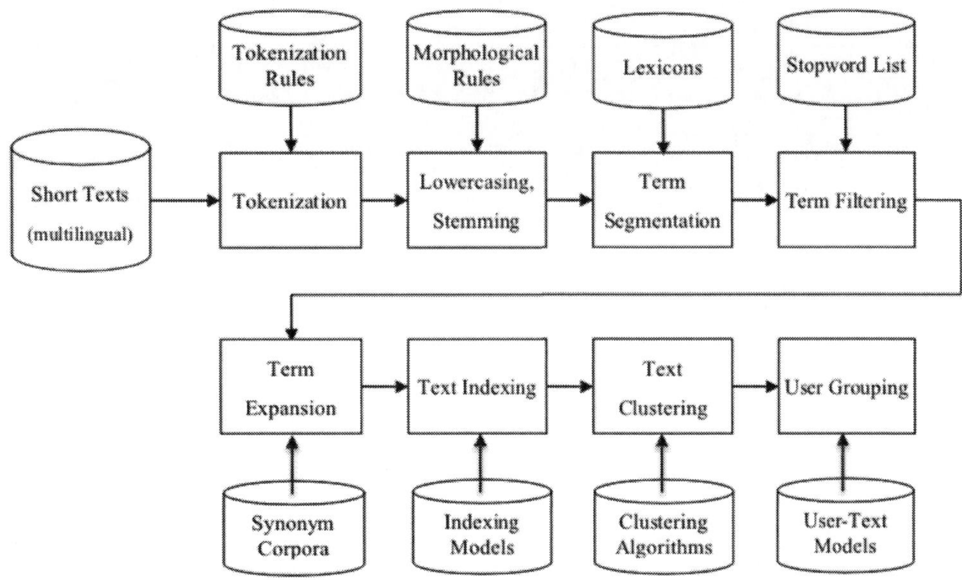

Figure 1: Pipeline steps of the SPM for processing short texts in an IRS system.

task in a certain language. At our early stage of development, each step would have options for selection by teachers or by NLP experts to best suit the educational activities in a certain course. At the later stage, we expect that the SPM should finally learn the options without human selection. For example, the tokenization need to transform all different digital numbers into a single numeric symbol for semantic clustering in general cases, but should leave the numbers intact in courses such as mathematics, where exact numbers from students are expected for accurate processing. The case also applies to the morphological step where lowercasing and stemming are applied for English semantic processing in general cases, but the morphological analysis should be turned off when, e.g., English is taught, or the expected answers are exact terms used by the students. This consideration would optimize the SPM for each educational activity, but may require years of fine-tuning when more and more activities are encountered in real-world applications. In fact, the CCR has at least 4780 teachers registered, 11,784 classrooms established, and 23,376 questions asked and 248,633 responses received. It really contains many valuable resources for NLP experiments and applications.

3   Demonstration

To have a concrete idea about the texts submitted by students via CCR, Table 1 shows a set of real-world texts in response to the question asked by a Taiwan university teacher of General Education of Science: "As a marine researcher, if someone presents the photos shown in Figure 2 to you and ask your opinion about the creature, what would you think of and what would you ask?"

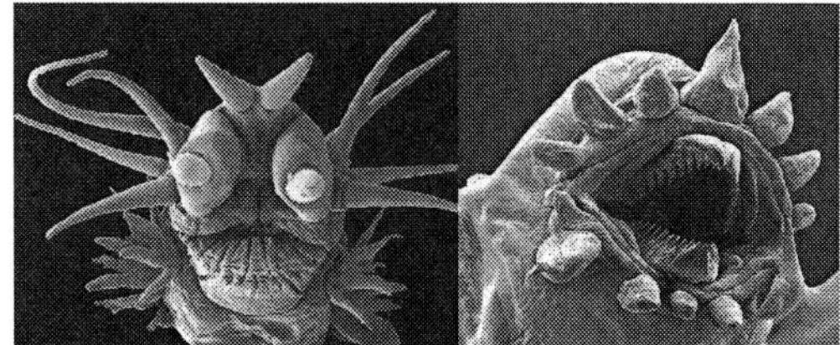

Figure 2: Photographs to trigger questions for students to respond.

As can be seen from Table 1, there are several characteristics in the students' responses: 1) meaningfulness punctuations, e.g., ID 3; 2) multi-lingual: English responses even in a Chinese

Student ID	In this table, there are 29 student responses to the question: "As a marine researcher, if someone presents the photos shown in figure to you and ask your opinion about the creature, what would you think of and what would you ask?"
1	1.發現地點 2. 推論有毒 3. 外星生物 地球沒有
3	1.好吃嗎。2.肉食性。3.牙齒很尖。4.深海魚。5.因為很醜==
4	What's its life cycle? I guess that it's a meat-eater. Maybe it's a parasite. Because it has a fixation structure.
5	他們有毒嗎？
6	他們看得到嗎？他們的食物可能是什麼？
9	他是生活在何種海域?!深度?!環境?!
11	它的體型大小
12	住在很深的海裡吧！眼睛很凸。牙齒很尖應該是食物動物！
15	呵呵呵呵呵
17	問題：在哪個海域發現的呢？特性：吃腐肉，極可能是古老的活化石。原因：場項特別、牙齒尖銳。生物：恐龍？！或其相關生物
18	問題：水深位置大約在何處。推測：疑似刺絲胞動物門，有攻擊力，有尖銳的外型
21	好奇怪
22	它有肛門嗎？
23	對光源有無反應
24	很像大英雄天團的噴火龍
25	我覺得它是人類的祖先。因為他有眼睛 有嘴巴 有牙齒。牠以細菌為主，牠屬於夜行性動物，睡眠時間為 12 小時 也就是半天，是個奇怪的生物！！！我想要 usb
27	海洋生物
28	深海生物，無視覺
29	爸爸
31	牠生活於海洋表層還深層？狩獵能力較強，因為牙齒以犬齒較多可進行撕裂，海洋深層消費者
32	發現的環境包含深度 身體外表特徵，實行生物分類 它的捕食習性
33	眼睛會感光嗎？肉食性動物，牙齒看起來很尖，深海的未知生物，因為看不出來是什麼種類的生物
34	神奇寶貝
35	肉食性的魚，在很深暗海
36	觸角是類似珊瑚的觸角嗎。應該是住在深海裡的雙種生物吧。
37	跟我同學很像
38	身體構造有那些特徵
39	這個生物是不是小小隻的？可能是吃浮游生物的，深海的生物，因為有觸手
43	這種生物有攻擊性嗎？應該住在深海？有照明的能力吧！這會不會是鯊魚和燈籠魚的合體

Table 1: Examples of text responses from students via CCR.

class, e.g., ID 4; 3) nonsense responses, e.g. ID 15, 24, 29, etc.; 4) very short texts, e.g., ID 5, 11, 27, etc.; and 5) non-topical texts, e.g. the last part of ID 25, where the student asks for a prize promised by the teacher who encourages the students to aggressively respond to the question for a USB storage device as a prize.

Characteristic 1 can be removed at the tokenization stage. Characteristic 2 could be translated using simple word-by-word translation (by way of multi-lingual lexicons or multilingual Word-Nets[5], such as BabelNet[6]), with translation tools such as Goslate[7], or customized machine translation techniques (Chuang and Tseng, 2008; Tseng et al., 2011). Characteristic 4 can be extended by synonym lexicons or multilingual WordNets to enrich the textual information. However, despite we have eHownet[8] resources from the ACLCLP (Association of Computational Linguistics and

[5] https://wordnet.princeton.edu/
[6] https://babelnet.org/
[7] https://pythonhosted.org/goslate/
[8] http://ehownet.iis.sinica.edu.tw/index.php

Chinese Language Processing), there is no guarantee that the synonyms or hypernyms in eHownet is able to cover the terms used in a class like the above. After these preprocessing, Characteristics 2, 3, 4, and 5 require an effective text clustering technique to distinguish them from the normal meaningful responses, such that the teacher could decide what to do for the improper responses. Once they can be isolated in real time, the teacher can, for example, ask the corresponding students to re-submitted their responses, or preset the system to prevent these texts from been submitted by the students.

To have an idea of how well existing clustering techniques can do for these texts, we have tried three approaches:

(1) Hierarchical Agglomerative Clustering (HAC) based on a hybrid way of term indexing, namely lexicon-based segmentation followed by a keyword extraction using the method of (Tseng, 1998, 2002; Tseng et al., 2010b), implemented in a well-debugged tool called CATAR (Tseng, 2010a; Tseng and Tsay, 2013), as shown in Figure 3.

(2) Latent Semantic Analysis (LSA) based on the word segmentation by jieba and a topic modeling tool genism without removal of any stopwords and punctuations, as shown in Figure 4.

(3) Latent Dirichlet Analysis (LDA) by jieba and gensim with stopwords and punctuations being removed, as shown in Figure 5.

From Figure 3 based on HAC, there are 3 multi-documents clusters and 16 singleton clusters. The result is generally reasonable, only a few texts, like ID 23 and 31, could not be grouped together with other similar texts. This is because a rigorous criterion is imposed on the HAC, i.e., complete linkage clustering such that ID 31 did not cluster into Cluster 3, despite it contains the salient term "牙齒" in Cluster 3. Also, the lexicon-based segmentation regards "深海", "海洋", and "海洋深層" as different terms, such that they are totally different features for text clustering. The above two reasons may also apply to the terms and texts, such as "光源" (ID 23), "感光" (ID 33), "暗海" (ID 35), and "夜行性" (ID 25), or "食物" (ID 6) and "肉食性" (ID 3, 33, and 35).

Figure 3: HAC clustering results.

Group ID	Student ID:
#1	3：1 好吃嗎。2 肉食性。3 牙齒很尖。…
	17：問題：在哪個海域發現的呢？…
	18：問題:水深位置大約在何處。…
	31：牠生活於海洋表層還深層 ？…
	33：眼睛會感光嗎？…
	36：觸角是類似珊瑚的觸角嗎，…
	39：這個生物是不是小小隻的？…
	43：這種生物有攻擊性嗎？…
#2	5: 他們有毒嗎?
	6: 他們看得到嗎? 他們的食物可能是什麼?
#3	11: 他的體型大小
	25: 我覺得它是人類的祖先。…
	32: 發現的環境包含深度 …
	37: 跟我同學好像
	38: 身體構造有那些特徵
#4	1: 發現地點　…
	4: What's its life cycle? …
	9: 他是生活在何種海域?! …
	22: 它有肛門嗎?
	23: 對光源有無反應
#5	12: 住在很深的海裡吧! 眼睛很凸 …
	24: 很像大英雄天團的噴火龍
	28: 深海生物，無視覺
	35: 肉食性的魚，在很深暗海
N/A	15: 呵呵呵呵呵
	21: 好奇怪
	27: 海洋生物
	29: 爸爸
	34: 神奇寶貝

Figure 4: LSA clustering results.

Group ID	Student ID
#1	1: 1. 發現地點　2. 推論有毒　… 5: 他們有毒嗎？ 6: 他們看得到嗎?… 21: 好奇怪 22: 它有肛門嗎？
#2	31: 牠生活於海洋表層還深層？ 39: 這個生物是不是小小隻的？ 37: 跟我同學好像 27: 海洋生物
#3	12: 住在很深的海裡吧！… 33: 眼睛會感光嗎？肉食性動物… 43: 這種生物有攻擊性嗎？… 36: 觸角是類似珊瑚的觸角嗎，… 9:　他是生活在何種海域?!… 15: 呵呵呵呵呵
#4	18: 問題:水深位置大約在何處。… 28: 深海生物，無視覺 3: 1 好吃嗎。2 肉食性。3 牙齒很尖。… 23: 對光源有無反應 32: 發現的環境包含深度 … 38: 身體構造有那些特徵 4: What's its life cycle? … 24: 很像大英雄天團的噴火龍 29: 爸爸
#5	17: 問題:在哪個海域發現的呢?… 35: 肉食性的魚，在很深暗海 11: 他的體型大小 25: 我覺得它是人類的祖先。… 34: 神奇寶貝

Figure 4: LDA clustering results.

To improve the performance such that the texts containing these semantically related terms being clustered together, it seems that LSA or LDA are better solutions as past studies have shown the possibility (Blei et al., 2003; Deerwester et al. 1990). Based on the HAC result, there are 3-5 clusters in this case. So we cluster the responses using 5 topics with LSA and LDA. Actually, this number: about 5 clusters for each set of responses, is a proper choice for science education based on the feedback of our co-investigator. However, Figure 4 and 5 shows that LSA and LDA alone cannot solve this short-text clustering problem better. They can sometimes lead to worse results. In addition to the shortage of textual information (short texts), there are other factors that influence the performance, such as feature extraction (whether to use 1-grams as features in Chinese short texts or not, such as "海", "光"), term expansion (whether to incorporate the term-level similarity, such as those between "感光" and "夜行性", or "食物" and "肉食性", into text clustering). Furthermore, these decisions may depend on the characteristics of the questions asked or classes taught. Therefore, we propose the pipeline SPM in Figure 1 to deal with this problem, so that in each step we could choose proper options for better performance.

To incorporate more semantic information into the SPM, we plan to use language resources such as eHownet, WordNet, and BabelNet for Chinese, English, and multilingual synonym expansion, respectively. Our future study would also use tools like word2vec (Mikolov et al., 2013) and concept map miner (Tseng et al., 2010; Tseng et al., 2012) to extract paradigmatically and/or topically similar terms for term expansion (Tseng et al., 2010). In addition to term expansion, utilization of contextual information of the short texts can be enhanced by machine translation (Tang et al., 2012). Direct clustering based on the continuous distributed representations of words, sentences, or paragraphs (Chinea-Rios et al., 2015; Mikolov et al., 2013) may also be worth of exploring. As a tradition in NLP research, further study will try all the promising combinations of the mentioned techniques to see which combinations perform best in which conditions.

As to the clustering performance evaluation, there are intrinsic and extrinsic measures, where the former measures the clustering quality directly and the latter measures the quality indirectly by applying the clustering result to other task and see if a good result can be obtained from the task. For intrinsic evaluation, measures like perplexity, Rand index, and Silhouette index have been used and we have implemented the latter two measures (Rand and Silhouette) in CATAR to help determine the number of clusters (Tseng, Lin, & Lin, 2007; Tseng & Tsay, 2013). For extrinsic evaluation, which is more suitable for the IRS applications, it depends on how the teacher would like the clustering results. Therefore, our strategies would implement different clustering techniques and intrinsic evaluation measures to suggest various cluster results for the teachers to choose a proper one. Before that, we had assisted the teachers to quickly understand a clustering result by providing some intrinsic evaluation result, i.e., the cluster descriptors as shown in Figure 3. In this way, we help the teachers to explore the students' responses in a period of time short enough during their lecturing activities using the IRS.

4 Conclusions

This paper describes our preliminary study of short text response clustering for mobile educational activities. We illustrate the characteristics of short text responses from the IRS, propose the SPM module for processing short texts, and demonstrate our implemented techniques via the CCR system. We also compare three clustering methods, and the results showed that theoretically better methods need not lead to better results, as there are various factors that may affect the final performance.

In real-case applications, the SPM module based on the LSA technique has been used online for two years, serving thousands of teachers. Informal evaluation from the responses of teachers, including those in Taiwan and Thailand, has shown that the proposed short-text clustering is applicable to their educational activities.

Acknowledgments

This study was partially supported by the Ministry of Science and Technology (MOST), Taiwan, R.O.C., under the grant: MOST 105-2221-E-003-020-MY2, MOST 106-2221-E-003-030-MY2, and MOST 107-2634-F-002-019-.

References

R. A. Bartsch, and M. Murphy. 2011. Examining the effects of an electronic classroom response system on student engagement and performance. *Journal of Educational Computing Research*, 44(1): 25-33. https://doi.org/10.2190/EC.44.1.b

I. Beatty, and W. Gerace. 2009. Technology-enhanced formative assessment: a research-based pedagogy for teaching science with classroom response technology. *Journal of Science Education and Technology*, 18(2): 146-162. https://doi.org/10.1007/s10956-008-9140-4

M. Birenbaum, and K. K. Tatsuoka. 1987. Open-ended versus multiple-choice response formats—it does make a difference for diagnostic purposes. *Applied Psychological Measurement*, 11(4): 385-395. https://doi.org/10.1177/014662168701100404

D. M. Blei, A. Y. Ng, and M. I. Jordan. 2003. Latent dirichlet allocation. *Journal of Machine Learning Research*, 3, 993-1022.

W. Cardoso. 2010. Clickers in foreign language teaching: a case study. *Contact: Teachers of English as a Second Language of Ontario*, 36(2): 36-55. http://spectrum.library.concordia.ca/36087/

T.-L. Chen, Y.-F. Lin, Y.-L. Liu, H.-P. Yueh, H.-J. Sheen, and W.-J. Lin. 2013. Integrating Instant Response System (IRS) as an in-class assessment tool into undergraduate chemistry learning experience: student perceptions and performance. In M.-H. Chiu, H.-L. Tuan, H.-K. Wu, J.-W. Lin, and C.-C. Chou (Eds.), *Chemistry Education and Sustainability in the Global Age* (pp. 267-275): Springer Netherlands.

Y.-T. Chien, and C.-Y. Chang. 2015a. Providing students with an alternative way to interact with the teacher in the silent classroom: Teaching with the CloudClassRoom technology. In *Proceedings of the Inaugural Asian Conference on Education & International Development*.

Y.-T. Chien, and C.-Y. Chang. 2015b. Supporting socio-scientific argumentation in the classroom through automatic group formation based on students' real-time responses. In M. S. Khine (Ed.), *Science education in East Asia: Pedagogical innovations and research-informed practices* (pp. 549-563): Springer International Publishing.

M. Chinea-Rios, G. Sanchis-Trilles, and F. Casacuberta. 2015. Sentence clustering using continuous vector space representation. In R. Paredes, J. S. Cardoso, and X. M. Pardo (Eds.), *Pattern Recognition and Image Analysis* (Vol. 9117, pp. 432-440): Springer International Publishing.

Z.-J. Chuang, and Y.-H. Tseng. 2008. NTCIR-7 experiments in patent translation based on open source statistical machine translation tools. In *Proceedings of the 7th NTCIR Workshop on Evaluation of Information Access Technologies: Information Retrieval, Question Answering, and Cross-Lingual Information Access*.

A. Deal. 2007. A teaching with technology white paper: classroom response systems. Retrieved from https://www.cmu.edu/teaching/technology/whitepapers/ClassroomResponse_Nov07.pdf

S. Deerwester, S Dumais, G Furnas, T. K. Landauer, and R. Harshman. 1990. Indexing by Latent Semantic Analysis. *Journal of the American Society for Information Science*, 41 (6): 391–407.

A. Gilbert. 2005. New for back-to-school: 'Clickers'. Retrieved from http://www.cnet.com/news/new-for-back-to-school-clickers/

J. H. Han. 2014. Closing the missing links and opening the relationships among the factors: a literature review on the use of clicker technology using the 3P model. *Journal of Educational Technology & Society, 17*(4): 150-168.

M. A. Hearst. 2015. Can natural language processing become natural language coaching? In *Proceedings of the 53rd Annual Meeting of the Association of Computational Linguistics.*

J. Hoffman. 2012. Speak up? Raise your hand? That may no longer be necessary. Retrieved from http://www.nytimes.com/2012/03/31/us/clickers-offer-instant-interactions-in-more-venues.html?_r=0

J. W.-S. Lee, and M.-l. Shih. 2015. Teaching practices for the student response system at National Taiwan University. *International Journal of Automation and Smart Technology*, 5(3): 145-150. https://doi.org/10.5875/ausmt.v5i3.862

T. Mikolov, I. Sutskever, K. Chen, G. S. Corrado, amd J. Dean. 2013. Distributed representations of words and phrases and their compositionality. In *Proceedings of the Advances in Neural Information Processing Systems.*

A. Morais, J. I. Barragués, and J. Guisasola. 2015. Using a classroom response system for promoting interaction to teaching mathematics to large groups of undergraduate students. *Journal of Computers in Mathematics and Science Teaching, 34*(3): 249-271.

K. Siau, S. Hong, amd F. F. H. Nah. 2006. Use of a classroom response system to enhance classroom interactivity. *IEEE Transactions on Education*, 49(3): 398-403. https://doi.org/10.1109/TE.2006.879802

K. F. Stanger-Hall. 2012. Multiple-choice exams: an obstacle for higher-level thinking in introductory science classes. *CBE Life Sciences Education, 11*(3): 294-306. https://doi.org/10.1187/cbe.11-11-0100

J. L. Tang, X. F. Wang, H. J. Gao, X. Hu, and H. Liu. 2012. Enriching short text representation in microblog for clustering. *Frontiers of Computer Science*, 6(1): 88-101. https://doi.org/10.1007/s11704-011-1167-7

Y.-H. Tseng. 1998. Multilingual keyword extraction for term suggestion. In *Proceedings of the 21st International ACM SIGIR Conference on Research and Development in Information Retrieval.*

Y.-H. Tseng. 2002. Automatic thesaurus generation for Chinese documents. *Journal of the American Society for Information Science and Technology, 53*(13): 1130-1138. https://doi.org/10.1002/asi.10146

Y.-H. Tseng. 2010a. Content Analysis Toolkit for Academic Research (CATAR). Retrieved from http://web.ntnu.edu.tw/~samtseng/CATAR/

Y.-H. Tseng. 2010b. Generic title labeling for clustered documents. *Expert Systems With Applications*, 37(3): 2247-2254. https://doi.org/10.1016/j.eswa.2009.07.048

Y.-H. Tseng, C.-Y. Chang, S.-N. R. Chang, and C.-J. Rundgren. 2010. Mining concept maps from news stories for measuring civic scientific literacy in media. *Computers & Education*, 55(1): 165-177. https://doi.org/10.1016/j.compedu.2010.01.002

Y.-H. Tseng, Z.-P. Ho, K.-S. Yang, and C.-C. Chen. 2012. Mining term networks from text collections for crime investigation. *Expert Systems With Applications*, 39(11): 10082-10090. https://doi.org/10.1016/j.eswa.2012.02.052

Y.-H. Tseng, C.-J. Lin, and Y.-I. Lin. 2007. Text mining techniques for patent analysis. *Information Processing and Management*, 43(5): 1216-1247. https://doi.org/10.1016/j.ipm.2006.11.011

Y.-H. Tseng, C.-L. Liu, C.-C. Tsai, J.-P. Wang, Y.-H. Chuang, and J Jeng. 2011. *Statistical approaches to patent translation for patentMT- experiments with various settings of training data.* In *Proceedings of the 9th NTCIR Workshop on Evaluation of Information Access Technologies: Information Retrieval, Question Answering, and Cross-Lingual Information Access.*

Y.-H. Tseng, and M.-Y. Tsay. 2013. Journal clustering of Library and Information Science for subfield delineation using the bibliometric analysis toolkit: CATAR. *Scientometrics, 95*(2): 503-528.

Chinese Grammatical Error Diagnosis

Based on CRF and LSTM-CRF model

Yujie Zhou[1], Yinan Shao[2], Yong Zhou[3,*]
[1]Department of Education Information Technology, East China Normal University,
[2] Harbin Institute of Technology Shenzhen Graduate School,
[3] Department of Education Information Technology, East China Normal University
*Corresponding author
Contact:yzhou@ied.ecnu.edu.cn

Abstract

When learning Chinese as a foreign language, the learners may have some grammatical errors due to negative migration of their native languages. However, few grammar checking applications have been developed to support the learners. The goal of this paper is to develop a tool to automatically diagnose four types of grammatical errors which are redundant words (R), missing words (M), bad word selection (S) and disordered words (W) in Chinese sentences written by those foreign learners. In this paper, a conventional linear CRF model with specific feature engineering and a LSTM-CRF model are used to solve the CGED (Chinese Grammatical Error Diagnosis) task. We make some improvement on both models and the submitted results have better performance on false positive rate and accuracy than the average of all runs from CGED2018 for all three evaluation levels.

1   Introduction

Nowadays, more and more foreigners take Chinese as their second language. Unlike English, Chinese has no verb tenses or pluralities, and meanwhile there are various ways to express the same meaning in Chinese, so Chinese has been considered as one of the most difficult languages in the world(Bo Zheng et al., 2016). Chinese as a Foreign Language(CFL) learners often make grammatical errors such as redundant words (R), missing words (M), word selection errors (S), and word ordering errors (W), due to language negative migration, over-generalization, teaching methods, learning strategies and other reasons. Natural Language Processing System(NLPS) which can detect and correct grammatical errors are important and invaluable to language learners. (Leacock et al., 2010). However, few grammar checking applications have been developed to support CFL learners. The goal of the CGED (Chinese Grammatical Error Diagnosis) task is to develop NLP (Natural Language Processing) techniques to automatically diagnose grammatical errors in Chinese sentences written by CFL learners.

In this paper, we use both a conventional linear CRF model (Lafferty et al., 2001) with specific feature engineering and a LSTM-CRF model to solve CGED task. Many researchers have already used these two models in the past few years, but our team make some improvement on both models. For CRF model, we integrate the syntactic feature into the CRF model. Character itself, POS feature and syntactic feature are used to generate 50 combinatorial features by template technology. As for LSTM-CRF model, most researchers use tag transition features only in CRF layer. The major improvement of our work is that more conventional sparse CRF features are incorporated into the CRF layer such as bag of POS n-grams features, words features, tag transition features, etc.

The rest of the paper is organized as follows: Section 2 gives the definition of the CEGD task. Section 3 introduces two methods we use to solve the CGED task. Section 4 describes the dataset we use, the evaluation results on the validation set and the test set. Section 5 discusses conclusion and future work.

2   Task Definition

The task of CGED is defined as follows: given a Chinese sentence, the goal of CGED tool is to diagnose four types of grammatical errors, including redundant words (R), missing words (M), words selection errors (S) and word ordering errors (W).

Proceedings of the 5th Workshop on Natural Language Processing Techniques for Educational Applications, pages 165–171
Melbourne, Australia, July 19, 2018. ©2018 Association for Computational Linguistics

他 [1] 们 [2] 是 [3] 不 [4] 但 [5] 我 [6] 父 [7] 母 [8]， [9] 而 [10] 且 [11] 是 [12] 人 [13] 生 [14] 的 [15] 先 [16] 辈 [17]。 [18]

Error Type	W	S
Error position-Start	3	16
Error position-End	5	17
Correction	他们不但是我父母，而且是人生的导师。	

Table 1: Two errors are found in the sentence above, one is word ordering error (W) from position 3 to 5, the other is word selection error (R) from position 16 to 17..

虽 [1] 然 [2] 吃 [3] 绿 [4] 色 [5] 的 [6] 食 [7] 品 [8] 是 [9] 对 [10] 身 [11] 体 [12] 健 [13] 康 [14] 很 [15] 有 [16] 好 [17] 处 [18]。 [19]

Error Type	R	M
Error position-Start	6	19
Error position-End	6	19
Correction	虽然吃绿色食品是对身体健康很有好处的。	

Table 2: Two errors are found in the sentence above, one is redundant word (R) error at position 6, the other is missing word (M) error at position 19.

The input sentence may contain one or more such errors. The developed tool should indicate each error type and its position in the given sentence. To be specific, if an input sentence contains the grammatical errors, the output of each error should include four items: the id of the sentence, the positions of starting and ending character at which the grammatical error occurs, and the error type which should be one of the defined errors: "R", "M", "S", and "W". Example sentences and corresponding notes are shown in Table 1 and Table 2.

3 Methodology

We use two different models to solve the CGED task. One is the traditional model based on Conditional Random Field (CRF) with specific feature engineering. Many researchers have chosen CRF based models to solve CGED2016 and CGED2017 task. From previous research, we know that the CRF model with carefully designed feature templates could maintain the performance with neural networks at the same level (Lung-Hao Lee et al., 2016), especially when the training data is not big enough. Another is LSTM-CRF model with conventional sparse CRF features. The LSTM-CRF model is also used by some researchers before (Bo Zheng et al., 2016). The research proved that LSTM is effective in various applications that involves sequence modeling. This time, we make some improvements on both CRF model and LSTM-CRF model.

3.1 CRF model with feature engineering

Conditional random fields (CRF), an extension of both Maximum Entropy Model (MEMS) and Hidden Markov Models (HMMs), has been used to solve some natural language processing problems such as word segmentation, information extraction and parsing. The CGED task can be considered as a sequence labeling problem which assigns each Chinese character in a sentence with a tag including the error types (R, M, S, W). CRF is a sequence labelling model with flexible feature space. Therefore, with given feature set and labeled training data, the CRF model can be used to solve the CGED task. The model can be defined as:

$$P(y|x) = \frac{1}{Z(x)} \exp\left(\Sigma_k \lambda_k f_k\right)$$

where Z(x) is the normalization factor, f_k is the feature sets and λ_k is the corresponding weight of the features. x is the sequence of the training sentences (the first column of Table 3), and y is the error type label (the forth column of Table 3) which includes O(Correct), R(Redundant words), M(Missing Words), S(Selection errors) and W(Word ordering errors). Tag 'O' indicates correct characters, 'B-X' indicates the beginning positions for errors of type 'X' and 'I-X' shows the middle or ending positions for errors of type 'X'.

For example, the label 'B-S' indicates this character is the beginning of a words selection error. The CRF model can generate the corresponding label sequence y according to the sequence data x. The second column of Table 3 is the POS(Part-of-speech) feature. The task is being solved at the character level. The POS tag was split of a word to character level by attaching position indicators ('B-' and 'I-') to the POS of a word. We use LTP Segmenter and Postagger which is a Chinese Language Technology Platform (Wanxiang Che et al., 2010) to tag the training sentences.

Character	POS	Parsing	Error
他	B-r	2	0
们	I-r	2	0
是	B-v	0	B-W
不	B-c	5	I-W
但	I-c	5	I-W
我	B-r	5	0
父	B-n	2	0
母	I-n	2	0

Table 3: A snapshot of a sample sentence

The third column of Table3 is syntactic feature of the character. Syntactic feature is the dependency parsing results of a sentence. Dependency parsing provides a representation of grammatical relations between words in a sentence. To be specific, dependency parsing can be used to identify the grammatical components of the subject in the sentence and analyze the relationship between the components. Figure 1 and Figure 2 shows the example of the dependency parsing. LTP is also used to parse the sentence. The output of the parsing of the sample sentence is "2:SBV 0:HED 5:ADV 5:ATT 2:VOB". Table 4 describe the meaning of these tags. The number means which word in the sentence is related to the current word. For example, 2:SBV means the 2th word "是" and the current word "他们" are the subject-predicate relationships . We can find out the grammatical relations of the sentence more clearly from the figures below. Figure 1 is the sentence with grammatical errors and Figure 2 is the correction. The number of the output is used as the syntactic feature.

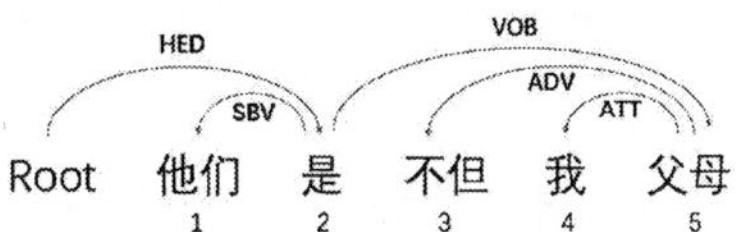

Figure 1: Dependency parsing of the sentence with grammatical errors

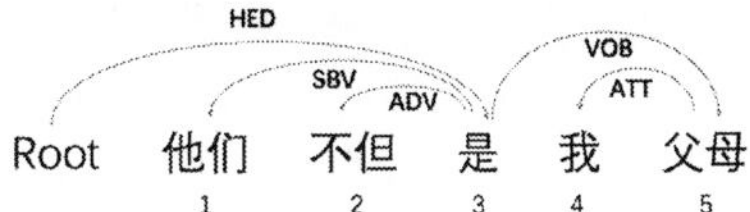

Figure 2: Dependency parsing of the correct sentence

Tag	Description
SBV	subject-verb
VOB	verb-object
IOB	indirect-object
FOB	fronting-object
DBL	double
ATT	attribute
ADV	adverbial
CMP	complement
COO	coordinate
POB	preposition-object
LAD	left adjunct
RAD	right adjunct
IS	independent structure
HED	head

Table 4: Description of syntactic features tag

Feature Templates

00-04: $Character_{i+k}$ (k=-2,-1,0,1,2)
05-09: POS_{i+k} (k=-2,-1,0,1,2)
10-14: $Parsing_{i+k}$ (k=-2,-1,0,1,2)
15-18: $Character_i/Character_{i+k}$ (k=-2,-1,1,2)
19-23: $Character_i/POS_{i+k}$ (k=-2,-1,0,1,2)
24-28: $Character_i/Parsing_{i+k}$ (k=-2,-1,0,1,2)
29-32: POS_i/POS_{i+k} (k=-2,-1,1,2)
33-37: $POS_i/Parsing_{i+k}$ (k=-2,-1,0,1,2)
38-41: $POS_i/Character_{i+k}$ (k=-2,-1,1,2)
42-45: $Character_i/Character_{i+k}/POS_{i+k}$ (k=-2,-1,1,2)
46-49: $POS_i/Character_{i+k}/POS_{i+k}$ (k=-2,-1,1,2)

Table 5: Feature templates

CRF++ (Kudo et al.,2007), a linear-chain CRF model software tool, is used to built the CRF model. To train a model with CRF++, we need to build some templates first. We use 50 templates to generate 50 combinatorial features which is listed in Table 5. The format of each template is %X[row, col], in which row is the number of row in a sentence and column is the number of column. The template %x[0,0]/%x[0,1] means the feature combining the current character and the next POS tag. Take the character "是" in sample sentence in Table 3 as an example, %x[0,0]/%x[0,1] represents "是/B-v".

3.2 LSTM-CRF model

LSTM-CRF model is currently a strong baseline in the task of sequence labeling. Compared with the conventional Bi-LSTM neural network, LSTM-CRF model can directly model probability distribution of the the label sequence by a CRF layer, and achieve better performance on several datasets (Z.Huang et al., 2015; X.Ma et al., 2016). An illustrative graph is shown in Figure 3. Under this framework, neural network (i.e. LSTM) is used to compute the features score in CRF, which are called neural features. These neural features are similar to the conventional sparse CRF features, which are directly used to compute the score of a given label sequence.

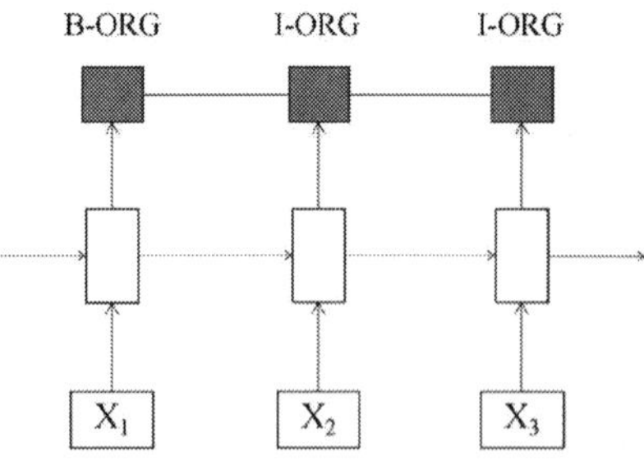

Figure 3: LSTM-CRF model

A LSTM-CRF model can efficiently capture past input features via a LSTM layer and other user specified sparse features (e.g. transition feature, n-gram feature.) via a CRF layer. In our case, plenty of features are considered, here we only take tag transition feature as an example for simplicity. Denoting a tag transition matrix $[A]$, where each $[A]_{i,j}$ models the transition score from i^{th} tag to j^{th} tag for a pair of consecutive time step. Note that this transition matrix is position

independent. De-noting the matrix of scores $f_\theta[x]_i^T$ are output by the network. The element $[f_\theta]_{[i]_t}$ of the matrix is the score output by the network with parameters θ, for the sentence $[x]_i^T$ and for the ith tag, at the tth word. The score of a sentence $[x]_i^T$ along with a path of tags $[i]_i^T$ is then given by the sum of transition scores and net-work scores:

$$s([x]_i^T, [i]_i^T, \theta) = \sum_{t=1}^{T} (w_1[A]_{[i]_{t-1},[i]_t} + w_2[f_\theta]_{[i]_t,t})$$

Here we modified the objective function to attend differentially to neural features and conventional CRF sparse features. It is worth noting that the dynamic programming can be used efficiently to compute $[A]_{i,j}$ and optimal tag sequences for inference. Then, the modified CRF layer models the conditional probability of possible output sequence s over input sequence x as:

$$p(s|x) = \frac{1}{Z(x)} \exp\{s([x]_i^T, [i]_i^T, \theta)\}$$

$s([x]_i^T, [i]_i^T, \theta)$ is the score of a sentence $[x]_i^T$ along with a path of tags $[i]_i^T$. $Z(x)$ is the normalization factor of all the possible paths of tags $[i]$ over input sequence x. For our LSTM CRF training, we use the maximum conditional likelihood estimation. For a training set$\{(x_i, i_i)\}$, the log-likelihood is given as:

$$\mathcal{L}_\mathcal{D}(W) = \sum_{i \in \mathcal{D}} \log p(i|x)$$

Maximum likelihood training chooses parameters W such that the log-likelihood $\mathcal{L}_\mathcal{D}(W)$ is maximized.

The training algorithm is giving as follows:

Algorithm 1 LSTM CRF training procedure
for each epoch do
for each batch do
1) neural network forward pass
forward pass for LSTM state
2) CRF layer forward and backward pass
3) neural network backward pass: backward pass for LSTM
4) update parameters
end
end

Table 6: the LSTM-CRF training procedure

In most LSTM-CRF based models (Z.Huang et al., 2015; X.Ma et al., 2016; M.Rei et al., 2016;

L.Kong et al., 2016; G. Lample et al., 2016), only tag transition features are considered in CRF layer. In our case, more conventional sparse CRF features are incorporated into the CRF layer. Specifically, we consider the following features defined over the inputs:

- Words features. Words that appear around the current position with a window of size 3.
- POS tags features. POS tags that appear around the current position with a window of size 3.
- Word n-grams features. Word n-grams that contain the current position, for n = 2, 3, 4.
- POS n-grams features. POS tags that contain the current position, for n = 2, 3, 4.
- Bag of words features. Bag of words that contains the current word, with a window of size 5.
- Tag transition features. Tag n-grams that contain the current position, for n = 2.

4 Experiments

4.1 Dataset

We collect datasets from CGED-HSK-2016, CGED-2017 and CGED-2018 as our training set and validation set. Table 7 shows the distributions of error types in both the training set and validation set. The ratio of training set size to validation set size is about 8:1. Besides the sentences with grammatical errors, 1539 correct sentences are added into the validation set.

	Training Set	Validation Set
Error	52313	6773
R	11598(22.17%)	3880(57.29%)
M	13931(26.63%)	991(14.63%)
S	23014(43.99%)	1620(23.82%)
W	3769(7.20%)	282(4.16%)

Table 7: The distributions of error types

4.2 Validation

We use the validation set to evaluate the results of the CRF models with and without syntactic feature. CRF-1 refers to the model with syntactic feature and CRF-2 refers to the model without syntactic feature. According to the results in Table 8, we can find out that syntactic feature does help to improve the performance of the CRF model. Therefore, CRF model with both Part-Of-Speech(POS) feature and syntactic feature is used in our final run.

	CRF-1	CRF-2
Accuracy	96.98%	96.34%
Precision	35.32%	31.53%
Recall	13.46%	12.28%
F1	19.49%	17.68%

Table 8: Evaluation results of CRF model on validation set for position level

We also thoroughly study the effectiveness of the handcraft features in our LSTM-CRF model. Experiment results are shown in Table 9. LSTM-CRF-1 refers to the LSTM-CRF model with handcraft features defined in section 3.2. LSTM-CRF2 refers to the LSTM-CRF model with no handcraft features (i.e. only tag transition feature is considered). As the experiment results shown that the feature engineering in CRF part can improve the performance (i.e. F1 value) about 2%, thus we use the LSTM-CRF1 model as our final model.

	LSTM-CRF-1	LSTM-CRF-2
Accuracy	97.28%	96.63%
Precision	33.10%	29.60%
Recall	15.76%	14.22%
F1	21.35%	19.21%

Table 9: Evaluation results of LSTM-CRF model on validation set for position level

4.3 Evaluation Results

In the CGED2018 shared task, there are 12 teams submitted the results, totally 32 runs. Among them, our team submitted three runs. Run1 and Run2 are based on the CRF model with different size of training set while Run3 is based on the LSTM-CRF model. The average of all runs is calculated from 32 runs of the 12 teams.

Table 10 shows the false positive rate of the 3 runs of our team and the average of all runs. FP (False Positive) is the number of sentences in which non-existent grammatical errors are identified as errors, so the lower the better. The best false positive rate of our team is 0.1255 (Run3) which is much lower than the average rate of all runs.

Table 11 Table 12 and Table 13 shows the evaluation result for detection level, identification level and position level. The submitted results of our

Submission	False Positive Rate
Run1	0.3470
Run2	0.3873
Run3	**0.1255**
Average of all runs	0.46685

Table 10: The False Positive Rate (The lower the better)

	Detection Level		
	Accuracy	Recall	F1
Run1	0.5923	0.5445	0.5993
Run2	0.5796	0.5536	0.5959
Run3	0.5762	0.3417	0.4745
Average of all runs	0.58701	0.63484	0.61310

Table 11: Evaluation Results for Detection Level

	Identification Level		
	Accuracy	Recall	F1
Run1	0.4767	0.2836	0.3556
Run2	0.4452	0.2740	0.3392
Run3	0.6139	0.1818	0.2805
Average of all runs	0.46223	0.41422	0.37791

Table 12: Evaluation Results for Identification Level

	Position Level		
	Accuracy	Recall	F1
Run1	0.1238	0.0667	0.0867
Run2	0.0901	0.0506	0.0648
Run3	**0.3745**	0.0858	**0.1397**
Average of all runs	0.17532	0.11386	0.12473

Table 13: Evaluation Results for Position Level

team have better performance on accuracy than the average of all runs from CGED2018 for all three evaluation levels, but all three runs do not perform well on recall rate. Table 13 indicates that Run 3 achieved the accuracy of 0.3745 for position level which is the most difficult level and it leads to the final F1 score of 0.1397 although the recall rate is still not above the average.

5 Conclusion and Future Work

In this paper, we thoroughly study the task of Chinese grammatical error diagnosis and propose two models to handle this issue. We use a conventional linear CRF with specific feature engineering and a LSTM-CRF model to solve this task. We make some improvements on these two models based on the previous research and get better performance on False Positive Rate and Accuracy than the average of all runs from CGED2018 for all three evaluation levels including detection level, identification level and position level, but all three runs do not perform well on recall rate which should be improved in the future . Future work includes explorations of semi-CRFs and neural semi-CRFs for the CGED shared task and exploring more task specific features such as phonology feature and grapheme feature.

Acknowledgments

This study was funded by Special Foundation for Graduate Students Attending International Conferences of East China Normal University.

References

John Lafferty, Andrew McCallum, and Fernando Pereira. 2001. *Conditional random fields: Probabilistic models for segmenting and labeling sequence data.* In Proceedings of ICML, pages 282-289.

Lunghao Lee, Rao Gaoqi, Liangchih Yu, Xun Endong, Baolin Zhang, and Liping Chang. 2016. *Overview of NLP-TEA 2016 shared task for Chinese grammatical error diagnosis.* In Proceedings of the 3rd Workshop on Natural Language Processing Techniques for Educational Applications, pages 40–48.

Bo Zheng, Wanxiang Che, Jiang Guo, and Ting Liu. 2016. *Chinese grammatical error diagnosis with long short-term memory networks.* In Proceedings of the 3rd Workshop on Natural Language Processing Techniques for Educational Applications, pages 49–56.

Po-Lin Chen, Wu Shih-Hung, Liang-Pu Chen, Ping-Che Yang, and Ren-Dar Yang. 2015. *Chinese grammatical error diagnosis by conditional random fields,* In Proceedings of The 2nd Workshop on Natural Language Processing Techniques for Educational Applications, pages 7–14.

Po-Lin Chen, Wu Shih-Hung, Liang-Pu Chen, and Ping-Che Yang. 2016. *Improving the selection error recognition in a Chinese grammar error detection system.* International Conference on Information Reuse and Integration, pages 525-530.

Jui-Feng Yeh, Chan-Kun Yeh, Kai-Hsiang Yu, Ya-Ting Li, and Wan-Ling Tsai. 2015. *Condition random dom fields-based grammatical error detection for Chinese as second language.* In Proceedings of The 2nd Workshop on Natural Language Processing Techniques for Educational Applications, pages 105–110.

Yajun Liu, Yingjie Han, Liyan Zhuo, and Hongying Zan. 2016. *Automatic grammatical error detection for Chinese based on conditional random field.* In Proceedings of the 3rd Workshop on Natural Language Processing Techniques for Educational Applications, pages 57–62.

Wanxiang Che, Zhenghua Li, and Ting Liu. 2010. *LTP: A Chinese language technology platform.* In Proceedings of the Coling 2010: Demonstrations, pages 13-16.

Taku Kudo. 2007. *"CRF++: Yet Another CRF toolkit",* https://taku910.github.io/crfpp/.

Zhiheng Huang, Wei Xu and Kai Yu. 2015. *Bidirectional LSTM-CRF models for sequence tagging.* Computer Science.

Xuezhe Ma and Eduard Hovy. 2016. *End-to-end sequence labeling via Bi-directional LSTM-CNNs-CRF.* In Proceedings of ACL, pages 1064-1074.

Lingpeng Kong, Chris Dyer and Noah A. Smith. 2016. In Proceedings of ICML.

Guillaume Lample, Miguel Ballesteros, Sandeep Subramanian, Kazuya Kawakami and Chris Dyer. 2016. *Neural architectures for named entity recognition.* pages 260-270.

Contextualized Character Representation for Chinese Grammatical Error Diagnosis

Jianbo Zhao, Si Li, Zhiqing Lin

Beijing University of Posts and Telecommunications

No.10 Xitucheng Road, Haidian District, Beijing, China

{zhaojianbo, lisi, linzq}@bupt.edu.cn

Abstract

Nowadays, more and more people are learning Chinese as their second language. Establishing an automatic diagnosis system for Chinese grammatical error has become an important challenge. In this paper, we propose a Chinese grammatical error diagnosis (CGED) model with contextualized character representation. Compared to the traditional model using LSTM (Long-Short Term Memory), our model have better performance and there is no need to add too many artificial features.

1 Introduction

With the rapid development of China, more and more non-native Chinese speakers begin to learn Chinese. Writing is a very important part of Chinese learning. However, there are some differences between Chinese and English, such as no changes in tense in Chinese, which makes it difficult for many Chinese learners to find their own mistakes in writing. Traditional Chinese learning methods cost a lot of labor and time, so it is very important to establish an automatic diagnosis system for Chinese grammatical error. This is also the purpose of this shared task.

The task of CGED2018[1] is to automatically diagnose grammatical errors in Chinese sentences written by second language learners. The errors include four types, redundant words (denoted as a capital "R"), missing words ("M"), word selection errors ("S") and word ordering errors ("W"). Table 1 shows examples of errors. The CGED system needs to detect the location of errors and gives the type of each error. For error typed S and M, the model can give at most three correct candidates.

Error Type	Error Sentence	Correct Sentence
R	大 家 合 作 无 间而救了那位病人。	大 家 合 作 无 间 救 了 那 位 病 人 。 (We saved that patient cooperatively.)
M	千万别人家添麻烦。	千 万 别 给 人 家 添 麻 烦。 (Don't bother others.)
S	怎 样 把 孩 子教养成人呢？	怎样把孩子抚养 成 人 呢 ？ (How to raise the child?)
W	我有强度高的思 维能力。	我有高强度的思 维能力。 (I have high-intensity thinking skills.)

Table 1: Examples of each error types

In this paper, we regard CGED task as a sequence labeling problem(Zheng et al., 2016) and propose a CGED model with contextualized character representation. This model have better considered the different semantics of words in Chinese texts. The experiment results show that our model have better result compared to the baseline without artificial features.

2 Contextualized Character Representation

2.1 Character Embedding

Words are the smallest unit of semantic expressions in Chinese texts. In different contexts, the same words may express different meanings. Also, the same situation exists for single characters. For example, the character "打" in word "一打" (a dozen) means dozen, in word "打鼓" (play the

---

[1] https://sites.google.com/view/nlptea2018/shared-task

Proceedings of the 5th Workshop on Natural Language Processing Techniques for Educational Applications, pages 172–179

Melbourne, Australia, July 19, 2018. ©2018 Association for Computational Linguistics

drum) means play. Therefore, we use the same character vector to represent the same character in different contexts is inaccurate, and sometimes there may be a big semantic deviation. To address this issue, we propose to use the contextualized character representation for CGED to solve the ambiguity problem.

2.2 Building Contextualized Character Representation

(Choi et al., 2016) puts forward that each dimension of a word vector may represent some semantic information of the word. But in different texts, the semantic information we need to use is different, so we need to ignore the unneeded semantic information. That is to say, under the different context conditions, we need to mask out some dimensions of the word embedding vectors. We take advantage of this method proposed in (Choi et al., 2016) for our model.

$$T = \frac{1}{M} \sum_{t=1}^{M} NN_\xi(x_t) \tag{1}$$

where x_t in our work represents the character representation in each time step. T represents the text representation. M is the max sequence length for the sentence. NN_ξ: $R^{C_E} \rightarrow R^{T_E}$ is a feedforward neural network parametrized by ξ. C_E is the character embedding size and T_E is the text representation size.

Then we use T to calculate the contextualized character vectors as input of traditional sequence labeling model of LSTM instead of the traditional character vectors.

$$mask = \sigma(W_m T + b_m) \tag{2}$$

$$x_t \leftarrow x_t \odot mask \tag{3}$$

where σ is the sigmoid activation function to control the output between 0 to 1. W_m is the weight of calculating $mask$ and b_m is the bias. $\odot$ is an element-wise multiplication.

We use the $mask$ to get the contextualized character representation which can better represent the meaning of characters and better obtain the information we need in the text.

The number of sentences	The number of characters	The average number of characters
402	19382	48.21

Table 2: Information of training set: The average number of characters represent the average number of characters of one sentence.

Error type	The number of error characters	The proportion of error characters in training set
R	281	1.44%
M	298	1.53%
S	797	4.11%
W	493	2.54%
all errors	1869	9.64%

Table 3: The number of errors in training set

3 Function of Save Model and Loss Function

3.1 Error Sparse Problem

In the given Chinese text, we find that a relatively long sentence may only contains one or two errors. Although one sentence may contain multiple errors but the number of errors is insufficient. In Table 2 and 3, we give the number of errors in CGED2018.

After dividing the errors into four categories, it can be seen that due to the small number of errors, it may not be conducive to the training of the model.

3.2 Function of Save Model

We use the traditional training method, accuracy, to train our model. However, when the development set has reached the greatest accuracy, the output of the model in test set is not good. Analyzing the result, we see that the model learns the correct part more, and learns the error information less. The model discriminates most of test sentences to be correct. Therefore, we propose to save the model no longer when the development set achieves the max accuracy, but when Eq. 4 is max in development set.

$$f_s = \frac{\sum_n \sum_i c_{ni}}{\sum_n \sum_i e_{ni}} \tag{4}$$

$$
c_{ni} = \begin{cases} 1 & p_{ni} = y_{ni} \ and \ (p_{ni} \neq 0 \ or \ y_{ni} \neq 0) \\ 0 & others \end{cases}
$$

$$(5)$$

$$
e_{ni} = \begin{cases} 1 & others \\ 0 & p_{ni} = 0 \ and \ y_{ni} = 0 \end{cases} \quad (6)
$$

where p represents the output label of the model of a character and y represents the ground-truth label.

The significance of Eq. 4 is that when we save the model, we expect the model to detect more wrong information and ignore some correct information. The model can capture more error information when there are fewer errors in the sentence.

3.3 Loss Function

Although the model can detect more error information but it is not enough, when we use Eq. 4 to save the model. From the table 6, 7, 8, 9, it can also be seen that although the results have improved but the increase is limited.

In the traditional LSTM model of sequence labelling, the cross-entropy loss function, Eq. 7, is generally used as its loss function.

$$
loss_1 = -\frac{1}{n} \sum_x [y \ln a + (1 - y) \ln(1 - a)] \quad (7)
$$

However, the problem that the number of correct characters in the dataset is much larger than the number of incorrect characters still exists. Therefore, the training of the model may have some problem. To address this issue, we add a loss function Eq. 8 to $loss_1$.

$$
loss_2 = -\frac{1}{n} \sum_x [y_m \ln a_m + (1 - y_m) \ln(1 - a_m)]
$$

$$(8)$$

$$
y_m = mask_r(y) \quad (9)
$$

$$
a_m = mask_r(a) \quad (10)
$$

where we use $mask_r$ to keep the correct place in the training tag, forcing the model to capture more error information. The overall loss function is Eq. 11.

$$
loss = (1 - \gamma)loss_1 + \gamma loss_2 \quad (11)
$$

Segmented sentence	2-gram	3-gram
我/自己/本身/偏好/于/男女/混合式/教育。	<本身 偏好> <偏好 于>	<自己 本身 偏好> <偏好 于 男女>

Table 4: Example of n-gram

where γ is a weight, indicates the importance of the error information that needs to be retained, and can be adjusted according to different tasks.

4 Correction System

Correct system we use in our model is the method proposed in (Chen et al., 2016). Since we mainly deal with the detection problem, we have simplified the method in (Chen et al., 2016) and only put forward one candidate correction.

(Chen et al., 2016) uses the method of calculating the n-gram score of each word to judge whether the word is correct or not and put forward correct candidates. If the original word has the highest score, the original word is considered to be correct. If the candidate word has a higher score than the original word, the original word is considered to be wrong. The candidate word with highest scoring is regarded as the correction.

$$
SL(S) = \sum_n \left(n \times \sum_{u \in SubStr(S,n)} \log(gsf(u)) \right)
$$

$$(12)$$

Eq. 12 gives the equation of length-weighted string log-frequency score $SL(S)$. Where S represents the sentence after word segmentation or character segmentation. $SubStr(S, n)$ represent all substring of sentence S with n words or characters. $gsf(\cdot)$ is the frequency of u. Obviously, matching a higher gram is more welcome than a lower gram. To increase the accuracy of correction, (Chen et al., 2016) adds weights to the different n-gram by their length to favor higher gram.

We use this score for errors typed S. In order to reduce the amount of calculation, we only keep the calculation of 2-gram and 3-gram, the example of n-gram of words is shown in table 4.

For the error which is typed with S is a word, we will calculate the SL score of the word. We use the dictionaries of characters with similar pronunciation and similar shape in (Wu et al., 2013) and convert characters into simplified Chinese[2]. We merged the two dictionaries to one dictionary of candidates for characters. When we choose the word to replace, we prefer to select the word that have only one character different from the original word. We replace each characters in the words and calculate the score separately. We select the candidate word with the highest score as the correct one.

For the error which is typed with S is a character, we calculate the SL score for the character. The candidate dictionary is directly used to replace the character and the score is calculated. The character with the highest score is considered to be correct.

For the error typed with M, we also use SL to calculate the score using 2-gram and 3-gram. We first search the words in the word dictionary which have the same character as the character labeled M. Then, calculate the candidates' score. We regard that the candidate with the highest score is the correct candidate.

5 Evaluation

5.1 Baseline

In this experiment, we build the Bi-LSTM model for sequence labelling as our baseline model. Unlike traditional sequence labeling, Chinese grammatical error diagnosis may result in inaccurate word segmentation due to existing errors, so we use character embeddings to replace word embeddings.

5.2 Hyper-parameter and Data

We use word2vec[3] to pretrain our character embeddings by wiki corpus[4]. We also use wiki corpus to build our n-gram dictionaries. The character embedding size is 400, the hidden units of Bi-LSTM is 256. We set the batch size is 32. We use Adam optimizer to train our model and the learning rate is 0.001.

The training data we use comes from NLPTEA2016 and NLPTEA2018 and we di-

---

	Train	Dev	Test 2016	Test 2017
Num_{sen}	7602	2402	3011	3154
Num_c	349230	112617	150826	141973
Num_{ec}	32117	10633	6680	8508

Table 5: Information of training data: Num_{sen} means the total number of sentences in each set. Num_c means the total number of characters. Num_{ec} represent the total number of error characters.

vide part of data from NLPTEA2016 to the development set. We use two test set from NLPTEA2016 and NLPTEA2017. Table 5 shows the data information in detail.

5.3 Evaluation Method

According to (Lee et al., 2016), the evaluation method includes three levels, detection level, identification level, position level. And this year add correction level.

Detection level: Determines whether a sentence is correct or not. If there is an error, the sentence is incorrect. In other words, the sentences are classified into two categories.

Identification level: The correct situation should be exactly the same as the gold standard for a given type of error. This can be considered as a multi-classification problem.

Position level: The system results should be perfectly identical with the quadruples of the gold standard.

Correction level: Characters marked as S and M need to give correct candidates. The model can recommend at most 3 correction at each error.

The following metrics are measured at detection, identification, position-level.

$$FalsePositiveRate = \frac{FP}{FP + TN} \quad (13)$$

$$Accuracy = \frac{TP + TN}{TP + FP + TN + FN} \quad (14)$$

$$Precision = \frac{TP}{TP + FP} \quad (15)$$

$$Recall = \frac{TP}{TP + FN} \quad (16)$$

$$F_1 = \frac{2 * Precision * Recall}{Precision + Recall} \quad (17)$$

[2]http://zh.wikipedia.org/wiki/Wikipedia: 繁简处理
[3]https://code.google.com/archive/p/word2vec
[4]https://dumps.wikimedia.org/zhwiki/latest/zhwiki-latest-pages-articles.xml.bz2

	False Positive Rate
Bi-LSTM	0.0136
Bi-LSTM+FS	0.0884
Bi-LSTM+loss_0.5	0.2073
Bi-LSTM+FS+loss_0.5	0.9831
Bi-LSTM+FS+loss_0.4	0.9519
Bi-LSTM+FS+loss_0.3	0.8571
Bi-LSTM+FS+loss_0.2	0.5491
Bi-LSTM+FS+loss_0.1	0.3028
Bi-LSTM+FS+loss_0.05	0.1832
Bi-LSTM+mask	0.7057
Bi-LSTM+mask+POS	0.7596

Table 6: Result on false positive rate: FS represents model that save model with new function and loss means the model with new loss function and the number after "_" is γ.

	Acc	Pre	Re	F_1
Bi-LSTM	0.5111	0.5	0.0143	0.0277
Bi-LSTM+FS	0.5064	0.4729	0.0829	0.141
Bi-LSTM +loss_0.5	0.5065	0.4888	0.2072	0.291
Bi-LSTM+FS +loss_0.5	0.4902	0.4894	0.9851	0.6539
Bi-LSTM+FS +loss_0.4	0.4829	0.4851	0.9375	0.6393
Bi-LSTM+FS +loss_0.3	0.4839	0.484	0.8404	0.6142
Bi-LSTM+FS +loss_0.2	0.4909	0.4813	0.5326	0.5056
Bi-LSTM+FS +loss_0.1	0.5005	0.4822	0.2948	0.3659
Bi-LSTM+FS +loss_0.05	0.5148	0.5096	0.199	0.2863
Bi-LSTM +mask	0.4899	0.4848	0.6943	0.5709
Bi-LSTM +mask+POS	0.5015	0.4937	0.7745	0.603

Table 7: Results on detection level: ACC represents accuracy. Pre means precision. Re is recall.

6 Result

In this part, we show our experiment results in the CGED2016 test set. Since the experiment results are similar on CGED2017 dataset, they are not given.

The first part of table 6, 7, 8, 9 shows the results of the comparison between the model using new function to save model, with the reconstruction loss function and the original model. The γ of the model with reconstructive loss is set to 0.5. It can be seen from the experiment that modifying the save function and rebuilding the loss function all have a good improvement on the error detection of the model. The results of mixing the above methods are also given. There is an improvement in error detection, but too many errors are detected and the correct information is ignored. So after that we modify the value of the weight γ in Eq. 11 to get more reasonable model.

The second part of table 6, 7, 8, 9 shows the different models with new function to save model and reconstructive loss for modifying the value of γ in Eq. 11. It can be seen that when the weight decreases, the false positive rate decreases significantly, which indicates that the model captures more correct information. When γ is 0.2 or 0.1 is more suitable for our task. When the weight is too large, false positive rate is too large indicates that the error is not detected, which is not consistent with the objectives of this task. At 0.05, the F1 values of all levels are too low, so we use 0.1 as the weight in the following experiments.

The third part of table 6, 7, 8, 9 shows the experimental results of our proposed model with new save function and reconstructive loss. γ is set to 0.1. The results from F1 show that the proposed model is improved compared to the baseline model. The model can also detect error information very well without artificial features. We also tried to add artificial information to the model to improve the experimental results, so we added POS (Part of Speech) information. Since we are dealing with characters, so we use POS for the character's corresponding word as the character's POS. It can be seen that POS is useful in Chinese error detection. For errors, POS may provide some information to help the model detect better.

Table 10, 11, 12, 13 shows the experiment results we submitted in CGED2018 in detection part. Table 14 show the results in CGED2018 in correction part. Since our model only proposes one candidate, the results on Correction and Top3 Correction are the same.

7 Related Work

Chinese grammatical error diagnosis task has been developed for a long time. From the initial statistical methods to the current machine learning, more and more attention has been paid to.

	Acc	Pre	Re	F_1
Bi-LSTM	0.5098	0.4048	0.0068	0.0134
Bi-LSTM+FS	0.4982	0.3788	0.0401	0.0725
Bi-LSTM +loss_0.5	0.4646	0.3039	0.0842	0.1419
Bi-LSTM+FS +loss_0.5	0.2557	0.2536	0.6919	0.3712
Bi-LSTM+FS +loss_0.4	0.2772	0.2713	0.5239	0.3575
Bi-LSTM+FS +loss_0.3	0.3064	0.2848	0.4256	0.3412
Bi-LSTM+FS +loss_0.2	0.4122	0.3431	0.2479	0.2878
Bi-LSTM+FS +loss_0.1	0.4579	0.349	0.1368	0.1965
Bi-LSTM+FS +loss_0.05	0.488	0.3735	0.0895	0.1443
Bi-LSTM +mask	0.361	0.3167	0.365	0.3392
Bi-LSTM +mask+pos	0.3752	0.3451	0.4902	0.405

Table 8: Results on identification level: ACC represents accuracy. Pre means precision. Re is recall.

	Acc	Pre	Re	F_1
Bi-LSTM	0.5041	0.0227	0.0003	0.0005
Bi-LSTM+FS	0.4643	0.0528	0.0043	0.008
Bi-LSTM +loss_0.5	0.3746	0.0101	0.0024	0.0039
Bi-LSTM+FS +loss_0.5	0.0239	0.0227	0.1256	0.0385
Bi-LSTM+FS +loss_0.4	0.0319	0.0261	0.0877	0.0402
Bi-LSTM+FS +loss_0.3	0.0553	0.0297	0.0612	0.04
Bi-LSTM+FS +loss_0.2	0.188	0.0346	0.0265	0.03
Bi-LSTM+FS +loss_0.1	0.3447	0.0648	0.0217	0.0325
Bi-LSTM+FS +loss_0.05	0.4107	0.0517	0.01	0.0168
Bi-LSTM +mask	0.1323	0.0582	0.0709	0.0639
Bi-LSTM +mask+pos	0.1965	0.1217	0.1729	0.1429

Table 9: Results on position level: ACC represents accuracy. Pre means precision. Re is recall

	False Positive Rate
Bi-LSTM+mask	0.5029
Bi-LSTM+mask+POS	0.5480

Table 10: Result on false positive rate in CGED2018

(Zhang et al., 2000) searched the optimal string from all possible derivation of the input sentence using operations of character substitution, insertion, and deletion with a traditional word 3-gram language model. (Chen et al., 2013) still used n-gram as the main method, and added Web resources to improve detection results. (Lin and Chu, 2015) used n-gram to establish a scoring system to better give correction options. (Yeh et al., 2017) based on n-gram used the KMP algorithm to speed up the search for correct candidates.

Due to the continuous rise of machine learning in recent years, the field of natural language processing is increasingly turning to machine learning. In the past few years, the diagnosis of Chinese grammatical errors has also been developing in machine learning. Grammatical error detection is usually considered as the sequence labeling task (Zheng et al., 2016). (Huang and WANG, 2016) used Bi-LSTM to annotate the errors in the sentence. (Shiue et al., 2017) combined machine learning with traditional n-gram methods, using Bi-LSTM to detect the location of errors and adding additional linguistic information, POS, n-gram. (Li et al., 2017) used Bi-LSTM to generate the probability of each characters, and used two strategies to decide whether a character is correct or not. (Liao et al., 2017) used the LSTM+CRF model to detect dependencies between outputs to better detect error messages. (yang et al., 2017) added more linguistic information on LSTM+CRF model, such as POS, n-gram, PMI score and dependency features.

8 Conclusion

As more and more people learn Chinese, the automatic diagnosis of Chinese grammatical error becomes more and more important. This paper proposes a contextualized character representation for CGED and related solutions for the error sparse problem, which are improved compared to the baseline approach.

In the future, we will add this contextualized character representation to models that are better at Chinese grammatical error diagnosis such as Bi-

	Acc	Pre	Re	F_1
Bi-LSTM +mask	0.6005	0.6331	0.6809	0.6562
Bi-LSTM +mask+POS	0.6236	0.6377	0.7584	0.6929

Table 11: Results on detection level in CGED2018: ACC represents accuracy. Pre means precision. Re is recall.

	Pre	Re	F_1
Bi-LSTM +mask	0.4134	0.3519	0.3802
Bi-LSTM +mask+pos	0.4084	0.4161	4122

Table 12: Results on identification level in CGED2018: Pre means precision. Re is recall.

	Pre	Re	F_1
Bi-LSTM +mask	0.0608	0.0504	0.0551
Bi-LSTM +mask+pos	0.0630	0.0609	0.0620

Table 13: Results on position level in CGED2018: Pre means precision. Re is recall.

	Pre	Re	F_1
Bi-LSTM +mask	0.33%	0.28%	0.30%
Bi-LSTM +mask+pos	0.92%	0.87%	0.90%

Table 14: Results on Correction Part in CGED2018: Pre means precision. Re is recall.

LSTM+CRF and consider better correction methods.

Acknowledge

This work was supported by National Natural Science Foundation of China (61702047), Beijing Natural Science Foundation (4174098) and the Fundamental Research Funds for the Central Universities (2017RC02).

References

Kuan-Yu Chen, Hung-Shin Lee, Chung-Han Lee, Hsin-Min Wang, and Hsin-Hsi Chen. 2013. A study of language modeling for chinese spelling check. In *Proceedings of the Seventh SIGHAN Workshop on Chinese Language Processing*, pages 79–83. Asian Federation of Natural Language Processing.

Shao-Heng Chen, Yu-Lin Tsai, and Chuan-Jie Lin. 2016. Generating and scoring correction candidates in chinese grammatical error diagnosis. In *Proceedings of the 3rd Workshop on Natural Language Processing Techniques for Educational Applications (NLPTEA2016)*, pages 131–139. The COLING 2016 Organizing Committee.

Heeyoul Choi, Kyunghyun Cho, and Yoshua Bengio. 2016. Context-dependent word representation for neural machine translation. *CoRR*, abs/1607.00578.

Shen Huang and Houfeng WANG. 2016. Bi-lstm neural networks for chinese grammatical error diagnosis. In *Proceedings of the 3rd Workshop on Natural Language Processing Techniques for Educational Applications (NLPTEA2016)*, pages 148–154, Osaka, Japan. The COLING 2016 Organizing Committee.

Lung-Hao Lee, Gaoqi RAO, Liang-Chih Yu, Endong XUN, Baolin Zhang, and Li-Ping Chang. 2016. Overview of nlp-tea 2016 shared task for chinese grammatical error diagnosis. In *Proceedings of the 3rd Workshop on Natural Language Processing Techniques for Educational Applications (NLPTEA2016)*, pages 40–48. The COLING 2016 Organizing Committee.

Xian Li, Peng Wang, Suixue Wang, Guanyu Jiang, and Tianyuan You. 2017. Cvte at ijcnlp-2017 task 1: Character checking system for chinese grammatical error diagnosis task. In *Proceedings of the IJCNLP 2017, Shared Tasks*, pages 78–83, Taipei, Taiwan. Asian Federation of Natural Language Processing.

Quanlei Liao, Jin Wang, Jinnan Yang, and Xuejie Zhang. 2017. Ynu-hpcc at ijcnlp-2017 task 1: Chinese grammatical error diagnosis using a bi-directional lstm-crf model. In *Proceedings of the IJCNLP 2017, Shared Tasks*, pages 73–77, Taipei, Taiwan. Asian Federation of Natural Language Processing.

Chuan-Jie Lin and Wei-Cheng Chu. 2015. A study on chinese spelling check using confusion sets and?n-gram statistics. In *International Journal of Computational Linguistics & Chinese Language Processing, Volume 20, Number 1, June 2015-Special Issue on Chinese as a Foreign Language*.

Yow-Ting Shiue, Hen-Hsen Huang, and Hsin-Hsi Chen. 2017. Detection of chinese word usage errors for non-native chinese learners with bidirectional lstm. In *Proceedings of the 55th Annual Meeting of the Association for Computational Linguistics (Volume 2: Short Papers)*, pages 404–410, Vancouver, Canada. Association for Computational Linguistics.

Shih-Hung Wu, Chao-Lin Liu, and Lung-Hao Lee. 2013. Chinese spelling check evaluation at sighan bake-off 2013. In *Proceedings of the Seventh*

SIGHAN Workshop on Chinese Language Processing, pages 35–42, Nagoya, Japan. Asian Federation of Natural Language Processing.

Yi yang, Pengjun Xie, Jun tao, Guangwei xu, Linlin li, and Si luo. 2017. Alibaba at ijcnlp-2017 task 1: Embedding grammatical features into lstms for chinese grammatical error diagnosis task. In *Proceedings of the IJCNLP 2017, Shared Tasks*, pages 41–46, Taipei, Taiwan. Asian Federation of Natural Language Processing.

Jui-Feng Yeh, Li-Ting Chang, Chan-Yi Liu, and Tsung-Wei Hsu. 2017. Chinese spelling check based on n-gram and string matching algorithm. In *Proceedings of the 4th Workshop on Natural Language Processing Techniques for Educational Applications (NLPTEA 2017)*, pages 35–38, Taipei, Taiwan. Asian Federation of Natural Language Processing.

Lei Zhang, Changning Huang, Ming Zhou, and Haihua Pan. 2000. Automatic detecting/correcting errors in chinese text by an approximate word-matching algorithm. In *Meeting on Association for Computational Linguistics*, pages 248–254.

Bo Zheng, Wanxiang Che, Jiang Guo, and Ting Liu. 2016. Chinese grammatical error diagnosis with long short-term memory networks. In *Proceedings of the 3rd Workshop on Natural Language Processing Techniques for Educational Applications (NLPTEA2016)*, pages 49–56, Osaka, Japan. The COLING 2016 Organizing Committee.

CMMC-BDRC Solution to the NLP-TEA-2018 Chinese Grammatical Error Diagnosis Task

Yongwei Zhang[1,2]**, Qinan Hu**[1,2]**, Fang Liu**[1,3]**, and Yueguo Gu**[1]

[1]China Multilingual & Multimodal Corpora and Big Data Research Centre, Beijing, China
[2]Institute of Linguistics, Chinese Academy of Social Sciences, Beijing, China
[3]School of Software and Microelectronics, Peking University, Beijing, China
zhangyw@cass.org.cn, qinan.hu@qq.com, liu_fang@pku.edu.cn, gyg@beiwaionline.com

Abstract

Chinese grammatical error diagnosis is an important natural language processing (NLP) task, which is also an important application using artificial intelligence technology in language education. This paper introduces a system developed by the Chinese Multilingual & Multimodal Corpus and Big Data Research Center for the NLP-TEA shared task, named Chinese Grammar Error Diagnosis (CGED). This system regards diagnosing errors task as a sequence tagging problem, while takes correction task as a text classification problem. Finally, in the 12 teams, this system gets the highest F1 score in the detection task and the second highest F1 score in mean in the identification task, position task and the correction task.

1 Introduction

With the development of Chinese economy and the growing popularity of Chinese culture, more and more foreigners begin to learn Chinese. However, Chinese and English are different. For instance, Chinese grammar is more flexible and more complex than English grammar and there are few morphological changes in Chinese. Consequently, it is quite difficult for the second language (L2) learners to master. In addition, the huge number of Chinese characters and no space between word and word cause the difficulty in Chinese natural language processing. In short, regarding how to use artificial intelligence to correct L2 learners, Chinese writing meets both opportunities and challenges.

In order to promote the development of automatic detection of syntactic errors in Chinese writing, the Natural Language Processing Techniques for Educational Applications (NLP-TEA) have taken CGED as one of the shared tasks since 2014. Thanks to the CGED task, some research achievements have been made in Chinese grammar error detection. Based on those previous research results, this paper puts forward a new thinking direction of enriching training dataset for the CGED task.

The structure of this article is as follows: Section 2 briefly introduces the CGED shared task. Section 3 introduces some related work. Section 4 talks about the methodology. Section 5 presents the data augmentation method used in the system, and section 6 shows the experiment result. Finally, conclusion and future work are drawn in Section 7.

2 Task Definition

CGED has been held in five consecutive years since 2014. It aims to develop a NLP system to automatically diagnose grammatical errors in Chinese sentences written by L2 learners. Such errors are divided into four types: redundant words ('R'), missing words ('M'), word selection errors ('S'), and word ordering errors ('W'). The input sentence may contain one or more such errors. For each sentence, the developed system would detect the following four levels (or tasks):

(1) Detection-level: whether the sentence is correct or not?

(2) Identification-level: which error types are embedded?

(3) Position-level: where the error positions occur?

(4) Correction-level: what is the correct

Proceedings of the 5th Workshop on Natural Language Processing Techniques for Educational Applications, pages 180–187
Melbourne, Australia, July 19, 2018. ©2018 Association for Computational Linguistics

word?

M and S type errors are required to offer 1 to 3 corrections. The other type errors only need to be identified.

The training dataset provided by CGED includes original error text, correct text, error types as well as error intervals. But the correct words of errors are not given explicitly. Table 1 shows two examples of the training dataset.

In table 1, there are two errors in example 1. One is S type from position 23 to 24, and the other is M type at position 28. There are also two errors in example 2. One is R type at position 8, and the other is W type from position 9 to 14. It has been found that, in example 1, '原故' is an error word and '缘故' is the correct form. Beside this, '了' is omitted in example 1.

3 Related Work

Yu and Chen (2012) proposed a CRF-based model to detect Chinese word ordering errors. In 2014, Cheng et al. (2014) proposed an SVM model to further study the Chinese word ordering problems. Lee et al. (2013) used a series of manual linguistic rules to detect grammatical errors in Chinese learners'writings. Lee et al. (2014) then further proposed a system which integrated both handcrafted linguistic rules and N-gram models to detect Chinese grammatical errors in sentences. Those two aforementioned models are based on linguistic rules, which need to be summarized manually. And because of the flexibility of Chinese syntax, the performance of existing models is not ideal. In recent years, artificial neural networks have been extensively used to do NLP tasks. However, due to the lack of large writing data of interlanguage, the performance of deep learning algorithms is limited a lot. In order to integrate more linguistic information into neural networks, HIT team (Zheng et al., 2016) used Part-of-Speech (POS) tag as a feature, and Alibaba team (Yang et al., 2017) further integrated Part-of-Speech-Tagging Score (POS Score), Point-wise Mutual Information (PMI), and dependency word collocation etc. into deep learning networks. These efforts made two teams achieved pretty good results in 2016 and 2017 CGED tasks respectively.

4 Methodology

We treat the first three tasks which are detection task, identification task and position task (DIP tasks) as a sequence tagging problem, and correction task as a classification problem.

4.1 Methodology of DIP Tasks

4.1.1 Model Description

Same with the methods used by HIT team (Zheng et al., 2016) and Alibaba team (Yang et al., 2017), we treat DIP tasks as a sequence tagging problem. Specifically, we tag each character of the sentences and then use the LSTM-CRF model (Huang et al., 2015) for training and prediction. Each character is tagged with BIO encoding (Collier and Kim, 2004), also the same as the method adopted by HIT team (Zheng et al., 2016) and Alibaba team (Yang et al., 2017). We use the bidirectional LSTM unit as the RNN model. The structure of the model we adopted in our research is shown in Figure 1.

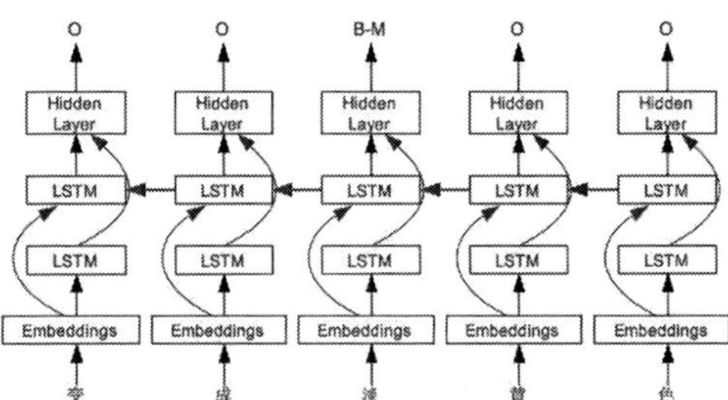

Figure 1: The structure of LSTM-CRF model we used.

4.1.2 Word Embedding Feature

We use char feature, POS feature, two char bigram features, and two char trigram features as the input features of the neural network. Language Technology Platform[1] (LTP) is used to segment words and do the POS tagging. If a word's POS tag is 'X', the POS tag of the first character of the word is 'B-X', and the POS tags of the rest characters of the word are all 'I-X'. When training bigram embeddings or trigram embeddings, we need to add a '^' character at the start of a sentence and a '$' character at the end of the sentence. In addition, in order to mark the missing words

---

[1]https://github.com/HIT-SCIR/ltp/

Example 1	Original Text	1 此 2 外 3, 4 吸 5 烟 6 也 7 影 8 响 9 了 10 美 11 观 12, 13 洁 14 白 15 的 16 牙 17 齿 18 因 19 为 20 吸 21 烟 22 的 23 原 24 故 25 而 26 变 27 成 28 淡 29 黄 30 色 31。32	
	Correct Text	此外，吸烟也影响了美观，洁白的牙齿因为吸烟的缘故而变成了淡黄色。	
	Error Type	S (word selection)	M (missing word)
	Error Interval	23, 24	28, 28
	Error-Correct Word	原故-缘故	-了
Example 2	Original Text	1 一 2 般 3 的 4 吸 5 烟 6 的 7 人 8 把 9 时 10 间 11 管 12 理 13 不 14 好 15。16	
	Correct Text	一般的吸烟的人管理不好时间。	
	Error Type	R (redundant word)	W (word ordering error)
	Error Interval	8, 8	9, 14
	Error-Correct Word	把-	时间管理不好-管理不好时间

Table 1: Two examples of training sentence of the CGED training dataset.

error occurred at the end of the sentence, a 'S' character is also need to be added at the end of the sentence. Figure 2 shows an example of the embedding features we used as the input for the neural networks.

```
变   BV    ^变    变成   ^^变    变成淡   O
成   IV    变成   成淡   而变成   成淡黄   O
淡   BA    成淡   淡黄   变成淡   淡黄色   B-M
黄   BN    淡黄   黄色   成淡黄   黄色。   O
色   IN    黄色   色。   淡黄色   色。$    O
。   BWP   色。   。$    黄色。   。$$     O
$   $     。$    $$     色。$    $$$      O
```

Figure 2: Embedding features of each character of '变成淡黄色。'. Each line represents one character's embedding features. These embedding features can be categorized as char feature, POS feature, two char bigram features, two char trigram features, and error tag. Different features are separated by using a tab character.

故' as a category, and '原故' as well as its context (N-gram) as the document.

In order to distinguish an error word from its left and right contexts, for correction task, we add a '_' character before and after the error word, a 'l' letter before each left word, and a 'r' letter before each right word. In addition to this, a prefix '__label__' is also required before the category name. And for M type error, we use '_M_' to denote the missing word, as shown in Figure 3.

```
__label__缘故  l因为  l吸烟  l的  _原故_  r而  r变成  r淡
__label__了    l原故  l而  l变成  _M_  r淡黄色  r。
```

Figure 3: The categories and their corresponding documents (texts) generated from example 1. Each line contains a category, followed by a corresponding document (text) which takes the error words, leftward three words, and rightward three words as its content.

4.2 Methodology of Correction Task

4.2.1 Model Description

The goal of text classification is to assign documents to one or multiple categories. Such categories can be spam v.s. non-spam, review scores or animal names. For correction task, the correct word can be seen as another type of category, and its context including its error form can be seen as a short document belonging to the category. In example 1, '缘故' is mistakenly written as '原故'. So we take '缘

However, using a text classifier to provide correct words also has a disadvantage—all proposed words must be correct forms of error words or missing words in the training dataset. The classifier can not provide correct words which do not contain. But the number of words that L2 learners used is limited. For this reason, text classifier can be used to provide correct words for the most common error words and missing words.

5 Data Augmentation

5.1 Rule format

The training dataset of CGED is relatively small for training neural network models. Increasing the scale of the training dataset may improve the performance of the models. We can study error rules from the training dataset of CGED. In addition, we find that L2 learners often make mistakes that native speakers are frequently to make. So, to identify linguistic mistakes often made by native speakers frequently also helps to identify linguistic errors of L2 learners. Therefore, there are two sources of data augmentation rules in this paper: (i) the training dataset of CGED; (ii)native speakers' error-prone language knowledge.

Error rules can be extracted from the training dataset of CGED, and be studied from the native speakers' error-prone language knowledge. And then, we can use those rules to generate more error sentences to enrich the training dataset. Therefore, error rule is an important medium for data augmentation.

The error rule consists of error type, error word, prefix of the error word, correct form of the error word (correct word), and suffix of the error word. The error rule types include S, M, and R types.

S-地-变-得-轻松
S-地-变-得-轻
M- -做-得-好
R-得-引--出来
R-得-引--出

Figure 4: An example of the rule format.

If figure 4, each line represents one error rule. The items of an error rule involved can be categorized as error type, error word, prefix, correct word, and suffix. Different items are separated by using a '-' character from left to right. The rule 'S-地-变-得-轻松' expressing the meaning of '变得轻松' is wrongly written as '变地轻松'.

5.2 Rules from CGED Training Dataset

The steps of extracting rules from the training dataset of CGED are indicated as follows:

(1) Count the number of sentences in each training document that contains the original error text and correct text, and discard documents that are not equal in number and cannot be corrected manually.

(2) Split the original error text and correct text of each document into sentences by LPT toolkit.

(3) Each error of the sentence can generate an error rule. The components of an error rule can be calculated based on the sentence original error text, correct text, and error interval. The prefix and suffix can be a word or a character. If it is a word, the left and right strings of the error word in the sentence need to do word segmentation respectively. After the word segmentation, the prefix becomes the rightmost word of the left string, and the suffix is the leftmost word of the right string.

For example, example 3 in Table 2 contains a S type error. Through the original text and error interval, we can know that '教养' is a bad word selection. The content before '抚养' in the correct text is the same as the content before '教养' in original text, and the content behind '抚养' in correct text is also the same as the content behind '教养' in original text. This can be inferred that the correct writing of '教养' should be '抚养' in this context. Therefore, the rules 'S -教养-孩子-抚养-成人' and 'S -教养-子-抚养-成' can be derived from the example 3.

Not all the correct form of an error word can be inferred. It is difficult to infer the correct word if the following conditions occur:

(1) Two errors have crossed position, or one error is contained in another.

(2) Two errors next to each other in position, but they are a S type error and a M type error.

(3) Two errors next to each other in position, but one of them is a W type error.

5.3 Rules from Native Speakers

There are many resources in Baidu WenKu[2], such as similar Chinese characters, commonly confused words, homonyms, and easily-misused characters, which are collected and uploaded by many teachers or students' parents. In addition, many Chinese researchers have written different kinds of books and dic-

___
[2] http://wenku.baidu.com/

Example 3	Original Text	₁怎₂样₃把₄孩₅子₆教₇养₈成₉人₁₀呢₁₁?₁₂
	Segment Text	怎样, 把, 孩子, 教养, 成人, 呢,?
	Correct Text	怎样把孩子抚养成人呢?
	Error Type	S (word selection)
	Error Interval	6,7
	Error-Correct Word	教养-抚养

Table 2: An example of training sentence that contains only one S type error.

tionaries to review these resources (Li, 2005; Pang, 2006; Ran, 2010; Tian, 2012; Ye, 1978).

Although all of the aforementioned resources can be converted to error rules. Although these resources provide only a correct word or an error word of an error rule, the prefix and suffix can be obtained from text corpus. We count the cluster (trigram) of the words in a textbook corpus, and the words located before or after the central words are regarded as prefixes or suffixes respectively. For example, the highest frequency clusters which take '录' as the central error word are '报录的', '记录下' and '听录音'. '录' and '陆' are easily-misused Chinese characters. Taking the misuse of '录' as '陆' for an example, we can generate the error rules of 'S-陆-报-录-的', 'S-陆-记-录-下' and 'S-陆-听-录-音' with the help of the high frequency clusters extracted from the textbook corpus.

In addition to the S type error, the M type error and the R type error can also be generated similarly. In order to reduce the number of rules and make the rules more accurate in predicting, the Chinese characters of the error word and correct word are all from the *Essential Chinese Dictionary* (Xu and Yao, 2009) and the top 1500 frequency characters high frequency in the list of the training dataset of CGED. These two wordlists contain 1,535 different Chinese characters. Based on the wordlists, 97.48% (49706/50471) of the correct words of the CGED dataset are formed.

5.4 Data Generation

5.4.1 Raw Data

In order to make the generated sentences more similar to the sentences written by L2 learners, we select candidate sentences from a textbook corpus, which covers 12 sets of textbooks compiled for foreign students and 7 sets of textbooks compiled for Chinese students, provided by the Research Center for Lexicology & Lexicography, the Chinese Academy of Social Sciences. Although large-scaled, it is still failed to provide enough candidate sentences. Therefore, we also select the People's Daily (1946-2017) provided by the Library of the Chinese Academy of Social Sciences as a supplementary corpus.

5.4.2 Preprocessing

The processing of text corpus includes the following steps:

(1) Use OpenCC[3] toolkit to convert all traditional CGED dataset to simplify dataset.

(2) Use LTP toolkit to do Chinese sentence segmentation.

(3) Filter the sentences by following methods: discard sentences whose characters are less than 5 or more than 40; discard sentences, in which the proportion of Chinese characters is less than 50%; if a sentence contains any character or word out of *National Syllabus of Graded Words and Characters for Chinese Proficiency* (Hanban, 2001) and *Chinese Proficiency Test Syllabus Level 1-6* (Hanban, 2010), the sentence should also be discarded.

The rest sentences are candidate sentences for generating error sentences.

5.4.3 Error Sentences Generation

Error sentences are generated based on error rules. We can replace the 'prefix+correct word+suffix'in a filtered candidate correct sentence with 'prefix+error word+suffix' to get an error sentence. For example, there is a correct sentence '他又当爹又当妈，把儿子抚养成人。' and an error rule 'S-教养-子-抚养-成'. When '子抚养成' in the sentence is replaced with '子教养成', a new error sentence '他又当爹又当妈，把儿子教养成人。' is generated. The newly generated training sentence is shown in table 3.

---

[3]https://github.com/BYVoid/OpenCC

Example 4	Original Text	1 他 2 又 3 当 4 爹 5 又 6 当 7 妈 8，9 把 10 儿 11 子 12 教 13 养 14 成 15 人。17
	Correct Text	他又当爹又当妈，把儿子抚养成人。
	Error Type	S (word selection)
	Error Interval	12,13
	Error-Correct Word	教养-抚养

Table 3: An example of training sentence generated from an error rule 'S-教养-子-抚养-成'.

6 Experiment Results

6.1 Implementation Details

We merge all the historical CGED training dataset and test dataset, and obtain 76,117 error sentences after sentence segmentation, of which 58,521 sentences have corresponding correct sentences. We use 80% of the error sentences and their corresponding correct sentences for training (119,414 sentences) and the rest for validation. In DIP tasks, we generated 79,131 rules from CGED dataset and 61,149 **different** rules from other corpus mentioned in section 5.4.1. With the help of these error rules, we generated 19,1331 error sentences. We use TensorFlow[4] to implement the LSTM-CRF model, and use FastText[5] directly for the correction task. We only use pre-trained embeddings for LSTM-CRF model which are pre-trained with the textbooks corpus and People's Daily (1946-2017) text corpus.

6.2 Results on Validation Dataset

We used the validation dataset to select the best hyper-parameters for both the LSTM-CRF model of DIP tasks and the classification model for correction task. From the results of table 4, it has been found that the model with added trigram embeddings performs better than that with only character embedding and bigram embeddings when using the same dataset. The model trained with increased new data is superior to the model that only trained with CGED dataset.

Table 5 shows the results of the correction task. MN refers to model N. For example, M2 refers to model 2. N stands for the number of aforementioned prefixes and suffixes in section 5.1. The smaller the N is, the more effective the model is.

[4]https://github.com/tensorflow/tensorflow
[5]https://github.com/facebookresearch/fastText

Detection Task			
Model	Precision	Recall	F1
CGED (U+B)	**0.6137**	0.6586	0.6354
CGED (U+B+T)	0.5686	**0.8102**	0.6682
CGED+G (U+B+T)	0.5969	0.7615	**0.6692**
Identification Task			
Model	Precision	Recall	F1
CGED (U+B)	0.4204	0.4236	0.422
CGED (U+B+T)	0.3973	**0.4974**	0.4418
CGED+G (U+B+T)	**0.4213**	0.4905	**0.4533**
Position Task			
Model	Precision	Recall	F1
CGED (U+B)	0.2995	0.2634	0.2803
CGED (U+B+T)	0.2499	0.2831	0.2655
CGED+G (U+B+T)	**0.3161**	**0.3057**	**0.3108**

Table 4: Results on Validation Dataset of DIP tasks. CGED indicates that only CGED training dataset is used. G stands for using generated dataset, U stands for character embedding, B stands for bigram embeddings, and T stands for trigram embeddings.

In table 5, model 1 has the best predictive effect, while the other models can predict the correct suggestions rather than model 1. Therefore, we take the results of model 1 as basis. If three results of the other four models are inconsistent with those of model 1, they will be taken as the priority result.

Correction Task (Top1)			
Model	Precision	Recall	F1
M1	**0.323**	**0.323**	**0.323**
M2	0.310	0.310	0.310
M3	0.297	0.297	0.297
M4	0.287	0.287	0.287
M5	0.278	0.278	0.278
Correction Task (Top3)			
Model	Precision	Recall	F1
M1	**0.136**	**0.408**	**0.204**
M2	0.130	0.389	0.195
M3	0.122	0.367	0.183
M4	0.121	0.362	0.181
M5	0.118	0.354	0.177

Table 5: Results on Validation Dataset of Correction task.

6.3 Results on Evaluation Dataset

While testing on the final evaluation dataset, we merged all the training dataset and validation dataset, and added generated sentences to retrain our models. Table 6 and Table 7 show the final results of DIP tasks and correction task.

We used the same parameters for training 9 different models, but obtained 9 different test results. Hence, we selected the best performing model in detection task in evaluating dataset of 2017 as run 1, and the best performing model in position task in evaluating dataset of 2017 as run 2. During this process, we didn't apply any model stacking.

Finally, 12 teams submitted 32 DIP task results. The first run of our system (run1) achieved the highest F1 scores in the detection task. In the identification task, the F1 of run1 and run2 ranked the second and the third respectively. And in the position task, the F1 of run2 gained third place among 32 results.

As for the correction task, the new task of this year, 9 teams submitted a total of 23 results. Run2 got better result than run1 in both top1 and top3 tasks. In top1 correction task, the F1 of run2 ranked 2/9 according to teams and 2/23 according to results, which is lower than the highest result by only 0.0001. In top3 correction task, the F1 of run2 ranked 2/9 according to teams and 3/23 according to results.

Detection Task			
Runs	Precision	Recall	F1
Run1	0.6736	**0.8621**	**0.7563**
Run2	**0.7266**	0.7408	0.7336
Identification Task			
Model	Precision	Recall	F1
Run1	0.4834	0.5952	0.5335
Run2	**0.5831**	**0.4955**	**0.5357**
Position Task			
Model	Precision	Recall	F1
Run1	0.2741	**0.3177**	0.2943
Run2	**0.3839**	0.2966	**0.3346**

Table 6: Results on Evaluation Dataset of DIP Tasks.

Correction Task (Top1)			
Runs	Precision	Recall	F1
Run1	0.1364	**0.1651**	0.1494
Run2	**0.1852**	0.1609	**0.1722**
Correction Task (Top3)		
Runs	Precision	F1
Run1	0.1432	0.1569
Run2	**0.1934**	**0.1798**

Table 7: Results on Evaluation Dataset of Correction Task.

7 Conclusion and Future Work

In this shared task paper, we mainly describe how to generate more error sentences based on the CGED training dataset and large filtered corpus. Based on the original training data and augmented data, we trained LSTM-CRF models ranking 1/12, 2/12 and 2/12 separately in DIP tasks. In the correction task, we regarded it as a classification problem and ranked 2/9. Our final submitted results achieved 2nd place in mean ranking. All of this proves the effectiveness of the data augmentation algorithm proposed in this paper.

In the future work, we will blend more grammatical features in error detection and correction, and integrate more second language teaching experience in the model.

References

Shuk-Man Cheng, Chi-Hsin Yu, and Hsin-Hsi Chen. 2014. Chinese word ordering errors detection and correction for non-native chinese language learners. In *Proceedings of COL-*

ING 2014, the 25th International Conference on Computational Linguistics: Technical Papers, pages 279–289.

Nigel Collier and Jin-Dong Kim. 2004. Introduction to the bio-entity recognition task at JNLPBA. In *Proceedings of the International Joint Workshop on Natural Language Processing in Biomedicine and its Applications, NLPBA/BioNLP 2004, Geneva, Switzerland, August 28-29, 2004*.

Hanban. 2001. *National Syllabus of Graded Words and Characters for Chinese Proficiency*. Economic Science Press.

Confucius Institute Headquarters Hanban. 2010. *Chinese Proficiency Test Syllabus Level 1-6*. The Commercical Press.

Zhiheng Huang, Wei Xu, and Kai Yu. 2015. Bidirectional LSTM-CRF models for sequence tagging. *CoRR*, abs/1508.01991.

Lung-Hao Lee, Li-Ping Chang, Kuei-Ching Lee, Yuen-Hsien Tseng, and Hsin-Hsi Chen. 2013. Linguistic rules based chinese error detection for second language learning. In *Work-in-Progress Poster Proceedings of the 21st International Conference on Computers in Education (ICCE-13)*, pages 27–29.

Lung-Hao Lee, Liang-Chih Yu, Kuei-Ching Lee, Yuen-Hsien Tseng, Li-Ping Chang, and Hsin-Hsi Chen. 2014. A sentence judgment system for grammatical error detection. In *Proceedings of COLING 2014, the 25th International Conference on Computational Linguistics: System Demonstrations*, pages 67–70.

Xingjian Li. 2005. *Similar Chinese Character Discrimination Dictionary*. Jiangsu Education Publishing House.

Chenguang Pang. 2006. *Common Similar Chinese Character Discrimination Dictionary*. World Publishing Corporation.

Hong Ran. 2010. *Similar Chinese Character Dictionary*. Foreign Language Teaching and Research Press.

Juanhua Tian. 2012. *Similar Chinese Characters Discrimination*. Shanghai Brilliant Publishing House.

Lin Xu and Xishuang Yao. 2009. *Essential Chinese Dictionary*. Foreign Language Teaching and Research Press.

Yi Yang, Pengjun Xie, Jun Tao, Guangwei Xu, Linlin Li, and Si Luo. 2017. Alibaba at IJCNLP-2017 task 1: Embedding grammatical features into lstms for chinese grammatical error diagnosis task. In *Proceedings of the IJCNLP 2017, Shared Tasks, Taipei, Taiwan, November 27 - December 1, 2017, Shared Tasks*, pages 41–46.

Yu Ye. 1978. *Easily-Misused Chinese Characters*. Shanghai Educational Publishing House.

Chi-Hsin Yu and Hsin-Hsi Chen. 2012. Detecting word ordering errors in chinese sentences for learning chinese as a foreign language. *Proceedings of COLING 2012*, pages 3003–3018.

Bo Zheng, Wanxiang Che, Jiang Guo, and Ting Liu. 2016. Chinese grammatical error diagnosis with long short-term memory networks. In *Proceedings of the 3rd Workshop on Natural Language Processing Techniques for Educational Applications (NLPTEA2016)*, pages 49–56, Osaka, Japan. The COLING 2016 Organizing Committee.

Detecting Simultaneously Chinese Grammar Errors

Based on a BiLSTM-CRF Model

Yajun Liu, Hongying Zan, Mengjie Zhong, Hongchao Ma

College of Information and Engineering, Zhengzhou University

liuyajun_gz@163.com, iehyzan@zzu.edu.cn

1837361628@qq.com, ma-hc@foxmail.com

Abstract

In the process of learning and using Chinese, many learners of Chinese as foreign language(CFL) may have grammar errors due to negative migration of their native languages. This paper introduces our system that can simultaneously diagnose four types of grammatical errors including redundant (R), missing (M), selection (S), disorder (W) in NLPTEA-5 shared task. We proposed a Bidirectional LSTM CRF neural network (BiLSTM-CRF) that combines BiLSTM and CRF without hand-craft features for Chinese Grammatical Error Diagnosis (CGED). Evaluation includes three levels, which are detection level, identification level and position level. At the detection level and identification level, our system got the third recall scores, and achieved good F1 values.

1   Introduction

With the rapid development of China's economy, "Chinese Fever" has been set off in the world and more foreigners begin to learn Chinese. Writing is an important part of Chinese learning, and the grammar is the basis of writing. In the process of writing and communicating with each other using Chinese, learners of Chinese as foreign language(CFL) may have grammar errors due to negative migration of their native languages.

Traditional learning methods for CFL rely on heavily manual work to point out grammar errors, which costs a lot of time and labor. In order to reduce the workload of manual identification, it is necessary to explore effective methods for Chinese Grammatical Error Diagnosis (CGED). In the field of natural language processing, CGED is a great challenge because of the flexibility and irregularity in Chinese, so a series of CGED evaluation tasks are arranged.

The CGED evaluation tasks provided a platform for many researchers to study the automatic detection of Chinese grammatical errors. The CGED 2018 evaluation task defines Chinese grammatical errors as four categories: redundant(R), selection (S), missing(M), disorder(W). As shown in Table 1, the example sentences corresponding to each error are given.

In this paper, we regarded the CGED 2018 shared task as a character-based sequence labeling task. We proposed a Bidirectional LSTM CRF(BiLSTM-CRF) neural network that combines LSTM and CRF for sequence labeling without any hand-craft features. Firstly, we use BiLSTM network to learn the information in the sentence and extract features, then we utilize CRF for sequence labeling to complete automatically Chinese grammatical errors detection.

Error Type	Error Sentence	Correct Sentence
R(Redundant)	时间是无价之宝的。	时间是无价之宝。 Time is priceless.
W(Word Order)	你采取几种方法应该帮助他们。	你应该采取几种方法帮助他们。 You should take several steps to help them.
M(Missing)	任何婴儿心都是白纸似的清白。	任何婴儿的心都是白纸似的清白。 Any baby's heart is white innocence.
S(Selection)	大家都知道吸烟是害健康的。	大家都知道吸烟是损害健康的。 Everyone knows that smoking is harmful to health.

Table 1: The examples given.

Proceedings of the 5th Workshop on Natural Language Processing Techniques for Educational Applications, pages 188–193
Melbourne, Australia, July 19, 2018. ©2018 Association for Computational Linguistics

The rest of this paper is organized as follows: Section 2 briefly introduces related work in this field. Section 3 introduces the model that we proposed. Section 4 discusses experiments and results analysis, including data preprocessing, hyperparameters and experiment results. Finally, conclusion and prospects are arranged.

2   Related Work

Automatic detection of grammatical errors is one of the most important tasks in the field of natural language processing. Researchers have already done a lot of work in the field of English grammatical errors diagnosis. For example, Helping Our Own (HOO) is a series of shared tasks in correcting textual errors (Dale and Kilgarriff,2011; Dale et al., 2012). The CoNLL2013 and CoNLL2014 shared tasks (Ng et al., 2013; Ng et al., 2014) focused on grammatical error correction, and many approaches were proposed, such as based N-gram language model methods (Hdez et al., 2014), statistical machine translation methods (Felice et al., 2014), machine learning methods (Wang et al., 2014), etc.

Compared with English, the study for Chinese grammatical errors diagnosis started later. The researchers also proposed many methods, such as statistical learning methods (Chang et al., 2012), ruled-based methods (Lee et al., 2013), and hybrid-based model methods (Lee et al., 2014).

However, due to the lack of corpora and the limitations of technology, the research progress is limited greatly. The CGED shared tasks (Yu et al., 2014; Lee et al., 2015, 2016; RAO et al., 2017) provided researchers with a good platform to present their work. In CGED2016 shared task, a CRF-based model achieved good precision (Liu et al., 2016) and a model based on CRF+LSTM get good results (Zheng et al., 2016). In CGED 2017, researchers used some features such as part of speech, collocation words, N-gram etc., and put forward the BiLSTM+CRF model to train models for each error type respectively, then analyzed the errors by model fusion, finally made great progresses for CGED (Xie et al., 2017; Liao et al., 2017).

In this paper, we propose a bidirectional LSTM CRF Neural Network (BiLSTM-CRF) for CGED. The model is described as follows:

(1) Different from the previous methods that train models for each error type, in our system, only one model is trained for all error types, and multiple error types are predicted at the same time.

(2) Our model captures sentence-level features based on the powerful long-term memory ability of BiLSTM and uses CRF for sequence labeling.

(3) The model only learns from word information without any handcraft features.

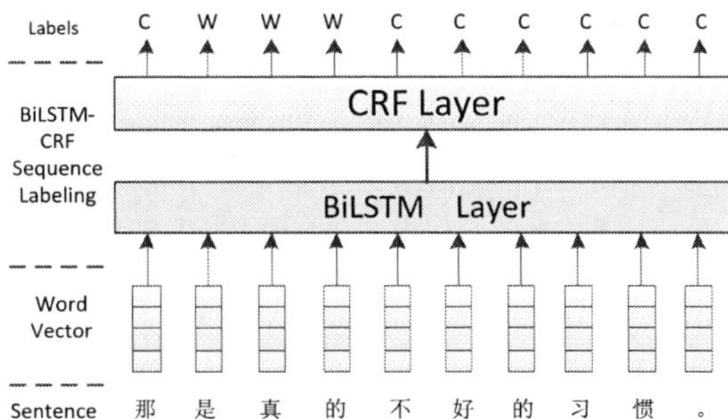

Fig 1 The proposed BiLSTM-CRF model.

3   Model

In this paper, we regard Chinese Grammatical errors diagnosis as the sequence labeling task based on character level, and the tag sets are R (Redundant), S (Selection), M (Missing), W (Word Order), C (Correct). The BiLSTM-CRF model presented in this paper is shown in Figure 1, which includes Embedding Layer, BiLSTM Layer and CRF layer.

(1) Embedding Layer: transforms the index of word into word vector.

(2) BiLSTM Layer: learns the information of each word and extracts features from sentence.

(3) CRF Layer: decodes and produces labels for words.

3.1   Embedding Layer

Embedding Layer aims to transform words into distributed representations which capture syntactic

189

and semantic meanings of words. Therefore, we use word embeddings to represent words in the sentence.

Given a sentence S, then we can describe it as $S = \{w_1, w_2, w_3, \ldots, w_{n-1}, w_n\}$, which contains a sequence of words, and each word is derived from a vocabulary V. Words are represented by distributional vectors $w \in R^d$ which are drawn from a word embedding matrix $W \in R^{|V| \times d}$. After Embedding Layer, then we can get X:

$$X = \{x_1, x_2, x_3, \ldots, x_{n-1}, x_n\}.$$

3.2 BiLSTM Layer

Due to the powerful long-term memory ability of LSTM, LSTM based neural networks, which have access to both past and future contexts, are proven to be effective in sequence labeling task. The hidden states in bidirectional LSTM can capture both past and future context information and accomplish sequence labeling for each token.

Basically, a LSTM unit is composed of three multiplicative gates which control the proportions of information to forget and to pass on to the next time step. Three components composite the LSTM-based recurrent neural networks: one input gate i_t with corresponding weight matrix $W^{(xi)}, W^{(hi)}, W^{(ci)}, b^{(i)}$; one forget gate f_t with weight matrix $W^{(xf)}, W^{(hf)}, W^{(cf)}, b^{(f)}$; one output gate o_t with corresponding weight matrix $W^{(xo)}, W^{(ho)}, W^{(co)}, b^{(o)}$. Formally, the formulas (1) to update an LSTM unit at time t are:

$$
\begin{aligned}
i_t &= \sigma(W^{(xi)}x_t + W^{(hi)}h_{t-1} + W^{(ci)}c_{t-1} \\
&\quad + b^{(i)}) \\
f_t &= \sigma(W^{(xf)}x_t + W^{(hf)}h_{t-1} + W^{(cf)}c_{t-1} \\
&\quad + b^{(f)}) \\
u_t &= tanh(W^{(xc)}x_t + W^{(hc)}h_{t-1} \\
&\quad + W^{(cc)}c_{t-1} + b^{(c)}) \\
c_t &= i_t \odot u_t + f_t \odot c_{t-1} \\
o_t &= \sigma(W^{(xo)}x_t + W^{(ho)}h_{t-1} + W^{(co)}c_t \\
&\quad + b^{(o)}) \\
h_t &= o_t \odot tanh(c_t)
\end{aligned}
\tag{1}
$$

where σ is the element-wise sigmoid function and $\odot$ is the element-wise product. x_t is the input vector at time t, and h_t is the hidden state vector storing all the useful information at (and before) time t.

Mathematically, the input of the BiLSTM layer is a sequence X of word vectors from Embedding Layer, where $X = \{x_1, x_2, x_3, \ldots, x_{n-1}, x_n\}$. The output of the BiLSTM Layer is a sequence of the hidden states for each input word vectors, denoted as $h = \{h_1, h_2, h_3, \ldots, h_{n-1}, h_n\}$. Each final hidden state is the concatenation of the forward $\overrightarrow{h_t}$ and backward $\overleftarrow{h_t}$ hidden states, then we can get h_t :

$$
\overrightarrow{h_t} = lstm(x_t, \overrightarrow{h_{t-1}}), \overleftarrow{h_t} = lstm(x_t, \overleftarrow{h_{t+1}})
$$
$$
h_t = [\overrightarrow{h_t}, \overleftarrow{h_t}]
$$

3.3 CRF Layer

Since there are many syntactic constraints in natural language sentences, the relationship among adjacent tags is very important for CGED shared task. If we simply transfer directly the hidden states of BiLSTM Layer to a Softmax layer for tag prediction, it is possible to break the syntactic constraints and it is difficult to consider the correlation among adjacent tags. Conditional random field (CRF) is the most commonly used method in structural prediction, and its basic idea is to use a series of potential functions to approximate the conditional probability of the output label sequence for the input word sequence.

The sequence of hidden states in the BiLSTM Layer can be described as $h = \{h_1, h_2, h_3, \ldots, h_{n-1}, h_n\}$, then we treat it as the input to the CRF Layer. The output of CRF Layer is our final prediction label sequence, we can see that $y = \{y_1, y_2, y_3, \ldots, y_{n-1}, y_n\}$, where $y_i \in Y$ and Y represents the set of all possible label sequences. So we can use the hidden state sequence to get the conditional probability of the output sequence, and the conditional probability is:

$$
\begin{aligned}
&p(y|h; W, b) \\
&= \frac{\prod_{i=1}^{n} exp(W_{y_{i-1}, y_i}^T h + b_{y_{i-1}, y_i})}{\sum_{y' \in Y} \prod_{i=1}^{n} exp(W_{y'_{i-1}, y'_i}^T h + b_{y'_{i-1}, y'_i})}
\end{aligned}
\tag{2}
$$

Where W, b is the two weight matrices, and the subscription indicates that we extract the weight vector for the given label pair (y_i, y_j). At the same time, in order to train the CRF Layer, we use the classical maximum conditional likelihood estimation to train our model. The final log-likelihood of the weight matrix is as follows:

$$
L(W, b) = \sum_{(h_i, y_i)} log\, p(y_i | h_i; W, b)
\tag{3}
$$

Finally, the Viterbi algorithm is used to train the CRF Layer and decode the optimal output sequence.

4 Experiments and Results Analysis

In this paper, based on the CGED series evaluations, we adopted the dataset of CGED 2016 and CGED 2018 shared tasks as out training dataset, then we manually deleted some incorrect sentences in the training set and rebuilt the dataset. The CGED 2017 test set was selected as the validation set and the CGED 2018 test set was used as the test set. We selected BiLSTM-CRF model for CGED 2018 shared task. This part mainly includes data preprocessing, parameter settings, results analysis on the validation set and the test set.

4.1 Data Preprocessing

Since the CGED evaluation task involves identification of incorrect boundary positions, word segmentation may cause the misalignment between the end points of words and corresponding error intervals. At the same time, it may also result in overlapping problems among multiple types of errors. Therefore, in this paper we employed characters for Chinese grammatical error diagnosis. Different from previous methods that trained models for each error type, only one model which can identity simultaneously four types of errors is trained in our system.

Using previous data preprocessing method (Liu et al., 2016), we extracted correct sentences and wrong sentences from the corpus according to the manual annotation, and then respectively marked characters with the corresponding labels that include redundant(R), missing(M), selection(S), disorder(W), correct (C). we give some preprocessing examples that are shown in Table 2.

Error sentence:	他们是不但我父母，而且是人生的先辈。
Correction sentence: 他们不但是我父母，而且是人生的导师。	
(They are not only my parents but also mentors in life.)	
Manual annotation: (3,5) W (16,17) S	
Preprocessing results：	
他/C 们/C 是/W 不/W 但/W 我/C 父/C 母/C，/C 而/C 且/C 是/C 人/C 生/C 的/C 先/S 辈/S。/C	
他/C 们/C 不/C 但/C 是/C 我/C 父/C 母/C，/C 而/C 且/C 是/C 人/C 生/C 的/C 导/C 师/C。/C	

Table 2: The examples of data preprocessing.

Methods		CRF	BiLSTM-CRF
False Positive Rate		**0.1881**	0.9643
Detection Level	Precision	**0.7514**	0.6016
	Recall	0.3093	**0.9481**
	F1-Score	0.4382	**0.7361**
Identification Level	Precision	**0.6328**	0.3375
	Recall	0.1763	**0.32**
	F1-Score	0.2758	**0.3285**
Position Level	Precision	**0.3913**	0.0015
	Recall	**0.0658**	0.0009
	F1-Score	**0.1126**	0.0011

Table 3: The results on the validation set.

4.2 Parameter Settings

In this paper, word vector is randomly initialized, and word vector dimension is 50. Here is the overview of optimized parameters:

- Word vector dimension   50
- Hidden size   50
- Adam learning rate   0.001
- Epoch   300

4.3 Experiments Results

In this paper, we use two different models to conduct experiments respectively, which are CRF model (M1) and BiLSTM-CRF model (M2).

CRF model: The CRF model adds a variety of grammatical features such as bigram and trigram features. The selection of features directly affects the performance of the model. Therefore, this experiment adopts the feature length of 7 and uses bigram and trigram to extract features.

BiLSTM-CRF model: The BiLSTM-CRF model combines LSTM and CRF for sequence labeling. Firstly, we use BiLSTM network to learn information in the sentence and extract features, then we utilize CRF for sequence labeling to complete automatically CGED shared work.

The results on the validation set: The valuation set used in this paper is the test set in the CGED2017 shared task. Two different models are used to conduct experiments on the valuation set, results are shown in Table 3.

From Table 3, we can see that CRF model has lower False Positive Rate (FPR) than BiLSTM-CRF model, and CRF model achieves better precision performance at the detection level and the identification level, because that CRF model has more features information such as bi-gram, tri-gram. However, CRF model and BiLSTM-CRF model are not good at position level. We think that our models are short of identification of position boundary. Next, we will focus on the position level by adding character position features.

The results on the test set: The test set is the test set in the CGED 2018 shared task. We submitted only one result in this task. The Table 4 lists the result Run1 we submitted and the test result based on CRF model.

At the error detection level and error identification level, our system achieves a third recall rate and gets a good F1 value. However, our system has a poor performance at the error position level and FPR. Since our system recognizes four types of errors at the same time, increasing the difficulty of recognition, it is easier to identify a correct sentence as an error sentence, it results in lower FPR performance on the test set. In addition, our system is based on character level, although the BiLSTM network has a powerful long-term memory function, the lack of word collocation information also results in lower position level efficiency. Another reason for low position level efficiency is that tag does not distinguish among locations. For example,

Error: 我/C 朋/C 友/C 的/C 努/C 力/C 真/C 是/C 可/S 看/S 的/C。/C
Correction: 我朋友的努力真是有效的。
(My friend's efforts are really effective)
In this sentence, "可看" should be corrected as "有效". There was no distinction in two "/S", so we think it leads to lower position level efficiency.

Methods		CRF	Run1
False Positive Rate		**0.0851**	0.9309
Detection Level	Precision	**0.8506**	0.5441
	Recall	0.3449	**0.9179**
	F1-Score	0.4908	**0.6926**
Identification Level	Precision	**0.7373**	0.3144
	Recall	0.17	**0.6266**
	F1-Score	0.2763	**0.4187**
Position Level	Precision	**0.5037**	0.0078
	Recall	**0.0615**	0.0189
	F1-Score	**0.1096**	0.0110

Table 4: The results on the test set.

5 Conclusion

On the basis of CGED series evaluation tasks, this paper proposes a neural network model based on BiLSTM-CRF, which is used for Chinese grammatical error detection. It has good effect at the detection level and identification level, especially the high recall rate. But it has low performance at the position level. Next, we will add some external features, such as parts of speech, character position features and collocation features to improve the performance of our system.

References

Chang, Ru-Yng, Chung-Hsien Wu, and Philips Kokoh Prasetyo. 2012. Error diagnosis of Chinese sentences using inductive learning algorithm and decomposition-based testing mechanism. *ACM Transactions on Asian Language Information Processing (TALIP)*, *11*(1), 3.

Dale, Robert, and Adam Kilgarriff. 2011, September. Helping our own: The HOO 2011 pilot shared task. In *Proceedings of the 13th European Workshop on Natural Language Generation* (pp. 242-249). Association for Computational Linguistics.

Dale, Robert, Ilya Anisimoff. 2012, June. HOO 2012: A report on the preposition and determiner error correction shared task. In *Proceedings of the Seventh Workshop on Building Educational Applications Using NLP* (pp. 54-62). Association for Computational Linguistics.

Felice, Mariano, et al. 2014. Grammatical error correction using hybrid systems and type filtering. In *Proceedings of the Eighteenth Conference on Computational Natural Language Learning: Shared Task* (pp. 15-24).

Gaoqi, R. A. O., et al. 2017. IJCNLP-2017 Task 1: Chinese Grammatical Error Diagnosis. *Proceedings of the IJCNLP 2017, Shared Tasks*, 1-8.

Hdez, S. David, and Hiram Calvo. 2014. CoNLL 2014 shared task: Grammatical error correction with a syntactic n-gram language model from a big corpora. In *Proceedings of the Eighteenth Conference on Computational Natural Language Learning: Shared Task* (pp. 53-59).

Lee, Lung-Hao, et al. 2013, November. Linguistic rules based Chinese error detection for second language learning. In *Work-in-Progress Poster Proceedings of the 21st International Conference on Computers in Education (ICCE-13)* (pp. 27-29).

Lee, Lung-Hao, et al. 2014. A sentence judgment system for grammatical error detection. In *Proceedings of COLING 2014, the 25th International Conference on Computational Linguistics: System Demonstrations* (pp. 67-70).

Lee, Lung-Hao, et al. 2015. Overview of the NLP-TEA 2015 Shared Task for Chinese Grammatical Error Diagnosis. *Proceedings of the 2nd Workshop on Natural Language Processing Techniques for Educational Applications* (*NLPTEA'15*), Beijing, China, 31 July, 2015, pp. 1-6.

Lee, Lung-Hao, et al. 2016. Overview of nlp-tea 2016 shared task for chinese grammatical error diagnosis. In *Proceedings of the 3rd Workshop on Natural Language Processing Techniques for Educational Applications (NLPTEA2016)* (pp. 40-48).

Liao, Quanlei, et al. 2017. YNU-HPCC at IJCNLP-2017 Task 1: Chinese Grammatical Error Diagnosis Using a Bi-directional LSTM-CRF Model. *Proceedings of the IJCNLP 2017, Shared Tasks,* 73-77.

Liu, Yajun, et al. 2016. Automatic Grammatical Error Detection for Chinese based on Conditional Random Field. In *Proceedings of the 3rd Workshop on Natural Language Processing Techniques for Educational Applications (NLPTEA2016)* (pp. 57-62).

Ng, Hwee Tou, et al. 2013. The CoNLL-2013 Shared Task on Grammatical Error Correction. *Seventeenth Conference on Computational Natural Language Learning: Shared Task*(pp.1-12).

Ng, Hwee Tou, et al. 2014. The CoNLL-2014 shared task on grammatical error correction. In *Proceedings of the Eighteenth Conference on Computational Natural Language Learning: Shared Task* (pp. 1-14).

Wang, Peilu, Zhongye Jia, and Hai Zhao. 2014. Grammatical error detection and correction using a single maximum entropy model. In *Proceedings of the Eighteenth Conference on Computational Natural Language Learning: Shared Task* (pp. 74-82).

Xie, Pengjun. 2017. Alibaba at IJCNLP-2017 Task 1: Embedding Grammatical Features into LSTMs for Chinese Grammatical Error Diagnosis Task. *Proceedings of the IJCNLP 2017, Shared Tasks,* 41-46.

Yu, Liang-Chih, Lung-Hao Lee, and Li-Ping Chang. 2014, November. Overview of grammatical error diagnosis for learning Chinese as a foreign language. In *Proceedings of the 1st Workshop on Natural Language Processing Techniques for Educational Applications* (pp. 42-47).

Zheng, Bo, et al. 2016. Chinese Grammatical Error Diagnosis with Long Short-Term Memory Networks. In *Proceedings of the 3rd Workshop on Natural Language Processing Techniques for Educational Applications (NLPTEA2016)* (pp. 49-56).

A Hybrid Approach Combining Statistical Knowledge with Conditional Random Fields for Chinese Grammatical Error Detection

Yiyi Wang   **Chilin Shih**

East Asian Languages and Cultures
University of Illinois at Urbana-Champaign
{ywang418, cls}@uiuc.edu

Abstract

This paper presents a method of combining Conditional Random Fields (CRFs) model with a post-processing layer using Google n-grams statistical information tailored to detect word selection and word order errors made by learners of Chinese as Foreign Language (CFL). We describe the architecture of the model and its performance in the shared task of the ACL 2018 Workshop on Natural Language Processing Techniques for Educational Applications (NLPTEA). This hybrid approach yields comparably high false positive rate (FPR = 0.1274) and precision (P_d= 0.7519; P_i= 0.6311), but low recall (R_d = 0.3035; R_i = 0.1696) in grammatical error detection and identification tasks. Additional statistical information and linguistic rules can be added to enhance the model performance in the future.

1 Introduction

Grammatical error detection is a growing area of research with general applications to grammar checking and Computer-Assisted Language Learning (CALL). NLPTEA shared task provides a platform for researchers to work on detecting the same types of grammatical errors, and evaluate the results on the same test set with predefined metrics(Yu et al., 2014; Lee et al., 2015, 2016; Rao et al., 2017) . Since NLPTEA 2014, the shared tasks focus on detecting and identifying four types of errors which are the most common grammatical mistakes made by CFL learners: word missing errors ("M"), word redundancy errors ("R"), word selection errors ("S"), and word ordering errors ("W"). The NLPTEA-2018 shared task focuses on identifying and correcting the above four types of errors made by CFL learners. The training data released by the task organizers contains 402 sentences written by Chinese language learners and corrected by native speakers of Chinese. The test data for the task consists of 3,548 sentences. The diagnose level evaluation metrics are based on three criteria: (1) detection-level: to distinguish grammatical and ungrammatical sentences; (2) identification-level: to identify error type; (3) position-level: to pin down error positions. Our model is designed to tackle the error detection task.

Most of the proposed methods for grammatical error detection employ supervised machine learning or deep learning approaches(Chen et al., 2016; Zheng et al., 2016; Chou et al., 2016) in recent years. Although neural networks model performs well for the complexity of the task in nature, CRFs still get steady application in the community. This paper proposes a integrated approach of combining CRFs, statistical information from Google n-grams and rule-based expert knowledge to detect the four types of errors. The method can yield high accuracy and precision, but low recall. To improve recall in the future, additional rules and statistical knowledge can be added to enhance model performance.

2 Data

In addition to the training data released by the task organizers, another data set containing 9,602 sentences with 23,518 types of grammatical errors employed in a similar shared task in NLPTEA 2016 is used in conjunction to train a CRFs model to detect all four types of grammatical errors. Table 1 is the distribution of the four types of errors in our training set.

Google Chinese Web 5-gram (Liu et al., 2010) is used to retrieve statistical information in the post-processing layer. The data is composed of around 883 millions of tokens generated from pub-

194

Proceedings of the 5th Workshop on Natural Language Processing Techniques for Educational Applications, pages 194–198
Melbourne, Australia, July 19, 2018. ©2018 Association for Computational Linguistics

	NLPTEA 2018	NLPTEA 2016	Total
M	298	6,202	6,500
R	208	5,270	5,478
S	474	10,426	10,900
W	87	1,620	1,707

Table 1: Distribution of Errors in training set.

licly accessible web pages written in Chinese characters. Low frequency n-grams occurring less than 40 times are filtered out. However, some frequently occurring typos, ungrammatical forms, idiosyncratic usages, even texts written by language learners and/or written in other languages such as in Japanese Kanji are kept in the final published version of the data, making it challenging to identify the subtleties of non-native speakers' writings. For example, the word "坑生素(antibiotic)" occurs 200 times in the data,in which it contains one misused character "坑(pit)" that shares similarities in orthography with the correct usage "抗(anti)". So, when the form "坑生素" is used in CFL writing, it would pass the grammar checker based on Google n-gram due to its high frequency. Another example is "知情达理(understanding and reasonable)" with 10,495 occurrences in the data. This is a case of portmanteau combining two idioms "知书达礼(well-educated and courteous)" and "通情达理(show common sense)", in which the misused character "知(to know)" shares semantic component with the correct character "通(to go through)".

Although these entries are considered as noises in the Google n-grams collection, they provide exemplary language mis-usage information by CFL learners, and can bring in valuable insights about the typical grammatical errors made by CFL learners that we can use in grammatical error detection task. We will discuss how to use the information to identify word selection and word order error in Section 3.3.

3 Model Components

The model is designed to feed the sentences into a CRFs model to detect four types of grammatical errors, and pass the results to a post-processing layer to further identify word selection and word order errors based on unigram and bigrams information retrieved from Google Chinese n-grams. We describe the data preprocessing, feature sets

selection of CRFs model, and post-processing step that modifies the CRFs output in the following sections.

3.1 Data Preprocessing

Since words are the basic element for many natural language processing tasks, and Chinese writing system by nature does not mark word boundaries, the first step of preprocessing is to segment the sentences into words. Stanford Word Segmenter is used to split the input sentences into sequences of words in terms of Peking University standard (Tseng et al., 2005) . Then the segmented sentences are fed into Stanford POS Tagger (Toutanova et al., 2003) to get parts of speech of each word. During the word segmentation and tagging processes, punctuations are treated as words, however, since they are not included in Google n-gram data, all the punctuations in the training set are removed to make the best use of available statistical information during the post-processing step. The sentences are presented as a three-column frame, with the first column as word, the second column as POS tagging, and the last one as error-detection output labels. Part of preprocessed training data is presented in Table 2.

Word	POS	Error
因此	AD	C
不仅	AD	C
靠	P	M
国家	NN	C
的	DEG	C
措施	NN	C
而且	AD	C
我们	PN	C
消费者	NN	C

Table 2: Example of preprocessed data.

3.2 Conditional Random Fields

CRFs (Lafferty et al., 2001) is a powerful model for predicting sequential labels with a wide range of applications in the NLP community, such as name entity recognition, POS tagging and parsing. The reason that CRFs is appropriate to model sequencing tasks is that it can take the contextual observations, usually a sequence of tokens as input and generates a sequence of labels as output, as in most of sequential labeling tasks.

The sequencing CRFs model, or linear chain CRFs, is well suited to the grammatical error detection task, as it can take the sentences as input sequences, and output the corresponding grammatical error labels. In our task, the output set is composed of five elements C, M, R, S, W, abbreviating for correct, missing, redundancy, selection and word ordering errors respectively.

CRFs provide a rich unconstrained feature set to represent data, and assigns a weight to each feature. Therefore, feature set construction can decide the expressive power of the model. We use 46 features in our model to represent the relationships between adjacent words, parts-of-speech, and their interaction in error prediction. CRF++ toolkit of Version 0.58 (?) is adopted in our model.

3.3 Post-Processing Layers

Two layers are added on top of the CRFs model to enhance performance by detecting grammatical errors based on the statistical information retrieved in Google Chinese n-grams. The first post-processing layer is applied to identify word selection error in terms of unigram information; the second layer is implemented to detect word-ordering error and word selection errors according to bigrams information.

3.3.1 Unigram Layer

The unigram layer applies to the words that are predicted as "C" in CRFs model to check the prediction accuracy by using unigram information; however, the words that are detected as errors will not be processed in this step. The post-precessing procedure of this step can be summarized as follows:

If a word is not a cardinal or ordinal number, the length of the word is not longer than two characters, and the occurrences of the word in Google unigram are less than 40,000 times, the original correct tag generated by CRFs is converted to a word selection error. The algorithm applied in this layer is shown Table 3 .

The rationale behind this design is that the frequencies of multisyllabic Chinese words decrease when their usages are unconventional. Therefore, when such expressions are found in CFL learner's writing, there are reasonable grounds to believe that word selection errors have occurred.

Since the corpus cannot include all the numbers and proper nouns, the words with relatively low frequencies, such as a proper noun "栋

Algorithm 1: *Tag C is converted to Tag S based on unigram statistics*

---

if   (output = "C"   *and*
       POS !="CD", "OD" or "NR"   *and*
       wordLength <=2   *and*
       wordFrequency <=40,000):
       "C" is changed to "S"

Table 3: Unigram algorithm.

杰(35,205)" and an ordinal number "第三百三十九(39,982)" are likely to bee grammatical expressions. For this reason, parts-of-speech knowledge is integrated with the frequency information to better identify errors. The frequency threshold is decided by descriptive statistics of Google n-grams data. Although this setting improves the model recall in this task, the rationality of setting this cut-off will be discussed further in Section 4. In this step, if a word "灵恬(214)" or "快子(15,700)" is marked as "C" by CRFs model with a non "CD, OD or NR" POS tagging, the predicted tag is changed to "S".

3.3.2 Bigrams Layer

This layer is used to further identify word selection and word order errors in terms of bigrams frequencies. If occurrences of bigrams are less than 1,000 times in the Google ngrams corpus, the range is detected as suspicious area that may contain grammatical errors. In this step, additional preprocessing is needed to chunk input sentences into bigrams with their corresponding frequencies in Google ngrams data. A preprocessed sentence as an example is shown in Table 4.

Since two words are contained in each suspicious area, the error type of individual word needs to be further decided. Unigram information is applied again to diagnose grammatical errors at the word level. The pseudo code used in this layer is presented Table 5.

If both of the words within the suspicious area have high word frequencies in the unigram data, such as "道(193,135,155)" and "吸烟(7,594,378)" in Row 3 of Table 4, the error may occur in the previous two words, if the previous bigrams also have low frequencies. In this case, both "道" and "吸烟" are correct words, however, the grammatical error occurs in the previous word "知不". Simi-

Bigrams		Frequency
他们	知不	0
知不	道	0
道	吸烟	354
吸烟	对	153,530
对	未成年	98,312
未成年	年	461
年	的	91,329,920
的	影响	47,251,277
影响	会	324,577
会	造成	6,907,267
造成	的	20,711,377
的	各种	19,073,836
各种	害处	524

Table 4: Example of preprocessed data.

larly, this procedure can be applied to check following bigrams to decide the error type of individual word within a suspicious area.

Algorithm 2: *Tag C is converted to Tag W or Tag S based on bigrams and unigram*

---

if (word1Frequency >=40,000 *and*
    word2Frequency >=40,000):
    if previousBigramsFrequency>=1000:
        word1 is marked as "C"
        word2 is marked as "S"
    if postBigramsFrequency>=1000:
        word1 is marked as "S"
        word2 is marked as "C"
    else:
        word1 is marked as "C"
        word2 is marked as "C"
else:
    for $word_i$Frequency <40,000:
        if $word_i$Length>1:
            swap characters to new bigrams
            if newBigramsFreq >1000:
                $word_i$ is marked as "W"
            else:
                $word_i$ is marked as "S"
        else:
            if $word_i$POS == "CD":
                $word_i$ keeps the tag "C"
            else:
                $word_i$ is marked as "S"

Table 5: Bigrams algorithm.

If the frequency of at least one word within a suspicious area is less than 40,000, it is possible to assume that at least one grammatical error appears within this area. For example, the bigrams "他们 知不" in Row 1 of Table 3, since the word "知不" has zero occurrence in unigram, we can identify it is an error. Then we can swap the characters, get a new bigrams "他们 不知" and check the frequency of the new bigrams in the corpus. Since the frequency of "他们 不知" is 73,080, the word "知不" is marked as a word order error; otherwise, the low frequency individual word is marked as a selection error.

In this step, word order and selection errors are further detected in terms of both statistical information and linguistic knowledge. Table 6 shows an example of re-marked tags after passing this layer.

Word	CRFs Tag	Post-processed Tag
他们	C	C
知不	S	W
道	C	C
吸烟	C	C
对	C	C
未成年	C	C
年	R	R
的	R	R
影响	C	C
会	C	C
造成	C	C
的	C	C
各种	C	C
害处	C	S

Table 6: Example of post-processed tags.

4 Results and Discussions

The model yields high precision, but low recall in the shared task. The detailed evaluation results are shown in Table 7.

Since the post-processed layers are designed to detect word selection and word order errors only, considering the large amount of word missing and redundancy errors in the test data, it is expected that some false negative elements are failed to be identified in this model. In the future, more statistical information and linguistic rules can be added to reinforce the performance of this hybrid model.

	Precision	Recall	F1
Detection	0.7519	0.3035	0.4324
Identification	0.6311	0.1696	0.2673
Position	0.2385	0.0536	0.0875

Table 7: Test results of hybrid model.

The evaluation results of using CRFs alone and the hybrid model we proposed are compared in Table 8. By adding the post-processed layer, there is a trade-off between precision and recall. The decrease in precision is possibly caused by the increase of false positive errors, because words with frequencies lower than 40,000 are marked as selection errors in the post-processed layer. Some words, such as "幽默性(19,928)" and "梧桐花(37,707)", even though with low frequencies, are grammatical expression in Chinese; however, they are identified as errors in the model by chance.

	Precision	Recall	F1
CRFs	0.8804	0.1444	0.2481
Hybrid	0.7519	0.3035	0.4324

Table 8: Comparison of CRFs model and hybrid model.

For the parameters setting in the post-processed layer, our model use 40,000 as the threshold for unigram, and 1,000 for bigrams. These two numbers are reached by observing the descriptive statistics of the data. Detailed corpus studies about the data distribution in Google n-grams can facilitate the parameter setting and in turn lead to better model performance in the future.

Since the post-layer is independent of the base model, it can be easily applied on top of other models, such as statistical, rule-based or hybrid models, to further promote the base model performance.

References

Po-Lin Chen, Shih-Hung Wu, Liang-Pu Chen, et al. 2016. Cyut-iii system at chinese grammatical error diagnosis task. In *Proceedings of the 3rd Workshop on Natural Language Processing Techniques for Educational Applications (NLPTEA2016)*, pages 63–72.

Wei-Chieh Chou, Chin-Kui Lin, Yuan-Fu Liao, and Yih-Ru Wang. 2016. Word order sensitive embedding features/conditional random field-based chinese grammatical error detection. In *Proceedings of the 3rd Workshop on Natural Language Processing Techniques for Educational Applications (NLPTEA2016)*, pages 73–81.

John Lafferty, Andrew McCallum, and Fernando CN Pereira. 2001. Conditional random fields: Probabilistic models for segmenting and labeling sequence data.

Lung-Hao Lee, Gaoqi Rao, Liang-Chih Yu, Endong Xun, Baolin Zhang, and Li-Ping Chang. 2016. Overview of nlp-tea 2016 shared task for chinese grammatical error diagnosis. In *Proceedings of the 3rd Workshop on Natural Language Processing Techniques for Educational Applications (NLPTEA2016)*, pages 40–48.

Lung-Hao Lee, Liang-Chih Yu, and Li-Ping Chang. 2015. Overview of the nlp-tea 2015 shared task for chinese grammatical error diagnosis. In *Proceedings of the 3rd Workshop on Natural Language Processing Techniques for Educational Applications (NLPTEA2015)*, pages 1–6.

Fang Liu, Meng Yang, and Dekang Lin. 2010. Chinese web 5-gram version 1 ldc2010t06. CD-ROMs.

Gaoqi Rao, Baolin Zhang, XUN Endong, and Lung-Hao Lee. 2017. Ijcnlp-2017 task 1: Chinese grammatical error diagnosis. *Proceedings of the IJCNLP 2017, Shared Tasks*, pages 1–8.

Kristina Toutanova, Dan Klein, Christopher D Manning, and Yoram Singer. 2003. Feature-rich part-of-speech tagging with a cyclic dependency network. In *Proceedings of the 2003 Conference of the North American Chapter of the Association for Computational Linguistics on Human Language Technology-Volume 1*, pages 173–180. Association for Computational Linguistics.

Huihsin Tseng, Pichuan Chang, Galen Andrew, Daniel Jurafsky, and Christopher Manning. 2005. A conditional random field word segmenter for sighan bake-off 2005. In *Proceedings of the fourth SIGHAN workshop on Chinese language Processing*.

Liang-Chih Yu, Lung-Hao Lee, and Li-Ping Chang. 2014. Overview of grammatical error diagnosis for learning chinese as a foreign language. In *Proceedings of the 1st Workshop on Natural Language Processing Techniques for Educational Applications*, pages 42–47.

Bo Zheng, Wanxiang Che, Jiang Guo, and Ting Liu. 2016. Chinese grammatical error diagnosis with long short-term memory networks. In *Proceedings of the 3rd Workshop on Natural Language Processing Techniques for Educational Applications (NLPTEA2016)*, pages 49–56.

CYUT-III Team Chinese Grammatical Error Diagnosis System Report in NLPTEA-2018 CGED Shared Task

Shih-Hung Wu*, Jun-Wei Wang
Chaoyang University of Technology,
Taichung, Taiwan, R.O.C
*Contact author: shwu@cyut.edu.tw

Liang-Pu Chen, Ping-Che Yang
Institute for Information Industry, Taipei, Taiwan, ROC.
{eit, maciaclark}@iii.org.tw

Abstract

This paper reports how we build a Chinese Grammatical Error Diagnosis system in the NLPTEA-2018 CGED shared task. In 2018, we sent three runs with three different approaches. The first one is a pattern-based approach by frequent error pattern matching. The second one is a sequential labelling approach by conditional random fields (CRF). The third one is a rewriting approach by sequence to sequence (seq2seq) model. The three approaches have different properties that aim to optimize different performance metrics and the formal run results show the differences as we expected.

1. Introduction

Learning Chinese as foreign language is getting popular. However, it is very hard for a foreign learner to write a correct Chinese sentence. We believe that a computer system that can diagnose the grammatical errors will help the learners to learn Chinese fast.

Since 2014, the NLP-TEA workshop provides a Chinese Grammar Error Detection (CGED) shared task to promote the research on diagnosis. The organizer provides learners' corpus tagged with error labels. There are four types of errors in the leaners' sentences: Redundant, Selection, Disorder, and Missing. The research goal is to build a system that can detect the errors, identify the type of the error, and point out the position of the error in the sentence (Yu et al., 2014). This year, the

CGED added a new requirement: for errors of missing words and word selection, systems are required to recommend at most 3 corrections. If one of the corrections of these instances is identical with gold standard, the instances will be regarded as correct cases.

In 2018, we sent three formal runs in three different approaches. The first two are based on previous works, the first one is a pattern-based approach by frequent error pattern matching and language model scoring; the second one is a sequential labelling approach by conditional random fields (CRF), which performs well in year 2015 and 2016. The third one is a new approach, called rewriting approach by sequence to sequence (seq2seq) model. In the following sections, we will introduce the three approaches, discuss the formal run results, and give conclusion and future works.

2. Previous Works

2.1 Pattern-Based Approach

The pattern matching approach is an old approach, which has been used in many previous works (Wu et al., 2010; Chen et al., 2011). The pattern contains frequent error terms, in which a character is replace by a similar one. This is based on an assumption that students often make mistake among similar characters (Liu et al., 2009). The advantage of pattern matching is stable, the many drawback is it cost a lot to collect the patterns.

The system is based on the previous work, the error pattern from a native student essay corpus in traditional Chinese. Before testing

Proceedings of the 5th Workshop on Natural Language Processing Techniques for Educational Applications, pages 199–202
Melbourne, Australia, July 19, 2018. ©2018 Association for Computational Linguistics

the system, the test data is transformed into traditional by MS-Word 2010.

2.2 Sequential Labelling Approach

The second one is a sequential labelling approach by conditional random fields (CRF), which performs well in CGED 2015 and 2016.(Chen et al., 2015; Chen et al., 2016b)

The sequential labelling approach is based on the conditional random field (CRF) model (Lafferty, 2001). CRF has been used in many NLP applications, such as named entity recognition, word segmentation, information extraction, and parsing. To apply it to a new task, it requires a specific feature set and labeled training data. The CRF model is regarded as a sequential labeling tagger. Given a sequence X, the CRF can generate the corresponding label sequence Y, based on the trained model. Each label Y is taken from a specific tag set, which needs to be defined in each task. How to define and interpret the label is a task-depended work for the developers.

Mathematically, the model can be defined as:

$$P(Y|X) = \frac{1}{Z(X)} \exp(\sum_k \lambda_k f_k) \qquad (1)$$

where $Z(X)$ is the normalization factor, f_k is a set of features, λ_k is the corresponding weight which will be learned in the training process. In the CGED task, X is the input sentence, and Y is the corresponding error type label. We define the tag set as: {O, R, M, S, D}, corresponding to no error, redundant, missing, selection, and disorder respectively. Table 1: A sample of the CRF sequential labeling dataset shows a sample of our working file. The first column is the input sentence X, and the third column is the labeled tag sequence Y. Note that the second column is the Part-of-speech (POS) of the word in the first column. The combination of words and the POSs will be the features in our system. The POS set used in our system is a simplified POS set provided by CKIP[1].

Term	POS	Tag
可是	C	0
有	Vt	0
一點	DET	0
冷	Vi	0
了	T	R
你	N	0
的	T	R
過年	Vi	0
呢	T	0

Table 1: A sample of the CRF sequential labeling dataset

Since the system is based on the previous work, the training set is the 2014, 2015, and 2016 CGED training dataset in traditional Chinese. The test data is also in transformed into traditional by MS-Word 2010.

3. Rewriting Approach

This year, we propose a new approach, called rewriting approach. Given a sentence with grammar errors, a system can rewrite it and output a sentence without grammar error. This idea is inspired from the RNN encoder-decoder models, which have been used in many deep learning researches. In such models, with the help of a large training set, a sequence can be transformed into another corresponding sequence. Amount them Sequence-to-sequence (seq2seq) models (Sutskever et al., 2014, Cho et al., 2014) have been applied successfully to a variety of NLP tasks such as machine translation, speech recognition, text summarization and conversation generation (Wu et al., 2017). In this task, we also adopt the seq2seq model as it is in Neural Machine Translation (NMT) which was the very first testbed for seq2seq model.

3.1 Seq2seq Model

Our rewrite approach system is built on TensorFlow Sequence to sequence (Seq2Seq) model [2] with the long-short-term-memory (LSTM). The training set is the 2017 and 2018 CGED training dataset.

---

[1] http://ckipsvr.iis.sinica.edu.tw/

[2] https://www.tensorflow.org/tutorials/seq2seq

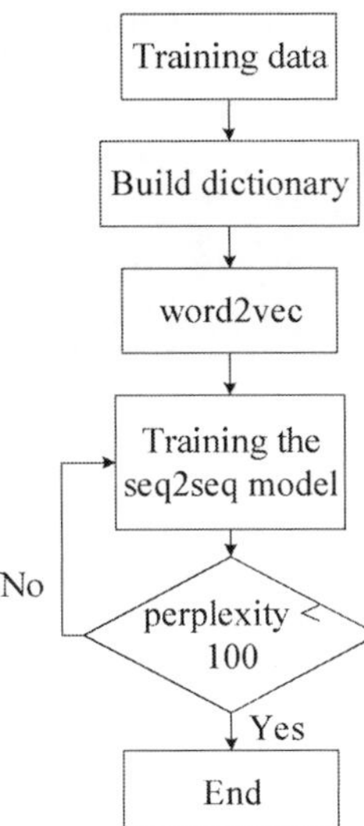

Figure 1. Training flowchart

3.2 Training the Seq2seq model

Figure 1 shows the training flowchart of our system. The first step is collecting all the vocabulary in the training corpus to build a dictionary. Then uses the word2vec model (Mikolov et al., 2013) to find the vector representation of each word. The sentences written by the students and the corresponding correct version sentences are used to train the seq2seq model. Since we do not have a validation set to find a better early stop point. The termination criterion of training is an empirical value, perplexity equal 100.

3.3 Preprocessing

The sentences are segmented by Jieba[3] word segmentation toolkit. The size of the vocabulary set is 5,424. The vocabulary is not very large, comparing to other the corpus used in other NLP tasks.

3.4 Post-processing

After the input is rewritten by the system, then the system will compare the rewritten sentence to the input sentence. We assume the rewritten one is the correct one and report the differences as grammar errors.

4. Experiment

4.1 Metrics

In the formal run, accuracy, precision, recall, and F-score are reported in three different levels. False positive rate is reported for the detection levels.

4.2 Formal Run result

The performance of our systems is shown in the following tables comparing to the average of all 32 formal runs in 2018. Table 2 shows the false positive rate; the only index that should be as low as possible. As we expected, the run1 pattern based approach gives the lowest FPR in all 32 runs.

Table 3 shows the performance evaluation

Submission	False Positive Rate
run1	**0.050**
run2	0.178
run3	1.000
Average of all 32 runs	0.467

Table 2:   The false positive rate.

in detection level. At this level, the run2 sequential labelling approach perform well in both accuracy and precision. The recall is also improved from the performance in 2016 (Chen et al, 2016a). The performance of rewriting approach gives highest recall and

	Detection Level			
	Accuracy	Precision	Recall	F1
run1	0.468	0.695	0.090	0.159
run2	**0.602**	**0.754**	0.428	0.546
run3	0.473	0.581	**0.845**	**0.688**
Average of 32 runs	0.587	0.667	0.635	0.613

Table 3:   Performance evaluation in Detection Level

high F1, however, poor accuracy and precision. This is also as we expected, since

---

[3] https://github.com/fxsjy/jieba

the training corpus is too small and the vocabulary size is also too small.

5. Conclusion and Future Works

This paper reports our approach to the NLP-TEA-5 CGED Shared Task evaluation. By comparing three different approaches, we find that the systems can be tuned to optimize different performance metrics.

Our system presents the best false positive rate in detection level by pattern matching approach and high accuracy, precision by sequential labelling approach and high recall and F1 by rewriting approach.

Due to the limitation of time and resource, our system is not tested under different experimental settings. In the future, we will use a larger corpus to train a better rewriting system to improve the performance on error diagnosis.

6. Acknowledgments

This study is conducted under the "III System-of-systems driven emerging service business development Project" of the Institute for Information Industry which is subsidized by the Ministry of Economic Affairs of the Republic of China.

Reference

Po-Lin Chen; Wu Shih-Hung; Liang-Pu Chen; Ping-Che Yang, (2016b) CYUT-III System at Chinese Grammatical Error Diagnosis Task, in Proceedings of The 3rd Workshop on Natural Language Processing Techniques for Educational Applications, Osaka, Dec 12, 2016.

Po-Lin Chen, Shih-Hung Wu, Liang-Pu Chen and Ping-Che Yang, (2016a) Improving the Selection Error Recognition in a Chinese Grammar Error Detection System, in Proceedings of the IEEE 17th International Conference on Information Reuse and Integration, July 28-30, 2016, Pittsburgh, PA, USA.

Po-Lin Chen; Wu Shih-Hung; Liang-Pu Chen; Ping-Che Yang; Ren-Dar Yang, (2015), Chinese Grammatical Error Diagnosis by Conditional Random Fields, in Proceedings of The 2nd Workshop on Natural Language Processing Techniques for Educational Applications, pages 7–14, Beijing, China, July 31.

Yong-Zhi Chen, Shih-Hung Wu, Ping-che Yang, Tsun Ku, and Gwo-Dong Chen (2011), Improve the detection of improperly used Chinese characters in students' essays with error model" Int. J. Cont. Engineering Education and Life-Long Learning, Vol. 21, No. 1, pp.103-116, 2011.

Chao-Lin Liu, Kan-Wen Tien, Min-Hua Lai, Yi-Hsuan Chuang and Shih-Hung Wu, (2009), "Capturing Errors in Written Chinese Words", in Proceedings of Joint conference of the 47th Annual Meeting of the Association for Computational Linguistics and the 4th International Joint Conference on Natural Language Processing of the Asian Federation of Natural Language Processing, Singapore, Aug. 3-5.

Cho, K. et al. (2014). Learning phrase representations using RNN encoder-decoder for statistical machine translation. In Proc. Conference on Empirical Methods in Natural Language Processing 1724–1734. arXiv preprint arXiv:1406.1078.

Lafferty, A. McCallum, and F. Pereira. (2001). Conditional random fields: Probabilistic models for segmenting and labeling sequence data. In Intl. Conf. on Machine Learning.

Mikolov, Tomas; et al. (2013). "Efficient Estimation of Word Representations in Vector Space". arXiv:1301.3781.

Ilya Sutskever and Oriol Vinyals and Quoc V. Le, (2014), Sequence to Sequence Learning with Neural Networks, Proc. NIPS. http://arxiv.org/abs/1409.3215.

Shih-Hung Wu, Yong-Zhi Chen, Ping-che Yang, Tsun Ku, Chao-Lin Liu, (2010), Reducing the False Alarm Rate of Chinese Character Error Detection and Correction, Proceedings of CIPS-SIGHAN Joint Conference on Chinese Language Processing (CLP), pages 54–61, Beijing, 28-29 Aug.

Shih-Hung Wu, Wen-Feng Shih, Che-Cheng Yu, Liang-Pu Chen, and Ping-Che Yang, (2017), CYUT-III Short Text Conversation System at NTCIR-13 STC-2 Task, in Proceedings of the 13rd NTCIR Conference on Evaluation of Information Access Technologies, Dec. 5-8, Tokyo Japan.

Yu, L.-C., Lee, L.-H., & Chang, L.-P. (2014). Overview of grammatical error diagnosis for learning Chinese as a foreign language. In Proceedings of the 1stWorkshop on Natural Language Processing Techniques for Educational Applications, 42-47.

Detecting Grammatical Errors in the NTOU CGED System by Identifying Frequent Subsentences

Chuan-Jie Lin and Shao-Heng Chen

Department of Computer Science and Engineering
National Taiwan Ocean University
{cjlin, shchen.cse}@mail.ntou.edu.tw

Abstract

The main goal of Chinese grammatical error diagnosis task is to detect word errors in the sentences written by Chinese-learning students. Our previous system would generate error-corrected sentences as candidates and their sentence likelihood were measured based on a large scale Chinese n-gram dataset. This year we further tried to identify long frequently-seen subsentences and label them as correct in order to avoid propose too many error candidates. Two new methods for suggesting missing and selection errors were also tested.

1 Introduction

The CGED (Chinese grammatical error diagnosis) tasks have been organized for 5 years (Yu *et al.*, 2014; Lee *et al.*, 2015; Lee *et al.*, 2016; Rao *et al.*, 2017). This task focuses on four kinds of errors in writing Chinese: using redundant words, missing words, arranging words in a wrong order, or using similar but incorrect words.

In our previous attempts in this task, our systems generated corrected-sentence candidates by different methods according to different error types. These candidates were scored by substring scoring functions (Lin and Chen, 2015). Although these systems were ranked in the middle place in the subtask of identification level, they tended to propose too many errors thus achieved rather low precisions.

This year we tried another approach to detect correct parts in a sentence before guessing positions of errors. The proposed methods in early and this year's tasks are explained in the following sections.

2 Identifying Frequent Subsentences

The main stage of the CGED tasks is to correct sentences written by Chinese-learning foreign students. The corrections were provided by Chinese teachers.

In our experience, corrections can be given in two levels. The first level is to make a sentence "correct" both in syntax and semantics. The second level is to make a sentence "better", which means the original sentence is also correct but there is a better paraphrase commonly used in Chinese. Unfortunately, our previous systems cannot distinguish the two different types of corrections. They will still propose suggestions when the original sentence is already a correct one.

In order to decrease the number of suggestions, we decided to trust the original sentences more. A simple approach is to detect frequently-seen long subsentences in Chinese. Only the positions not covered by the frequent subsentences can be candidates of grammatical errors. Our referencing database of frequent subsentences is the Chinese Web 5-gram dataset[1], which collects substrings occurring more than 20 times on the Internet.

The steps to identify frequent subsentences are described as follows. All substrings (with at least three Chinese characters) in the original sentence are looked up in the Chinese Web 5-gram dataset. All matched substrings in the original sentence are considered "correct". If two substrings overlap with at least one Chinese character (or two characters for substrings no longer than 4 Chinese characters), they are merged into one longer substring. After the matching process, only those words not covered by any substring can be deleted (as redundant errors), replaced (as selection errors), or

---

[1] https://catalog.ldc.upenn.edu/LDC2010T06

Proceedings of the 5th Workshop on Natural Language Processing Techniques for Educational Applications, pages 203–206
Melbourne, Australia, July 19, 2018. ©2018 Association for Computational Linguistics

switched (as disorder errors). And only the positions not inside any matched substring can have additional words being inserted (as missing errors).

An example of identifying frequent subsentences is given here. The second sentence in the Query 200405109523201166_2_1x2 in the training data is "我認為吸煙的壞處比長處更多". We can match three subsentence in the Google 5-gram dataset:

我認為吸煙的	128
吸煙的壞處	2111
處更多	25635

The first two are further merged into one larger subsentence. So the identified frequent subsentences in the original sentence can be shown in brackets as [我認為吸煙的壞處]比長[處更多].

After substituting "長處" (advantage) with its synonym "好處" (advantage) by the methods described in Section 3.4, a longer subsentence "好處更多" can fully cover the previous identified frequent subsentence "處更多". Therefore, an error will be reported as a Selection Error here.

好處更多	12938

3 Correction Candidate Generation

3.1 Character or Word Deletion (Case of Redundant)

Generating correction candidates in the case of Redundant type is quite straightforward: simply removing any substring in an arbitrary length. However, in order not to generate too many unnecessary candidates, we only do the removal under three special cases: removing one character, removing two-adjacent characters, and removing one word whose length is no longer than two Chinese characters. This method is the same as in the previous CGED tasks.

3.2 Character Insertion (Case of Missing)

The idea of generating correction candidates in the case of Missing type is to insert a character or a word into the given sentence. But it is impractical to enumerate candidates by inserting every known Chinese characters or words. We observed the CGED 2015 training set (Lin and Chen, 2015) and collected 34 characters which were frequently missing in the essays written by Chinese-learning foreign students, as they occurred at least three times and covered 73.7% of the missing errors in the CGED 2015 training set. Insertion happens between characters or words as usual.

A new idea to find insertion candidates was tested this year. Instead of inserting frequently missing characters, we directly discovered the n-gram string with the highest frequency in the Google 5-gram dataset. Take the sentence of the Query 200405205525200106_2_2x1 "這個團體的目的是減少邊走邊抽的人" as an example. When considering inserting characters in the position between "抽" and "的", we found the longest most-frequent n-gram string is "邊抽煙的人" (a person smoking at the same time) which is the correct Missing Error.

3.3 Substring Moving (Case of Disorder)

Generating correction candidates in the case of Disorder type is also straightforward: simply moving any substring in any length to another position to its right (not to its left so that no duplication will be produced). This method is the same as in the previous CGED tasks.

3.4 String Substitution (Cases of Selection)

The first case of selection errors is the misuse of prepositions. To generate the correction candidates for preposition substitutions, we first extracted all prepositions in the Academia Sinica Balanced Corpus (ASBC for short hereafter, cf. Chen *et al.*, 1996). An input sentence is word-segmented and POS-tagged automatically beforehand. Correction candidates are generated by replacing each preposition (whose POS is "P") in the given sentence by other prepositions.

The second case of selection errors is the misuse of synonyms. As we known, even synonyms cannot freely replace each other without considering context.

To generate the correction candidates for synonym substitutions, we consulted a Chinese thesaurus, Tongyici Cilin[2] (the extended version; Cilin for short hereafter). A given sentence is word-segmented beforehand. Correction candidates are generated by replacing each word in the given sentence by its synonyms in Cilin if any.

---

[2] http://ir.hit.edu.cn/
    http://www.ltp-cloud.com/

The third case of selection errors is the misuse of words which were lexically similar to the correct ones. It is possible that the writer tried to use a word but misused another word with similar looking, such as "仔細" (carefully) and "細節" (details).

To generate but not over-generate the correction candidates for similar string substitutions, we first collected all 2-character words in the Google 5-gram dataset. Correction candidates are generated by replacing each 2-character word in the given sentence by another 2-character word having at least one character in common, such as "仔細" and "細節" where "細" appears in both words, or "合適" (suitable, *adjective*) and "適合" (suiting, *verb*) where both characters appear in both words. Examples of similar string substitution are given in the next page.

A new idea to find selection candidates was tested this year. We searched the Google 5-gram dataset and extracted the n-gram string with the highest frequency which differed with the original sentence with only one or two characters.

Take the second sentence of the Query 200405109523200578_2_1x2 "吸煙也是各人的人權" as an example. When considering replacing the character "各", we found the longest most-frequent n-gram string is "是個人的人權" (is a personal human right) which is the correct Selection Error.

4   Substring Scoring Functions

In our previous work (Lin and Chen, 2015), we have defined a sentence likelihood scoring function to measure the likelihood of a sentence to be common and correct. This function uses frequencies provided in the Chinese Web 5-gram dataset in a way described as follows.

Chinese Web 5-gram consists of real data released by Google Inc. which were collected from a large amount of webpages in the World Wide Web. Entries in the dataset are unigrams to 5-grams. Frequencies of these n-grams are also provided. Some examples from the Chinese Web 5-gram dataset are given in the left part of Table 1.

In order to avoid interference of word segmentation errors, we decided to use substrings instead of word n-grams as the scoring units of likelihood. When scoring a sentence, frequencies of all substrings in all lengths are used to measure the likelihood.

Frequencies of substrings are derived by removing space between n-grams in the Chinese Web 5-gram dataset. For instances, n-grams in the left part of Table 1 will become the strings in the right part, where length of a substring is measured in bytes and a Chinese character often occupies 3 bytes in UTF-8 encoding. Note that if two or more different n-grams are transformed into the same substring after removing the space, they become one entry and its new frequency is the summation of their original frequencies. Simplified Chinese words were translated into Traditional Chinese in advanced.

Some notations are explained as follows. Given a sentence S, let $SubStr(S, n)$ be the set of all substrings in S whose lengths are n bytes, and **Google String Frequency** $gsf(u)$ be the frequency of a string u in the modified Chinese Web 5-gram dataset. If a string does not appear in that dataset, its gsf value is defined to be 1 (so that its logarithm becomes 0).

Equation 1 gives the equation of **length-weighted string log-frequency score** $SL(S)$. Each substring u in S contributes a score of the logarithm of its Google string frequency weighted by u's length n. The value of n starts from 6, because most content words are not shorter than 6 bytes (i.e. two Chinese characters).

$$SL(S) = \sum_{n=6}^{len(S)} \left(n \times \sum_{u \in SubStr(S,n)} \log(gsf(u)) \right) \qquad \text{Eq 1.}$$

This function was also explained in the work of Lin and Chu (2015). Please refer to that paper for examples of how to compute the sentence generation likelihood scores.

5   Run Submission

We planned to submit two runs this year. One run was produced with the previous system, i.e. generating error-correction candidates and choosing the ones with the highest length-weighted substring scores. The other run was produced by identifying frequent subsentences and then proposing errors containing in longer, more frequent n-gram strings found by new candidate generating methods.

Unfortunately, due to some errors in our procedures, only the one run was produced which reported as many errors as our previous system. We will finish the correct experiment as soon as possible to see the real performance of the newly proposed methods.

Two different strategies to identify frequent subsentences have been observed on the training data, where two thresholds are defined as follows. The **length threshold** (*lenTh*) defines the confident level of a subsentence in length (in Chinese characters). All subsentences no shorter than the length threshold are marked as "correct". The **frequency threshold** (*frqTh*) defines the confident level of a subsentence in frequency. All subsentences with a high frequency are also marked as "correct", even though their lengths might be short. The correction-candidates inside these "correct" subsentences are discarded.

Table 1 shows the evaluation results at the position level in the training data with different combination of length thresholds and frequency thresholds. The results suggest that trusting subsentences with at least 8 Chinese characters or appearing at least 900000 times in the Internet can reduced the erroneous proposal of corrections in a best way.

6   Conclusion

This paper describes the design of our Chinese grammatical error diagnosis system. This is our fourth attempt in the CGED tasks. Long frequent subsentences in the original sentences were identified in the first step. An error could be proposed only if it was not covered by a longer "correct" subsentences. Two runs were planned to be submitted. One run was produced with the previous system, i.e. generating error-correction candidates and choosing the ones with the highest length-weighted substring scores. The other run was produced by identifying frequent subsentences and then proposing errors containing in longer, more frequent n-gram strings found by new candidate generating methods.

References

Liang-Chih Yu, Lung-Hao Lee, and Li-Ping Chang (2014) "Overview of Grammatical Error Diagnosis for Learning Chinese as a Foreign Language," *Proceedings of the 1st Workshop on Natural Language Processing Techniques for Educational Applications (NLPTEA '14)*, pp. 42-47.

Lung-Hao Lee, Liang-Chih Yu, and Li-Ping Chang (2015) "Overview of the NLP-TEA 2015 Shared Task for Chinese Grammatical Error Diagnosis," *Proceedings of The 2nd Workshop on Natural Language Processing Techniques for Educational Applications (NLP-TEA 2), the 53rd Annual Meeting of the Association for Computational Linguistics and the 7th International Joint Conference on Natural Language Processing of the Asian Federation of Natural Language Processing (ACL-IJCNLP 2015)*, pp. 1-6.

Lung-Hao Lee, Gaoqi Rao, Liang-Chih Yu, Endong Xun, Baolin Zhang, and Li-Ping Chang (2016). "Overview of the NLP-TEA 2016 Shared Task for Chinese Grammatical Error Diagnosis," *Proceedings of the 3rd Workshop on Natural Language Processing Techniques for Educational Applications (NLPTEA '16)*, pp. 40-48.

Gaoqi Rao, Baolin Zhang, Endong Xun (2017) "IJCNLP-2017 Task 1: Chinese Grammatical Error Diagnosis," *Proceedings of the 8th International Joint Conference on Natural Language Processing (IJCNLP), Shared Tasks*, pp. 1-8.

Chuan-Jie Lin and Shao-Heng Chen (2015) "NTOU Chinese Grammar Checker for CGED Shared Task," *Proceedings of The 2nd Workshop on Natural Language Processing Techniques for Educational Applications (NLP-TEA 2), the 53rd Annual Meeting of the Association for Computational Linguistics and the 7th International Joint Conference on Natural Language Processing of the Asian Federation of Natural Language Processing (ACL-IJCNLP 2015)*, pp. 15-19.

Chuan-Jie Lin and Wei-Cheng Chu (2015) "A Study on Chinese Spelling Check Using Confusion Sets and N-gram Statistics," *International Journal of Computational Linguistics and Chinese Language Processing (IJCLCLP)*, Vol. 20, No. 1, pp. 23-48.

lenTh	frqTh	F-score (%)
20	1000000	8.9160
10	1000000	8.9244
8	1000000	8.9823
5	1000000	7.9004
20	900000	9.1603
10	900000	9.1647
8	**900000**	**9.2144**
5	900000	7.9651
20	500000	8.8235
10	500000	8.8280
8	500000	8.9185
5	500000	7.9507

Table 1: Performance of Error Proposal at the Position Level in the Training Data.

Author Index